The SCO Performance Tuning Handbook

Gina Miscovich / David Simons

P T R Prentice Hall
Englewood Cliffs, New Jersey 07632

Library of Congress Cataloguing-in-Publication Data

Editorial/production supervision: *Mary P. Rottino*
Cover design: *Karen Marsilio*
Cover photographs: *Westlight Computer Graphics Collection*
Manufacturing manager: *Alexis Heydt*
Acquisitions editor: *Mark L. Taub*

Published by P T R Prentice Hall
Prentice-Hall, Inc.
A Paramount Communications Company
Englewood Cliffs, New Jersey 07632

The publisher offers discounts on this book when ordered in bulk quantities.
For more information contact: Corporate Sales Department, P T R Prentice Hall,
113 Sylvan Ave., Englewood Cliffs, NJ 07632.
Phone (201) 592-2863 Fax (201) 592-2249

Printed in the United States of America

10 9 8 7 6 5 4 3 2 1

ISBN 0-13-102690-9

Prentice-Hall International (UK) Limited, *London*
Prentice-Hall of Australia Pty. Limited, *Sydney*
Prentice-Hall Canada Inc., *Toronto*
Prentice-Hall Hispanoamericana, S.A., *Mexico*
Prentice-Hall of India Private Limited, *New Delhi*
Prentice-Hall of Japan, Inc., *Tokyo*
Simon & Schuster Asia Pte. Ltd., *Singapore*
Editora Prentice-Hall do Brasil, Ltda., *Rio de Janeiro*

Table of Contents

List of Figures

List of Tables

Foreword

Over the past ten years, the success of Open Systems software running on industry-standard hardware has exceeded even the most optimistic projections. SCO has been a leader in this effort with its SCO UNIX, SCO MPX, SCO Open Desktop, and SCO Open Server products. These products are being actively embraced by large and small corporations all over the world who understand the benefits of open and multi-vendor software and hardware solutions.

As the popularity of Open Systems solutions on industry-standard hardware continues to grow, we are seeing more and more attempts by Information Processing Professionals to push these systems to their limits. And we are seeing a corresponding demand from them for information on optimizing the performance of these systems.

This book presents the most detailed and comprehensive account available today of how to get the most out of SCO Open Systems software products. Gina and David are senior members of SCO's Operating System development staff. Over the past two years, they have done groundbreaking work in SCO's Performance Engineering Group. As such, they are ideally suited to write this book. They have done a remarkable job, and I am sure you will agree with me as you read through their work.

Doug Michels
Co-Founder, Senior Vice President, and Chief Technology Officer
The Santa Cruz Operation, Inc.

Preface

This is the book for people who want to improve the performance of their SCO® UNIX®, SCO MPX™, Open Desktop® and Open Server™ systems. This book provides information about what affects a computer system's performance so you can decide how to allocate system resources for optimal performance.

This book uses an integrated, system-oriented approach to understanding how resources are used. Rather than describing the performance characteristics of individual operating system subsystems, such as disk or memory management, we look at the applications, operating system, network connectivity, and hardware environment as a complete system. An understanding of how these components interact is necessary to maximize the efficient use of the resources.

This book specifically refers to tuning the following SCO products: SCO UNIX 3.2v4.2, SCO MPX 3.0, Open Desktop 3.0 and Open Server 3.0. Most of what is described applies to other versions of these SCO products, although they are not specifically referred to in the descriptions. The features described in these chapters that are not available in earlier releases are explicitly noted in the text.

Intended Audience

The information in this book is for anyone who wants to improve the performance of their SCO system. We present the material for people at all levels of technical and performance tuning experience. We assume you have a basic understanding of your computer system and are somewhat familiar with the tools, such as sar(ADM), that are used for monitoring the system. We also assume some shell programming experience as well as a basic understanding of configuring networks and Open Desktop systems. If you are not familiar with these tools, you still need this book, but may also need to refer to the appropriate System Administrator's Guide shipped with the operating system for additional information.

About This Book

We provide a combination of technical descriptions and case studies to help you understand how to maximize system performance. We include the test programs and data collection scripts from the case studies on a floppy disk so you can try them on your system.

The primary goal of system tuning is to allocate software and hardware resources so that the operations executed by the computer system go as fast as possible. System tuning increases the efficiency of everyone using the system by minimizing the time they wait for operations to complete. Figure P-1 summarizes the types of information provided in this book.

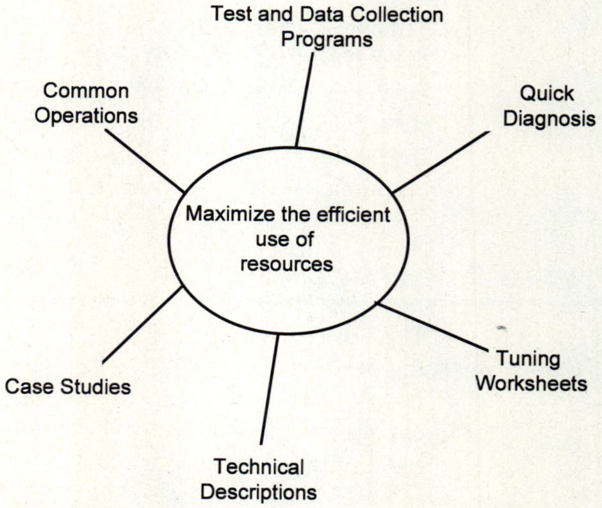

Figure P-1: Types of Information Provided in This Book

The *performance* of a system is defined to be the amount of time a specific operation takes to complete. The amount of time depends on the interactions between the hardware and software that take place in order to complete the task.

Tuning is the optimal allocation of hardware and software resources such that the duration of the operation is minimized. Tuning also requires balancing the often conflicting needs of a computer user community and the company budget. The user community may require more resources as they develop more and more uses for the computing environment, but a company finance department may not have additional money to spend on new hardware to match those increased demands. Unless you understand how the system resources are used, you can spend money on more hardware, but end up with no performance benefit.

In this book, we use an approach that analyzes the typical operations that computer systems execute. These *common operations* provide a way of looking at the entire system as you actually use it: to accomplish certain tasks in a minimum amount of time. The technical descriptions in each of the chapters focus on how a given resource fits into the chain of resource interactions required to complete an operation. The impact of changing that resource is clear because you can see where it fits with the other resources, thus helping you prioritize resource allocation decisions.

Road Map of This Book

This material in this book is divided into the following sections:

- Introduction and description of the step-by-step tuning method. This chapter also describes the worksheets.
- Technical information describing resource interactions, resource monitoring, and optimal allocation suggestions
- Case studies showing how the step-by-step method can be used to tune operations in simple and more complex environments
- Sample test programs and data collection scripts included on the floppy disk

The chapters are summarized as follows:

Chapter 1 presents an overview of performance tuning, the step-by-step method and the worksheets. The step-by-step method and the worksheets save time by eliminating much of the guesswork previously associated with performance tuning.

Chapter 2 presents the technical background on the interactions that occur when common operations are executed on SCO UNIX. This chapter is the foundation on which the other technical chapters are built.

Chapter 3 presents a case study for tuning a file read and write operation on SCO UNIX.

Chapter 4	presents the technical background on the interactions that occur when common operations are executed on SCO MPX. This chapter illustrates the differences in behavior between SCO UNIX and SCO MPX and provides more information on tuning SCO MPX than does any other existing book. This chapter also includes some special tuning hints for Oracle® Version 7 and Sybase® SQL Server™ release 10.0.
Chapter 5	presents two case studies showing how to tune a system running SCO MPX. The tuning issues that are exposed after an additional processor is installed are also illustrated.
Chapter 6	presents the technical background on the interactions that occur on an Open Desktop system. This chapter includes a description of SCO UNIX memory management because a memory shortage is the most common resource shortage in an Open Desktop environment.
Chapter 7	presents a case study showing the effects of memory shortage on system performance. This case study shows how to determine the optimal amount of additional memory required to alleviate the memory shortage.
Chapter 8	presents technical background on how connections are set up and monitored in a networked environment. The additional complexity of multiple machines cooperating to complete an operation is addressed. This chapter refers to the other product chapters, and so builds on and integrates the information presented in those chapters.

Chapter 9 presents technical background on common client/server operations, such as remote file access. The additional complexity of tuning multiple machines presented in Chapter 8 is addressed in more detail in this chapter. This chapter includes a description of tuning remote file access operations in the NFS® environment.

Chapter 10 presents a series of case studies showing how to tune systems executing typical client/server operations. A case study showing how to tune the NFS environment is also included.

Chapter 11 presents a case study showing how to tune an Oracle® Version 7 system by following the seven-step method. This case study features a multiprocessor system that contains Intel™ Pentium™ processors.

Chapter 12 presents a case study showing how to tune Informix®-OnLine by following the seven-step method.

Chapter 13 presents guidelines for building a high performance system and highlights the key tuning concepts presented in this book.

Appendix A contains blank worksheets to use when the common operations are tuned with the step-by-step method. These worksheets are also annotated for easy future reference. Worksheets for Informix-OnLine and Oracle are also provided.

Appendix B contains some suggestions for saving memory on an Open Desktop, Open Server, SCO UNIX or SCO MPX system.

Appendix C includes reference documentation for each of the test and data collection programs included on the floppy disk.

Appendix D is a special patch for the SCO NFS environment that improves performance of remote file access.

The product chapters focus on presenting system and resources interactions, because our experience in performance tuning has shown that understanding interactions is far more relevant to performance tuning than in-depth understanding of the internal workings of a single area. Each resource involved in the completion of an operation is described as follows:

- Technical background describes how the resource works and what configurable variables control that resource.

- How to monitor the resource. This section begins with the stopwatch symbol that appears in the margin next to this text.

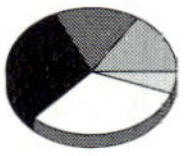

- How to tune the resource for improved performance. This section begins with the pie chart symbol that appears in the margin next to this text. The pie chart symbolizes those tuning situations where a fixed amount of resource must be allocated among a variety of uses.

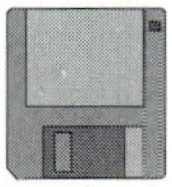

- The floppy disk margin symbol highlights where the test programs and data collection tools provided on the floppy disk are used in the case studies.

HINT

Hints scattered throughout the text highlight special tips to make performance tuning for that operation easier.

Each chapter concludes with a "Quick Diagnosis Summary" that summarizes the common operation, the key monitoring tools and tuning concepts presented in that chapter.

How to Use This Book

If you are approaching performance tuning for the first time, then we recommend reading all of Chapter 1, reading the product chapters and corresponding case studies, and then focussing on the product chapter and case studies that match the SCO products and operations that you want to optimize. Read all of the case studies to become familiar with the test and data collection programs provided on the floppy disk. To begin tuning, either write a new test program or modify the existing test programs. Use the knowledge you have gained from the product chapters to decide how to optimally allocate resources.

If you are familiar with performance tuning, then read Chapter 1 and the case studies to become familiar with the test and data collection programs provided on the floppy disk. After you decide what you want to improve, modify or write a new test program, monitor the resource usage pattern and start tuning. Read the technical descriptions to discover more information about the resource interactions for the operations that you are tuning.

Developing Your Understanding

Our approach eliminates much of the guesswork previously associated with performance tuning. The systematic method also helps you prioritize what resources should change so your time is used most effectively. Successful tuning often involves balancing between contrasting needs, so understanding exactly how your resources are used allows you to precisely identify what must be balanced in order to achieve the optimal solution. Understanding how the balance point is achieved and how the inevitable trade-offs are made will help you achieve the best performance.

Do not give up if you do not understand all of the information presented in this book. Developing a thorough understanding is often a series of small enlightenments that occur over time. Unlike many other system administration tasks, mistakes in tuning can often be made without drastic consequences. The framework presented in this book helps you avoid the more extreme mistakes and also provides a learning structure from which you can develop your understanding over time. Systematic experimentation is often the best way to learn about what is really happening on the system, and this method recognizes that experience plus some good guessing are also essential tools when performance tuning.

Good luck!

Acknowledgments

A number of people have contributed to the successful completion of this project.

We would like to thank Ed Whalen, Tom Rhodes, Bernie Luksich, Chuck Maples, Doug Strain, Michael Stephens (thanks for the power!), Andy Dixon and the rest of the crew all over the world at Compaq for sharing their knowledge, experience and hardware with us. A special thanks also to Gordon Larimer at Oracle for his expertise and patience in supporting us.

Graham Moore and Brian Foster at SCO Ltd. contributed to the shells scripts that are included on the floppy disk. John Simons was also a good source of information. Chris Stott showed an exceptional amount of understanding during the entire project.

The reviewers of this book, Alec Parker, Roger Snyder, Darin Carlson and Mary Lou Nohr helped shape the structure of the material. A very special thanks to Darin for being consistently "beautiful" and for making especially insightful and constructive comments. Seth Katz contributed enormously at the beginning of this project by helping us clarify what we were trying to do.

The project was consistently kept on track by our editor at Prentice-Hall, Mark Taub. He also deserves credit for thinking of the idea in the first place. Excellent and essential production debugging tools (ghostscript) were provided by the folks at Aladdin Enterprises and the Free Software Foundation. Production expertise and green rice were provided by Edwin Datschefski.

We hope you enjoy reading this book as much as we enjoyed writing it.

Gina Miscovich and David Simons

Chapter 1

Introduction to SCO Performance Tuning

This chapter introduces the concepts that are used throughout this book to explain how resources are used, monitored, and changed to maximize the speed of operations.

The first part of this chapter discusses some problems that tuning can solve. The second part discusses a model of a computer system and uses that model to explain the primary tuning goals. The final part describes a systematic method for performance tuning that helps you understand how system resources are used.

Reasons For Performance Tuning

Performance tuning benefits all computer users by making more efficient use of the existing environment so everyone gets more out of the hardware and software investment.

For example, at XYZ company, end of the month inventory and sales reports are generated for the auditors and financial controllers. Every month the users complain to the system administrator: "My terminal takes so long to update the screen that I cannot keep track of what I am entering, can't you fix it?"; "Retrieving data across the network is so slow that I cannot get any work done, why can't you fix it?"; "You know this happens every month, why haven't you done something about it?" You know that a problem exists, but you have many other problems to deal with that occur more frequently than once a month, and, besides, you are really not quite sure how to solve it. This scenario is one example of a computer system whose resources could be more optimally allocated to avoid those end of the month complaints.

Another reason for tuning is that in most computing environments, the demands placed on the system increase over time as more and more uses are found. The increased demand means increased use of resources, and tuning allows you to make the most efficient use of the resources you have. Understanding the resource usage also helps you determine whether a hardware upgrade would be beneficial and, if so, what kind of hardware upgrade would most enhance system performance.

Having a systematic method to collect information provides a way of determining whether available hardware is a limiting factor to increased performance, thereby helping you justify hardware upgrades, should they be necessary. Being able to identify where upgraded hardware will benefit the users provides you with useful information to influence the money allocation decisions. Should additional money become available, you will be in a position to spend that money for maximum performance benefit. Because compromising resource usage is an inevitable part of administering a system in a commercial environment, understanding the system interactions helps you make those decisions in ways that benefit a majority of users.

The resource idea that underlies this book extends to time as well. Time is often limited because the computing environment is in use 24 hours a day, so improvements must be implemented before the commercial interests of the business start to be adversely affected. Time is also limited because system administrators are often responsible for far more than the performance of the system and can devote only a small amount of time to performance tuning tasks. When confronted with a very limited time to devote to tuning, please remember that, unlike many other administration projects, tuning can be done in small increments over a long period of time.

Understanding the Core Tuning Concepts

The core goal of this approach to system tuning is to minimize the number of intermediate storage locations that must be searched to complete a given operation. This goal is central to tuning because each time an additional storage location is searched to retrieve data, completion of the operation is delayed. This core goal may be viewed differently in different performance tuning contexts, but the central concept remains.

The following section describes a unifying model for the application, the operating system, and the hardware environment that underlies what is presented in this book.

The computer system contains two types of storage: *permanent* and *temporary*. Permanent storage areas, such as disks, are generally slower to access than temporary storage areas such as main memory.

For example, a word processing application might maintain two copies of what is displayed on the screen, one for updating when the user is typing in characters and one as a copy of what is actually displayed on the screen. The screen updated with the new characters is then compared with the one that is actually displayed on the screen. The differences between the two are transferred to the video hardware for display on the screen. Although these additional screens occupy space in main memory, they allow the application to update the screen more quickly, because a smaller amount of data is sent to the hardware for screen update. To reduce display update time, this application requires an *intermediate storage location*. Many applications and operating systems use the intermediate storage location technique to improve performance.

Underlying hardware resources, such as main memory, are allocated to implement intermediate storage areas. The operating system copies data and instructions from the permanent storage areas into temporary storage locations when needed by the applications running on the system. Underlying hardware resources, such as the CPU, are needed to complete this copy operation. The underlying hardware is therefore used for two purposes: to contain the intermediate and permanent storage locations and to move the data and instructions between storage areas.

The intermediate storage areas required by applications and the operating system often share the same underlying resource. The primary difference between these data storage areas is where they are located in the search for the data. When an application requires some data, it searches the various intermediate storage locations until that data is found. If the application finds the data in the first storage area searched, then the application can continue the operation without additional searching. Thus, delay caused by searching for the required data is minimized.

Each search of an intermediate data storage area requires underlying hardware resources to complete the search and to copy the data from the data storage area to a place where the application can use the data. Because each search delays the completion of the application's operation, the core goal of performance tuning is to minimize the amount of searching that occurs when completing a given operation. Figure 1-1 shows the differences in searching when an application finds the data earlier in the search chain.

If the computer system runs multiple applications or the application is a complex one, many different intermediate storage locations are sharing the same underlying hardware resources. The application's needs for rapid information access must be balanced with the increased demands on the underlying hardware for more and/or larger intermediate storage areas to access that information rapidly. This balance is what makes resource allocation and tuning less straightforward than some other administration tasks.

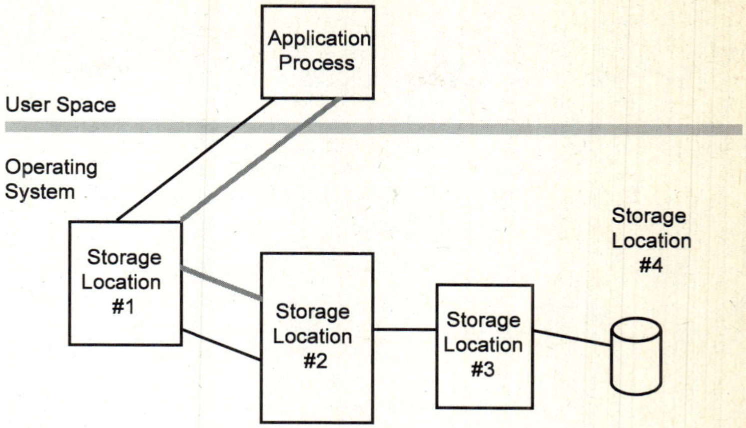

Figure 1-1: The application searches for the information in intermediate storage locations. These intermediate storage locations can located in the application as well as in the operating system. The application continues searching each location in turn until the data is found. The more intermediate storage locations that must be searched in order to find the data, the longer the operation. The black lines indicate what happens when the data is not found until the application searches the permanent storage location. The gray line indicates what happens when the data is found in the second storage location. Because a shorter pathway is taken when the data is found in storage location #2 rather than in storage location #4, the application uses fewer resources to find the data and completes the operation in a shorter period of time.

Common operations provide a framework for decreasing the amount of time an application spends searching for information. By analyzing how the intermediate storage locations cooperate to complete an operation, a clear relationship between the intermediate storage location and duration of the operation is developed. This clear relationship provides the information necessary to make optimal resource allocation decisions.

Seven Steps Towards Improved System Performance

This section describes seven steps towards improving system performance. Figure 1-2 summarizes the steps. Appendix A contains blank tuning worksheets for all the operations and applications discussed in this book. Appendix A also contains annotated worksheets that describe the data that should be entered at each step.

The worksheets are provided as a framework for collecting resource usage information and deciding on new resource allocations. The worksheets contain the tunables and resources that should be monitored for the common operation.

The floppy disk contains test programs that automatically collect the correct data, and extract it for entry into the worksheet. See Appendix C for more information on the floppy disk programs.

Step 1. Decide what to improve.

☑ Select the appropriate worksheet for the common operation.

⇩

Step 2. Identify the limited and unlimited resources.

☑ Note any limited resources on the worksheet by marking them with an asterisk (*).

⇩

Step 3. Determine how to measure the operation and test its current performance.

☑ Note the test result on the worksheet in the column marked **Now.**

⇩

Step 4. Set a realistic performance goal.

☑ Note this on the worksheet in the column marked **Your Goal.**

⇩

Step 5. Identify the resources to monitor and decide which monitoring tools to use.

☑ The worksheets list the appropriate resources.

⇩

Step 6. Run the test with the monitoring tools and monitor the resource usage and record the test results.

☑ Enter the initial values of the tunables and note the resource usage in the column marked **Initial Values**. Note the test results under the column called **Monitoring.**

⇩

Step 7. Decide how to change the resource allocation; rerun the tests and note progress toward the goal. Iterate until either the goal is reached, or until a limited resource is encountered.

☑ Determine whether to increase or decrease the resource/tunable. Note the new tunable values in the column marked **Test #1** and the test results under the column **Res #1.** Use the rest of the columns for the results of subsequent test iterations.

☑ When the goal is reached, implement the new resource allocation.

Figure 1-2: Summary of Performance Tuning Steps

In the future, if system performance changes for the same or similar operations, the worksheets serve as reminders of what was changed and why, and so the tuning process can start at step 6 with some testing and monitoring of resources without losing any essential information.

The rest of this section describes the steps and the worksheets in more detail.

Step 1. Decide what to improve.

☑ Select the appropriate worksheet for the common operation.

Determining as precisely as you can what needs to be improved is critical to successful tuning. The problem must be clearly defined so the data collection and analysis is well focused and efficient. The common operations are designed to help focus the data collection and analysis around commonly occurring situations. Table 1-1 lists the common operations.

Operation	Description
Calculations	This operation covers situations where the computer performs CPU-intensive operations, such as calculating cells in a spreadsheet.
File Read and Write	This operation covers situations where information stored in the filesystem is retrieved and written.
Direct Disk Access	Some databases prefer this alternative method of accessing disk information for increased performance.
Display Update and Character Echo	This operation covers how quickly characters that are typed in at the keyboard are displayed on the screen. The resource interactions vary considerably with the operating system.

Table 1-1: Common Tunable Operation Summary

The four operations can be divided into two categories: easily measurable operations and more subjective ones. The first three operations in the table are easily measurable with existing SCO UNIX commands, such as time(C). The last one is more subjective and varies greatly among environments. A subjective operation is one that measures how quickly the application interacts with the user; thus it is often not precisely measurable with a commonly available command. For example, operations involving character echo and screen updating cannot be measured with time(C) and instead rely on user observations as to when the screen update has completed.

Because subjective operations are visible to the user, they are often a common source of complaints regarding system performance. An example of a subjective operation is the time required for the character to be echoed on the screen after it is typed in at the keyboard. The completion of the operation requires two levels of user interaction: typing in the key on the keyboard and watching the display for the appearance of the character. Without supplementary hardware and/or software to measure precisely when the key was pressed and precisely when the character appeared, the time between the two events must be reported by the user. Because the duration of the operation is generally quite short and the variability among user reflexes is quite large, measuring this operation involves a level of subjectivity not encountered in the easily measurable tasks.

The common operations concept can help to narrow the scope of what is being investigated, thereby simplifying tuning of both measurable and subjective operations. An ill-defined operation almost guarantees time wasted repeating work and revisiting resource allocation decisions. Since resource allocation decisions must often be made in a resource-constrained environment, priorities must be set regarding resource usage. A well-defined operation provides an effective framework for making such priority decisions.

☑ Once you have decided what you want to improve, go to Appendix A and find the tuning worksheet that matches the SCO product and the operation that you want to improve.

⇩

Step 2. Identify the limited and unlimited resources.

☑ Note any limited resources on the worksheet by marking them with an asterisk (*).

A *resource* is anything used by either the hardware or the software in the completion of a given operation. A resource can be hardware or software. An example of a hardware resource is the physical memory installed in the machine. An example of a software resource is an intermediate storage location configured as part of the application.

Resources also include time and money, since these often have a great impact on how much can be invested in the quest for optimal system performance. Identifying what is limited early in the tuning process helps clarify what might reasonably be expected in terms of performance improvement and so contributes towards the setting of realistic improvement goals in step 3.

The pattern of resource usage has a great impact on system performance. If a resource is in continual short supply, then the time necessary to complete an operation that uses that resource will be increased dramatically. Increasing the supply of that resource either by increasing the actual amount available or by reducing the number of applications using it is critical to shortening the duration of that operation.

Tuning is made more complex by a common situation in which one minor resource shortage causes more serious resource shortages elsewhere in the system. You might spend time increasing the latter resource without any increase in performance because the initial resource shortage remains. An understanding of how the system uses resources and how to monitor the usage of those resources helps you uncover the fundamental resource shortage and implement a solution. Uncovering such fundamental problems is essential to effective system tuning.

☑ The predefined worksheets list the underlying hardware and software resources used by each common operation in the **Resources to Monitor** section. With some worksheets, the **Resources to Monitor** section is continued on a second page.

⇩

Step 3. Determine how to measure the operation and test its current performance.

☑ Note the test result on the worksheet in the column marked **Now.**

A reliable measurement procedure is essential to determining whether a new resource allocation has reduced the time for the operation.

The requirements of a reliable measurement procedure are as follows:

- Results must be reproducible and consistent.

  Reproducible means that if someone else runs the test with the exact same environment, they can reproduce your results. *Consistent* means that the results from a set of test runs are within a small margin of error, where *small* is a percentage of what is being measured and for how long. If a test takes 2 hours, then variations of 10 or 20 seconds may be acceptable, whereas if a test takes 15 seconds, then variations of 5 seconds are not acceptable. If such a large variation occurs in the test results, then determining the improvement of any resource allocation changes becomes difficult, because some of the improvement seen may be inadvertently caused by the variation in the test results.

  Having a reliable test procedure will reduce the amount of time needed for tuning. You can be confident in the resource allocation decisions made, because the test results will reflect genuine improvements.

  If you are focusing on reducing the duration of a subjective operation, then setting up a reliable measurement procedure is a bit more difficult. Repeatable tests can be set up with macros and shell scripts, and stopwatches can be used to time the operations. Ensure that you clarify precisely when you start and stop timing. In order to achieve repeatable results, a simple rule to follow is the test should take a minimum of 20 or 30 seconds. In most cases, this length is long enough to reduce the effect of any inherent variability in the test. Increasing the test period improves both consistency and reproducibility.

The test case need not be complicated, as long as it tests the correct behavior. In some cases, a simple printing of a very long file to the screen when the system is under normal use is enough to test the update display operation.

- The procedure must actually measure what you want to improve.

  Because designing such a test can sometimes be quite time-consuming, use the tests included on the floppy disk as examples to help design a test procedure. Industry-standard benchmarks can also be used to measure various performance behaviors of a system. Such tests may be more applicable. By its nature, a test measuring a subjective operation may require more test design in order to measure the appropriate behavior. The more effort put toward test design, the quicker and more reliable the rest of the tuning process becomes.

- The environment in which the procedure is used must only vary in the experimental parameters, the rest being as consistent as possible.

  Ideally, the only difference between the previous test run and the current run is the new resource allocation. If more than the resource allocation has changed between runs, isolating the effect of changing parameters is difficult. Well-controlled test procedures are essential to conclusively determining whether resource changes increase or decrease the test duration. We recognize that perfectly controlled test environments are often impossible to set up in a commercial computing environment. If you can make the environment reasonably well-controlled, then the analysis will be that much more reliable, thereby optimizing the use of your time.

After you have implemented the test procedure, run the tests on the target environment to get an idea of current performance. These values will be used as a basis for evaluating whether changing the resource allocation has increased or decreased the time for the operation. Run the tests at least three times to see if the test produces stable results and use the average of those results as an initial starting point.

☑ Enter the results of the initial tests under the column marked **Now.** With some worksheets, this column will appear on the second page of the worksheet.

⇩

Step 4. Set a realistic performance goal.

☑ Note this on the worksheet in the column marked **Your Goal.**

Considering the limited resources and where you are now, define a performance improvement goal. The goal can be relative, for example, "25% reduction in the amount of time taken by this operation," or it can be absolute, for example "this operation should take no longer than 30 seconds." What is realistic depends on the computing environment and what you can change; there are no general rules for determining what is a realistic improvement goal.

☑ Enter the goal in the worksheet under the column marked **Your Goal**. In some cases, this column appears on the second page of the worksheet.

⇩

Step 5. Identify the resources to monitor and decide which monitoring tools to use.

☑ The worksheets list the appropriate resources.

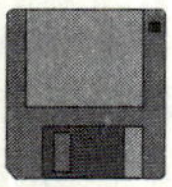

Use the monitoring tools described in each chapter to monitor the resource. The test programs on the floppy disk provide a template for how data should be collected. In general, the resources are monitored with the sar -o command and then the data is extracted with the utilities provided on the floppy disk.

⇩

Step 6. Run the test with the monitoring tools and monitor the resource usage and record the test results.

☑ Enter the initial values of the tunables and note the resource usage in the column marked **Initial Values**. Note the test results under the column called **Monitoring**.

Run the test with the monitoring tools enabled. Because monitoring tools use resources as well, running them may impact the test results. Record any differences in the test results in the worksheet.

☑ If results vary when the monitoring tools are run with the test, enter this adjusted result under the **Monitoring** column. Enter the initial values of the tunables in the **Tunables** section under the **Initial Values** column. In the **Resources to Monitor** section, note the usage level of the resources in the rows corresponding to those resources under the **Initial Values** column. In some cases, the **Resources to Monitor** section appears on the second page of the worksheet.

⇩

Step 7. Decide how to change the resource allocation; rerun the tests and note progress toward the goal. Iterate until either the goal is reached, or until a limited resource is encountered.

☑ Determine whether to increase or decrease the resource/tunable. Note the new tunable values in the column marked **Test #1** and the test results under the column **Res #1.** Use the rest of the columns for the results of subsequent test iterations.

☑ When the goal is reached, implement the new resource allocation.

This step is iterative and initially involves a decision about whether to increase or decrease the size of the intermediate storage locations used in the common operation. You make this decision based on the resource usage patterns observed in step 6. After you implement the first decision, run the test again to see whether progress toward the goal has been made. If the goal is not reached, look at the resource usage pattern, change the resource allocation again and run the test again.

☑ Enter the increase or decrease decisions for the appropriate tunables in the **Tunables** section. Enter new values for the tunables in the column under **Test #1**.

With the new resource allocation, run the tests again with the monitoring tools enabled to see the effect of the first set of changes.

☑ Enter the new test results under the column marked **Res #1**. Enter the new resource usage pattern in the **Resources to Monitor** section. Any additional observations can be noted in the margins.

In some cases, you may need to change two or more tunables in order to see a difference in performance. Such situations are noted in the description of the common operation in the product chapters so please read them carefully to ensure that you understand any relationships between tunables.

Based on the progress towards the goal made in this experiment, continue to change the tunables until either the goal is reached or until you encounter a limiting resource that prevents further progress. Knowing what is limited and unlimited allows you to see immediately if the goal needs to be adjusted because of a limiting resource.

☑ When you have reached the goal, record the final tunable values, resource usage patterns, and test results in the appropriate sections of the worksheet along with any comments you may have regarding the results. File the tuning worksheet with the system logbook so you can refer to it if additional performance tuning needs arise.

We recommend a program of frequent monitoring of system performance and resource usage patterns. Frequent monitoring allows you to further develop an understanding of precisely how the hardware and software are used and how effective the initial tuning phase has been. More incremental changes may be necessary as the usage pattern of the machine changes. Based on the tuning worksheet, select some key resources to monitor. You can implement the monitoring by setting up a regularly executed job, such as one called from cron(ADM), that executes the tools you used to monitor the selected resources.

The computing environment is always changing and this frequent monitoring allows you to forecast if and when more tuning is required before performance degrades significantly. Often new releases of applications will require additional memory and disk space. This is another ideal time to reexamine the environment to see if additional tuning or a hardware upgrade is necessary for optimal performance of the new application.

If Your System Fails To Improve...

We have sometimes found that the method described here does not yield a performance improvement. This failure can occur for a variety of reasons, some of which are outlined here and some of which are illustrated in the case studies.

The most common reason why you may not see a performance improvement is that the day-to-day variations of the system resource usage patterns cannot be isolated sufficiently to implement a reliable test procedure. In such cases, you will need to explore more thoroughly the resource usage patterns under a variety of system load situations and perhaps use more than one common operation combination to characterize system performance behavior. This approach is particularly applicable to complex client/server computing environments, where many different types of applications are supported in a heterogeneous computing network. The more you understand about how the applications are using resources in a variety of situations, the more successful you will be in tuning those complex systems.

Another reason that performance improvement is not achieved is because of a fundamental hardware limitation. Our experience has shown this hardware limitation often occurs either in the I/O subsystem or in physical memory availability. Software tuning improves problems caused by a hardware limitation such as a very slow disk running in a database system, but software cannot make the disk service requests any faster. In such cases, the solution which saves the most time is to upgrade the slow disk. Since that purchase often involves money, a trade-off between time and money must be made within the commercial constraints of the environment.

A third reason we have found is that occasionally an application is somehow constrained by its design because of internal contention on a resource, such as access to a special file. Multiple copies of the application that run in a multiuser environment and that require access to the same file will prevent performance improvement unless simultaneous access to that file is somehow implemented. Although rare, such a situation can be very frustrating, because tuning and hardware upgrades do not make any difference in performance.

All of the mechanisms described in this chapter provide you with more information on what is happening on the system. The more information you have about how the system is used, the better prepared you will be to respond efficiently to any issues which might arise regarding performance or other aspects of system administration.

Chapter 2

Common SCO UNIX Operations

This chapter is the foundation for the rest of the product chapters. This chapter presents the technical background for each common operation in detail. A *common operation* describes actions that are typically executed by computerrs.

The rest of the chapters in this book assume an understanding of the material presented in this chapter. The technical descriptions assume a minimal understanding of the SCO UNIX operating system concepts such as process. Some understanding of hardware concepts, such as system bus and disk adapter is also assumed.

A quick note about the monitoring tools used throughout the chapters is included before the common operation description begins.

Each resource involved in the operation is described in the order in which the resource is encountered during execution of the common operation. For example, when an application accesses filesystem information, the first operating system resource or intermediate storage location encountered is the *namei cache*. The namei cache maps the filename specified by the application to the data structure the operating system uses to represent that file.

The common operations described in this chapter are as follows:

- File read and write operations are common in an SCO UNIX environment, so this is the first operation described. A detailed example showing how to tune this operation following the seven- step method is presented in the SCO UNIX File Operation Case Study chapter following this chapter.

- The direct disk access interface is often used by databases for improved throughput and greater control over how the database records travel between the database server and the disks. Some comments on database layout are also included in this section.

- The calculation, or CPU-intensive operation are encountered when the speed of the CPU is the primary factor limiting the performance of the operation. Much of what occurs on the system requires the CPU, so the availability of the CPU is often critical to good performance. The final common operation in this chapter describes display update and character echo scenarios where serial terminals are connected to servers.

All of the common operation descriptions assume that sufficient memory is installed in the system to satisfy the memory needs of all the processes required to complete the operation. The impact of memory shortages is described in the Common Open Desktop Operations chapter. The discussion of SCO UNIX memory management is postponed until the Common Open Desktop Operations chapter because memory shortages occur frequently in an Open Desktop environment.

The chapter concludes with a Quick Diagnosis Summary highlighting some of the key monitoring tools and behaviors discussed in this chapter.

A Word About Monitoring Tools

The monitoring tools used in this chapter are as follows:

- sar(ADM) for essential resource monitoring
- timex(C)/time(C) to time the performance analysis tests and operations

- ps(C) to find out how the application process uses some system resources

Running sar consumes operating system resources just like any other application and may affect the test results. When sar runs, it uses CPU time to collect the data. When sar records the information, it also writes files to the filesystem. sar uses all of the resources described in the filesystem operation section.

The scripts on the floppy disk use the sar -o option to collect all the statistics and then extract the appropriate worksheet data.

To understand the impact of sar on the resource usage pattern, run sar when no other applications are running and note the average number of filesystem and disk operations with sar -b/ sar -d. After starting the test program, run sar again and monitor the number of filesystem and disk operations with sar -b/sar -d.

The difference in filesystem resource usage statistics between simply running sar and running sar with the performance analysis test is normally smaller than 5%. If the number of operations is greater than 5%, then consider increasing the intensity or length of the performance test program so the number of filesystem operations from sar becomes a much smaller proportion of the filesystem activity.

Do a similar analysis on the CPU usage to ensure that the CPU statistics are not significantly different when sar is running. Always run the test with and without sar to assess the impact of the filesystem operations.

HINT:

To speed the filling in of the worksheet, run sar with the -o option (all options) to direct the output to a file. Use the sar processing script included on the floppy disk, sar2oswks, to isolate the data required for the worksheet.

This book does not attempt to replace the information on these tools contained in the SCO manuals. Instead, this book complements the SCO manuals. Please refer to the SCO manual set for more information on the monitoring tools if the information is not provided in this book.

Some of the options specified for sar are not available for releases prior to SCO UNIX 3.2v4.2. Please check the SCO documentation for the release installed on the system for the definitive list of sar options supported by the particular release.

File Read And Write Operations

This section describes what happens when an application reads from or writes to a file stored in the filesystem. The resources are presented in the order that they are encountered by the operating system during a file read or write operation. Figure 2-1 summarizes the resources that are discussed in this section.

When an application reads data from a file, data is transferred from the filesystem to the operating system intermediate storage location known as the buffer cache. The data is then copied from the buffer cache to the application storage area. When the application writes data to a file in the filesystem, the information is copied from the application storage area to the buffer cache and then eventually to the filesystem on the disk.

Synchronous File Access

Applications can access filesystem data in either a *synchronous* or *asynchronous* manner. Synchronous access ensures that all the data the application writes to the filesystem is actually on the disk before the application proceeds. Applications requiring an extra level of data integrity, such as databases using the filesystem, often use the synchronous interface for essential information, such as log files.

Asynchronous File Access

With asynchronous access, the application data is written to the operating system intermediate storage location, the buffer cache. The application continues executing instead of waiting for the data to be written to the disk. The data in the buffer cache is written to the disk by a separate system process called *bdflush*. The bdflush mechanism is described in more detail in the Buffer Cache section.

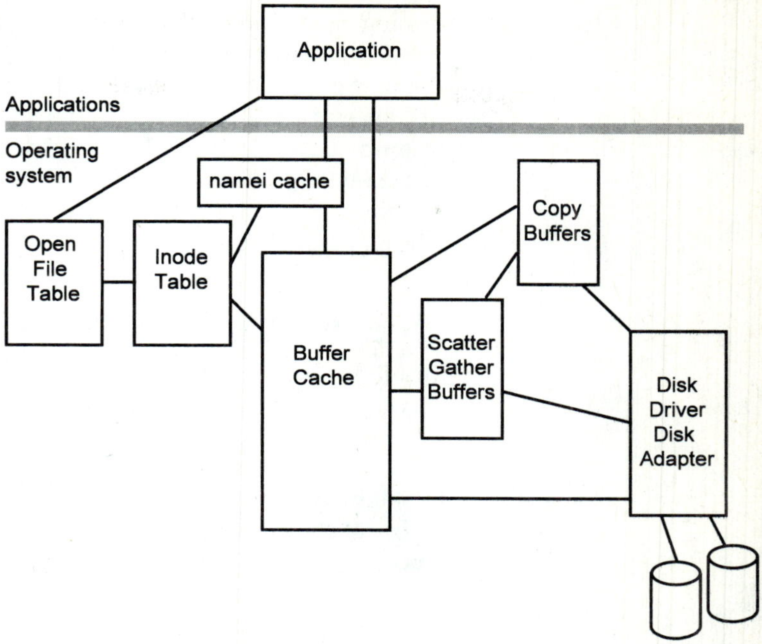

Figure 2-1: Intermediate Storage Locations and Resources In A File Read or Write Operation. Before the client application can access file data, the name of the file must be mapped to an inode. The operating system maintains a list of the most recent filename mappings in the namei cache. The operating system must also add the open file to its internal list of open files. The buffer cache is another intermediate storage location for the filesystem data. The scatter/gather buffers are used when a group of requests that are scattered in memory reside next to each other on the disk. The copy buffers are used only when the disk adapter cannot access memory above 16 Mbytes and some of the buffers in the buffer cache are located above this boundary. Neither scatter/gather nor the copy buffers are used for every disk transfer. The disk adapter manages the disk hardware. The disk provides permanent storage.

The tuning recommendations contained in the following sections apply primarily to asynchronous filesystem access, since that is the most commonly used method. If you want to improve the performance of synchronous filesystem access, then concentrate on the recommendations from the copy buffer section through to the disk adapter and disks. Pay special attention to the filesystem layout recommendations, as these apply to both synchronous and asynchronous filesystem access.

Application Storage and Behavior

Applications often use memory to reduce the amount of information that must be transferred to and from the disk or other permanent storage locations. If the application stores frequently accessed information in memory, then the information is immediately available. Because no disk transfer is necessary, the operation is shorter and requires less CPU time. The file access operation uses less CPU time, so more CPU time is available for other operations. Using memory to store new information can also reduce disk activity, because the application may need to store less information on the disk.

Table 2-1 summarizes how to monitor some of the resources used by an application process.

Behavior	Command	Column
The amount of CPU time used by the process	ps -el	TIME
The amount of memory used by the process	ps -el	SZ
State of the process	ps -el	S
Number of ready-to-run processes	sar -q	runq-sz

Table 2-1: How to Monitor Application Resource Usage

ps -el

The ps command provides a snapshot of process activity when the command is executed. The TIME column shows the amount of CPU time accumulated by the process since the process started. Over time, the values reported in this column for the active processes should increase.

The SZ column shows the amount of memory, in Kbytes, occupied by the process. The amount of memory shown in the SZ column is equal to the size of the text area plus the size of the data area plus the size of the stack. Other special types of memory, such as shared memory, are also included in the value. The value in the SZ column may grow as the process runs because it allocates more memory. Monitoring this value over time shows which processes require more memory as they run.

The S column shows the state of the process when the ps command is executed. The states that affect the performance of the process are as follows:

- *O* means the process is actually running on the processor
- *S* means the process is suspended, or *sleeping*, waiting for access to a resource
- *R* means the process is waiting to run on the CPU
- *B* means the process is waiting for memory

If the process should continually display the status B, then the performance of this process is affected by a system memory shortage. Please see the Common Open Desktop Operations chapter for more information on memory shortages.

Performance monitoring tools are provided with many applications to help monitor the effectiveness of memory used by the application. Check the application documentation to see if any tools are provided and for further help in tuning the application. Any such additional measurement should be noted on the tuning worksheet.

sar -q The average number of ready-to-run processes as shown in the runq-sz column is an indication of whether enough processes are available to keep the CPU busy. Process management and scheduling is discussed in more detail in the Calculations section of this chapter.

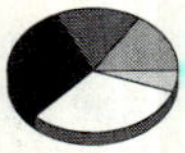

In terms of tuning, some applications are extensively configurable and others have no configuration options. Database applications are often very configurable, and tuning their resource usage often yields significant performance improvement. Check the application documentation for information on tuning resource allocation.

When you are deciding how to change the system's resource allocation, you need to find the balance between many uses of memory. One application process may run faster when using more memory, but other application processes receive little or no benefit.

Avoid increasing the amount of memory used by an application to such a degree that paging or swapping begin. If paging or swapping occurs, either reclaim memory by reducing other memory usage or reduce the amount of memory used by your application until paging and swapping cease. See the Common Open Desktop Operations chapter for a complete description of tuning when a memory shortage occurs.

The Namei Cache

SCO UNIX uses the namei cache to map the pathname specified by the application to a filesystem data structure describing the file's characteristics and location on the disk. This filesystem data structure is called an *inode*.

The first time an application accesses a filename, a copy of the filename is stored in the namei cache for other applications to access. When a name cannot be found in the namei cache, the operating system makes either one or two read requests to another intermediate filesystem storage location, the buffer cache.

If the size of the directory is less than or equal to 10 Kbytes, then only one read request occurs; otherwise two read requests occur. The first request obtains the location of the directory, and the second retrieves the first 1 Kbyte of the directory. If the name is not found in the first 1 Kbyte of the directory, the next 1 Kbyte of the directory is read. This read operation requires another two requests for data from the buffer cache. All such buffer cache and disk accesses can cause performance degradation because more intermediate storage locations must be searched before the data can be retrieved.

If the buffer cache does not contain any of the required information; then a disk transfer must take place to obtain the data. Extending the size of the namei cache can therefore reduce the number of requests processed by the buffer cache and can also reduce the number of disk requests.

S5CACHEENTS

The size of the namei cache is determined by the configurable variable S5CACHEENTS. Each entry in the cache occupies 40 bytes. The larger the cache, the more likely the operating system will find a filename without accessing the disk.

S5HASHQS

For efficient searching, the operating system maintains a separate indexed list of entries in the namei cache. The value of the configurable variable S5HASHQS determines the number of index lists. Each entry in the indexed list occupies 8 bytes. The average number of namei cache entries associated with an index is calculated by dividing the value of S5HASHQS into the value of S5CACHEENTS as shown by the following equation:

$$\frac{S5CACHEENTS}{S5HASHQS} = average\_list\_length$$

The namei search time decreases as the value of S5HASHQS increases, because the average length of the indexed lists is shorter. When modifying S5CACHEENTS, adjust S5HASHQS until the ratio of S5CACHEENTS divided by S5HASHQS is less than or equal to four.

Figure 2-2 shows how these tunables affect the configuration of the indexed lists. Indexed lists are also implemented in the inode table and the buffer cache, so this diagram applies to those intermediate storage locations as well.

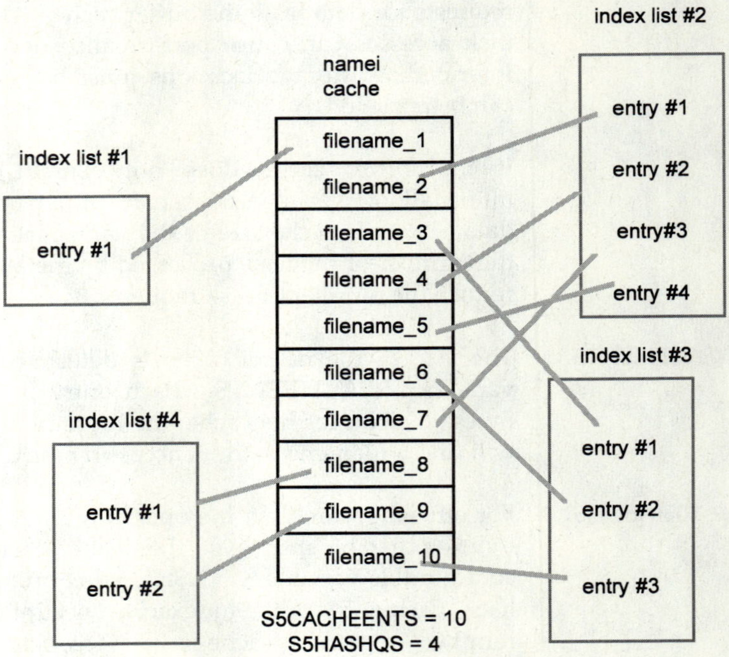

Figure 2-2: This diagram shows how the values configuring the data structure size and the nmber of lists affects the average length of the lists. With S5CACHEENTS equal to 10 and S5HASHQS equal to four, the average length of the indexed lists is 10/4, or 2.5. Because this ratio is an average length, some of the lists will contain a number of entries greater than three, and others will contain a number less than three. One-half an entry is not possible.

Symbolic Links

A symbolic link is a special type of file that actually references another file. A symbolic link can be used across filesystems to present a consistent filesystem hierarchy to users even if the underlying file hierarchy varies, for example with remotely mounted filesystems. For example, a symbolic link called */u/username* can refer to the actual directory */host/systemname/u/username/text*. In this way, the hierarchy presented to the user is consistent no matter where the files are located.

When the operating system locates a name within a pathname that is a symbolic link, the operating system must locate the actual file, directory or device node that is referenced by the symbolic link. The operating system opens the file referenced by the symbolic link, obtains the actual file pathname, and then opens the actual file specified by the symbolic link.

All the read operations for the symbolic link and actual file information occur as described in this section. Because the symbolic link has been accessed to obtain the actual file information, the inode for the symbolic link must also be updated. If the inode is stored in the buffer cache, the inode can be updated without accessing the disk. The buffer cache is explained in more detail later in this section.

Table 2-2 summarizes how to monitor the namei cache.

Behavior	**Command**	**Column**
Number of filenames located in the cache	sar -n	c_hits
Number of filenames not located in cache	sar -n	cmisses
Cache efficiency	sar -n	hit %
Total number of filename requests processed by namei cache	sar -n	cmisses plus c_hits

Table 2-2: Monitoring Namei Cache Efficiency

sar -n

The c_hits column shows the average number of filenames that were found in the namei cache during the time increment specified when sar was invoked. The higher this value, the more effective the namei cache. For example, if this value is 20, then a filename was successfully found in the cache 20 times, and at least 20 requests to the buffer cache have been saved.

The cmisses column shows the average number of filenames that were not found in the namei cache during the time increment specified when sar was invoked. Each time the operating system does not find a filename in the cache, at least one request to the filesystem is made to complete the filename mapping. The lower the value reported by cmisses, the fewer accesses to the buffer cache for filesystem information.

The hit % column is a ratio of cache efficiency. The value in this column is calculated by dividing the value in c_hits by the sum of cmisses and c_hits as shown by the following equation:

$$\frac{c\_hits}{c\_hits + cmisses} = hit\ \%$$

The efficiency of the cache rises as this percentage rises because a greater proportion of filename mapping requests are satisfied with the information present in the cache.

The average number of filename mapping requests made by application processes can be calculated by adding the values shown in the c_hits and cmisses columns.

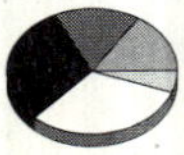

The performance of those applications accessing filenames can be increased by raising the values of both S5CACHEENTS and S5HASHQS in proportion until the cache hit rate is above 90%. When modifying S5CACHEENTS, adjust S5HASHQS until the ratio of S5CACHEENTS divided by S5HASHQS is less than or equal to four. If the ratio is greater than four, the time required to find the correct entry in the cache is increased, thereby possibly compromising the expected performance improvement. Setting S5HASHQS to a prime number will also improve the distribution of the entries in the indexed lists.

The performance of applications that access many different files may also improve if S5CACHEENTS is increased. Increasing this configurable variable may prove to be a more efficient use of memory than increasing the size of the buffer cache to handle all the filesystem requests.

Each additional entry in the cache consumes only 40 bytes so configuring the cache until the hit rate is close to 100% does not significantly increase the memory usage of the operating system.

The Inode Table and Open File Table

The operating system stores information about all the open files and directories that the applications are currently using in the inode and open file tables. An inode describes various attributes about the file or directory, such as size, type, and access permissions. Location information for the file or directory on the filesystem is also kept in the inode. The open file table is the operating system's list of all open files.

When the application closes a file or directory, the operating system removes the inode from the table and places it on another list, called the inode freelist. The inode freelist is maintained by the operating system. The entry in the open file table is also removed.

When another file is opened and an inode is requested, the operating system first checks to see if the inode is located on the freelist or if the inode is already in the inode table. If the operating system finds the inode in either of these locations, then the operating system returns a *file descriptor* to the application with no further searching. After the application has opened a file, the file descriptor is the data structure that the application uses to access the file.

If the operating system does not find the correct inode, then the operating system allocates an inode from the freelist, and the operating system updates this inode with the correct information for the newly opened file. In order to update the information in this data structure for the inode table, the operating system retrieves the information from the filesystem. Retrieving the information in this way requires at least one transfer of information from the buffer cache to the inode table, which degrades performance.

NINODE

The number of inodes that the operating system stores in the inode table is determined by the configurable variable NINODE. An insufficient number of entries in the inode table affects the operation of applications as well as their performance. If the operating system runs out of entries in this table, the operating system displays the following message:

```
CONFIG:ifreeget - Inode table overflow (NINODE =
x exceeded)
```

When this message appears, the operation fails, and an error is returned to the application that initiated the operation. If this message appears, increase NINODE to ensure proper application execution.

Each inode table entry itself occupies 76 bytes, plus an additional 96 bytes for operating system filesystem bookkeeping information.

NHINODE

For efficient searching, the operating system maintains a set of indexed lists of inode table entries, similarly structured to the lists described in the namei cache section. The number of indexes is determined by the value of NHINODE; the length of each of the lists is determined by dividing NINODE by NHINODE as shown by the following equation:

$$\frac{NINODE}{NHINODE} = average\_list\_length$$

The optimal ratio of NINODE divided by NHINODE is less than or equal to four.

When an inode change is critical, the updated inode is written synchronously to the filesystem. Because inodes contain essential file information, the synchronous update ensures that the valuable data is written to the filesystem before continuing. With less critical information, the inode update occurs asynchronously.

NFILE

The number of open files is configured with NFILE. As with the inode table, when the operating system runs out of entries in the open file table, it displays the following error message:

```
CONFIG:falloc - File table overflow (NFILE = x)
```

where x is equal to the current value of NFILE.

Each entry in the file table occupies 12 bytes.

Table 2-3 summarizes how to monitor the usage of the inode and open file tables.

Behavior	**Command**	**Column**
Number of open file table entries used	sar -v	file-sz
Number of times the operating system ran out of open file table entries	sar -v	ov
Number of inode table entries used	sar -v	inod-sz
Number of times the operating system ran out of inode table entries	sar -v	ov

Table 2-3: How to Monitor Open File and Inode Table Usage

sar -v

The file-sz column shows the average number of entries in the open file table. The inod-sz column shows the average number of entries in the inode table for each time interval specified when sar was invoked. Both columns display information in the form xx/yy, where xx shows how many file entries or inodes are actually in use, and yy shows how many are configured. This number is the value of NFILE or NINODE.

The usage percentage can be calculated by dividing the maximum number of entries used by the total number of entries in the table as shown by the following equation:

$$\frac{Maximum\_number\_used}{Total\_number\_configured} = Percentage\_used$$

The number of times no entries were available in the table is shown by the ov column displayed next to the usage statistics for that table.

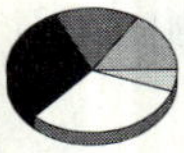

The first priority for tuning these data structures is to ensure that the operating system has sufficient inode and open file table entries to support the number of processes on the system. Applications may not function correctly without a sufficient number of entries in these tables.

When the value of NINODE is increased, the likelihood of locating the inode in the table rises, thereby reducing the number of requests to the buffer cache and the number of disk requests. Reducing the number of requests to the buffer cache and to the disks reduces the delay in completing the filesystem operation.

If the inode and open file table utilization is more than 80%, increase the relevant parameter until the usage is below 80%. Increase NHINODE so the ratio of NINODE divided by NHINODE is less than or equal to four.

The Buffer Cache

The operating system uses the buffer cache to reduce the total amount of disk activity caused by applications accessing the filesystem.

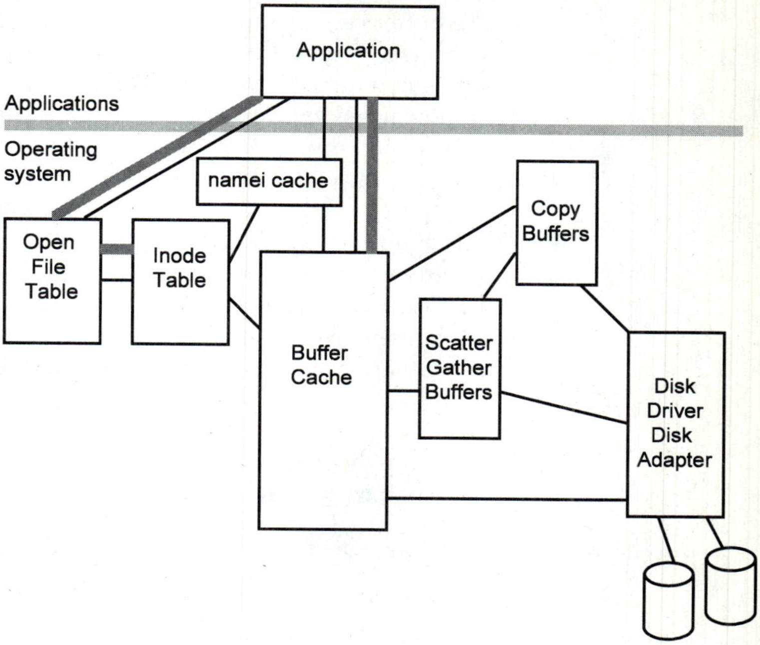

Figure 2-3: The thin black line shows the data path when the application accesses filesystem information for the first time. All of the caches must be filled with accesses from the disk. The gray line shows the data path when the application accesses the same filea data again and the data is still in the buffer cache. The second path is much shorter than the first, so the time required for the second data access is shorter than for the first.

The buffer cache consists of 1 Kbyte data storage locations, known as *buffers.* These buffers occupy memory and contain copies of filesystem data. The buffer cache reduces the amount of disk traffic caused by applications reading filesystem information by retaining a copy of the filesystem information in memory after it has been retrieved from the disk. If another application requires access to the data or the same application requires access to the data again, the application can access it in the buffer cache instead of retrieving it again from the disk. The time required for a filesystem read operation is therefore equal to the time required to locate the correct buffer in the cache. Because memory access is faster than disk access, the time required to find a buffer in the cache is much less than the time required to retrieve the data from the disk. Figure 2-3 compares the data path when a buffer is not found in the buffer cache to the data path when the buffer is contained in the buffer cache.

BDFLUSHR

The buffer cache improves the performance of filesystem write operations by allowing the application to write its data to the buffer cache instead of forcing the application to wait for a disk transfer to complete. A separate system process, *bdflush,* then writes all of the modified filesystem data contained in the buffer cache to the disk at intervals specified by the configurable variable BDFLUSHR. The application continues executing as if the data had been written to the disk, but actually the data is not written until bdflush transfers all of the modified data to the disk or until the operating system needs to recycle the buffer. This mechanism is known as *delayed write*

NAUTOUP

The configurable variable NAUTOUP determines how old the data in the buffer must be before it is written to the disk. The age is denoted in seconds.

The buffer cache reduces the amount of disk traffic caused by applications writing filesystem data in two ways:

- If a buffer contained in the buffer cache is modified more than once in the interval between bdflush transfers, then only the final version of the data is transferred to the disk. If the intermediate version had been written to the disk, the second modification would have cancelled out the first modification, so the first disk transfer was not required. In this case, the data was changed before it was written to the disk, so a write was *saved* by the buffer cache.

- The process of writing out an entire set of modified buffers allows the collection of the write requests into larger requests. The disk is used more efficiently because more data can be transferred per disk request.

The operating system manages buffers by means of a *least recently used* algorithm. This algorithm preserves frequently used data and recycles buffers containing data that is not used as often. The algorithm works as follows:

- The operating system keeps track of when the buffers were last accessed, so when a new buffer is required, the new data writes over the most infrequently accessed buffer.

- If a buffer contains data which needs to be written to the disk, the operating system writes the data to the disk without waiting for bdflush to run. The operating system writes the buffer to the disk without bdflush when a buffer is required.

- If the application needs the data after the data has been expelled from the buffer cache, the data must be retrieved from the disk again.

With the least recently used algorithm, more data can be stored in a larger buffer cache, thereby postponing the time when the data must be expelled because of other filesystem requests. The number of disk transfers is reduced because the data can be held in the cache for a longer period of time. If the buffer cache is small and many applications are accessing the filesystem, a larger cache can reduce the number of disk transfers because more filesystem data can be stored in the buffer cache.

MAXBUF, NBUF

The size of the buffer cache is controlled by the configurable variables MAXBUF and NBUF. If the value of NBUF is equal to zero, the operating system automatically determines the size of the buffer cache, based on the total amount of physical memory in the system. The value of the MAXBUF variable is an upper bound for the operating system's decision.

The size of the buffer cache is printed when the operating system initializes. The message is:

```
kernel: i/o bufs  = xxxk
```

where xxx is the number of buffers the operating system configured if the value of NBUF is zero or is the value of NBUF. This message can also be found in */usr/adm/messages*.

NHBUF

For efficient searching, the operating system maintains a set of indexed lists of buffers in the buffer cache. The value of NHBUF determines the number of indexed lists. The larger this index, the more quickly the operating system can locate the correct buffer, because the average length of each list is shorter. The average length of each indexed list is specified by the ratio of NBUF divided by NHBUF as shown by the following equation:

$$\frac{NBUF}{NHBUF} = average\_list\_length$$

The optimal ratio is equal to four.

Each buffer occupies 1098 bytes, including operating system bookkeeping information, and each indexed list entry occupies 16 bytes.

Table 2-4 summarizes how to monitor the buffer cache.

Behavior	Command	Column
Number of logical read requests per second	sar -b	lread/s
% of read requests found in the cache	sar -b	%rcache
Number of read operations to the disk (due to cache miss) per second	sar -b	bread/s
Number of logical write requests per second	sar -b	lwrit/s
% of writes saved by keeping data in the cache	sar -b	%wcache
Number of write operations to the disk per second	sar -b	bwrit/s

Table 2-4: How to Monitor the Buffer Cache

sar -b

The sar statistics account for reads in two stages. The first stage of the read is attempting to obtain the information from the buffer cache. This read is called a *logical read* because no physical devices were involved. If the data was not found in the buffer cache, then the second part of the read must occur. The second part of the read operation involves accessing the disk where the filesystem data is stored.

The average number of logical read requests to the buffer cache per second is shown in the lread/s column. The percentage of logical reads satisfied by information already stored in the buffer cache is shown in the %rcache column. The higher the percentage, the more disk requests are avoided, and the more efficient the cache. If the data is not found, the information must be retrieved from the disk. The bread/s shows the number of read requests that were not found in the cache during the second stage of the read operation.

The sar statistics also account for filesystem write operations in two stages. The first stage of a write operation is the transfer of the modified data to the buffer cache. This part of the transfer is known as a *logical write*. The second stage of the write is the transfer of the data to the physical device.

The average number of logical write requests to the buffer cache per second is shown in the lwrit/s column. The value shown in the bwrit/s column is the average number of write requests per second made to write buffers to the filesystem. These write operations occur because bdflush recycles buffers containing delayed write data and applications execute synchronous write operations.

The value in the %wcache column provides an indication of the number of disk write requests that are avoided because the buffer was modified before being transferred to the disk. If data is frequently modified while in the buffer cache before being written to the filesystem, then disk write requests are reduced because only the last modification is actually copied to the disk. None of the intermediate modifications are transferred to the disk. Because data to be written to the filesystem is actually written to the filesystem only at specified intervals, a buffer may be modified more than once before it is written to the filesystem.

An important difference between the buffer cache and the application storage area is the sharing of the buffer cache among all applications running on the system. Memory used for the buffer cache benefits all application processes accessing the filesystem. Other applications may also benefit, because more processor time is available. More processor time is available because the filesystem accesses take less CPU time to complete. A balance is therefore needed between the application's use of memory and the size of the buffer cache.

Before deciding to increase the amount of memory allocated to the buffer cache, examine the amount of available memory on the system as reported by sar. See the Common Open Desktop Operations chapter for more information on determining the amount of free memory. If the system is currently swapping or paging, increasing the size of the buffer cache may result in reduced performance because the increased paging or swapping activity negates the improvement in disk efficiency caused by a larger buffer cache.

For such a system, file read and write performance may be improved by reducing the size of the buffer cache until paging and swapping cease. For a system where little paging activity occurs, try increasing the size of the buffer cache until either paging begins or the cache efficiency statistics reported by sar indicate an optimal size. See the Common Open Desktop Operations chapter for more information on paging and swapping.

The primary cache efficiency statistic is the read hit rate reported by %rcache. Typical application environments execute many more filesystem read operations than write operations, so tuning the buffer cache until %rcache is maximized will improve the performance of filesystem operations. In most cases, when the cache hit rate is more than 98%, further increases to the size of the buffer cache minimally improve filesystem performance. The most common exception to this guideline is when the applications executing on the system are constantly updating inodes. Since most of these inode update operations are synchronous, increasing the size of the buffer cache has no benefit.

HINT:

If the performance test program creates many files, a majority of the test program's filesystem operations will be synchronous because the inode updates for file creation are synchronous. Because of the high percentage of synchronous writes, increasing the size of the buffer cache will not significantly increase performance.

Whenever the value of NBUF is increased, increase the value of NHBUF until the ratio of NBUF divided by NHBUF is less than or equal to four. The shorter the lists, the shorter the time required to find the correct buffer. The value of NHBUF should always be a power of two.

Increasing the length of time between bdflush operations by increasing the value of BDFLUSHR reduces the total amount of disk activity, because buffers are written to the disk less frequently. However, as the value of BDFLUSHR increases, so does the risk of lost data should the system unexpectedly terminate, as in a power cut for example.

The data loss occurs because not all of the application data is on the disk when the system stops. The data that is to be written to the disk in a delayed write manner is stored only in memory and so cannot be readily recovered when the system is restored. When the system is terminated by init(M), reboot(ADM), or haltsys(ADM), the operating system ensures that all vital data is transferred to the disk before the system stops.

To avoid inadvertent loss of data, users can execute a sync(ADM) command that causes all the unwritten buffer cache data to be added to the disk driver's request list in preparation for transfer to the disk. Applications can also execute a special function also called sync. Applications and users executing this function or command may cause a long list of requests to be sent to the disk driver, thereby causing a temporary backlog in the processing of disk requests.

Reducing BDFLUSHR to values less than or equal to five can improve operations that continuously write large amounts of filesystem data. The system process bdflush runs more frequently, so the data is written continuously rather than in large and infrequent bursts.

When the value of NAUTOUP is increased, the bdflush process transfers fewer buffers to the disk on each scan through the buffer cache because fewer buffers of that age will be found. With a lower age, bdflush finds more buffers of that age, and more data is transferred on each scan. Reducing NAUTOUP may help reduce the amount of data written each time bdflush runs.

The Scatter/Gather Feature

Scatter/gather is a performance optimization that allows separate filesystem requests to be grouped together as a single request. Only requests whose destinations are physically located next to each other on the disk can be grouped.

Some intelligent disk adapters support the scatter/gather feature with minimal operating system intervention.

Other disk adapters require the operating system to build the group of requests in a temporary work area, which can then be transferred to the disk driver as one large request. If the disk adapter does not support scatter/gather directly, then the operating system copies the data into a temporary work area before transferring it to the disk.

When the operating system initializes, the disk adapters that use the Sdsk subsystem print a message that indicates whether scatter/gather is supported. If the adapter supports scatter/gather, then the following message is shown in the Comment column:

```
fts=xxsx
```

where the x represents additional configuration information and the s specifies whether scatter/gather is supported.

NMPHEADBUF For disk adapters that support scatter/gather directly in hardware, the operating system keeps track of each scatter/gather request with a special data structure called a *buffer header*. The operating system assigns one buffer header to each outstanding scatter/gather request for these types of adapters. The number of buffer headers is controlled by the value of NMPHEADBUF. Each scatter/gather buffer header occupies 72 bytes.

MPBUF NFor disk adapters that do not support scatter/gather directly in hardware, the number of simultaneous scatter/gather requests that can be composed in the temporary work area is determined by the configurable variable NMPBUF. The value of NMPBUF is expressed in units of 16 Kbytes. Each temporary work area occupies 16 Kbytes, so to avoid wasting memory, increase the value of NMPBUF only when necessary. If the value of NMPBUF is equal to zero, the operating system automatically allocates a number of temporary work areas based on the amount of available memory.

Table 2-5 summarizes how to monitor the scatter/gather resource usage pattern.

Behavior	**Command**	**Column**
Number of scatter/gather requests per second to hardware that supports scatter/gather	sar -h	mphbuf/s
Number of times per second buffer headers were not available	sar -h	omphbuf/s
Number of times per second a temporary work area has been allocated	sar -h	mpbuf/s
Number of times per second a temporary work area could not be allocated	sar -h	ompb/s

Table 2-5: How to Monitor Scatter/gather

sar -h The frequency of scatter/gather requests issued by the operating system per second is shown in the mphbuf/s column. This column is greater than zero if the disk adapter supports scatter/gather without requiring operating system intervention.

The omphbuf/s column shows the number of times the operating system required buffer headers and none were available. When no buffer headers are available, each disk request is sent to the disk adapter individually.

The mpbuf/s column shows the number of scatter/gather requests made to disk adapters that do not have hardware support for scatter/gather.

In some cases, the operating system allocates one of these temporary work areas when loading application binaries into memory, so this number may be greater than zero even if the disk adapter supports scatter/gather at the hardware level. However, if this value is consistently greater than one, then the disk adapter does not support scatter/gather and performance may be improved by upgrading the disk adapter to one that does.

The number of times per second the operating system runs out of temporary work space is shown by the ompb/s column. If the operating system runs out of temporary work space, then the scatter/gather pathway is not used for this set of disk requests. The only time the operating system suspends the process when temporary work space is not available is when the operating system is copying application binaries into memory.

The first priority for tuning scatter/gather is to ensure that a sufficient number of buffer headers and temporary work areas are available. A sufficient number are available when the values displayed in the ompb/s and omphbuf/s columns are always equal to zero. Running out of buffer headers or temporary work areas delays the completion of the filesystem operation because this performance optimization cannot be used. Ensure that increasing NMPBUF does not cause the system to begin paging or swapping, as this increase in disk activity caused by paging or swapping negates any potential performance benefit of increasing NMPBUF.

If the values shown in the mpbufs/s column are greater than zero, then the operating system is building scatter/gather requests, and performance of filesystem operations can be improved by replacing this disk controller with one that supports scatter/gather directly in the adapter. Data copying is reduced, and the requests are sent to the disk adapter without operating system intervention.

The Copy Buffer Mechanism

Some disk adapters are restricted in their ability to access some memory locations referenced by the buffer cache. The most common restriction is an inability to directly access physical memory located above the 16 Mbyte boundary. Since the buffer cache can reside anywhere in physical memory, buffers may be located above the 16 Mbyte memory boundary. These disk adapters cannot directly access these buffers because of a hardware limitation.

The memory access limitation is common among ISA and some MCA disk adapters. Check the hardware documentation for information regarding such limitations.

NCOPYBUF

The operating system compensates for this inability to access memory locations above 16 Mbytes by providing an intermediate transfer area called a *copy buffer* for copying the buffer cache data to a location that is accessible to the disk adapter. Copy buffers are used by both file read and write operations when the disk adapter cannot access the buffer cache data directly. The number of copy buffers is determined by the configurable variable NCOPYBUF.

Each copy buffer occupies 1 Kbyte of memory.

When a copy buffer is used, an additional transfer operation occurs for the data on its way to and from the disk. This additional transfer operation requires the CPU to copy the data from one memory location to another, thereby increasing the amount of CPU time required to complete the file read or write operation. Copying data also reduces the efficiency of the Level 2 cache, which also affects performance. Level 2 caches are described in the Calculations section later in this chapter.

PLOWBUFS

The location of the buffer cache in memory is controlled by setting the value of the configurable variable PLOWBUFS. This variable sets the percentage of *low buffers*, which are buffers that should be located below the 16 Mbyte boundary. The higher the value, the greater number of buffers the operating system tries to locate below this boundary. Since many hardware devices also require access to the memory below 16 Mbytes, the actual number of buffers located below 16 Mbytes may not be equal to the percentage specified by PLOWBUFS. Figure 2-4 shows how copy buffers are used to complete the transfer of data to and from the disk.

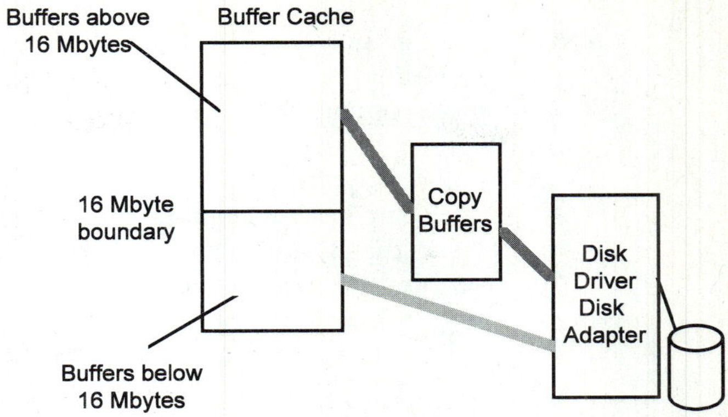

Figure 2-4: The buffers above 16 Mbytes must be copied to the copy buffers before they can be transferred to the disk adapter because the disk adapter cannot access memory above 16 Mbytes. The buffers below 16 Mbytes can be transferred directly to the disk adapter.

When the operating system initializes, it prints a message indicating the total number of buffers allocated and the number that are located above 16 Mbytes. The message shown is:

```
kernel: i/o buffers = xx (hi bufs = yy)
```

where xx is the total number of buffers allocated and yy is the number of buffers above 16 Mbytes. If the "hi bufs" is not displayed, then the operating system has not allocated any buffers above 16 Mbytes.

Table 2-6 summarizes how to monitor copy buffer usage.

Behavior	Command	Column
Number of copy buffers used per second	sar -B	cpybuf/s
Frequency of copy buffer exhaustion	sar -B	slpcpybuf/s

Table 2-6: How to Monitor Copy Buffer Usage

sar -B

The cpybuf/s column shows how frequently per second the operating system uses copy buffers. The greater the value the more copying that is occurring.

The slpcpybuf/s column shows how many times per second the operating system required a copy buffer, but none was available. When this situation occurs, the process requiring the copy buffer is suspended until a copy buffer is available. If the process is suspended, then the completion of the filesystem operation is delayed, and performance is adversely impacted.

If the operating system did not allocate any buffers above 16 Mbytes, then do not monitor copy buffer usage.

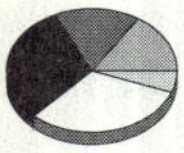

Copying data for filesystem transfers introduces an extra step in the filesystem operation, thereby adversely impacting performance. If a disk adapter with a memory access restriction must be used, then ensure that the number of copy buffers required is sufficient.

Reduce the amount of copying by increasing the value of PLOWBUFS so more buffers are directly accessible by the disk adapter. Remember that the value of this tunable can be overridden by the operating system because of a shortage of memory below the 16 Mbyte boundary, so increasing this value may have no effect. Check the initialization messages to see what the operating system actually allocated.

If changing the value of PLOWBUFS does not affect the number of buffers above 16 Mbytes, check the values reported by slpcpybuf/s. When this value is greater than zero, increase NCOPYBUF until this value reaches zero. Each copy buffer uses 1 Kbyte of memory, so make sure the system does not start to page or swap when NCOPYBUF is increased. The effects of paging and swapping are described in the Common Open Desktop Operations chapter.

The Disk Driver, Disk Adapter, and Disks

The disk driver manages the transfer of data from the buffer cache to the disks by controlling the disk adapter hardware.

In SCO UNIX, when the operating system is ready to transfer data from the buffer cache to the filesystem on the disk, the operating system calls the disk adapter routine xxstrategy() on behalf of the process requesting the transfer to the disk. The xx in xxstrategy() is the unique prefix specifying the appropriate disk driver. The xxstrategy() routine adds all the requests from all processes to a list. The disk driver then takes each disk request off the list and sends it to the disk adapter. Figure 2-5 shows the pathway of the request from the application to the disk.

SDSKOUT

The value of SDSKOUT specifies the maximum number of simultaneous requests that can be queued for each SCSI disk. This configurable variable applies only to SCSI disks whose drivers used the Sdsk mechanism. When the request list for that disk reaches the length specified by SDSKOUT, the operating system must wait for the list to shorten before it can add the request to the list. The operating system suspends the process that initiated the disk request until the request list is shorter than SDSKOUT.

After the disk request is successfully added to the list, the disk driver sends the request to the disk adapter. Notification that the request is complete is accomplished by the device sending an interrupt to the disk driver. The operating system handles the interrupt by executing the disk driver interrupt service routine, xxintr(). This disk driver routine resets the state of the disk adapter and then notifies the process that started the disk request that the request is complete. If the process was suspended, the operating system changes the state of the process from waiting-on-device-I/O to ready-to-run and adds the process to the ready-to-run process list. Process scheduling is discussed in more detail in the Calculations section.

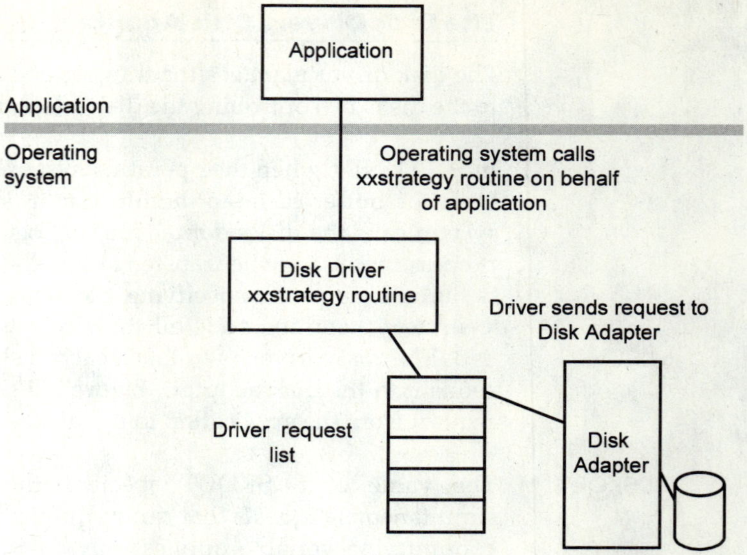

Figure 2-5: The operating system calls the xxstrategy routine to add the application request to the driver's list of requests. The xxstrategy routine is called on behalf of the application. This routine is the entry point to the driver for all filesystem requests no matter how many intermediate storage locations, such as scatter/gather buffers and copy buffers, were accessed on the way to the disk. The driver sends the request to the disk adapter for servicing. The driver request list is managed in the most optimal manner for that particular disk adapter.

Disk Adapter

The disk adapter, or disk controller, is the hardware that transfers data to and from the disks in response to commands from the disk driver. Disk adapters vary considerably in their features and performance. Table 2-7 suggests some common features that improve disk subsystem performance and why.

Feature	Benefits
Disk mirroring	Parallelization of read requests and disk storage duplication, so in case of one disk failure, the other disk still contains a copy of the data
Disk striping	Parallelization of read and write requests
On-board caches	Higher throughput for both reads and writes because waiting for disk to service requests is eliminated
32-bit	Higher throughput and no copy buffers
Bus master DMA	Setup and execution of data transfers without involving the primary CPU
Scatter/gather	Higher throughput by grouping requests together to avoid setting up separate transfer for each request

Table 2-7: Disk Adapter Features and Benefits

The connection between the adapter and the disk usually conforms to an industry standard, such as ESDI (Enhanced Small Disk Interface), IDE (Integrated Drive Electronics), or SCSI (Small Computer Systems Interface). The capacities of these different interfaces vary; these capacities are normally not tunable with software. When the connection between the adapter and the disk is busy, the time taken for the data to reach the disk increases because the adapter must wait for the connection to become available. Waiting generally occurs in configurations running disk-intensive applications with a maximum, or close to maximum, number of disks attached to the connection.

The time taken for the disk to service the request also depends on the speed of the disk and how the data on the disk is arranged. If the data is spread over the disk, the disk heads must travel a longer distance than if the information is close together. The further the disk heads must travel, the longer the disk operation takes. The layout of data is covered in the next section.

Table 2-8 summarizes how to monitor the disk driver and disk adapter usage.

Behavior	Command	Column
Number of 512-byte blocks handled by the disk driver per second	sar -d	blks/s
Absolute number of requests made to the disk per second	sar -d	r+w/s
Proportion of time spent waiting on the disk driver's list versus amount of time required to service the request	sar -d	avque
Amount of time for driver to process request	sar -d	avwait
Amount of time required for disk to service the request	sar -d	avserv
Average number of SCSI disk requests per second	sar -S	reqblk/s
Average number of times per second that a process was suspended because the SCSI disk queue was full	sar -S	oreqblk/s

Table 2-8: How to Monitor Disk Driver and Adapter Usage

sar -d

The blks/s column shows the average number of 512 byte blocks transferred to the disk per second. All requests are converted to 512 byte units regardless of what the size of the original request.

The r+w/s column shows the average number of requests made to the disk driver per second. This number does not take into account size, only the number of requests made.

The avque column shows the amount of time requests spent waiting in the driver's list versus the amount of time the disk took to service the request. This ratio gives an idea of how long the disk service time is compared to the amount of time spent waiting to access the disk.

The amount of time in milliseconds between adding the request to the list and the driver starting the actual disk request is shown in the avwait column. This value is an indication of how much time the request spends in the driver's queue as opposed to the time required for the disk to service the request.

The amount of time in milliseconds between the driver starting the disk request and the driver receiving the interrupt completion notification is shown in the avserv column. This is an average time for all the requests processed by each disk drive during the time interval specified in sar.

sar -S The reqblk/s column shows the average number of requests per second made to each SCSI disk. The oreqblk/s column shows the average number of times per second a process had to be suspended because the SCSI disk list was full. If this value is greater than zero, then either increase SDSKOUT or examine the distribution of disk utilization to see if perhaps this disk is receiving more requests than others and possibility causing delay. This statistic is only available with the SCO MPX mpsar maintenance supplement.

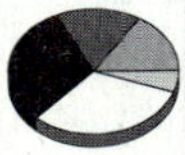

Some drivers are configurable and some are not. Check the hardware documentation for any information on disk driver configurable variables. Even if the driver is not configurable, monitoring the disk subsystem resource usage is important because changing resource allocations elsewhere in the system can increase CPU availability, allowing more applications to run, thereby increasing disk activity.

The amount of time a disk request waits in the driver's list indicates the ability of the disk subsystem to handle the disk workload. Monitoring these statistics shows whether the applications generate disk requests faster than the disk subsystem can service them. If these values increase, then the disk subsystem cannot keep up. If the values stay the same, then the disk subsystem can keep up with the level of disk requests.

If the buffer cache hit rates are less than 90%, then increasing the size of the buffer cache will reduce the number of read and write requests to the disk adapter. Increase the size of the buffer cache only if the system will not start paging or swapping as a result.

In some cases, such as those shown in the case studies following this chapter performance can continue to increase with cache hit ratios greater than 90%. The case studies show how a series of tests can help to determine the optimal size of the buffer cache.

The more performance features that the disk adapter supports, the shorter the duration of any disk request.

Filesystem Layout

Data in files and directories is stored on the filesystem in arrangements specified by the filesystem type. A DOS filesystem stores data differently than does an AFS (Acer Fast Filesystem) or EAFS (Extended Acer Fast Filesystem) filesystem. The degree of control over data layout varies among different filesystems.

Both AFS and EAFS divide the disk into a number of 1 Kbyte blocks. Each block is assigned a unique number for easy recognition. The blocks a file occupies on the disk depends on the size of the file and the availability of contiguous blocks

Although the file appears to the application as one contiguous area of the disk, the blocks allocated on the disk to store the file data may not be contiguous. For example, if the first 1 Kbyte of the file is held in block n, the second 1 Kbyte may not be in block n+1. If the file is larger than ten blocks, then only the first ten blocks are stored in blocks that can be referenced in one step. The rest of the file is stored in blocks that must be referenced by first accessing filesystem information that refers to the locations where the rest of the file is stored. This reference is known as an indirect reference because the first location contains an address pointing to the actual location of the information.

When writing data to the filesystem, the operating system tries to allocate physically contiguous areas on the disk to store the data.

If the data is physically contiguous, then the time required to access the data is reduced. The time required for a disk to service a file read or write operation is directly proportional to the distance the disk heads must move to retrieve the data. The more the disk heads must move, the longer the time to retrieve the data.

Fragmentation

The allocation of contiguous areas on the disk is limited by the size of the file and also by the age of the filesystem. When the filesystem is created, available filesystem blocks map to physically contiguous areas on the disk. Over time, the amount of physically contiguous disk space is reduced because as files are created and destroyed, the location of the available space becomes fragmented. This fragmentation decreases the likelihood that new filesystem data can be written in a contiguous manner, thereby degrading the performance of access to that data.

The file read and write operations take the shortest amount of time when the disk heads have to move the least. The amount of time required to write filesystem data to the disk is also affected by the amount and location of free space on the filesystem. The lower the amount of free space on the filesystem, the longer the operating system takes to find space to store new data. This time is compounded if the filesystem is highly fragmented.

No tools are available to accurately monitor the filesystem fragmentation. A rough test case can be constructed that indicates how performance is degrading because of filesystem fragmentation. Construct a program that writes a file whose size is 5% of the filesystem and time the synchronous write of that file. If the performance test duration increases from one month to the next, then fragmentation is affecting file write operation performance.

The following guidelines can be used to plan an optimal filesystem layout:

- When using a disk adapter that supports grouping a set of smaller disks into one large virtual disk, configure the filesystem on this large virtual disk. Since smaller physical disks can simultaneously service the large filesystem requests, a greater degree of parallelism in request handling is possible.

Greater parallelism decreases the time required to access filesystem information.

- Rearrange the filesystem information so that frequently accessed files are located on separate disks. With such a layout, the amount of work each disk completes will be more equal. If one disk is processing many more requests than another disk, the busy disk could take longer to process requests and this increase in time could adversely impact performance.

- Disk mirroring also improves filesystem access. In many cases, the majority of filesystem accesses are read operations. With disk mirroring, both disks can service different read requests simultaneously, and the duration of the file read operation decreases.

If the amount of time required to write a file that is approximately 5% of the filesystem size increases dramatically, then fragmentation is likely to be affecting the filesystem write performance. See the SCO Open Desktop and Open Server System Administrator Manuals for instructions on how to reinitialize the filesystem.

When a filesystem is nearly full, the operating system spends longer locating available space, and the space is less likely to be contiguous. For optimal write performance, ensure that at least 5% of the filesystem is free. If the filesystem is nearly full, remove any unwanted files or move files to another disk.

Direct Disk Access

The direct disk access interface allows an application to access the data on the disk without using any filesystem mechanisms. An application using direct disk access must define the layout of the data on the disk instead of relying on the operating system to define it. No intermediate caching mechanisms are provided by the operating system for direct disk access, unlike those that are provided by the operating system for filesystem operations, such as the buffer cache.

Direct disk access is used primarily by databases to increase performance and the amount of control over the data. Since the path to the data on the disk is short, the performance of databases benefits from using direct disk access rather than filesystem operations.

Figure 2-6 summarizes the resources that are described in this section. Note that the pathway between the client application and the disk driver, disk adapter is much shorter than in the filesystem operation.

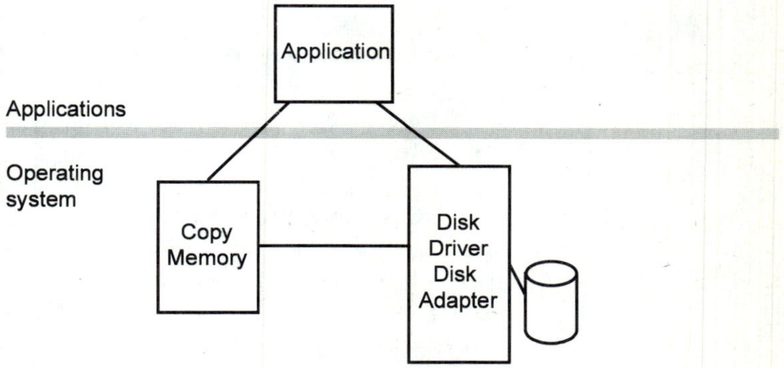

Figure 2-6: The client application uses copy memory only when the disk adapter cannot access storage locations above 16 Mbytes and the client application's data resides above 16 Mbytes. If the disk adapter can access storage locations above 16 Mbytes, then the data flows directly from the client application to the disk driver.

The Application and Direct Disk Access

To use the direct disk access interface, the application allocates an area of memory for the data that is to be transferred to or from the disk. In the case of a database, this area might be an area of shared memory that contains copies of records located on the disk. The database may manage this shared memory area similarly to the filesystem buffer cache. In such cases, the shared memory area is a key intermediate storage location that can increase performance by storing data in memory that normally resides on the disk.

Whether the size of these memory areas is configurable depends on the application. Databases generally support changing the size of the area to a size appropriate for the hardware and software configuration. Many databases also support configuring the frequency with which the versions of the records on disk are updated with the version of the records in memory.

The frequency of update affects the number of requests made to the disk driver and so affects performance. In addition, some databases prevent new transactions from being processed while the updating of disk and memory records occurs. This situation may negatively affect performance when the database usage is such that database processes must wait until the full update is complete.

When the application uses direct disk access, it must specify the physical location of the data on the disk. Some database applications use indexes to map data to physical locations on the disk. Often the index may also be stored on the disk, and the application may need to issue an additional disk request to retrieve the index before the application can access the actual data. The configuration of these indexes may also be configurable in the database.

The direct disk interface supports both synchronous and asynchronous I/O, or AIO, operations. Synchronous operations are those that require the requesting process to wait until the operation is complete.

Asynchronous I/O

Asynchronous operations are those that do not require the requesting process to wait. The application process that requests data asynchronously can continue other processing until the data is available from the disk. Using asynchronous operations implies that the application has other work that it can do while waiting for the disk transfer to complete.

HINT:

Use AIO for both Oracle Version 7 and Sybase SQL Server System 10 for improved performance. Be sure to configure both the application and the operating system to use AIO. See the SCO Open Desktop and Open Server System Administrator's Guide for information on configuring AIO in the operating system. See the appropriate database administrator's manual for information on configuring the database to use AIO.

NPBUF

The application disk transfer requests are passed to the disk driver with minimum operating system intervention. The operating system keeps track of the direct disk access requests by associating a special control block with the request. The total number of control blocks is specified by the configurable variable NPBUF. The value of NPBUF determines the maximum number of simultaneous direct disk access requests that can occur.

Each special control block occupies 76 bytes of memory.

The tools used to monitor application resource usage are the same as those described in the File Read and Write Operation section. In addition, databases often supply resource monitoring tools that allow the usage of memory and disks to be monitored independently of the operating system. Table 2-9 shows how to monitor the frequency of direct disk access requests.

Behavior	**Command**	**Column**
Average number of direct disk requests per second	sar -h	pbuf/s
Number of times per second that a process was suspended because no control blocks were available	sar -h	spbuf/s

Table 2-9: How to Monitor Direct Disk Access Requests

sar -h

The average number of direct disk access requests made by all the processes on the system per second is shown by the pbuf/s column. This value also includes all the page faults that involve copying a page from the swap device. Page faults are described in more detail in the Common Open Desktop Operations chapter. If no paging or swapping is occurring on the system and the duration of the test decreases, the value of pbuf/s may increase because the frequency of disk requests increases.

Whenever the operating system runs out of control blocks, the operating system suspends any other processes making a direct disk access request until one of the control blocks becomes available. The average number of times per second that the number of control blocks is exhausted is reported in the spbuf/s column. Running out of control blocks causes delay to the completion of the operation.

Tuning direct disk access involves the following actions:

- Ensuring that sufficient control blocks are available for the frequency of direct disk requests
- Optimizing the size of the application's storage area
- Optimizing the layout of the data on the disks used by the application
- Configuring AIO in both the application and the operating system if the application can use it

Ensure that a sufficient number of operating system control blocks are available at all times to complete the direct disk operation with no delay.

When the application uses direct disk access, the operating system does not provide any intermediate storage locations to reduce the number of disk requests. With no intermediate storage locations provided by the operating system, the layout of the data significantly affects the transfer time between the application and the disk. Some suggestions for optimal data layout are included here and in the database case studies.

Many applications supply specific tools to monitor the effectiveness of memory and disk usage. Check the documentation provided with the application for information describing how to tune the memory, disks, and data layout used by the application.

Depending on the nature of the application, increasing the size of the application storage area may reduce the number of disk requests, thereby minimizing the delay in accessing the data. With some databases such as Oracle, the size of this area can be increased until the system starts to page or swap.

When the size of the application's storage is changed, other application tunable variables may also need to change. In some cases, such as with Informix, these other tunables may be expressed as percentages of memory used by the application. In the case of Informix, when the value of BUFFERS is increased, the absolute values of these other tunables may become very large and possibly less optimal. Please see the application documentation for more information.

If the system is already paging and swapping, then consider reducing the size of this application storage area until paging and swapping cease. Also consider reducing the size of other applications or operating system data structures until paging and swapping cease. Installing additional physical memory will also alleviate the memory shortage and stop paging and swapping activity. See the Common Open Desktop Operations chapter for more information on alleviating memory shortages.

The Copy Memory Mechanism

Copy memory is used when the memory location specified by the application for the information transfer is not accessible to the disk adapter. Some disk adapters are restricted in the memory locations they can access, and copy memory allows these disk adapters to be used even when the application specifies a memory location outside the range of the disk adapter. Copy memory is used by direct disk access in a fashion similar to the use of copy buffers in filesystem operations.

All memory is accessible by EISA and most MCA disk adapters. However, ISA adapters can typically access only memory located below 16 Mbytes. Installing more than 16 Mbytes of memory when using a disk adapter that can only access memory below 16 Mbytes of memory means that some disk transfer operations may involve the additional step of either copy buffers or copy memory.

For a write operation, the operating system copies the data from the application storage area to an intermediate storage location in preparation for transfer to the disk. In the case of a read operation, the operating system initiates the disk request, but instead of specifying the application's destination memory location, the operating system specifies the intermediate storage location. After the data is retrieved from the disk, the operating system copies the data from the intermediate storage location to the application's destination memory location.

DMAABLEBUF

The size of the intermediate storage location is determined by the configurable variable DMAABLEBUF. The value of DMAABLEBUF is in units of 4 Kbytes, so each copy buffer occupies 4 Kbytes of memory. The operating system allocates copy memory only if it detects that a driver may require it.

Table 2-10 summarizes how to monitor the usage of copy memory.

Behavior	Command	Column
Number of copy memory buffers used per second	sar -h	dmabuf/s
Frequency that the copy memory resource was exhausted	sar -h	sdmabuf/s

Table 2-10: How to Monitor Copy Memory Usage

sar -h

The dmabuf/s column shows the average number of times copy memory is used per second. Each time copy memory is used, the operating system copies anywhere from 1 byte to 4 Kbytes of data to the intermediate storage area. If this value is greater than zero, then at least one of the disk adapters cannot, or is not configured to, access memory above 16 Mbytes.

The sdmabuf/s column shows the average number of times per second that a process had to wait for access to copy memory. When copy memory runs out, the process is suspended until some copy memory is available. If this value is greater than zero, then increase DMAABLEBUF until the values in this column are zero or until the system begins to page or swap, whichever comes first.

When applications use direct disk access, the value of DMAABLEBUF should be increased in proportion to the amount of memory installed above the 16 Mbyte boundary. Memory set aside for copying cannot be used for any other purpose, so ensure sufficient memory is available before increasing the value of DMAABLEBUF. Increase this value until either sdmabuf/s is equal to zero, or until the system starts to page or swap.

With 16 Mbytes of memory or less, set DMAABLEBUF equal to four. In addition, use this value if the system contains disk adapters that can address all the installed memory because the floppy disk requires access to copy memory.

The frequency of copy memory usage may increase when the size of the application storage area is increased. The frequency increases when the additional memory used by the application is not accessible to the disk adapter. The increased copying may negate any potential performance improvement normally seen by increasing the size of the application storage area.

The Disk Driver, Disk Adapter, and Disks

The disk driver manages the disk adapter hardware. Managing the hardware includes taking the direct disk requests and sending them to the disk adapter. The disk driver maintains a list of requests that are waiting for service by the disks. The disk adapter is the hardware that transfers the data from memory to the disk.

If the application is using synchronous direct disk access, then the application is suspended until the request is serviced by the disk adapter and the application process is notified that the request is complete. When the request is complete, the operating system changes the state of the application from suspended or *sleeping* to ready-to-run. The application resumes execution when the operating system determines that the ready-to-run process is the most appropriate process to assign to a CPU.

If the disk adapter has an on-board read or write cache, then the request may complete before the process is suspended, whereupon the process simply continues execution. If the process can continue, two context switches are saved and any delays due to process scheduling are avoided. Performance of direct disk access is therefore greatly improved with an on-board cache.

If the application is using asynchronous direct disk access, then the application sends the request and continues execution. Databases often use this mode to achieve maximum transaction throughput with minimum delay. Notifying the application that the request is complete is achieved through a variety of mechanisms depending on how this mode is configured and the asynchronous support provided by the disk driver.

Table 2-11 summarizes how to monitor the disk usage.

Behavior	Command	Column
Number of direct disk access read requests per second	sar -b	pread/s
Number of direct disk access write requests per second	sar -b	pwrit/s
Number of disk requests per second	sar -d	r+w/s
Number of 512-byte requests handed by the disk driver per second	sar -d	blks/s
Proportion of time spent waiting on the list versus amount of time required to service the request	sar -d	avque
Amount of time for driver to process request	sar -d	avwait
Amount of time required for disk to service the request	sar -d	avserv

Table 2-11: How to Monitor Disk Driver and Adapter Use

sar -b

The pread/s column shows the average number of times per second application processes made read requests via the direct disk access interface. The pwrit/s column shows the same information but for write requests. Both of these values are averages over an interval of one second.

Determine the frequency of direct disk requests by adding the pwrit/s and pread/s column. The values shown for both pwrit/s and pread/s are not itemized per disk driver or per disk. The values reported do not account for asynchronous direct disk access.

The sar -d options described in the Disk Driver, Disk Adapter and Disks section of the File Read and Write Operation section are used to monitor the amount of disk activity using the direct disk interface. The values reported by sar -d do not separate direct disk access activity from filesystem activity.

To increase the speed of direct disk access requests, try the following techniques:

- Rearrange the data on the disks so that the number of requests to each disk and disk adapter are spread evenly. The number of requests to each disk can be monitored with the sar -d options described previously.

- To spread the workload, add another disk adapter and either move some of the disks to the new disk adapter or add more disks to the new adapter. When attempting to spread the work evenly, ensure that the newly configured disks can handle the load by monitoring the values reported in avwait and avserv after reconfiguration. If the reported values decrease after the reconfiguration, then the new configuration is more optimal than the previous one. If the reported values increase, or are still unequal, then the new configuration has not improved the disk efficiency.

- Use disk mirroring to improve the parallelization of disk read requests. Most systems show a higher number of read requests than write requests. Mirroring increases parallelization of read requests by allowing both disks to service disk adapter read requests simultaneously.

- Use data striping to improve the parallelization of disk read and write requests. Striping spreads the data in small increments across multiple disks, so a large disk request could be serviced by multiple disks simultaneously.

- Install a cache on the disk adapter so that requests access the cache instead of waiting for the disk.

- Free memory so the size of the application storage area can be increased. This technique only works for applications, such as databases, that manage their direct data access area in a similar fashion to the operating system filesystem buffer cache.

Because the speed of direct disk access requests is dependent on the capacity of the disk adapter and disks, sometimes the only way to significantly increase performance is to upgrade the hardware.

If system monitoring shows regular peaks of disk activity, the length of the intervals between these peaks may be configurable in the application. Some applications support changing the amount of disk activity that occurs at each interval in addition to the changing length of the interval.

Data Layout

The layout of the data on the disks affects the speed at which the disk can service the requests. The further the disk heads travel to retrieve the data, the longer the duration of the operation.

Databases are the most common users of direct disk access. Fortunately, these applications tend to be highly configurable, so a great deal of control can be exercised over the layout of the database on the disk subsystem. Use any database disk monitoring tools to determine the frequency of access for the different parts of the database. If no database tools are provided, use sar -d to help determine which disks are heavily loaded, then rearrange the data to spread the workload more evenly.

If possible, lay out the database so that the amount of traffic to each disk is about equal. This layout prevents one disk from becoming a bottleneck for the database transaction. The additional time required to plan an optimal database layout is more than compensated for by the dramatic performance gains that are possible with an optimally laid-out database.

In general, use as many disks as possible to maximize the parallelism in disk request servicing. Spreading the database over multiple disks allows more user queries to be serviced simultaneously, thereby increasing throughput. In such cases, a large number of small disks is preferably to one very large disk.

The database case studies in Chapters 11 and 12 discuss some additional layout guidelines specific to Informix and Oracle.

CALCULATIONS

Calculations are the most CPU intensive of all the common operations. This type of operation is especially sensitive to the capacity of the processor and its availability. Therefore, the goal of tuning the calculation operation is to increase CPU availability. The resources described in this section are summarized in Figure 2-7.

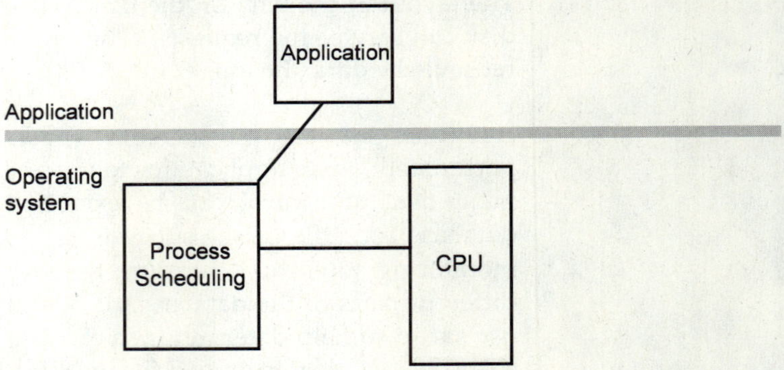

Figure 2-7: Process scheduling controls the application access to the CPU. In SCO UNIX, the CPU is shared among many applications and the operating system.

Because this section focuses on understanding how the applications and the operating system use the CPU resource, the information in this section can be applied to more than just calculating applications. The availability of the CPU affects the duration of many operations, not just calculating ones.

Application Behavior

When an application executes any operation, the instructions to be executed must be present in memory, as must any information that is required for the operation.

SCO UNIX copies into memory only the parts of an application binary that are needed for execution. This practice improves performance because a user does not wait for the entire binary to be transferred from the disk. Less physical memory is needed because memory is used to store only essential information. When an application executes instructions that are not present in memory, SCO UNIX automatically retrieves the necessary instructions from the disk. The file read operation retrieves the instructions from the disk because the application's instructions are stored in a file in the filesystem.

Monitoring the application's use of resources is the same for the calculating operation as for the filesystem operation.

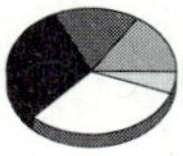

Maximizing CPU availability is the key aspect of tuning for the calculating process. Paging and swapping affect the performance of the calculation by taking CPU time away from the calculation and using it for managing the memory shortage. If calculations are to complete in the shortest amount of time, the system should not be paging or swapping.

Process Scheduling

In a multitasking operating system such as SCO UNIX, Open Desktop and SCO MPX, multiple application processes must share the CPU resource. The operating system manages the CPU resource by giving each application process an opportunity to run on the CPU. This mechanism is called *time-slicing*.

MAXSLICE

The maximum amount of time an application process can use the processor in one turn is specified by the configurable variable MAXSLICE. MAXSLICE is specified in units of clock ticks, which is currently set to one hundredth of a second. If the value of

MAXSLICE is 100, then the maximum amount of time the process can use the processor in one turn is one second. When the process time slice has expired and no other ready-to-run processes are available, the process may continue running for another time slice. Figure 2-8 shows the transitions from the various states that a process can have in SCO UNIX process scheduling.

Normally, application processes are suspended before their time slice expires because the process accesses a resource that is not immediately available, as shown by line A in Figure 2-8. When a requested resource is not available, the process is suspended and the operating system selects another process to run on the CPU, as shown by line B. The mechanism of suspending one process and starting another is called *context switching*. When the resource that the first process wishes to access becomes available, the operating system modifies the state of the process from waiting to ready-to-run, then adds it to the "ready-to-run" list. This transition is shown by line C.

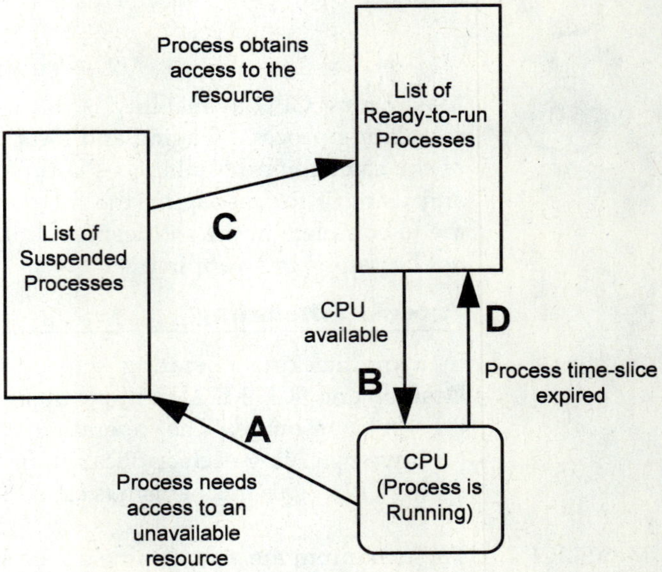

Figure 2-8: How processes move between different states

SCO UNIX selects a process to run from the ready-to-run list according to process priorities. These process priorities are assigned by the operating system and can be influenced by the user with the nice(C) command. The priority values range from 0 to 127, with 0 representing the highest priority and 127 the lowest.

The operating system selects a new process to run when any of the following situations occur:

- The process currently on the processor has made a resource request and the process cannot proceed until the request is complete. In this case, the process is suspended and another process is chosen to run. When the operating system switches from one process to another, the operating system executes a context switch.

- The time slice for the current process has expired. Because SCO UNIX is a time-sharing operating system, each process can run on the processor for a fixed length of time before it must relinquish the processor for possible use by another ready-to-run process. This transition is shown by line D in Figure 2-8.

- A request for a previously suspended process has completed, and the process that was suspended is a higher priority process than the one currently running.

The priority of every ready-to-run process is reduced every second if the process has been running on the CPU. This reduction in priority ensures that all ready-to-run processes execute eventually because the priority of the processes actually running on the CPU is reduced. The amount the priority is reduced is based on how recently the process used the processor and how much CPU time was actually used. The more recently the process used the CPU, the more the priority is reduced. The greater the amount of CPU time used by the process, the more the priority is reduced. This adjustment also takes into account any nice(C) value set by the user.

Process priorities are also adjusted for those processes that have not recently used the CPU or that have used only a small amount of CPU time. The priorities of these processes is increased every second. The amount the priority is increased is based on how long ago the process used the CPU and how much CPU time was used.

System Process

In addition to application processes, the operating system runs a special type of process called a *system process*. A system process is similar to an application process, except the system process is considered part of the operating system. The system process occupies memory and consumes CPU resources when executing. The system process also occupies a slot in the process table. The Common Open Desktop Chapter describes the activity of some key system processes that affect performance.

HINT:

The activity of both system and user processes can be monitored using ps(C). The ps -ef commands displays the accumulated CPU time in the TIME column.

Although not directly related to performance, the operating system maintains some configurable process-related bookkeeping as follows:

NPROC

The operating system maintains a list of processes in a table called the *process table*. The size of this table is controlled by the configurable variable NPROC. Each entry in the process table occupies 372 bytes.

MAXUP

The operating system allows a user, as defined by a user id, to create additional processes. The maximum number of additional processes that a single user can create is controlled by the variable MAXUP. If MAXUP is increased, then consider increasing NPROC to ensure that sufficient space is available in the process table for these additional processes.

Table 2-12 shows how to monitor process scheduling.

Behavior	Command	Column
Number of ready-to-run processes	sar -q	runq-sz
Number of context switches	sar -w	pswch/s

Table 2-12: How to Monitor Process Scheduling

sar -q

The runq-sz column shows the average size of the ready-to-run process list over the interval specified when sar was invoked. The longer this list, the more ready-to-run processes are available for the CPU to execute, and the less likely that the CPU is idle because no ready-to-run processes exist.

HINT:

Monitor the total number of ready-to-run processes to understand if all the calculating processes are ready-to-run all the time. If the number shown by runq-sz is much less than the total number expected, some of the calculating or CPU-intensive processes may be waiting on resource access instead of waiting for the CPU.

sar -w

The pswch/s column shows the average number of context switches per second completed by the operating system. A context switch occurs when the operating system suspends one process in favor of another process.

Configure SCO UNIX scheduling in two ways:

- Use the nice command to set the priority of a process
- Reduce the maximum time a process can use the CPU in any one turn

The nice command reduces the priority of an application process, which means that the operating system selects higher priority processes to run before selecting the application process whose priority was modified Only the superuser, or root, can raise the priority of an application process.

Reducing the value of MAXSLICE causes the operating system to context-switch between application processes more often. If most of the processes on the system are CPU-intensive, then reducing the value of MAXSLICE increases the feeling of responsiveness of the application process but does not actually shorten the duration of the operation. This effect is produced because each process executes for a shorter period of time, but more frequently, so users constantly see a small amount of work occurring rather than an intermittent large amount of work.

When the system has a majority of ready-to-run processes and runs with %wio less than 3%, then reducing MAXSLICE may have an effect. In general, reducing MAXSLICE has little effect since a majority of application processes are suspended because of waiting for resource access rather than because their time slice expired.

Processor

Once the instructions and the data for the calculation are copied into memory, the capacity of the processor and the operating system scheduling dictate how quickly the calculation completes. A faster processor completes a calculation more quickly than does a slower processor because each instruction takes less time to execute.

CPU Caches

The CPU has two types of caches. The internal, or on-chip cache, is a fixed size and is located on the chip. The *Level 2* (L2) cache, is external to the chip. Different size L2 caches are available and some machines allow upgrade of the existing L2 cache to a larger one. Some machines do not support the installation of an L2 cache.

CPU caches improve performance by keeping copies of frequently accessed information in special hardware that the CPU can access more quickly than it can access normal physical memory. The computation, or any other operation, takes the shortest time when all the necessary information is in the processor's cache, because the CPU does not need to access memory or the disk to complete the operation.

If the information must be retrieved from memory, the duration of the calculation increases because of the time taken for the information to travel from main memory to the processor cache.

A larger processor cache improves performance because more frequently accessed information can be stored in the special cache hardware. The CPU retrieves the information from the cache instead of accessing memory.

Processor caches can be implemented in a number of ways. When a memory location stored in the cache is modified, a *write-through* cache forces the processor to wait for the memory to be updated, whereas a *write-back* cache allows the processor to continue processing during the update.

On some computers, the processor cache is configured only to cover a particular region of memory. When the cache does not cover an area of memory, all accesses to that memory require the processor to wait while the data is obtained. Normally the first 16 Mbytes of memory are covered by the cache, but in some cases this may be lower.

HINT:

Check the hardware documentation for the type and size of cache supported by the system. Since cache performance and size varies widely, follow the recommendations of the hardware documentation. If the system contains more memory than is covered by the cache, consider purchasing a larger cache for improved performance of all operations, not just calculations.

Once all of the required information is in the processor cache, the operation can continue uninterrupted. If the time slice of the process expires, the process is suspended and another process from the ready-to-run list is started.

CPU speed and floating point

If the processor can complete the calculation, or any other similar CPU-intensive operation, without any other system interactions, a processor running at double the speed will complete the calculation in half the time.

If the calculation requires floating point, then performance is improved by ensuring that all of the CPUs support floating point. With the exception of the Intel 486SX, Intel i486™ or later CPUs support floating-point operations directly in the hardware. Intel i386™ CPUs do not support floating point in the hardware without the addition of a i387™ floating point co-processor. Calculations involving floating point on i386 systems without an i387 are slowed significantly because the floating point instructions must be emulated by a program called the *floating point emulator*.

The floating point emulator uses many normal CPU instructions to complete operations that can be executed in one instruction on a floating point processor. Using software to emulate hardware adds to the overhead of the calculation and impacts performance.

Monitor the CPU usage with the tools described in Table 2-13.

Behavior	**Command**	**Column**
Percentage of time the CPU is idle with no ready-to-run processes to execute	sar -u	%idle
Percentage of time the CPU is idle waiting for I/O to complete and no other ready-to-run processes to execute	sar -u	%wio
Percentage of time the CPU spends executing application processes	sar -u	%usr
Percentage of time the CPU spends executing the operating system	sar -u	%sys

Table 2-13: How to Monitor CPU Usage

sar -u The %idle column of sar -u shows the percentage of time that the processor has spent idle during the time interval specified when sar was invoked. Idle means that the CPU has no work to do because no processes are ready-to-run, and no processes are waiting-for-device-I/O requests to complete.

The %wio column shows the percentage of idle time accumulated by the processor waiting-for-device-I/O requests to complete. This statistic does not include waiting for network I/O to complete. Time is accumulated here only if the system has no other processes that are ready-to-run, but processes are waiting-for-device-I/O to complete. In this case, all the processor can do is wait for the I/O to complete. Reducing %wio by increasing the I/O resources or otherwise increasing the number of processes that can run improves performance.

The %usr column shows the percentage of time spent by the processor executing all the application processes running on the system. Optimal tuning increases the amount of CPU time available to execute application processes.

The %sys column shows the percentage of time spent by the processor executing the operating system. Tuning SCO UNIX so that this time is reduced means more CPU time is available for application processes. Additional CPU time increases application performance only if there are application processes that could be executed. If the application processes are all waiting for device I/O to complete, then decreasing the amount of %sys time increases the amount of %wio time and does not increase performance.

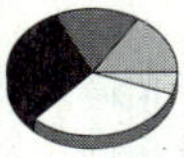

The CPU usage statistics show how the CPU is spending its time executing processes. When the CPU is idle while waiting for I/O or just plain idle, the CPU resource is not used efficiently and performance could be improved by minimizing %idle and %wio in favor of %usr time. Tuning to increase the availability of the CPU benefits all application processes running on the system and not just calculations.

For a calculating or other CPU-intensive operation with no paging and swapping occurring, by far the largest value for CPU usage should be in the %usr column. The %sys value for both operations should be low, as the operating system is only involved in such operations when it schedules the calculating processes.

When the operating system is running other application processes besides calculating processes, then the CPU may spend more time executing the operating system on behalf of the other application processes.

Because sar uses some resources, some of the %sys and %usr activity is due to the background data collection and processing. If the calculating processes are accessing large spreadsheets and paging or swapping is occurring, then parts of the calculating processes may be transferred to the swap area. When the calculating process is selected to run on the processor, that part of the process that was transferred to the swap area is transferred back to memory. The effects of paging and swapping are described in more detail in the Common Open Desktop Operations chapter.

If other application processes are running with the calculating processes, then tuning these other operations to use less processor time benefits the calculating processes by increasing the amount of CPU time available.

Display Update and Character Echo

This section describes the resources used when executing the following types of operations:

- Simple character echo when the user is typing at the keyboard and interacting with the csh(C) or sh(C) shells.
- Complex application display update

Much of the resource usage is the same in both of these scenarios. The key difference is that the shell programs require minimal resources to echo characters to the screen, while the more complex applications may require more resources to update the display. This section addresses configurations where serial terminals are connected to the computer. X terminals and networking are covered in the Monitoring Client/Server Connections and Common Client/Server Operations chapters.

When a user presses a key on the terminal's keyboard, the terminal sends information to the computer across the serial connection. The serial adapter then transfers the character from the serial connection to the serial driver.

The key underlying hardware resource affecting all serial terminal operations is the CPU. The availability of the CPU has a direct impact on these operations, and so increasing the availability of the CPU is the primary goal of tuning this operation. The tuning recommendations for increasing CPU availability from the Calculations section also apply to this operation. Figure 2-9 summarizes the resources described in this section.

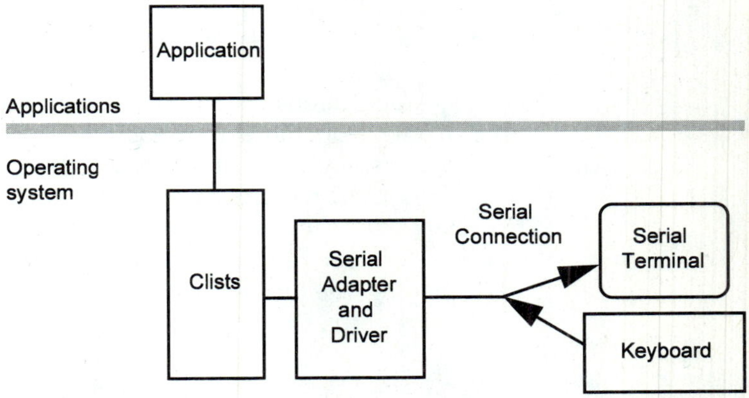

Figure 2-9: The user types keys at the keyboard. These characters are transmitted over the serial connection and received by the serial adapter and driver. The driver copies them into a clist. The application reads the characters from the clist. When the application must display information, the information is sent to the serial driver by copying it to a clist. The serial driver copies the information in the clist to the serial adapter, which then transmits it to the serial terminal for display on the screen.

Application Behavior

The application generates the text to be displayed on the terminal's screen. The application can combine the display update operation with one or more operations in order to generate the text to be displayed. A database, for example, may access different records stored on the disk in order to display a form for the user to view.

In such cases, the duration of the operation to retrieve the data to be displayed impacts the duration of the entire display update operation. In such environments, monitor both operations and balance the resource needs of both operations.

Many applications provide monitoring tools so the application resource usage pattern can be monitored from within the application as well as by the standard operating system tools.

Some applications use simple character echo to display characters, and others do more processing or formatting of the characters before displaying them. For example, when the user runs the Bourne shell, the characters are echoed with minimal operating system intervention. However, a word processing application often formats the screen after the key is entered as part of displaying the new characters in the screen. The amount of resources used varies considerably between these two operations.

Application resource usage is monitored for this operation in the same way as for the filesystem operation. Check the application documentation to see if any tools are provided, and for further help in tuning the application. Any additional information measured should be noted on the tuning worksheet.

Tuning the display update operation involves the following actions:

- Optimally allocating the resources used by the application in the display update
- Maximizing the amount of CPU time available

Adjusting the resources used by the application so that no shortages occur benefits the display update operation as well as other operations executed by the application.

Most of the suggestions in this book are targeted at reducing the amount of CPU time consumed by the system to increase the amount of CPU time available to application processes. If other application processes are executing at the same time as the display update, tuning these other operations so they use less processor time reduces the time taken by the display update and character echo.

Clists

The CPU copies each character that the application wants to display to a temporary character storage area, called a *clist*. The characters are stored in the output clist until the serial driver passes them to the serial adapter. The CPU is also required to process characters received from the terminal when the serial driver copies all characters received from the terminal to an input clist.

NCLIST

The total number of clists is determined by the value of the configurable variable NCLIST. The size of each clist is 76 bytes.

If the operating system runs out of input or output clists, one of the following messages appears on the console:

```
putc - Out of clists (NCLIST = X exceeded); Y
failures so far
getcf - Out of clists (NCLIST = X exceeded); Y
failures so far
putcbp - Out of clists (NCLIST = X exceeded); Y
failures so far
```

where X is the current value of NCLIST and Y is the number of times the operating system tried to allocate a clist and failed. If either of these message appear, then potentially 64 or more characters could have been lost.

Flow Control

Transmission of characters is regulated using a mechanism called *flow control*. Many types of flow control are implemented in the hardware and software. The concept underlying most of them is to ensure that the destination does not lose characters because the destination is too busy to receive them. When the destination raises flow control, the source stops sending until the destination is ready for characters again. In this case, the destination or the source could be the computer, the application process, the serial adapter, or the terminal.

For example, when the amount of data copied to the output clist exceeds a certain threshold value, the operating system starts transferring the characters to the serial adapter. When the operating system starts transferring the characters, it also suspends the application from writing any more characters until some of them have been sent to the terminal. The operating system restarts the application and resumes copying characters to the output clist when there is room on the output clist for more characters. The time taken to update the display or echo characters includes all the time the application was suspended. Figures 2-10 and 2-11 show the interaction when the serial terminal cannot keep up with the number of characters sent by the application and the operating system.

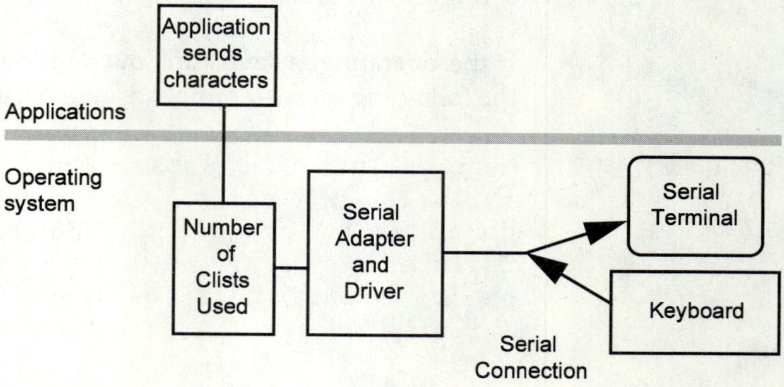

Figure 2-10: The serial terminal is able to receive all of the characters transmitted to it by the computer. The number of clists used is low because the serial terminal and computer are matched in their capacity to transmit and receive characters.

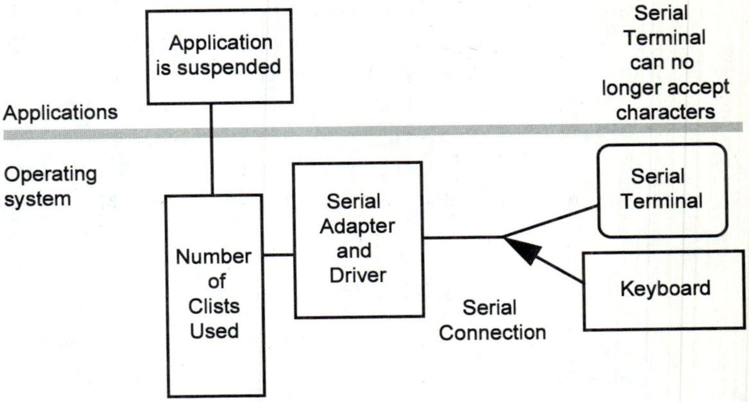

Figure 2-11: When the serial terminal can no longer keep up with the number of characters transmitted by the computer, the serial terminal asserts flow control and the computer stops sending the characters. The number of clists used increases because the operating system must store the characters while the serial terminal cannot receive them. Eventually the application is suspended when too many characters are waiting to be sent to the terminal. Once the serial terminal begins receiving characters, the number of clists used decreases and the operating system begins to execute the application.

Because of flow control, any resource shortage in the pathway of the character may cause delays and other resource shortages, as the senders buffer the characters waiting for the destinations to receive characters again. For example, if the serial terminal is very slow and the system is optimally tuned for display update, the operating system may see the terminal asserting flow control frequently and so is forced to store the characters until the terminal is ready to accept them.

The operating system may run out of clists because it cannot send characters to the terminal as quickly as the application processes generate them. In this case, increasing the number of clists does not solve the underlying resource limitation and does not improve the performance of the display update on the slow terminal. Discovering the underlying resource shortages is important to improving performance in situations where computers, or computers and terminals, cooperate to complete operations.

Table 2-14 summarizes how to monitor clist usage.

Behavior	Command	Column
Number of times per second the operating system ran out of clists	sar -g	ovclist/s
Number of times per second that the serial adapter has detected an overflow	sar -g	ovsiohw/s

Table 2-14: How to Monitor clist Usage

sar -g

The number of times each second the operating system ran out of clists is shown in the ovclist/s column. If this value fluctuates, then flow control at some stage in the character's pathway may be causing the operating system to store these characters and run out of clists.

The number of times per second that the serial adapter detected and overflow condition is reported in the ovsiohw/w column. A value greater than zero indicates mismatched hardware. For example, the serial adapter may be too slow for the sending device. Try decreasing the baud rate to stop the overflow conditions.

The usage pattern for clists can provide clues as to whether all the source and destination locations in the character's pathway can keep up with the level of activity generated by the applications. Flow control causes delay to the display update and character echo operations and can cause exhaustion of resources, such as clists.

Memory allocated for clists cannot be used for any purpose other than communicating with serial terminals, so consider reducing NCLIST if clist usage is low. Pseudo-ttys, such as those used with remote login, also use clists.

The Serial Adapter and Driver, Serial Connection, and Terminals

The serial adapter driver manages the serial adapter by transferring characters between the clists and the serial adapter. The amount of CPU time needed to transfer the characters varies among serial adapters. Intelligent serial adapters provide additional hardware to shift the work from the CPU to the serial adapter. This shifting of work means the CPU is available for executing other operations.

When a character is received by the serial driver, two different types of processing may occur on that character, depending on how the application expects to receive the characters. If some control character processing is to be handled by the application, then the driver is configured to perform *canonical processing* on the characters. If the application wants to receive all the characters exactly as they are typed in, including control characters, then the driver does not do any processing. This mode is called *raw mode,* because the characters are transferred to the application exactly as they are received.

HINT:

Intelligent serial I/O adapters are also called *smart* cards. The amount of work these cards can accomplish varies with manufacturer and also with how the cards are configured. Understanding how to configure these cards optimally for the environment maximizes the performance benefit of using them. Matching the capacity of the cards to the capacity of the machine is important to good performance. Monitoring tools are sometimes provided with these cards, so check the documentation for any additional performance monitoring tools and tunables.

The time taken for data to travel from the serial adapter to the terminal depends on the baud rate of the serial connection. The higher the baud rate, the quicker the transfer. A serial connection using a slow baud rate increases the time taken by the display update and character echo operations. If the application generates characters at a much greater rate than the serial line can transfer them, the use of clists will increase because the characters must be stored prior to sending them over the serial connection.

The serial terminal displays characters taken from the serial connection. The time taken to update the display is increased if the terminal cannot keep up with the data being transferred from the host computer because the terminal blocks further transmissions until the backlog is completed. This case is another example of flow control. To reduce the likelihood of flow control, most terminals have a buffer which stores characters until they can be processed. Usually the serial connection is not able to transfer characters quickly enough to cause a serial terminal to block further transfers.

HINT:

A terminal host is not always the main computer. Terminal concentrators allow many terminals to be connected to one computer. System performance is improved because much of the overhead associated with serial processing is removed from the CPU. Performance of the entire system is improved because the CPU is available for other operations.

Table 2-15 summarizes how to monitor the serial driver, serial adapter and connections.

Behavior	Command	Column
Number of raw mode characters processed per second	sar -y	rawch/s
Number of canonical mode characters processed per second	sar -y	canch/s
Frequency of interrupts received for sending more characters	sar -y	xmtin/s
Average number of characters transmitted per second	sar -y	outch/s
Average number of characters received per second	sar -y	inch/s
Frequency of interrupts received for receiving characters	sar -y	rcvin/s

Table 2-15: How to Monitor Serial Driver Usage

sar -y The number of characters processed by the driver per second is shown in the rawch/s and canch/s columns. Peaks and troughs in the reported values may indicate a flow control problem related to the availability of the CPU to process characters. Whether a problem exists can be corroborated by the values reported in the xmtin/s and rcvin/s columns. If these values also fluctuate, then the availability of the CPU is affecting the ability of the serial driver to process characters. Peaks and troughs may also indicate sporadic use of the terminals by the users.

The columns outch/s and inch/s report on the average number of characters transmitted and received per second. If the reported values fluctuate and the number of application processes is constant, then flow control could be causing the operating system to temporarily store characters.

For non-intelligent cards, the CPU is required to handle all the interrupts generated as a result of receiving and sending characters. If xmtin/s and rcvin/s are consistently high, the system is receiving a large number of interrupts, so an intelligent serial adapter may benefit performance of display updates. The other applications running on the system also benefit because more CPU time is available for application execution instead of interrupt handling.

QUICK DIAGNOSIS SUMMARY

This section highlights the key monitoring tools and tuning guidelines described in this chapter.

CPU Usage

For an overall picture of the system resource usage, examine CPU usage with the following tools listed in Table 2-16.

Behavior	Command	Column
Percentage of time the CPU is idle with no ready-to-run processes to execute	sar -u	%idle
Percentage of time the CPU is idle waiting for I/O to complete and no other ready-to-run processes to execute	sar -u	%wio
Percentage of time the CPU spends executing application processes	sar -u	%usr
Percentage of time the CPU spends executing the operating system	sar -u	%sys

Table 2-16: How to Monitor CPU Usage

Almost all operations benefit from minimizing %wio, %idle, %sys time in favor of %usr time. If %wio goes down and %idle goes up or %idle goes down and %wio goes up, then look in detail at resource usage pattern for all the processes running on the system to uncover the resource shortage preventing processes from becoming ready-to-run.

File Read and Write Operations

The key behaviors for filesystem operations are listed in Table 2-17.

Behavior	Command	Column
Number of read requests per second	sar -b	lread/s
Percentage of read requests found in the cache	sar -b	%rcache
Number of read operations to the disk (due to cache miss) per second	sar -b	bread/s
Number of write requests per second	sar -b	lwrit/s
Number of write operations to the disk per second	sar -b	bwrit/s
Number of 512-byte block requests handled by the disk driver	sar -d	blks/s
Absolute number of requests made to the disk	sar -d	r+w/s
Proportion of time spent waiting on the list versus amount of time required to service the request	sar -d	avque
Amount of time for driver to process request	sar -d	avwait
Amount of time required for disk to service the request	sar -d	avserv

Table 2-17: Key Filesystem Operation Behaviors

Filesystem operations can be improved by the following techniques:

- Tuning the buffer cache to maximize %rcache value. When the cache hit rate is more than 98%, further increases to the size of the buffer cache minimally improve filesystem performance.
- Planning the filesystem layout to maximize the ability of the disk subsystem to handle these requests in parallel and to minimize the disk head travel.
- Increasing the capacity of the disk subsystem to match the level of activity required by the application processes. Onboard caches, striping, mirroring, and 32-bit bus master DMA are some features that improve performance.

In all cases, do not increase filesystem resources if the system is paging or swapping.

Direct Disk Access

In addition to the disk usage behaviors listed above, the key behaviors for direct disk access are listed in Table 2-18.

Behavior	Command	Column
Average number of direct disk requests per second	sar -h	pbuf/s
Frequency that a process was suspended because no control blocks were available	sar -h	spbuf/s

Table 2-18: Key Direct Disk Access Behaviors

Performance of applications using direct disk access can be improved by the following techniques:

- Ensuring that a sufficient number of direct access control blocks are always available

- Rearranging the data on the disks so that number of requests to each disk and disk adapter are spread evenly

- Using disk mirroring and striping to improve the parallelization of disk read and write requests

- Installing a cache on the disk adapter so that requests access the cache instead of waiting for the disk. This feature improves performance of direct disk access more so than for filesystem operations.

Display Update and Character Echo

The key resources to monitor for display update and character echo are listed in Table 2-19.

Behavior	Command	Column
Number of times the operating system ran out of clists	sar -g	ovclist/s
Number of raw mode characters processed per second	sar -y	rawch/s
Number of canonical mode characters processed per second	sar -y	canch/s
Average number of characters transmitted	sar -y	outch/s
Average number of characters received	sar -y	inch/s

Table 2-19: Key Display Update and Character Echo Behaviors

The performance of display update and character echo can be improved by the following actions:

- Increase CPU availability
- Install an intelligent serial adapter
- Match the capabilities of the sending and receiving machines and terminals in order to avoid delays caused by flow control

Chapter 3

SCO UNIX Case Study

This case study shows how a read and write file operation can be tuned with the seven step method in a multiuser environment. The relationships between increasing the buffer cache, adding more and/or faster disks, and installing a ramdisk are explored. This chapter assumes some familiarity with the material presented in the Common SCO UNIX Operations chapter, especially the File Read and Write Operation section.

This example is designed to show how you can analyze the data recorded on the worksheets, draw conclusions regarding resource shortages, and change the resource allocations to increase efficiency and improve performance. This example uses tools provided on the floppy disk to run the test and collect appropriate resource usage statistics. The relevant statistics are extracted with another utility and entered into the worksheets that are included at the end of this chapter. The worksheets are provided in the examples as a sort of appendix to show where the data originated. The data presented in the graphs and bar charts in the example description highlights the worksheet data relevant to that particular operation.

The Seven Step Method

The performance of the file read and write operation is the subject of this investigation.

Step 1. Decide what to improve.

☑ Select the appropriate worksheet for the common operation.

The SCO UNIX Operating System Tuning worksheet is the appropriate worksheet. Completed worksheets for all the tests run in this example are included at the end of this chapter.

⇩

Step 2. Identify the limited and unlimited resources.

☑ Note any limited resources on the worksheet by marking them with an asterisk (*).

All hardware resources except for the disk subsystem are limited. A hard disk and disk adapter may be borrowed temporarily in order to verify whether additional hardware improves performance. Figure 3-1 shows the hardware configuration.

⇩

Step 3. Determine how to measure the operation and test its current performance.

☑ Note the test result on the worksheet in the column marked **Now.**

The fileop shell script is a mixture of typical file read and write operations. This shell script simulates 10 users executing a combination of simple file read and more complex file read and write operations.

The fileop script operates on a directory hierarchy created by ctree, also included on the floppy disk. Each process receives a list of 100 files on which to execute file operations. These files are randomly selected by the fileop script. Four read operations are executed for every write operation. The script provides a great deal of flexibility regarding source and target filesystem location, so each portion of the file operation can be closely investigated.

The following command lines show how the ctree utility is used to create two directories each containing 100 32 Kbyte files:

```
ctree -f 100 -d 1 -s 32768 -n data1
ctree -f 100 -d 1 -s 32768 -n data2
```

Figure 3-1 shows the hardware configuration and how the data flows.

In order to keep the test environment as stable as possible, once the file lists are created, the same lists are used for subsequent test runs. The initial test duration is 245 seconds.

Step 4. Set a realistic performance goal.

☑ Note this on the worksheet in the column marked **Your Goal.**

The goal is to reduce the duration of the test by approximately 50%. An additional goal is to determine whether the existing disk adapter and disk combination can support the level of filesystem activity on the system.

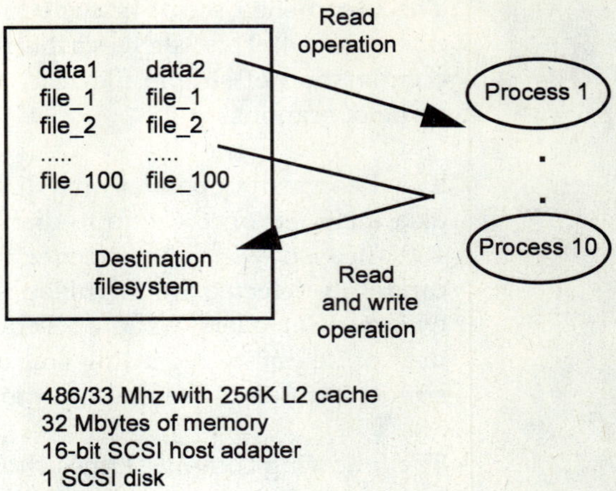

Figure 3-1: Processes 1 through 10 execute a combination of read and read/write operations on files located in the directories data1 and data2. The read operation reads the files in data1 and data2 from the file lists set up by fileop. The read and write operation copies files from the file list to the destination filesystem.

⇩

Step 5. Identify the resources to monitor and decide which monitoring tools to use.

☑ The worksheets list the appropriate resources.

The standard SCO UNIX Operating System Tuning Worksheet contains all the resources that should be monitored for the filesystem operation.

The fileop script automatically runs sar when the option -sar is specified. The utility tune2wks extracts the relevant tunable information for the first part of the operating system worksheet. The utility sar2oswks extracts the appropriate data from the sar data files for entry into the resource monitoring section of the worksheet.

⇩

Step 6. Run the test with the monitoring tools and monitor the resource usage and record the test results.

☑ Enter the initial values of the tunables and note the resource usage in the column marked **Initial Values**. Note the test results under the column called **Monitoring.**

With the monitoring tools enabled, the duration of the operation increases to 259 seconds. Since sar writes its data to the filesystem and uses the CPU, this increase is expected. These results and initial tunable values are noted in Worksheet 3-1.

Initial Observations: One Disk

First check the CPU and memory usage patterns, and then examine the intermediate storage locations for the filesystem operation.

The CPU spent only 10% of its time executing user applications. 58% of the time was spent executing the operating system. At no point in the test did the CPU become idle with no work to do, but 32% of the time was spent idle waiting-for-device-I/O transfers to complete. A %wio value of 32% indicates that for one-third of the time, no processes were ready-to-run because they were waiting-for-device-I/O transfers to complete. Exploring the reason for the delays in I/O completion is the first path to investigate.

This system contains a sufficient amount of memory because neither paging nor swapping occur. With free memory averaging 14,336 pages, the system has sufficient memory to allow an increase in the size of a number of the filesystem intermediate storage locations to reduce the amount of %wio.

The average length of the ready-to-run list is 5.2 over the duration of the test. This average number seems rather high considering the amount of %wio. With %wio greater than zero, at some points during the test, the size of the ready-to-run list was equal to zero.

Some possible reasons for the %wio may be because of inefficient filesystem intermediate storage allocation. Examine the resource usage pattern for each of the filesystem locations. These locations are described in more detail in the Common SCO UNIX Operations chapter.

The namei cache hit rate is 99%. For the fileop script, such a high value is expected because the size of the name cachei is 256 entries, as indicated by S5CACHEENTS. Although each process started by fileop accesses at least 100 files, all of these files are selected from the list of 200 files created by ctree. Once the namei cache is filled, all the mapping requests are satisfied directly from the cache. S5HASHQS is equal to 61, which is approximately 1/4 of S5HASHQS. This setting is optimal for SCO UNIX.

The open file table and inode table had sufficient space for the test. The file table maximum size was 98 entries, and since the table is currently 350, the size of this table could be reduced if no additional file activity is expected on the system.

The inode table had a maximum of 116 entries. The value of NINODE is currently 450, and could be reduced if no additional file activity is expected on the system. The value of NHINODE is 128, though, so NINODE/NHINODE is greater than three, which is optimal for SCO UNIX.

The buffer cache shows a %rcache efficiency of 83%. Considering that a high proportion of the file data can be re-used, this statistic is lower than expected. The automatic buffer cache read-ahead feature should be activated quite frequently in this test case, hopefully causing the cache to be even more efficient. The buffer cache read-ahead is more effective when file access is sequential, as it is in this test case.

Higher cache efficiency would be seen with read-ahead because the filesystem blocks that are read asynchronously for read-ahead may be requested by a process. The process could then retrieve data from the buffer cache without having to access the rest of the file system, generating a cache hit.

The statistics also show that most of the requests to the filesystem are reads. Some of these reads will be satisfied by the buffer cache, and some of them will be satisfied by retrieving the data from the disk if the data is not found in the buffer cache. Increasing the proportion of requests that are satisfied by the buffer cache access will improve performance.

The scatter/gather statistics, as indicated by mphbufs/s, show that on average 21 scatter/gather buffer headers are used per second. The operating system did not run out of these data structures, however. Increasing the value of NMPHEADBUF would therefore have no benefit.

If the system is running the SCO MPX mpsar Maintenance Supplement, then statistics showing the usage of Sdsk control blocks are available. These statistics show that although 41.15 requests per second were made for Sdsk control blocks, the operating system never ran out of these data structures. Increasing SDSKOUT would have no benefit.

The sar -d statistics show that the disk subsystem is, on average, 100% busy for the duration of the test. 100% means that for the duration of the test, at least one disk request was on the disk driver's list during the test. The average time a request spent on the disk driver's request list was 62 milliseconds, while the average time the disk took to service the request was 83 milliseconds.

Considering the disk is always busy, the likelihood that the 32% of the CPU time spent idle waiting-for-device-I/O is caused by the processes waiting for the disk to service requests is high. Increasing the size of the buffer cache should reduce the number of disk requests by allowing more data to be held in an intermediate storage location.

With plenty of memory, the buffer cache can be increased without causing the system to page or swap. To determine the optimal size of the cache, a series of tests where the buffer cache is increased for each test was executed. This buffer cache increase provides a framework for each of the test series described in this chapter.

Any increase in NBUF may also require an increase in NHBUF to keep the length of the indexed lists in the buffer cache as short as possible. The current value of NHBUF is 256. When NBUF is increased to 1024, the ratio of NBUF/NHBUF = 1024/256 = 4, which is fine for SCO UNIX.

For the first test series, the following tunables are changed:

- NBUF increased to 1024, 2048, etc. up until 8192
- NHBUF increased as the required by the ratio of NBUF and NHBUF

⇩

Step 7. Decide how to change the resource allocation; rerun the tests and note progress toward the goal. Iterate until either the goal is reached, or until a limited resource is encountered.

☑ Determine whether to increase or decrease the resource/tunable. Note the new tunable values in the column marked **Test #1** and the test results under the column **Res #1.** Use the rest of the columns for the results of subsequent test iterations.

☑ When the goal is reached, implement the new resource allocation.

Tests Series #1: One disk

The first series of tests involves increasing the values of NBUF and NHBUF and running the fileop program on the same hardware environment. For each change in the tunable, the operating system must be relinked and rebooted. Figure 3-2 shows the test results for the different sizes of buffer cache. The changes in the cache efficiency for the larger buffer caches is shown in Figure 3-3.

Figure 3-3 shows how the buffer efficiency increases, but not linearly. When the buffer cache grows beyond six Mbytes, the rate of efficiency increase slows. The increase in cache efficiency should have resulted in a decrease in the disk activity. Figure 3-4 shows how the number of 512-byte blocks handed by the disk decreased as the buffer cache increased.

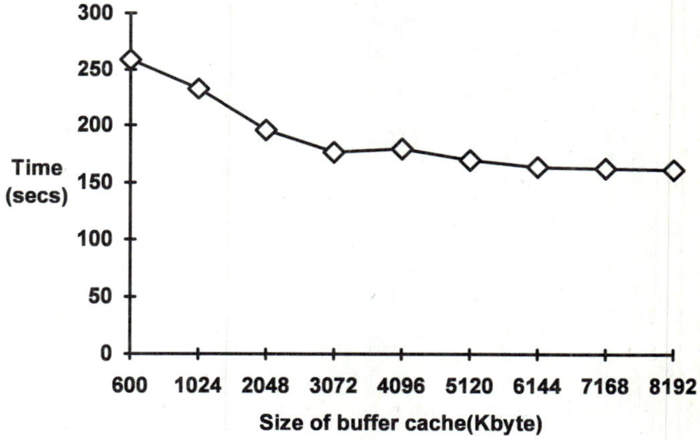

Figure 3-2: fileop Test Results for Different Size Buffer Caches on One disk

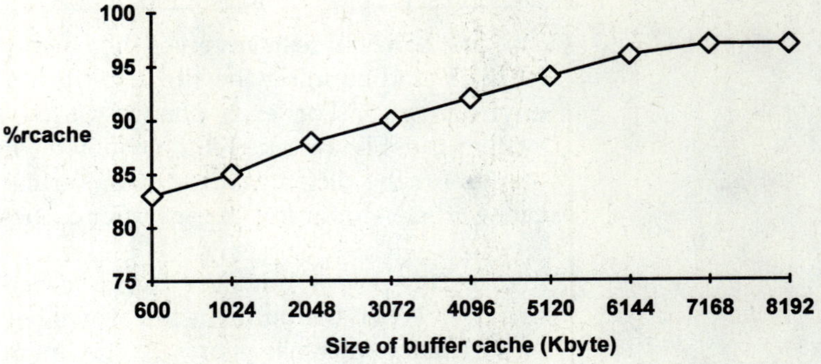

Figure 3-3: Increases in Cache Efficiency as the Buffer Cache Increases

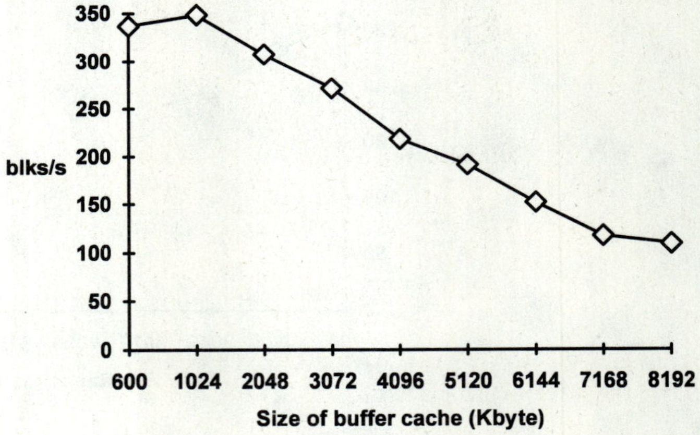

Figure 3-4: Number of Blocks Processed by the Disk as the Buffer Cache Grows

The number of blocks processed by the disk follows the pattern expected as the buffer cache efficiency increased. Above six Mbytes, the number of blocks processed continues to decrease, but at a slower rate.

Figure 3-5 shows how the amount of time required to process each disk request changes as the number of blocks decreases.

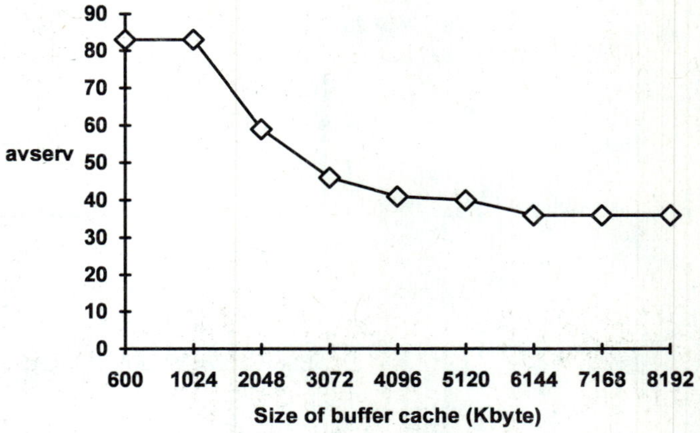

Figure 3-5: Relationship Between avserv and Size of Buffer Cache

The amount of time the disk required to service the request decreases along with the increase in cache efficiency. Most of the reduction occurred between one and three Mbytes. The rate of reduction slows above six Mbytes. This behavior is similar to the other statistics for this test series.

The service time, as indicated by avserv, is still 40 milliseconds even with an optimal %rcache, so the next step is to understand what the benefits would be of using a faster disk and disk adapter. No configuration options are supported by the current disk adapter, so increasing the speed of the disk subsystem with the existing hardware is not possible.

The decrease in the amount of disk activity as the buffer cache increases also results in a decrease in the amount of %wio as shown in Figure 3-6.

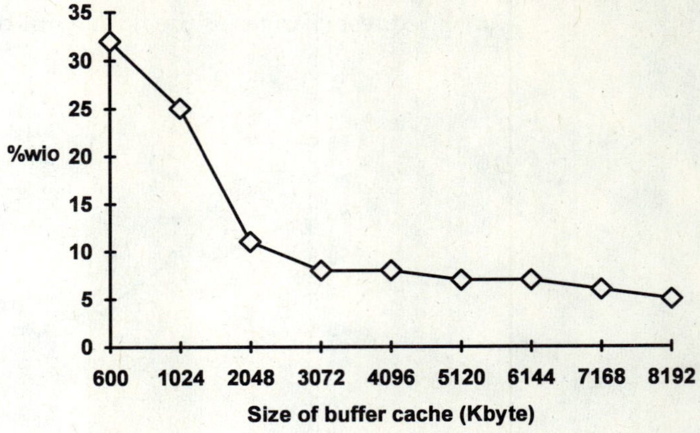

Figure 3-6: %wio as Buffer Cache Increases

Figure 3-6 corroborates the original theory that decreasing the amount of %wio would result in shorter test times. However, the goal is 132 seconds, and the current test result is 162 seconds, so more tests are necessary.

Test Series #2: Move Reads to a Faster Disk

This set of tests moves the read operations from the first disk to a second, faster disk. The new disk adapter supports full 32-bit addressing and bus master DMA. The write operations remain on the first disk. Once again, the same tests for different size buffer caches were run and the results are summarized in Figure 3-7.

In order for the test conditions to be as similar as possible, the two directories containing the files, *data1* and *data2*, are copied to the new filesystem created on the new disk. Symbolic links are created between the original *data1* directory and the new *data1* directory. The overhead for a symbolic link is an additional inode access as described in Chapter 2.

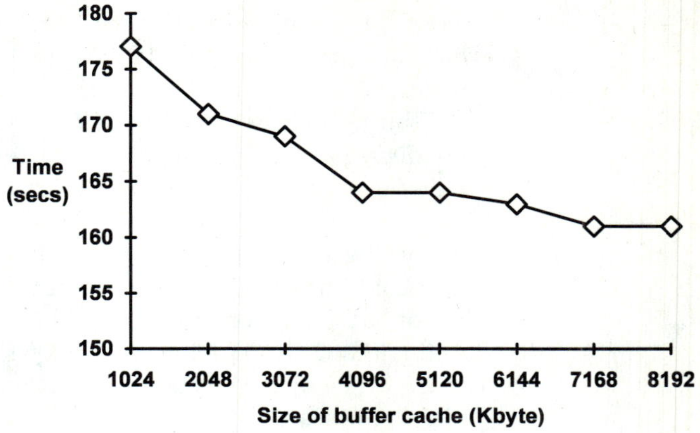

Figure 3-7: Test Results With New Disk and Disk Adapter

With a smaller buffer cache, the test is faster with the additional disk and disk adapter, and shows a similar performance increase as the size of the buffer cache increases. However, at a size of eight Mbytes, the duration of the test with one disk is almost equal to the duration of the test with two disks. The amount of %wio does not vary significantly during the test as shown in Figure 3-8.

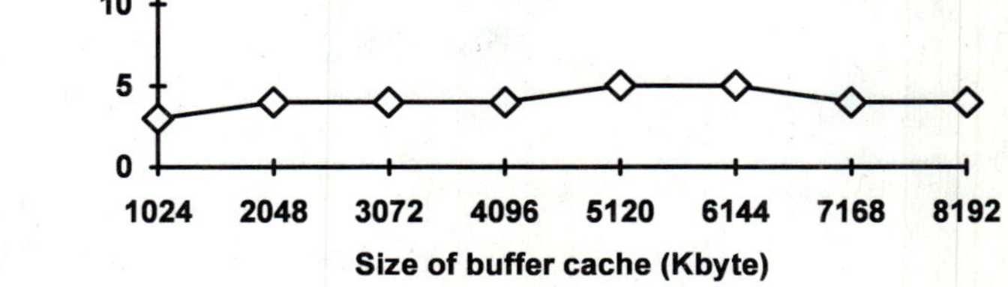

Figure 3-8: Amount of %wio

With a one Mbyte buffer cache and one disk the operation took 233 seconds, but with two disks, the operation took only 177 seconds. The additional disk in the second configuration allowed the greater number of disk requests that are the consequence of the small buffer to be serviced more quickly. The benefit of the second disk decreases as the buffer cache size is increased, because more of the filesystem requests are satisfied without accessing the disks.

At a cache size of eight Mbytes, the additional disk causes no significant improvement. This result illustrates how increasing the size of an intermediate storage location early in the series of locations that are searched for filesystem data, such as the buffer cache, can be more effective than adding faster hardware at a later point in the search..

The use of the second disk did improve the service time on the original disk. The service time is now 26 milliseconds with an eight Mbyte buffer cache rather than the 36 milliseconds recorded with only one disk. However, the additional disk and disk adapter perform better than the first disk as shown in Figures 3-9 and 3-10. Both of these graphs show that the blks/s decreased as the size of the buffer cache increased.

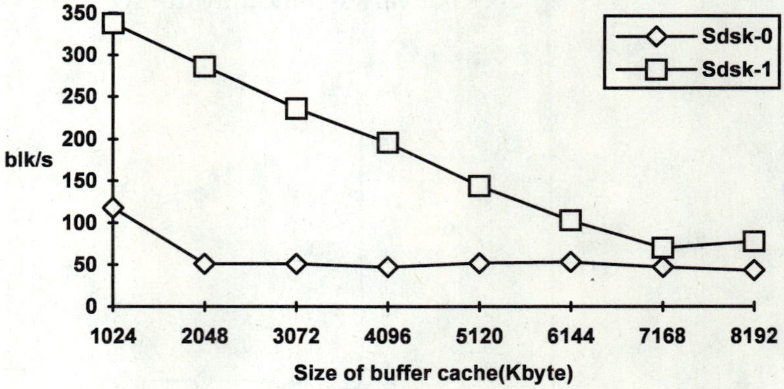

Figure 3-9: Comparison of Blocks Handled By New (Sdsk-1) and Old (Sdsk-0) Disks

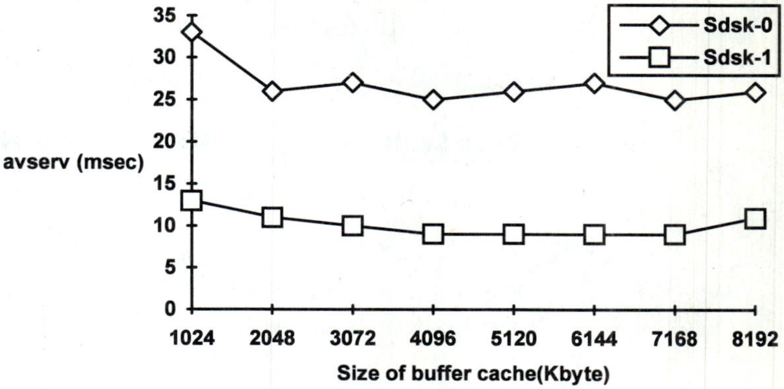

Figure 3-10: Comparison of avserv Time Between New (Sdsk-1) and Old (Sdsk-0) Disks

The amount of file data in the test is equal to the 200 files multiplied by the size of those files as shown by the following equation:

$$200 * 32768 = 6 \text{ Mbytes}$$

Since much of the file data is read by multiple processes, the cache must be at least six Mbytes for maximum read efficiency. Additional filesystem information, such as inodes and directory blocks, can also be stored in the cache for increased efficiency. The file writes will force the contents of some of the read buffers out of the buffer cache. Considering the total amount of data that could be stored in the cache, the optimal size should be greater than six Mbytes. This theory corresponds to the behavior seen as the cache grows to six Mbytes. The additional two Mbytes is probably sufficient to store the extra information, which is probably why continuing to increase the size beyond eight Mbytes shows no benefit.

Since none of the other filesystem resources are in short supply, the only other area to explore is the final point in the filesystem search chain, the disk adapter and disk.

The trend of decreased disk activity on the first disk, Sdsk-0, stops at two Mbytes as shown in Figure 3-9. This behavior is unexpected and so should be explored further.

Test Series #3: Move Reads and Writes to Faster Disk

Assuming the first disk cannot keep up with the frequency of write activity, the writes are now redirected to the second disk. The writes are redirected by setting up a symbolic link between the original write directory and the new write directory on the second disk. The results from these tests are shown in Figure 3-11.

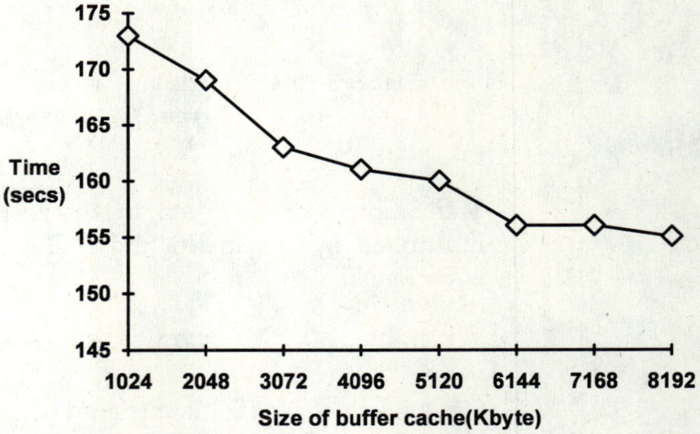

Figure 3-11: Test Results When Both Read and Write Operations are On New Disk

Performance improved only slightly over the first and second configurations. Figure 3-12 shows the change in %wio for this test.

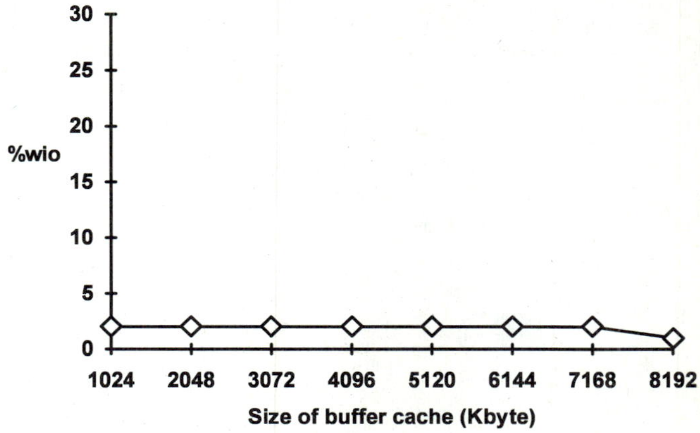

Figure 3-12: Amount of %wio

The amount of %wio has dropped a small amount with this configuration.

Figures 3-13 and 3-14 show the changes in blks/s and avserv time with reads and writes directed to the faster disk.

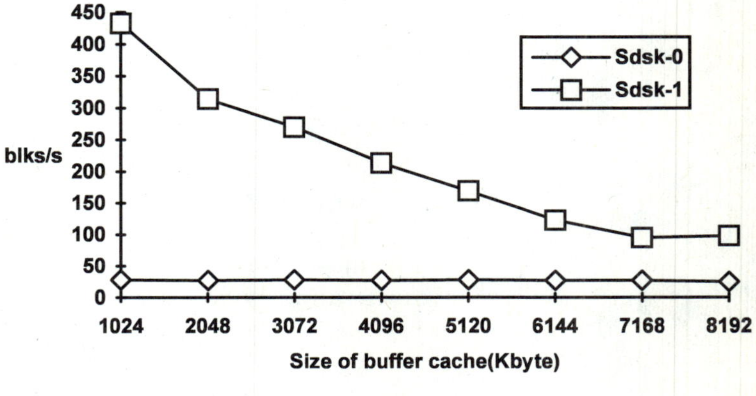

Figure 3-13: Changes in blks/s as Buffer Cache Increases

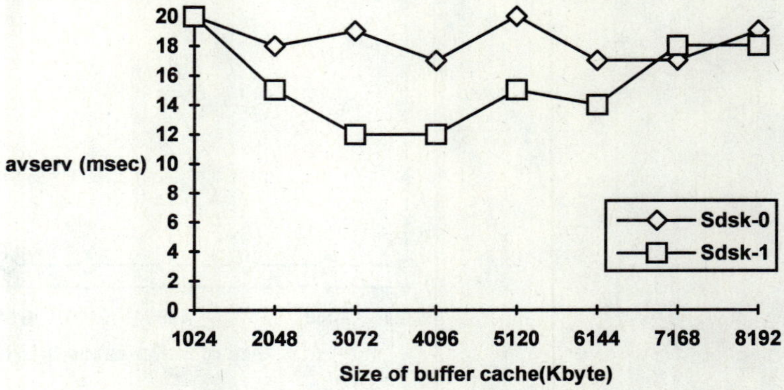

Figure 3-14: Changes in avserv as Buffer Cache Increases

The change in avserv behavior at six Mbytes does not correspond to the reduction in the number of blocks handled by the disk. One possible explanation is that the disk requires a longer time to access the filesystem blocks because the heads have to travel farther. The direct cause and effect relationship of the increase is difficult to prove at this point, however.

Figure 3-13 shows that even with all reads and writes occurring on the second disk, the first disk is still handling requests. One source of those requests is sar as it writes the data to the filesystem. The second source of these requests is the fileop script.

The fileop script is a shell script. The shell interpreter creates pipes that facilitate communication between the processes that are created when some shell commands are executed. Creating pipes involves allocating inodes on the root filesystem, which is located on the first disk.

If sar was causing the majority of disk activity on the first disk, increasing the size of the buffer cache would affect the number of blocks processed. The sar command uses normal write operations to access its data files in the filesystem. Pipes, however, require the allocation and updating of inodes, which are synchronous write operations. Increasing the size of the buffer cache does not improve the performance of synchronous write operations.

Test Series #4: Two Disks and a ramdisk

To prove that the disk activity on the first disk is caused by pipes, another set of tests is run where pipes are configured to use a ramdisk. A ramdisk is a filesystem that uses memory rather than a physical disk. For transient data such as the data transferred through pipes, a ramdisk is a useful mechanism for improving performance. A ramdisk should be used only for data that does not need permanent storage. A ramdisk stores data in memory and that data can be lost should the system unexpectedly stop.

The following command:

```
makeram 2Mb -pipe
```

creates a two Mbyte ramdisk. The makeram utility is included on the floppy disk. Figure 3-15 shows the test results for different size buffer caches after configuring the ramdisk.

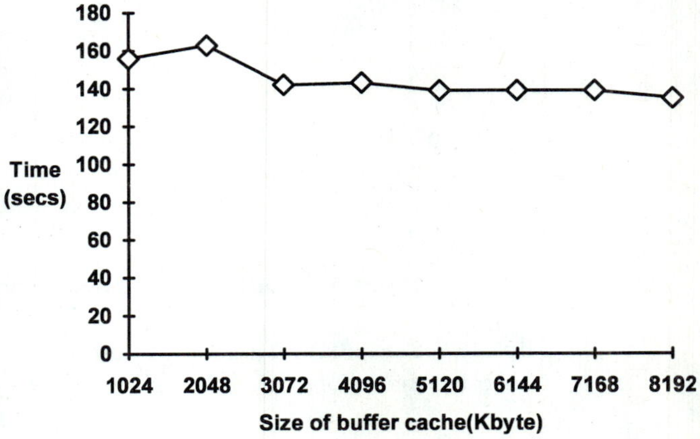

Figure 3-15: Two Disks and a ramdisk Test Results

The behavior of the test as the size of the buffer cache grows has changed dramatically. No longer does performance improve as the size of the buffer cache is increased. A synchronous write to memory to allocate and update the pipe inode uses fewer resources and is much quicker than a synchronous write to the disk, so the ramdisk benefits overall system performance. This benefit extends to the smaller size buffer caches as well as the larger ones. Less memory is required to achieve better performance because system resources are allocated more efficiently.

The amount of %wio has not changed in this configuration.

As expected, the amount of activity on the first disk has decreased and the amount of activity on the second disk has remained the same. Figure 3-16 shows these statistics for different size buffer caches.

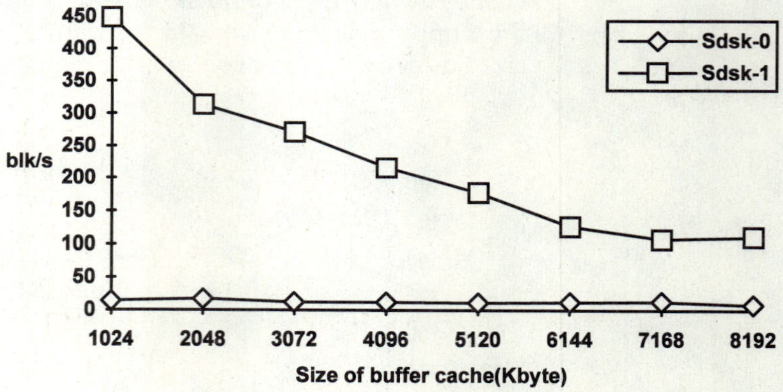

Figure 3-16: Disk Activity After Installing the ramdisk

Because the behavior of the system changed so dramatically, the need for the second hard disk should be re-examined.

Test Series #5: One Disk and a ramdisk

Since the disk activity to the first disk has decreased significantly after reconfiguring the ramdisk, perhaps the slower disk and disk adapter is sufficient for the level of filesystem activity with the ramdisk configured. Try an experiment by reconfiguring the reads and writes back to the original disk and start again.

Figure 3-17 shows the test results with the first disk only plus the ramdisk. With a small buffer cache, the second disk helps performance, but as the size of the cache increases, the difference between the configurations diminishes to just seven seconds.

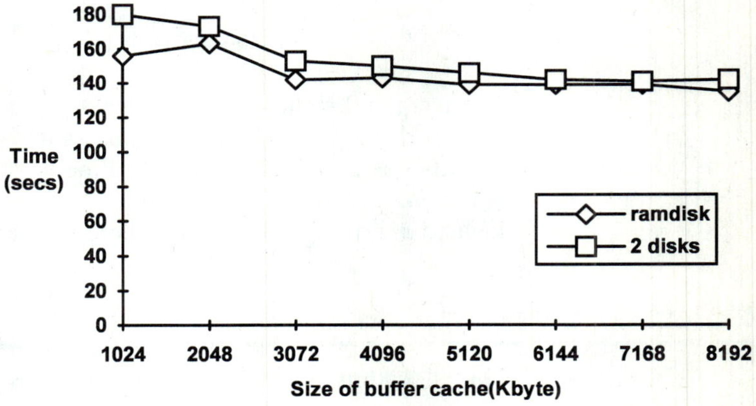

Figure 3-17: Comparison Between ramdisk and Two Disk Test Results

The amount of time spent %wio has increased slightly with this configuration, as shown by Figure 3-18. Because the first disk is so much slower than the second, this increase in %wio is expected.

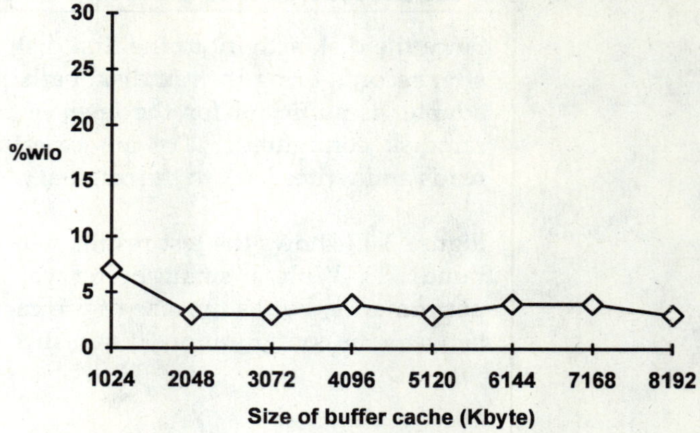

Figure 3-18: Amount of %wio

The test results show that the same performance can be achieved in two different ways at two different costs. Since the machine already has a sufficient amount of memory, the cheaper alternative is to configure a ramdisk and increase the size of the buffer cache, instead of adding a second disk and disk adapter.

CONCLUSIONS

The allocation and update of inodes, with only a few exceptions, always occurs synchronously. Pipes require inodes, but since the data in a pipe is transient, a ram-based filesystem can be installed to improve the time taken to allocate pipe inodes. Performance increases when the amount of pipe activity is high enough to adversely affect the disk subsystem, as shown in this case.

Increasing the size of intermediate storage locations also increases the efficiency of the system by ensuring that the application waits the shortest possible time for access to a resource.

This example shows the importance of understanding the resource usage patterns of the filesystem operation and how that understanding can achieve greater performance at no extra cost.

Worksheet 3-1: SCO UNIX Operating System Tuning Worksheet for One Disk

Tunables	Initial Values	Test #1	Test #2	Test #3	Test #4
*Installed Memory	64Mb				
Application Storage					
GPGSLO, GPGSHI	25 40				
MAXSC, AGEINTERVAL	8 31				
S5CACHEENTS, S5HASHQS	256 61	450			
NFILE	350				
NINODE, NHINODE	450 128				
NBUF, NHBUF	600 256	1024 256	2048 1024	3072 2048	4096 2048
BDFLUSHR, NAUTOP	30 10				
NCOPYBUF, PLOWBUFS	100 30				
NMPBUF, NMPHEADBUF	4 100				
NPBUF, DMAABLEBUF	40 16				
SDSKOUT	4				
*Disk Configuration, Data Layout	1 SCSI disk				
NCLIST	120				
NPROC, NREGION	100 300				
NSCRN, CTBUFSIZ	0 128				
Display adapter, colors	n/a				
Mouse Settings	n/a				
Other Memory Used	n/a				

Worksheet 3-2: SCO UNIX Operating System Worksheet for One Disk

Resources to Monitor	Initial Values	Test #1	Test #2	Test #3	Test #4
Free Memory, Free swap	14336 196608	14262 196608	13996 196608	13730 196608	13462 196608
Blocks Swapped in/out	0.0 0.0	0.0 0.0	0.0 0.0	0.0 0.0	0.0 0.0
Pages Reclaimed	0.00	0.00	0.00	0.00	0.00
CPU: %usr, %sys, %wio, %idle	10 58 32 0	11 64 25 0	13 76 11 0	14 78 8 0	13 78 8 0
Scheduling: runq-sz, swpq-sz, pswch/s	5.2 0 95	7.0 0 101	8.8 0 112	9.8 0 110	10.1 0 108
Namei Cache	99%	99%	99%	99%	99%
File Table, Inode Table	98 0 116 0	97 0 114 0	96 0 115 0	98 0 113 0	86 0 104 0
Buffer Cache %rcache Reads: bread/s lread/s Writes: bwrit/s, lwrit/s	83 126 757 42 208	85 129 866 45 221	88 129 1035 24 256	90 114 1131 21 285	92 89 1142 20 294
Scatter/Gather: mpbuf/s, ompb/s, mphbuf/s, omphbufs/s	0 0 21 0	0 0 21 0	0 0 18 0	0 0 15 0	0 0 12 0
Copy Buffers	0 0	0 0	0 0	0 0	0 0
Direct Disk Requests	0 0	0 0	0 0	0 0	0 0
Copy Memory	0 0	0 0	0 0	0 0	0 0
Sdsk Request Blocks	41.15 0	39.82 0	36.82 0	32.40 0	28.29 0
Disk Driver : %busy avque, r+w/s, blks/s, avwait, avserv	100 2 41 337 62 83	100 2 40 348 55 83	100 2 37 307 44 59	100 2 32 271 33 46	100 2 28 218 46 41

Now	Your Goal	Monitoring	Res #1	Res #2	Res #3	Res #4
245	130	259	233	196	177	180

Worksheet 3-3: SCO UNIX Operating System Tuning Worksheet for One Disk

Tunables	Initial Values	Test #5	Test #6	Test #7	Test #8
Installed Memory	64 Mb				
Application Storage	n/a				
GPGSLO, GPGSHI	25 40				
MAXSC, AGEINTERVAL	8 31				
S5CACHEENTS, S5HASHQS	256 61				
NFILE	350				
NINODE, NHINODE	450 128				
NBUF, NHBUF	600 256	5120 4096	6144 4096	7164 4096	8192 4096
BDFLUSHR, NAUTOP	30 10				
NCOPYBUF, PLOWBUFS	100 30				
NMPBUF, NMPHEADBUF	4 100				
NPBUF, DMAABLEBUF	40 16				
SDSKOUT	4				
Disk Configuration, Data Layout	1 SCSI disk				
NCLIST	120				
NPROC, NREGION	100 300				
NSCRN, CTBUFSIZ	0 128				
Display adapter, colors					
Mouse Settings					
Other Memory Used					

Worksheet 3-4: SCO UNIX Operating System Worksheet for One Disk

Resources to Monitor	Initial Values	Test #5	Test #6	Test #7	Test #8
Free Memory, Free swap		13175 196608	12909 196608	12637 196608	12334 196608
Blocks Swapped in/out		0.0 0.0	0.0 0.0	0.0 0.0	0.0 0.0
Pages Reclaimed		0.00	0.00	0.00	0.00
CPU: %usr, %sys, %wio, %idle		14 79 7 0	14 79 7 0	14 80 6 0	14 81 5 0
Scheduling: runq-sz, swpq-sz, pswch/s		11.0 0 104	10.8 0 94	10.0 0 93	10.7 0 . 93
Namei Cache		99%	99%	99%	99%
File Table, Inode Table		97 0 115 0	99 0 114 0	98 0 114 0	97 0 114 0
Buffer Cache %rcache Reads: bread/s, lread/s Writes: bwrit/s, lwrit/s		94 75 1192 20 310	96 55 1220 21 318	97 37 1257 21 333	97 33 1250 21 333
Scatter/Gather: mpbuf/s, ompb/s, mphbuf/s, omphbufs/s		0 0 10 0	0 0 8 0	0 0 6 0	0 0 5 0
Copy Buffers		0 0	0 0	0 0	0 0
Direct Disk Requests		0 0	0 0	0 0	0 0
Copy Memory		0 0	0 0	0 0	0 0
Sdsk Request Blocks		24.4 0	21.63 0	17.78 0	16.07 0
Disk Driver : %busy avque, r+w/s, blks/s, avwait, avserv		99, 2 24 191 54 40	77 3 22 151 59 36	65 3 18 117 78 36	58 3 16 109 65 36

Now	Your Goal	Monitoring	Res #1	Res #2	Res #3	Res #4
245	130	259	170	164	163	162

Worksheet 3-5: SCO UNIX Operating System Tuning Worksheet for Reads on Second Disk

Tunables	**Initial Values**	**Test #1**	**Test #2**	**Test #3**	**Test #4**
Installed Memory	64Mb				
Application Storage					
GPGSLO, GPGSHI	25 40				
MAXSC, AGEINTERVAL	8 31				
S5CACHEENTS, S5HASHQS	256 61				
NFILE	350				
NINODE, NHINODE	450 128				
NBUF, NHBUF	600 256	1024 256	2048 1024	3072 2048	4096 2048
BDFLUSHR, NAUTOP	30 10				
NCOPYBUF, PLOWBUFS	100 30				
NMPBUF, NMPHEADBUF	4 100				
NPBUF, DMAABLEBUF	40 16				
SDSKOUT	4				
Disk Configuration, Data Layout	reads on 2nd disk				
NCLIST	120				
NPROC, NREGION	100 300				
NSCRN, CTBUFSIZ	0 128				
Display adapter, colors					
Mouse Settings					

Worksheet 3-6: SCO UNIX Operating System Tuning Worksheet for Reads on Second Disk

Resources to Monitor	Initial Values	Test #1	Test #2	Test #3	Test #4
Free Memory, Free swap		14289 196608	14013 196608	13735 196608	13466 196608
Blocks Swapped in/out		0.0 0.0	0.0 0.0	0.0 0.0	0.0 0.0
Pages Reclaimed		0.00	0:00	0.00	0.00
CPU: %usr, %sys, %wio, %idle		14 84 3 0	13 83 4 0	14 82 4 0	14 82 4 0
Scheduling: runq-sz, swpq-sz, pswch/s		10.7 0 116	10.9 0 106	10.5 0 99	10.7 0 92
Namei Cache		99%	99%	99%	99%
File Table, Inode Table		98 0 113 0	97 0 114 0	87 0 106 0	98 0 113 0
Buffer Cache %rcache Reads: bread/s lread/s Writes: bwrit/s, lwrit/s		85 171 1157 58 305	88 145 1196 24 321	90 122 1222 22 323	92 101 1247 21 334
Scatter/Gather: mpbuf/s, ompb/s, mphbuf/s, omphbufs/s		0 0 26 0	0 0 19 0	0 0 15 0	0 0 13 0
Copy Buffers		0 0	0 0	0 0	0 0
Direct Disk Requests		0 0	0 0	0 0	0 0
Copy Memory		0 0	0 0	0 0	0 0
Sdsk Request Blocks		42.95 0.00	33.08 0.00	28.72 0.00	25.57 0.00
Disk Driver : %busy avque, r+w/s, blks/s, avwait, avserv		52 1 16 118 3 33	29 3 11 51 60 26	32 4 12 51 81 27	28 4 11 47 68 25

Now	Your Goal	Monitoring	Res #1	Res #2	Res #3	Res #4
245	130	259	177	171	169	164

Worksheet 3-7: SCO UNIX Operating System Tuning Worksheet for Reads on Second Disk

Tunables	Initial Values	Test #5	Test #6	Test #7	Test #8
Installed Memory	64Mb				
Application Storage					
GPGSLO, GPGSHI	25 40				
MAXSC, AGEINTERVAL	8 31				
S5CACHEENTS, S5HASHQS	256 61				
NFILE	350				
NINODE, NHINODE	450 128				
NBUF, NHBUF	600 256	5120 4096	6144 4096	7164 4096	8192 4096
BDFLUSHR, NAUTOP	30 10				
NCOPYBUF, PLOWBUFS	100 30				
NMPBUF, NMPHEADBUF	4 100				
NPBUF, DMAABLEBUF	40 16				
SDSKOUT	4				
Disk Configuration, Data Layout	all reads on 2nd disk				
NCLIST	120				
NPROC, NREGION	100 300				
NSCRN, CTBUFSIZ	0 128				
Display adapter, colors					
Mouse Settings					

Worksheet 3-8: SCO UNIX Operating System Tuning Worksheet for Reads on Second Disk

Resources to Monitor	Initial Values	Test #5	Test #6	Test #7	Test #8
Free Memory, Free swap		13179 196608	12908 196608	12610 196608	12303 196608
Blocks Swapped in/out		0.0 0.0	0.0 0.0	0.0 0.0	0.0 0.0
Pages Reclaimed		0.00	0.00	0.00	0.00
CPU: %usr, %sys, %wio, %idle		14 81 5 0	14 81 5 0	14 81 5 0	14 82 4 0
Scheduling: runq-sz, swpq-sz, pswch/s		10.9 0 94	10.9 0 92	10.4 0 80	10.9 0 85
Namei Cache		99%	99%	99%	99%
File Table, Inode Table		98 0 113 0	97 0 115 0	98 0 115 0	97 0 115 0
Buffer Cache %rcache Reads: bread/s lread/s Writes: bwrit/s, lwrit/s		94 77 1312 21 335	96 55 1261 23 337	97 38 1281 21 344	97 40 1281 21 346
mpbuf/s, ompb/s, mphbuf/s, omphbufs/s		0 0 10 0	0 0 8 0	0 0 5 0	0 0 5 0
Copy Buffers		0 0	0 0	0 0	0 0
Direct Disk Requests		0 0	0 0	0 0	0 0
Copy Memory		0 0	0 0	0 0	0 0
Sdsk Request Blocks		21.56 0	19.12 0	15.73 0	15.11 0
Disk Driver : %busy avque, r+w/s, blks/s, avwait, avserv		29 5 11 52 94 26	32 4 12 53 92 27	28 5 11 47 88 25	26 5 10 43 93 26

Now	Your Goal	Monitoring	Res #5	Res #6	Res #7	Res #8
245	259	130	164	163	161	161

Worksheet 3-9: SCO UNIX Operating System Tuning Worksheet for Reads and Writes on Second Disk

Tunables	Initial Values	Test #1	Test #2	Test #3	Test #4
Installed Memory	64Mb				
Application Storage					
GPGSLO, GPGSHI	25 40				
MAXSC, AGEINTERVAL	8 31				
S5CACHEENTS, S5HASHQS	256 61				
NFILE	350				
NINODE, NHINODE	450 128				
NBUF, NHBUF	600 256	1024 256	2048 1024	3072 2048	4096 2048
BDFLUSHR, NAUTOP	30 10				
NCOPYBUF, PLOWBUFS	100 30				
NMPBUF, NMPHEADBUF	4 100				
NPBUF, DMAABLEBUF	40 16				
SDSKOUT	4				
Disk Configuration, Data Layout	all reads and writes on 2nd disk				
NCLIST	120				
NPROC, NREGION	100 300				
NSCRN, CTBUFSIZ	0 128				
Other Memory Used					

Worksheet 3-10: SCO UNIX Operating System Tuning Worksheet for Reads and Writes on Second Disk

Resources to Monitor	Initial Values	Test #1	Test #2	Test #3	Test #4
Free Memory, Free swap		14285 196608	14013 196608	13709 196608	13465 196608
Blocks Swapped in/out		0.0 0.0	0.0 0.0	0.0 0.0	0.0 0.0
Pages Reclaimed		0.00	0.00	0.00	0.00
CPU: %usr, %sys, %wio, %idle		13 85 2 0	14 84 2 0	14 84 2 0	14 84 2 0
runq-sz, swpq-sz, pswch/s		10.9 0 114	10.9 0 109	10.4 0 99	10.6 0 95
Namei Cache		99%	99%	99%	99%
File Table, Inode Table		97 0 114 0	96 0 113 0	89 0 108 0	97 0 114 0
Buffer Cache %rcache Reads: bread/s lread/s Writes: bwrit/s, lwrit/s		86 171 1188 59 317	88 148 1218 22 327	90 126 1260 22 337	92 99 1272 21 343
Scatter/Gather: mpbuf/s, ompb/s, mphbuf/s, omphbufs/s		0 0 24 0	0 0 18 0	0 0 16 0	0 0 12 0
Copy Buffers		0 0	0 0	0 0	0 0
Direct Disk Requests		0 0	0 0	0 0	0 0
Copy Memory		0 0	0 0	0 0	0 0
Sdsk Request Blocks		41.56 0.00	33.13 0.00	28.94 0.00	25.17 0.00
Disk Driver : %busy avque, r+w/s, blks/s, avwait, avserv (Sdsk-0)		20 1 10 28 1 20	18 1 10 27 3 18	18 1 9 28 5 19	17 1 10 27 7 17
Sdsk-1		63 1 31 433 1 20	1 36 1 23 314 6 15	24 2 19 270 8 12	18 2 15 214 10 12

Now	Your Goal	Monitoring	Res #1	Res #2	Res #3	Res #4
245	130	259	173	169	163	161

Worksheet 3-11: SCO UNIX Operating System Worksheet for Reads and Writes on Second Disk

Tunables	Initial Values	Test #5	Test #6	Test #7	Test #8
Installed Memory	64Mb				
Application Storage					
GPGSLO, GPGSHI	25 40				
MAXSC, AGEINTERVAL	8 31				
S5CACHEENTS, S5HASHQS	256 61				
NFILE	350				
NINODE, NHINODE	450 128				
NBUF, NHBUF	600 256	5120 4096	6144 4096	7168 4096	8192 4096
BDFLUSHR, NAUTOP	30 10				
NCOPYBUF, PLOWBUFS	100 30				
NMPBUF, NMPHEADBUF	4 100				
NPBUF, DMAABLEBUF	40 16				
SDSKOUT	4				
Disk Configuration, Data Layout	all reads and writes on 2nd disk				
NCLIST	120				
NPROC, NREGION	100 300				
NSCRN, CTBUFSIZ	0 128				
Other Memory Used					

Worksheet 3-12: SCO UNIX Operating System Tuning Worksheet for Reads and Writes on Second Disk

Resources to Monitor	Initial Values	Test #5	Test #6	Test #7	Test #8
Free Memory, Free swap		13183 196608	12912 196608	12639 196608	12338 196608
Blocks Swapped in/out		0.0 0.0	0.0 0.0	0.0 0.0	0.0 0.0
Pages Reclaimed		0.00	0.00	0.00	0.00
CPU: %usr, %sys, %wio, %idle		14 83 2 0	15 83 2 0	15 83 2 0	15 84 1 0
runq-sz, swpq-sz, pswch/s		10.6 0 97	10.6 0 88	10.7 0 86	10.8 0 88
Namei Cache		99%	99%	99%	99%
File Table, Inode Table		89 0 107 0	97 0 114 0	98 0 113 0	97 0 114 0
Buffer Cache %rcache Reads: bread/s lread/s Writes: bwrit/s, lwrit/s		94 77 1289 22 347	96 56 1316 19 354	97 41 1316 20 357	97 39 1335 23 365
Scatter/Gather: mpbuf/s, ompb/s, mphbuf/s, omphbufs/s		0 0 10 0	0 0 7 0	0 0 5 0	0 0 5 0
Copy Buffers		0 0	0 0	0 0	0 0
Direct Disk Requests		0 0	0 0	0 0	0 0
Copy Memory		0 0	0 0	0 0	0 0
Sdsk Request Blocks		21.20 0.00	18.24 0.00	16.07 0.00	15.08 0.00
Disk Driver : %busy avque, r+w/s, blks/s, avwait, avserv (Sdsk-0)		19 2 10 28 14 20	18 2 10 27 10 17	17 2 10 27 10 17	17 2 9 25 12 19
Sdsk-1		18 2 12 169 13 15	11 2 8 123 15 14	11 2 6 95 22 18	10 2 6 98 24 18

Now	Your Goal	Monitoring	Res #1	Res #2	Res #3	Res #4
245	130	259	160	156	156	155

Worksheet 3-13: SCO UNIX Operating System Tuning Worksheet For Two Disks Plus ramdisk

Tunables	Initial Values	Test #1	Test #2	Test #3	Test #4
Installed Memory	64Mb				
Application Storage					
GPGSLO, GPGSHI	25 40				
MAXSC, AGEINTERVAL	8 31				
S5CACHEENTS, S5HASHQS	256 61				
NFILE	350				
NINODE, NHINODE	450 128				
NBUF, NHBUF	600 256	1024 256	2048 1024	3072 2048	4096 2048
BDFLUSHR, NAUTOP	30 10				
NCOPYBUF, PLOWBUFS	100 30				
NMPBUF, NMPHEADBUF	4 100				
NPBUF, DMAABLEBUF	40 16				
SDSKOUT	4				
Disk Configuration, Data Layout	2 disks, ramdisk pipes				
NCLIST	120				
NPROC, NREGION	100 300				
NSCRN, CTBUFSIZ	0 128				
Other Memory Used					

Worksheet 3-14: SCO Operating System Tuning Worksheet For Two Disks Plus ramdisk

Resources to Monitor	Initial Values	Test #1	Test #2	Test #3	Test #4
Free Memory, Free swap		13799 196608	13531 196608	13252 196608	12970 196608
Blocks Swapped in/out		0.0 0.0	0.0 0.0	0.0 0.0	0.0 0.0
Pages Reclaimed		0.00	0.00	0.00	0.00
CPU: %usr, %sys, %wio, %idle		14 85 2 0	14 84 2 0	15 84 1 0	14 84 2 0
Scheduling: runq-sz, swpq-sz, pswch/s		9.0 0 86	8.5 0 72	9.1 0 63	9.1 0 58
Namei Cache		99%	99%	99%	99%
File Table, Inode Table		98 0 115 0	98 0 115 0	97 0 116 0	87 0 107 0
Buffer Cache %rcache Reads: bread/s lread/s Writes: bwrit/s, lwrit/s		85 180 1238 59 343	88 151 1280 21 355	90 130 1323 20 371	92 103 1319 20 367
Scatter/Gather: mpbuf/s, ompb/s, mphbuf/s, omphbufs/s		0 0 25 0	0 0 19 0	0 0 16 0	0 0 12 0
Copy Buffers		0 0	0 0	0 0	0 0
Direct Disk Requests		0 0	0 0	0 0	0 0
Copy Memory		0 0	0 0	0 0	0 0
Sdsk Request Blocks		35.99 0.00	27.11 0.00	21.35 0.00	17.96 0.00
Disk Driver : %busy avque, r+w/s, blks/s, avwait, avserv (Sdsk-0)		9 1 3 14 3 27	10 1 4 17 3 26	7 1 2 12 13 41	8 1 3 12 14 31
Sdsk-1		50 1 33 449 0 15	23 1 23 313 4 10	21 2 20 271 5 11	18 2 15 216 7 12

Now	Your Goal	Monitoring	Res #1	Res #2	Res #3	Res #4
245	130	259	156	163	142	143

Worksheet 3-15: SCO UNIX Operating System Tuning Worksheet For Two Disks Plus ramdisk

Tunables	Initial Values	Test #5	Test #6	Test #7	Test #8
Installed Memory	64Mb				
Application Storage					
GPGSLO, GPGSHI	25 40				
MAXSC, AGEINTERVAL	8 31				
S5CACHEENTS, S5HASHQS	256 61				
NFILE	350				
NINODE, NHINODE	450 128				
NBUF, NHBUF	600 256	5120 4096	6144 4096	7168 4096	8192 4096
BDFLUSHR, NAUTOP	30 10				
NCOPYBUF, PLOWBUFS	100 30				
NMPBUF, NMPHEADBUF	4 100				
NPBUF, DMAABLEBUF	40 16				
SDSKOUT	4				
Disk Configuration, Data Layout	2 disks, ram pipes				
NCLIST	120				
NPROC, NREGION	100 300				
NSCRN, CTBUFSIZ	0 128				
Other Memory Used					

Worksheet 3-16: SCO UNIX Tuning Worksheet For Two Disks Plus ramdisk

Resources to Monitor	**Initial Values**	**Test #5**	**Test #6**	**Test #7**	**Test #8**
Free Memory, Free swap		12697 196608	12422 196608	12149 196608	11858 196608
Blocks Swapped in/out		0.0 0.0	0.0 0.0	0.0 0.0	0.0 0.0
Pages Reclaimed		0.00	0.00	0.00	0.00
CPU: %usr, %sys, %wio, %idle		15 84 1 0	15 84 1 0	15 83 1 0	15 84 1 0
Scheduling: runq-sz, swpq-sz, pswch/s		8.9 0 53	9.0 0 47	8.8 0 47	8.2 0 46
Namei Cache		99%	99%	99%	99%
File Table, Inode Table		96 0 116 0	97 0116 0	97 0 116 0	99 0 116 0
Buffer Cache %rcache Reads: bread/s lread/s Writes: bwrit/s, lwrit/s		94 86 1359 20 377	96 57 1351 21 378	97 48 1377 21 383	97 48 1406 20 391
Scatter/Gather: mpbuf/s, ompb/s, mphbuf/s, omphbufs/s		0 0 10 0	0 0 7 0	0 0 6 0	0 0 6 0
Copy Buffers		0 0	0 0	0 0	0 0
Direct Disk Requests		0 0	0 0	0 0	0 0
Copy Memory		0 0	0 0	0 0	0 0
Sdsk Request Blocks		14.02 0.00	10.50 0.00	9.11 0.00	7.99 0.00
Disk Driver : %busy avque, r+w/s, blks/s, avwait, avserv (Sdsk-0)		7 2 2 11 40 47	9 2 2 12 38 37	10 2 3 13 49 38	7 2 1 8 61 56
Sdsk-1		15 2 12 177 9 12	11 2 8 127 14 14	10 2 7 108 16 16	10 2 7 111 15 15

Now	**Your Goal**	**Monitoring**	**Res #5**	**Res #6**	**Res #7**	**Res #8**
245	130	259	139	139	139	135

Worksheet 3-17: SCO UNIX Operating System Tuning Worksheet for One Disk Plus ramdisk

Tunables	Initial Values	Test #1	Test #2	Test #3	Test #4
Installed Memory	64Mb				
Application Storage					
GPGSLO, GPGSHI	25 40				
MAXSC, AGEINTERVAL	8 31				
S5CACHEENTS, S5HASHQS	256 61				
NFILE	350				
NINODE, NHINODE	450 128				
NBUF, NHBUF	600 256	1024 256	2048 1024	3072 2048	4096 2048
BDFLUSHR, NAUTOP	30 10				
NCOPYBUF, PLOWBUFS	100 30				
NMPBUF, NMPHEADBUF	4 100				
NPBUF, DMAABLEBUF	40 16				
SDSKOUT	4				
Disk Configuration, Data Layout	1 disk, ram pipes				
NCLIST	120				
NPROC, NREGION	100 300				
NSCRN, CTBUFSIZ	0 128				
Other Memory Used					

Worksheet 3-18: SCO UNIX Operating System Tuning Worksheet For One Disk Plus ramdisk

Resources to Monitor	Initial Values	Test #1	Test #2	Test #3	Test #4
Free Memory, Free swap		13752 196608	13520 196608	13242 196608	12971 196608
Blocks Swapped in/out		0.0 0.0	0.0 0.0	0.0 0.0	0.0 0.0
Pages Reclaimed		0.00	0.00	0.00	0.00
CPU: %usr, %sys, %wio, %idle		14 79 7 0	15 82 3 0	15 82 3 0	14 82 4 0
Scheduling: runq-sz, swpq-sz, pswch/s		7.2 99	8.5 85	9.0 74	9.0 80
Namei Cache		99%	99%	99%	99%
File Table, Inode Table		96 0 116 0	97 0 116 0	97 0 116 0	97 0 116 0
Buffer Cache %rcache Reads: bread/s lread/s Writes: bwrit/s, lwrit/s		86 57 1090 55 291	88 147 1194 21 328	90 124 1230 21 340	92 101 1240 21 340
Scatter/Gather: mpbuf/s, ompb/s, mphbuf/s, omphbufs/s		0 0 24 0	0 0 19 0	0 0 16 0	0 0 13 0
Copy Buffers		0 0	0 0	0 0	0 0
Direct Disk Requests		0 0	0 0	0 0	0 0
Copy Memory		0 0	0 0	0 0	0 0
Sdsk Request Blocks		41.21 0.00	32.95 0.00	26.91 0.00	23.11 0.00
Disk Driver : %busy avque, r+w/s, blks/s, avwait, avserv		100 2 41 409 52 71	95 2 33 322 16 29	71 2 27 274 27 27	58 3 23 227 40 25

Now	Your Goal	Monitoring	Res #1	Res #2	Res #3	Res #4
245	130	259	180	173	153	150

Worksheet 3-19: SCO UNIX Operating System Tuning Worksheet For One Disk Plus ramdisk

Tunables	Initial Values	Test #5	Test #6	Test #7	Test #8
Installed Memory	64Mb				
Application Storage					
GPGSLO, GPGSHI	25 40				
MAXSC, AGEINTERVAL	8 31				
S5CACHEENTS, S5HASHQS	256 61				
NFILE	350				
NINODE, NHINODE	450 128				
NBUF, NHBUF	600 256	5120 4096	6144 4096	7168 4096	8192 4096
BDFLUSHR, NAUTOP	30 10				
NCOPYBUF, PLOWBUFS	100 30				
NMPBUF, NMPHEADBUF	4 100				
NPBUF, DMAABLEBUF	40 16				
SDSKOUT	4				
Disk Configuration, Data Layout	1 disk, ram pipes				
NCLIST	120				
NPROC, NREGION	100 300				
NSCRN, CTBUFSIZ	0 128				
Other Memory Used					

Worksheet 3-20: SCO UNIX Operating System Tuning Worksheet For One Disk Plus ramdisk

Resources to Monitor	Initial Values	Test #5	Test #6	Test #7	Test #8
Free Memory, Free swap		12689 196608	12420 196608	12145 196608	11846 196608
Blocks Swapped in/out		0.0 0.0	0.0 0.0	0.0 0.0	0.0 0.0
Pages Reclaimed		0.00	0.00	0.00	0.00
CPU: %usr, %sys, %wio, %idle		14 82 3 0	14 82 4 0	15 81 4 0	16 81 3 0
Scheduling: runq-sz, swpq-sz, pswch/s		9.0 0 73	8.9 0 54	8.8 0 49	8.9 0 51
Namei Cache		99%	99%	99%	99%
File Table, Inode Table		98 0 116 0	96 0 117 0	98 0 116 0	97 0 115 0
Buffer Cache %rcache Reads: bread/s lread/s Writes: bwrit/s, lwrit/s		94 80 1281 19 351	95 60 1309 22 359	96 47 1326 19 364	97 46 1343 23 368
Scatter/Gather: mpbuf/s, ompb/s, mphbuf/s, omphbufs/s		0 0 10 0	0 0 8 0	0 0 6 0	0 0 7 0
Copy Buffers		0 0	0 0	0 0	1 0
Direct Disk Requests		0 0	0 0	0 0	0 0
Copy Memory		0 0	0 0	0 0	0 0
Sdsk Request Blocks		17.94 0.00	15.02 0.00	11.81 0.00	11.16 0.00
Disk Driver : %busy avque, r+w/s, blks/s, avwait, avserv		48 3 18 183 53 27	43 4 15 148 81 29	36 4 12 117 77 30	37 4 11 121 111 33

Now	Your Goal	Monitoring	Res #1	Res #2	Res #3	Res #4
245	130	259	146	142	141	142

Chapter 4

Common SCO MPX Operations

This chapter describes operations that are typically executed on the SCO MPX multiprocessor environment. SCO MPX is an extension to SCO UNIX that allows multiple processors to run simultaneously. Since SCO MPX is an extension to SCO UNIX, the same operations are described in this chapter as are described in the Common SCO UNIX Operations chapter.

Tuning SCO MPX involves considering all of the same resource allocations discussed in the SCO UNIX chapter, but with the added complication of multiple processors simultaneously executing applications and the operating system.

The chapter begins with a technical description of SCO MPX, covering some of the special features of multiprocessor hardware and SCO MPX. The technical background behind the key tuning goals are also described in this section. Because SCO MPX is an extension to SCO UNIX, only the differences between SCO UNIX and SCO MPX are described in this chapter. This technical description assumes some understanding of the material presented in the Common SCO UNIX Operations chapter.

The operations section begins with the calculation operation because that is most illustrative of the SCO MPX process scheduling concepts. This section also shows the performance improvements that can be achieved when many independent processes are running on the machine.

The file read and write operation and the display update and character echo operations follow the same outline as their corresponding descriptions in the Common SCO UNIX Operations chapter.

Chapter 5 contains a case study showing what happens to a system when an additional processor is activated by installing SCO MPX. The changes in resource allocation that normally accompany the installation of an additional processor are also explored.

How SCO MPX Works

SCO MPX enables the operating system to use the additional CPUs installed in the computer system to run more application processes at the same time. The more capacity the entire system has for parallel execution, the greater the performance benefit of installing SCO MPX. Multiprocessor machines supported by SCO MPX have special performance features that are not found in ordinary uniprocessor machines.

In order for SCO MPX to run on a particular multiprocessor hardware platform, the machine must conform to the following requirements:

- All of the processors must be able to use the same memory address to access the same memory location. For example, if the first CPU accesses some data located at hexadecimal physical address 0xC0001000, the second CPU can access that same data using the same physical address, 0xC0001000. In addition, all of the memory in the machine must be accessible by all of the processors.

- Interrupts must be implemented among all of the CPUs in order to facilitate rapid hardware-oriented communication. These special purpose interrupts are known as *interprocessor interrupts* and are distinguished from normal device interrupts by special purpose hardware. Interprocessor interrupts are used by the hardware manufacturer and SCO MPX to implement a variety of features. The features and their implementation vary widely among different platforms, so check the hardware documentation for more information. Interprocessor interrupts are not configurable by the system administrator and should normally never be changed. Interprocessor interrupts are also called *interCPU interrupts*.

- The integrity of the data must be guaranteed by the hardware platform, since multiple processors, all having L2 caches, are accessing data simultaneously. The integrity of the data means that when one processor updates an address that is also located in another processor's cache, the other processor's cache entry is either invalidated or updated with the new value. Guaranteeing the integrity of cache data is known as *cache coherency*. Usually this feature requires some very complex hardware logic, so the implementation of cache coherency varies greatly among hardware manufacturers. Check the hardware documentation for more information on what type of cache coherency is provided by the hardware platform.

Internal CPU cache

Most multiprocessor platforms have two levels of caches. The first cache is commonly known as the *on-chip* or *internal CPU cache*. With i486 and later processors, this cache is internal to the processor and is mostly used for the pre-fetching of instructions and data. Additional parallel internal caches on the Pentium processor are also available to increase simultaneous instruction and data execution.

L2 cache

The second cache found on multiprocessor systems is commonly known as the *L2*, or level-two, cache. This cache is called L2 because it is accessed only when the CPU does not find the required information in the internal, or level one, CPU cache. This cache is external to the CPU.

The size and behavior of these L2 caches vary considerably among the multiprocessor platforms supported by SCO MPX. The two most common types of L2 caches are known as *write-through* and *write-back*. A write-through cache stores copies of the data, or instructions, read from memory inside the cache. The write operation requires the location in physical memory to be updated prior to the CPU continuing execution.

A write-back cache stores both memory reads and writes inside the cache and implements some advanced logic to ensure that the data inside of these caches is not corrupted when two or more processors update the memory locations. Because cache coherency can occur at the speed of the hardware without interference by the operating system, performance is maximized.

In addition to advanced caching technology, multiprocessor machines differ from uniprocessor machines in their internal bus architectures. Many multiprocessor machines are implemented with a high-speed bus that connects only memory and processor cards. Some multiprocessor machines allow high speed I/O cards to connect to this high-speed bus as well. The speed with which the CPUs access memory is critical to good multiprocessor performance.

The high-speed memory/CPU bus connects to a *compatibility* bus by a number of different mechanisms. The compatibility bus is primarily used for expansion cards, such as additional disk adapters and network interface cards, and so is normally ISA, MCA, or EISA.

The mechanisms for connecting the high speed memory/CPU bus vary greatly among multiprocessor hardware implementations. No matter what the mechanism, it is transparent to the operating system. Figure 4-1 shows an example block diagram for a multiprocessor hardware platform.

Multiprocessor machines are more complex than uniprocessor machines. Their hardware architectures also vary. Consequently, the range of hardware performance is large. Even though the same release of SCO MPX may run on all of these platforms, the performance of the same applications on the same operating system varies because of the underlying hardware differences. Understanding the capabilities of the underlying hardware is important to understanding the performance capacity of the system.

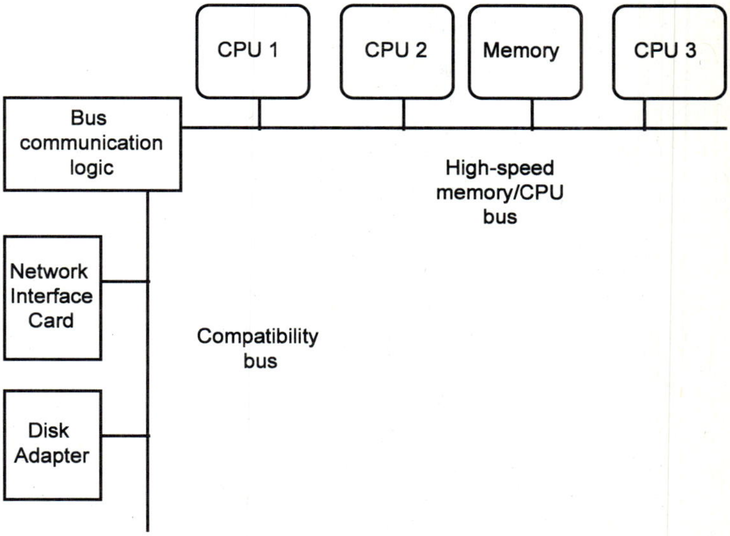

Figure 4-1: The CPUs and memory are connected to the high-speed CPU/memory bus. The high-speed bus communicates with the compatibility bus through special bus communication logic. The compatibility bus can support ISA, EISA or MCA. Devices, such as network interface cards and disk adapters, are connected to the compatibility bus.

After The Installation of Another Processor

After the installation of another processor, the processing capacity of the system increases dramatically. Increased processing capacity means that potentially more applications can run simultaneously. More running applications means that the previously installed hardware resources are in much greater demand, thereby increasing the likelihood that the underlying hardware resource will be unable to meet the demand. If underlying hardware shortages exist, the increase in system performance after installing another processor may not be as great as expected. Shortage of hardware resources is the most common reason that system performance does not increase after another processor is added.

When considering the installation of another processor, always consider adding more memory, disks/disk adapters, or network capacity to match the increased processing capacity. In addition to possibly needing more underlying hardware resources, the installation of SCO MPX introduces new tuning concepts that are not encountered in a uniprocessor environment. These new concepts are discussed in the following sections.

Contention for Resources

A fundamental tuning theme underlying the descriptions in this chapter is *maximize performance by minimizing resource contention*. Resource contention occurs whenever more than one process must wait to access a resource because another process is currently using the resource.

For example, when two users run the same application at the same time, both users may require simultaneous access to the same application resource because two processors could be running the application at the same time on behalf of both users. One user may be forced to wait while the other user finishes accessing the resource, thereby reducing the amount of time the processes can execute simultaneously. Figure 4-2 shows the interaction when two processes have to compete for access to one resource.

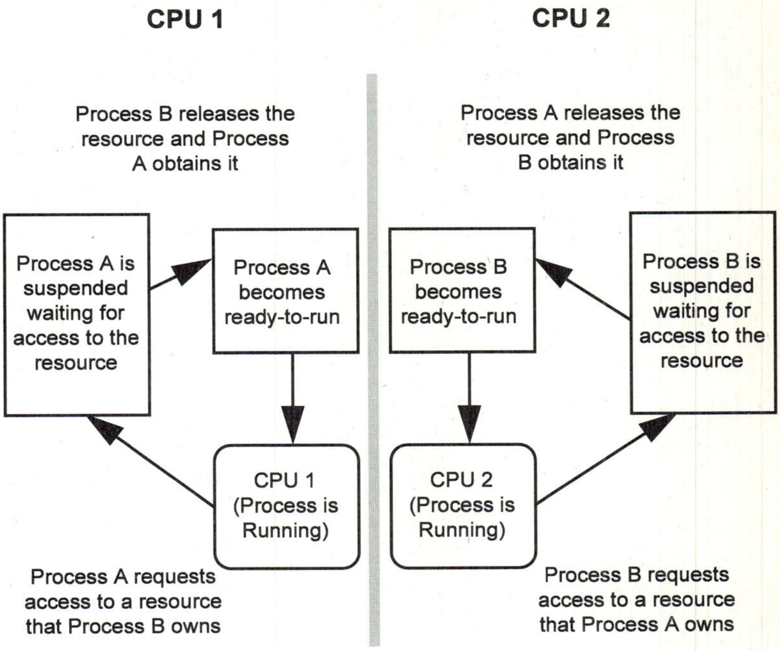

Figure 4-2: Process A and B cannot execute in parallel because of their mutual need to access the same resource. On CPU 1, Process A runs until it requires access to the resource owned by Process B. Process A is suspended until Process B releases the resource. If no other ready-to-run processes are available, CPU 1 will be idle until Process B releases the resource. On CPU 2 a similar interaction occurs. Process B runs and releases the resource. Process A runs and obtains the resource. When Process B needs the resource, Process A owns it, so Process B is suspended until Process A releases it. If the resource were freely available to both of them, then Process A and B could execute simultaneously and performance would be maximized. This diagram assumes that no other processes are running on the system.

Contention reduces the capacity of the operating system to simultaneously execute processes on the separate CPUs. The more contention for resources and the less frequently application processes can execute simultaneously. The benefit of each additional CPU is reduced because the CPU spends part of its time idle instead of running processes. The level of simultaneous execution supported by the system is often known as the degree of *parallelism* because, with no contention, each application process executes in parallel on the different CPUs.

Scaling

The terms *scaling* and *scalability* are frequently used to describe a measure of the performance improvement obtained when an additional processor is installed. For example, 95% scaling or scalability means that when a second CPU is added to the system, performance improves by 95%. That is, a test runs 1.95 times faster than before the addition of the second processor. Scaling can also define the amount of additional work the system can do with the additional processor. For example, if a system can support 50 users with a certain response time, after an additional processor is added, then, at 90% scaling, the machine can support 95 users with that response time.

A high degree of scaling is possible when application processes can complete operations without competing with other processes for access to resources. Resource contention inhibits good scaling, since the process cannot access a resource needed to complete an operation because another process is using the resource. When contention occurs, the operating system suspends the application process that is waiting for the resource, as shown in Figure 4-2. When the resource becomes available, the process is put on the ready-to-run list and is assigned to a CPU at the appropriate time. When the process is suspended, the time required to complete the operation is lengthened, thereby reducing the performance benefit of the additional CPU.

HINT:

In some cases, a general idea of the amount of contention on a multiprocessor system can be found by examining the number of ready-to-run processes. Run mpsar -q and look at the values reported in the runq-sz column. This value is the average number of processes per second that are waiting for access to a CPU. If the actual number of processes waiting is always greater than one, then adding a CPU may benefit performance, because that waiting process can run on the additional CPU. If this number is less than one, then system performance may be improved by reducing contention.

A Word About Monitoring Tools

The SCO MPX monitoring tools used in this chapter are described in the SCO MPX Multiprocessor Extension Release 3.0 User's Guide. This book does not attempt to replace the information in that document, so please refer to it for more detailed information on how to run the tools and for other information not covered in this book.

In addition to the standard SCO UNIX monitoring tools, the SCO MPX specific tools used in this chapter are:

- mpsar(MP)
- cpusar(MP)
- mpstat (MP)

Although mpsar, cpusar and sar share some of the same functionality, throughout this chapter each of the tools is named explicitly to avoid confusion.

The primary impact of running mpsar and cpusar is on resource usage as shown by the values reported for filesystem and disk activity. To understand the impact of mpsar on the reported values, run mpsar -b with no other processes and note the average number of filesystem operations. After starting the test process or processes, run mpsar again and monitor the number of filesystem operations.

HINT:

When monitoring resource usage, run mpsar with the -o option to collect data for all CPUs simultaneously. With this option, the CPU data remains synchronized. Synchronized data makes analysis simpler because CPU activity at different intervals can be easily compared.

The command mpstat provides a useful snapshot of system activity. Bar charts for each CPU display the proportion of time spent in the operating system and executing user applications. This command uses a noticeable amount of CPU time itself, so keep that fact in mind when using mpstat to collect data on CPU utilization.

The mpsar and cpusar monitoring tools are not available in releases prior to SCO MPX 3.0. Results for SCO MPX reported by sar prior to SCO MPX 3.0 are incompatible with the results reported by mpsar and cpusar. mpsar and cpusar should be used for monitoring SCO MPX. The SCO MPX mpsar Maintenance Supplement also includes some additional mpsar/cpusar options that are referred to in this chapter.

Interrupt Handling

Device interrupts are handled differently on multiprocessor machines from how they are handled on uniprocessor machines. On a uniprocessor machine, interrupts can be serviced only by one processor.

Depending on the capabilities of the hardware, a particular interrupt can either be serviced by one processor or by several processors. This feature is known as *distributed interrupts*. Some multiprocessor systems support distributed interrupts and some do not. The operating system automatically assigns the interrupts based on the capability of the machine and the types of drivers that are configured. The operating system assigns interrupts to the first CPU for drivers that are not multithreaded. Multithreading is described later in this chapter.

If an interrupt vector is shared between a multithreaded driver and a non-multithreaded driver, then the operating system must assign the interrupt vector to the first CPU. Careful configuration of the multithreaded and non-multithreaded device drivers so that multithreaded drivers share only with multithreaded drivers ensures that the operating system has the most flexibility in the assignment of interrupts. If possible, configure different drivers to use different interrupts rather than sharing the same interrupt.

HINT:

Use the mthread utility to determine which drivers are multithreaded. This utility is available on the SCO MPX mpsar Maintenance Supplement.

Table 4-1 summarizes how interrupt behavior can be monitored.

Behavior	Command	Columns
View assignment of interrupts to CPUs	displayintr*	A table is displayed whose columns are CPU number and whose rows contain the abbreviated driver name.
Interrupt activity per CPU per second	cpusar -j *	vector contains the name of the driver assigned to that interrupt. ints/s contains the number of interrupts processed by that CPU per second.

Table 4-1: How to Monitor Interrupt Behavior

* displayintr and cpusar are available only in SCO MPX 3.0 or later releases. See the SCO MPX 3.0 User's Guide for more information.

displayintr The displayintr command detects the case when more than one interrupt handler is assigned to an interrupt number and notes this case with a parenthetical "S" after the name of the interrupt handler. Because the operating system executes each interrupt handler associated with a vector, sharing interrupts means the operating system executes more instructions for every interrupt received, and this may affect the responsiveness of the operating system to device interrupts.

cpusar -j The command cpusar -j shows two columns. The vector column shows the name of the interrupt handler, and the ints/s column shows the average number of interrupts per second that are processed by the handler. The larger the value of ints/s, the more interrupts handled by that vector.

The displayintr and cpusar command shows the prefix for each of the drivers with an interrupt handler. Use the abbreviations and the information in */etc/conf/cf.d/mdevice* to convert this prefix to a full device name.

If interrupt numbers have more than one interrupt handler assigned to them, performance may be improved by reconfiguring such that each interrupt vector has only one interrupt handler assigned to it.

Some adapters operate more optimally if more than one card of the same type are installed at the same interrupt number, and others perform more optimally if the cards are installed at different interrupt numbers. Check the adapter hardware documentation for any recommendations.

CALCULATIONS

Calculation operations provide a good starting point for understanding the differences between a uniprocessor and multiprocessor system because they are CPU-intensive. Figure 4-3 lists the resources that are described in this section.

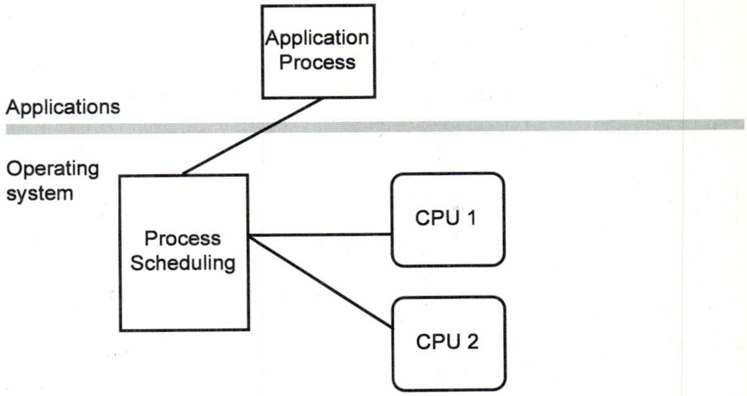

Figure 4-3: The application process must share the CPUs with other application processes. SCO MPX process scheduling controls application access to the CPUs.

To avoid repetition, only the differences from SCO UNIX are described, so please read this section after reading the Calculations section in the Common SCO UNIX Operations chapter.

Application Storage and Behavior

The most critical aspect of tuning applications for SCO MPX is to minimize resource contention between all the application processes on the system. Each time the application accesses a file or some other shared data structure, contention may become an issue when multiple users run this application. When multiple users start the application simultaneously, multiple processes are created. With multiple processors, these processes may execute simultaneously, thereby exposing underlying resource contention that may not occur on a uniprocessor system.

When these multiple processes need to access some shared information, only one process may be able to access this information at a time. The other processes that need to access the information must wait until the first process relinquishes its control of the information. After the process gives up control of the information, another process can access it. Any other waiting processes are still suspended until the process that just acquired control of the resource relinquishes it.

Resource contention can take many forms. For example, multiple users may require access to a file containing the template used to display information retrieved from a database. When multiple users are running application processes on multiple processors, each application process must wait its turn to access this file in order to display records to the user. Even though multiple processes could be running simultaneously because of multiple CPUs, in reality only one application process at a time can run because of the contention on the template file. Because only one process at a time executes in a uniprocessor environment, the other processes must wait for the CPU before accessing the template file, so contention does not occur. This contention reduces the amount of parallelism and decreases the benefit of the additional CPU.

Every time a process waits for access to shared information, a delay occurs. These delays adversely impact the amount of performance difference observed after installation of an additional CPU. Check the application configuration to see if sufficient application resources are available for a multiprocessor environment.

The duration of the calculation is also adversely affected if all the necessary memory pages for the application and the data cannot be held in memory. If the operating system must page or swap to complete the calculation, then additional delays will occur.

The usage of the CPUs in the system can provide some information on whether or not performance can be improved. The behaviors that should be monitored are summarized in Table 4-2.

Behavior	**Command**	**Column**
Percentage of time the CPU(s) spends executing application processes	mpsar -u and cpusar -u	%usr
Percentage of time the CPU(s) spends executing the operating system	mpsar -u and cpusar -u	%sys
Percentage of time the CPU(s) is idle waiting for I/O to complete with no other ready-to-run processes to execute	mpsar -u and cpusar -u	%wio
Percentage of time the CPU(s) is idle with no ready-to-run processes to execute	mpsar -u and cpusar -u	%idle

Table 4-2: How to Monitor Processor Usage

mpsar -u

The command mpsar monitors the usage statistics of all processors installed on system.

The %usr column shows the percentage of time spent by all processors executing all applications running on the system. The percentage is an average over all the processors. For example, if CPU 1 spends 60% of time executing applications and CPU 2 spends 40% of time executing applications, the value reported by mpsar is 50%.

The %sys column shows the percentage of time the processors spent executing the operating system. Tuning that reduces operating system resource contention decreases the percentage of CPU time allocated to operating system execution.

A decrease in the %sys values reported by mpsar means more CPU time is available for executing applications. This additional CPU capacity increases application performance only if the application processes are ready-to-run. If applications are not ready-to-run, then this extra CPU time may become %wio or %idle time instead.

The %wio column shows the percentage of time spent by all the processors waiting-for-device-I/O to complete. Time is accumulated here only if there are no other ready-to-run processes on the system so all the processor can do is wait for the I/O to complete. Reducing %wio by increasing the I/O resources or otherwise increasing the number of ready-to-run processes improves performance. This statistic does not include waiting for network I/O to complete.

The %idle column shows the percentage of time spent by all the processors waiting with no work to do. If the values shown in this column are greater than zero, no ready-to-run and waiting-for-device-I/O processes exist on the system. Whenever the column is greater than zero, application processes may be experiencing resource contention or no ready-to-run processes are available to keep the CPUs busy.

For example, if a calculating process shares a set of formulas with another calculating process, and the access to the formulas is controlled via semaphores, then only one process at a time can execute the formulas. If these are the only two processes on a two CPU system, then %idle will be approximately 50%, because only one of the processors can execute a calculating process at any time since both processes need access to the formulas. Having two copies of the formulas allows both calculating processes to execute simultaneously, and %idle will be 0%.

cpusar -u

The command cpusar displays information similar to that of mpsar, except the statistics are reported for individual CPUs instead of for the entire system. The cpusar command provides a more detailed and accurate picture of the usage pattern for each of the processors installed.

Paging and swapping affect the performance of the calculation and should be minimized to reduce both application and operating system contention for resources. When a system is swapping or paging, processors spend time managing the additional transfers to and from disk, and processors can become idle waiting for transfers to complete. The same paging and swapping tuning guidelines described in the Common Open Desktop Operations chapter apply to SCO MPX.

Optimally tuned calculating applications show CPU usage statistics with a majority of %usr time and a small amount of %sys time. Ideally, the amount of %idle and %wio time should be close to zero for all the CPUs.

SCO MPX process scheduling

With one processor, SCO UNIX process scheduling considers only *when* a process runs on the single processor. Both SCO UNIX and SCO MPX determine when a process should be executing by evaluating relative process priorities. These process priorities are assigned by the operating system and can be influenced by the user through the nice command. The priority values range from 0 to 127, with 0 representing the highest priority and 127 the lowest.

Figure 4-4 shows how processes move through various states in SCO MPX with two processors. In both SCO UNIX and SCO MPX, the operating system selects a new process to run when any of the following situations occur:

- The process currently running on the processor has made a resource request, and the process cannot proceed until that request is complete. This transition is shown by line A. In this case, the process is suspended and the operating system chooses another process to run on that CPU.

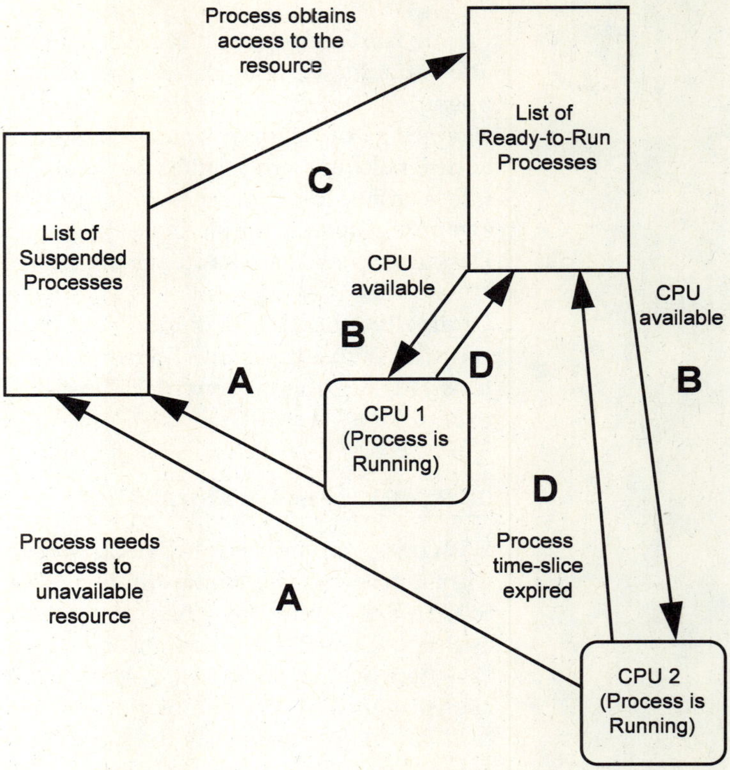

Figure 4-4: A process runs on CPU 1 or CPU 2 until it requests access to an unavailable resource. The process then joins the list of suspended processes as shown by line A. When the resource is available, the process moves to the list of ready-to-run processes, as indicated by line C. When either CPU 1 or CPU 2 become available, the process starts running on that CPU as shown by line B. Because only one copy of the application process exists no matter how many processors are installed in the machine, running processes on different CPUs does not involve any more work on the part of the operating system than does running it on the same processor.

- The time slice for the current process has expired. This transition is shown by line D. Because both SCO UNIX and SCO MPX are time-sharing operating systems, each process can run on a CPU for a fixed length of time before it must be prepared to relinquish the CPU in favor of another ready-to-run process.

- A resource requested by a previously suspended process is now available, as shown by line C, and the process that was suspended is a higher priority process than the one currently running. The lower priority process is suspended, as shown by line D, and the higher priority process starts running. This transition is shown by line B.

SCO MPX differs from SCO UNIX in that SCO MPX also considers which processor, or *where*, a process executes as well as when it will run.

In some cases, the operating system is restricted in where it can run a process. For example, the process may be assigned to a specific processor because it requires access to a floating-point coprocessor that is available only on a particular processor. SCO MPX scheduling transparently handles all restrictions.

SCO MPX scheduling does not allow a single process to be simultaneously executed on more than one CPU, so an additional processor does not shorten the duration of a single process executing calculation operations.

For example, consider a calculation that normally takes 60 seconds to complete. For simplicity, assume:

- No paging or swapping activity

- The time required to load the application and data into memory from the disk is small in proportion to the length of time required for the calculation

- The calculating process is always ready-to-run

With one CPU installed, simultaneously start two of these calculating processes that require 60 seconds of CPU time. Although both processes use only 60 seconds of CPU time, the operating system scheduling ensures that both processes had equal access to the CPU at regular intervals. Therefore, the duration of each calculation is 120 seconds.

With two processors installed, each processor executes one of the calculating processes. Both calculations now take only 60 seconds. The time is reduced by half because sharing the CPU is not necessary with only two ready-to-run processes, because one can run on each processor installed. Examples of SCO MPX scheduling are described in the next chapter.

SCO MPX also differs from SCO UNIX because the additional processors must be kept running even when the ready-to-run list is empty. When the ready-to-run list is empty and a particular CPU has no work to do, the operating system executes an *idle process* at a very low priority. This idle process is a special system process that runs on the CPU until a ready-to-run process is available for the CPU to execute. Because the idle process appears like a genuine process to the monitoring utilities, some of the statistics reported by the monitoring tools must be adjusted for the number of idle processes. The specific adjustments are listed in the section on the monitoring tools.

Some of the statistics for the idle processes can be seen with the ps -el command. Each idle process is named "CPUx idle process" in the listing, where x is the number of the CPU, starting at one for the first installed CPU. The TIME column shows the amount of CPU time accumulated by each idle process since the system was booted. The idle process is always either in a ready-to-run or running state.

Table 4-3 shows the process scheduling behavior and the statistics used to it.

Behavior	Command	Column
Average number of ready-to-run processes during the time interval specified	mpsar -q	runq-sz
Average amount of time the ready-to-run list was occupied	mpsar -q	%runocc
Average number of non-idle processors during the time interval	cpusar -u	%idle
Average number of context switches per second	mpsar -w	pswch/s

Table 4-3: How to Monitor Process Scheduling

mpsar -q

The values reported for the runq-sz, or size of the ready-to-run list, must be adjusted to take into account the idle processes. Each CPU in the system has an associated idle process. These processes are always either running or on the ready-to-run list, so to get an actual picture of the number of ready-to-run and running processes, subtract the total number of CPUs from the numbers reported in this column.

The version of mpsar on the SCO MPX mpsar Maintenance Supplement calculates the number of ready-to-run processes excluding the idle processes. The subtraction of number of CPUs is not necessary if this Maintenance Supplement is installed.

The value reported in %runocc is the percentage of time that the ready-to-run list contains at least one ready-to-run process during the interval specified when mpsar was invoked. The %runocc is almost always reported as 100% because of the idle processes.

cpusar -u

The amount of time each CPU in the system spends idle is reported by the %idle column of cpusar -u. Execute cpusar for each CPU installed in the system to see the total distribution of

%idle time. If the number of ready-to-run processes is less than one, then the CPU may become idle because no processes are ready-to-run. No ready-to-run processes is usually an indicator of contention or an insufficient amount of work for the CPUs to complete.

mpsar -w

The average number of context switches per second, pswch/s, is an indication of the frequency with which processes are relinquishing the CPUs or being suspended by the operating system. A context switch occurs when the operating system suspends one process in favor of another process. What is a *normal* level of context switches varies, so normal must be defined within the setting of the test environment. The number of context switches can be modified changing the tunable variables described in the following section.

No performance change after the addition of a CPU can be observed in any situation where the number of ready-to-run and running processes is less than the number of CPUs installed. If the number of processes on the system is large, but only one of them is ready-to-run at any point in time, then the additional CPUs will not be fully utilized because there are no processes for them to execute.

Because different application environments often require different types of scheduling for optimal performance in a multiprocessor environment, SCO MPX process scheduling is configurable. All of these variables are located in */etc/conf/pack.d/crllry/space.c*. In all cases, changing the values of these variables requires the operating system to be relinked and rebooted.

primove

To ensure all ready-to-run processes execute eventually, the priority of every ready-to-run process is reduced every second if the process has been running on the CPU. The amount the priority is reduced is based on how recently the process used the processor and how much CPU time was actually used. The more recently the process used the CPU, the more the priority is reduced. The greater the amount of actual CPU time used by the process, the more the priority is reduced. This adjustment also takes into account any nice value set by the user.

If the priority of a process changes beyond a certain threshold, then SCO MPX moves the process from one ready-to-run list to another as part of its normal bookkeeping. The threshold is defined by the variable primove located in the file */etc/conf/pack.d/crllry/space.c.*

The variable primove should be set to a value between 0 and 20. Values close to 20 can significantly affect process scheduling by favoring one set of processes over another, thereby reducing the opportunity for some ready-to-run processes to run.

Increasing the value of primove can improve performance for the following reasons:

- The amount of operating system bookkeeping decreases because moving a process from one priority list to another requires more CPU time. With many processes, the operating system may execute this bookkeeping frequently, thereby reducing the amount of CPU time available to application processes.

- The higher the value, the less sensitive the operating system scheduler becomes to changes in the priority of ready-to-run processes. A lower priority process may execute for a longer period than with lower values of primove. The longer the process runs on the processor, the more optimally the L2 cache is used, since the information in the cache is used as long as possible.

Conversely, increasing the value of primove can also decrease performance for these reasons:

- SCO MPX is less sensitive to changes in priority because processes are selected for running by a scan of the lists in order of priority. If the priority of a process has increased but the process has not been moved to a new list, then another, possibly lower priority, process may be selected in place of the higher priority process.

dopricalc

The priority adjustments based on accumulated amount of CPU time can be avoided by changing the value of dopricalc in the file */etc/conf/pack.d/crllry/space.c*. The value one enables these priority adjustments and the value zero disables them.

When running applications that make frequent I/O requests, such as databases, performance may be improved by setting dopricalc to zero. With dopricalc set to zero, the application process, such as a database server, continues to service requests until the server makes an I/O request. This behavior is optimal since the database runs without being suspended because of other ready-to-run processes. Ensuring that a database server runs as long and as often as possible is critical to good database transaction performance.

Because the process is running on that processor for longer periods of time, the number of context switches is also reduced, and the efficiency of the L2 cache is increased. However, setting dopricalc to zero reduces access to the CPUs by lower priority processes, so some processes may never run.

preemptive, loadbalance

The *preemptive* and *loadbalance* variables control whether the operating system stops lower priority processes that are currently executing on the CPU in favor of higher priority processes that have just become ready-to-run, placing the lower priority process on the ready-to-run list.

Processes are suspended while waiting for access to a resource or for an I/O transfer to complete. Each suspended process is assigned a priority based on the importance of the resource or operation. The priority does not change while the process is on the ready-to-run list, and the value is independent of the priority at which the process normally runs.

When the I/O transfer completes or the resource becomes available, the process is made ready-to-run at the assigned priority. Normally, if this priority is higher than that of another currently running process (on the current or other CPU), the lower priority process is suspended in favor of the higher priority process.

Because priorities are constantly checked, the highest priority processes are always running.

The variables preemptive and loadbalance determine the number of processors that are checked for lower priority processes when the higher priority process becomes ready-to-run. Both of these variables change the behavior guaranteeing that the highest priority processes are always running.

The variable preemptive controls whether the current processor is checked, and loadbalance controls whether the other CPUs are checked for lower priority processes. If preemptive is set to one, then the priority of the process currently executing on the CPU responsible for changing the state of the ready-to-run process is compared to the ready-to-run process; if the ready-to-run process is higher priority, the currently executing process is suspended. If preemptive is set to zero, this CPU is not checked and the higher priority ready-to-run process is not immediately executed.

If loadbalance is one, then the priority of the processes currently running, except for the process on the current processor, is compared with the ready-to-run process, and, if any of the currently running processes are lower priority than the ready-to-run process, the ready-to-run process starts executing in favor of the lower priority process. Figures 4-5 and 4-6 show how loadbalance and preemptive change scheduling behavior.

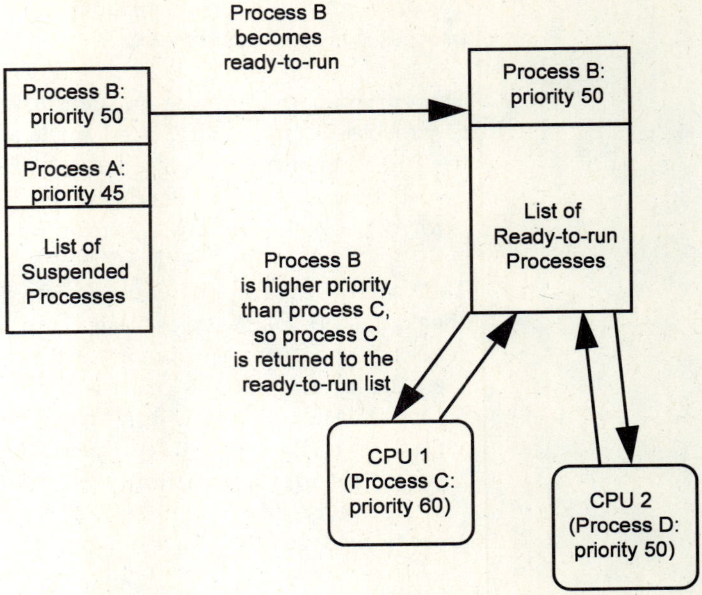

Figure 4-5: With loadbalance and preemptive equal to one, when process B becomes ready-to-run, the operating system will force process C to relinquish the CPU in favor of process B. Process D continues to run on CPU 2. When process A becomes ready-to-run, the operating system will place process D back on the ready-to-run list, and allow process A to use the CPU. In this fashion, the operating system ensures that the highest priority processes are always kept running. This diagram assumes the transitions occur before process priorities are recalculated. The recalculation of priorities may affect the selection of the processes from the ready-to-run list.

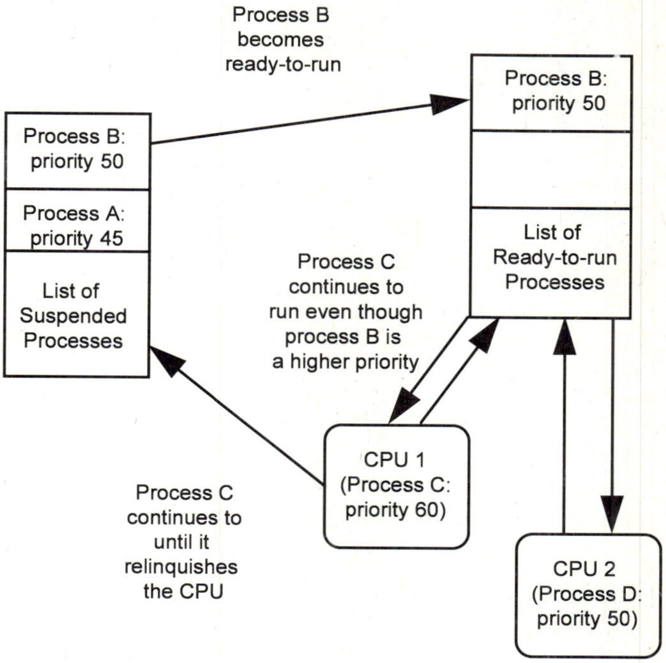

Figure 4-6: With preemptive and loadbalance set to zero, when process B becomes ready-to-run, it will remain in the ready-to-run list until process C relinquishes the CPU by requesting access to an unavailable resource. Process C may also relinquish the CPU when its time-slice expires. When process A becomes ready-to-run, it will also remain on the ready-to-run list even though it is the highest priority process on the system. Because the highest priority processes are not always running, lower priority processes may run on the CPU for longer periods of time than higher priority processes. This diagram assumes these transitions occur before process priorities are recalculated.

Setting preemptive and loadbalance to zero reduces the amount of time the operating system spends comparing process priorities and reduces the amount of context switching between processes. This setting can increase performance by reducing the amount of CPU time consumed by the operating system for process scheduling. However, setting these variables to zero also decreases the operating system's responsiveness to priority changes, and so there is no longer any guarantee that the highest priority processes are running at any given time.

In addition, if a process is suspended because of waiting for resource access, that resource may not be efficiently used. When the resource is released and the process that was suspended becomes ready-to-run, even though the process waiting for the resource has a higher priority than the processes currently executing, the ready-to-run process must wait until one of the lower priority processes relinquishes the CPU.

When loadbalance and preemptive are set to one, the operating system suspends the lower priority process in favor of the ready-to-run process, thereby reducing the delay and increasing the likelihood that the ready-to-run process can obtain the resource for which it was waiting.

cache_affinity

The variable *cache_affinity* controls whether the operating system favors some CPUs over the other CPUs when selecting a CPU to run a given process. For example, if a process was running on the second CPU and is now suspended, then when the process becomes ready-to-run, the operating system may select the second CPU for that process over any other CPU.

This favoritism is a performance optimization that encourages efficient L2 cache usage. L2 caches are quite large, and often the information in the cache remains valid for a suspended process even though another process has been running on that CPU. If the suspended process becomes ready-to-run and can then begin executing on the CPU where it was running previously, the L2 cache is not refilled, bus traffic is reduced, and performance is improved.

Whether the information in the cache is still valid depends on the nature of the applications that are running on the system and the amount of time the process is suspended.

HINT:

Some relational databases, such as Oracle Version 7, run optimally with the scheduler variables set the following way: loadbalance, preemptive, dopricalc, and cache_affinity all equal to zero. These settings ensure the database server processes run as long and as often as possible.

If cache_affinity is set to one, then the operating system may select a lower priority ready-to-run process that previously executed on that CPU over a higher priority ready-to-run process that has been in the ready-to-run list longer. Since ready-to-run processes that have been waiting for the CPU for a shorter period of time may be selected over higher priority processes that have been waiting longer, some low priority processes may end up running more frequently than others.

If cache_affinity is zero, then the highest priority ready-to-run process is always selected, independently of where the process may have executed previously. This setting may allow the CPU time to be more evenly distributed between ready-to-run processes.

The Processor

Once the application and the data for the calculation are copied into memory, the speed of the processor and the operating system scheduling dictate how quickly the calculation completes. A faster processor can complete a calculation more quickly than a slower processor because each instruction takes less time to execute.

CPU speed and L2 caches

In order for the application to complete the calculation, both the data and the instructions for the calculation are copied from the disk to memory. While the data and instructions are copied from memory to the processor cache, the high-speed memory/CPU bus is unavailable to any other processors that might wish to transfer information from memory to cache.

The processor waiting to access the bus is suspended until the other CPU's memory transfer is complete. If the processor running the calculation is the one that has to wait until another processor completes its CPU/memory transfer, then the duration of the calculation increases because of the delay in accessing the high-speed memory bus. The amount of bus traffic adversely affects scaling because processors must wait to access memory.

Once the required information is in the processor cache, the calculation continues uninterrupted, subject only to operating system process scheduling and regular bookkeeping.

Different multiprocessor machines have different types of L2 caches. The cache behavior can be configured on some machines with the system's hardware configuration utility. A write-through cache forces the processor to wait until an update to the memory location completes. A write-back cache updates the location in the cache and so does not cause the processor to wait for the memory update to complete.

In some application environments, a write-through cache generates more CPU/memory bus activity then does a write-back cache, and so bus traffic is reduced if a write-back cache is configured in the machine. Larger caches also improve performance by reducing bus traffic.

For maximum calculation performance on a multiprocessor system, all processors should be able to perform floating point operations.

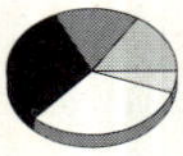

A system optimally tuned for quick calculation response should have the following characteristics:

- %wio less than 5% for all CPUs. A value greater than five for %wio on one processor is acceptable while running mpsar or cpusar because of the additional file activity generated by mpsar and cpusar.

- %idle less than 5% for all CPUs. If the value is greater than five, then an insufficient number of ready-to-run processes is affecting the efficient use of CPUs.

For a calculation operation running when no paging and swapping are occurring, by far the largest value should be in the %usr column for each processor running a calculating process. The %sys value for both cpusar and mpsar should be low, as the operating system is involved in calculations only when it schedules the calculating processes. Some of the %sys and %usr activity may be due to the data collection and processing activity of cpusar and mpsar.

With multiple processes performing calculations, performance may be improved by more equally sharing CPU time among them. To evenly split the allocation of CPU time, try reducing the value of MAXSLICE, reducing the value of primove, and setting cache_affinity to zero.

File Read And Write Operations

The resources used by SCO MPX to complete file read and write operations are similar to those used by SCO UNIX. The primary consideration for optimizing this type of operation for SCO MPX is to reduce the amount of contention for the underlying resources. Since a typical SCO MPX system runs a larger number of processes than does a uniprocessor system, the probability of delays caused by multiple processes requiring simultaneous access to these resources is increased dramatically.

Figure 4-7 summarizes the resources that are discussed in this section. This diagram is exactly the same as Figure 2-1 in the Common SCO UNIX Operations chapter and is included here for easy reference.

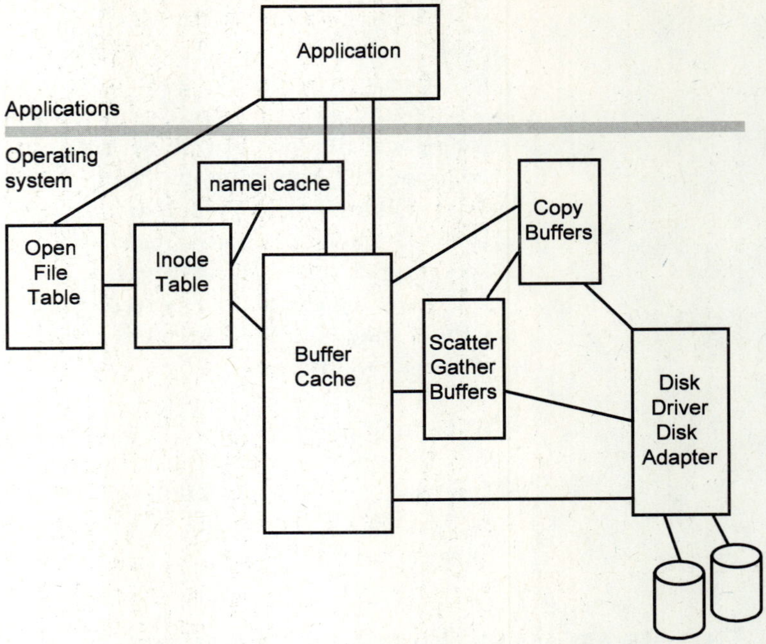

Figure 4-7: Intermediate Storage Locations and Resources In A File Read or Write Operation. Before the client application can access file data, the name of the file must be mapped to an inode. The operating system maintains a list of the most recent filename mappings in the namei cache. The operating system must also add the open file to its internal list of open files. The buffer cache is another intermediate storage location for the filesystem data. The scatter/gather buffers are used when a group of requests that are scattered in memory reside next to each other on the disk. The copy buffers are used only when the disk adapter cannot access memory above 16 Mbytes and some of the buffers in the buffer cache are located above this boundary. Neither scatter/gather nor the copy buffers are used for every disk transfer. The disk adapter manages the disk hardware. The disk provides permanent storage.

Application Storage and Behavior

Reducing any delays that multiple application processes encounter when accessing resources is the primary tuning goal. With complex applications such as databases, the most optimal way of reducing application contention is to tune the application. With other types of applications, rearranging the application's data on the filesystem can improve performance. This rearrangement can be especially beneficial if the application makes frequent searches through files in the filesystem. The data can often be rearranged to allow more application processes to access the same information simultaneously, perhaps by copying it to a different filesystem.

The exact cause of application resource contention is difficult to determine. Application specific tools are often provided to monitor resource usage.

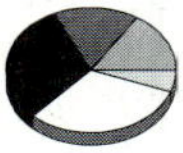

Complex server-oriented applications such as databases generally provide guidance for optimal resource allocation. Check the application documentation for these recommendations.

If the application provides any specific tunables, add these to the worksheet to help obtain the complete resource usage pattern.

The Namei cache

The namei cache operates identically between SCO UNIX and SCO MPX. The SCO UNIX chapter describes the operation and tuning of the namei cache in more detail.

mpsar -n

The information reported by mpsar -n is identical to the information reported by sar -n. Please see the Common SCO UNIX Operations chapter for more information.

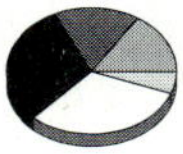

After an additional processor is installed, the average number of filename mapping requests may increase dramatically because more application processes can request filesystem information simultaneously. The hit % reported by mpsar decreases as a result.

If hit % decreases, increase the performance of those applications accessing filenames by increasing the values of S5CACHEENTS and S5HASHQS until the cache hit rate is above 90%.

When modifying S5CACHEENTS, adjust S5HASHQS until the ratio S5CACHEENTS divided by S5HASHQS is less than or equal to one as shown by the following equation:

$$\frac{S5CACHEENTS}{S5HASHQS} <= 1$$

This ratio defines the average length of the indexed lists used to optimize the search through the namei cache. If the ratio is greater than one, the time required to find the correct entry in the cache is increased, thereby potentially negating the expected performance improvement.

Contention is reduced with a larger namei cache because requests for filenames are more likely to be satisfied by the namei cache, instead of being passed to the buffer cache or to the disk.

The Inode Table and Open File Table

The inode table and open file tables work identically in SCO UNIX and SCO MPX. Please see the Common SCO UNIX Operations chapter for more information on the operation of these tables.

mpsar -v

The information reported by mpsar -v is the same as the information reported by sar -v. Please see the Common SCO UNIX Operations chapter for more information.

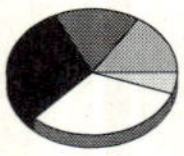

After an additional processor is installed, the value of NINODE and NFILE may need to be increased because of the rise in the number of processes that are running. The operating system should have sufficient inodes and open file entries to support the number of processes on the system to ensure proper functioning of the applications.

If the inode or open file table utilization is more than 80%, increase NINODE until the usage is below 80%. The value of NHINODE must be a power of two, and the ratio of NINODE divided by NHINODE must be less than or equal to one as shown by the following equation:

$$\frac{NINODE}{NHINODE} <= 1$$

This ratio is the average length of the indexed lists that are searched to find the inode. If the ratio is greater than one, the time required to find the correct entry in the table is increased, thereby potentially negating the expected performance improvement.

The Buffer Cache

The buffer cache works in the same manner in SCO MPX as it does in SCO UNIX. Most applications require access to files at some point, so optimal configuration of the buffer cache is critical to good performance.

mpsar -b

The information reported by mpsar -b is the same as the information reported by sar -b. Please see the Common SCO UNIX Operations chapter for more information.

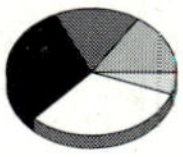

After an additional processor is installed, the number of processes that require simultaneous access to information in the filesystem increases dramatically. Careful tuning of the buffer cache can ensure that these applications encounter minimal delays in accessing filesystem data.

Buffer cache usage can be optimized by the following actions:

- Provided no paging or swapping occurs, increase the size of the buffer cache until the %rcache is greater than 90%

- Increase NHBUF until the ratio of NBUF divided by NHBUF is less than or equal to one-half as shown by the following equation:

$$\frac{NBUF}{NHBUF} <= \frac{1}{2}$$

  Even if the value of NBUF is not changed, increase NHBUF until the ratio of NBUF divided by NHBUF is correct. This usually means a value of NHBUF the power of two greater than 2 * NBUF. The ratio of NBUF divided by NHBUF is the average length of each indexed list, so the shorter the lists, the shorter the time required to find the correct buffer.

The size of the buffer cache may need to be increased by a considerable amount in order to achieve a read cache efficiency of 90% or more. Do not increase the size of the cache beyond the point where paging or swapping occurs. With plenty of free memory, try to achieve %rcache rates of 95% or more.

For example, if %rcache prior to adding the processor was equal to 90%, then for every 100 read requests to the buffer cache, 10 disk requests occur. After addition of the processor, double the number of application processes are running, so the number of read requests increases to 200. With a 90% hit rate, 20 disk requests occur. The amount of disk activity has doubled even though the cache efficiency rate is constant. Increasing the cache efficiency rate to 95% reduces the number of disk requests to 10, but requires more memory.

Depending on the application usage pattern and the amount of memory installed, the size of the buffer cache may reach 48 Mbytes or more of memory to achieve a high cache efficiency. Increasing the buffer cache by a considerable amount requires more memory, and is an example of where adding a processor may mean adding more memory so that both the hardware and software can be optimally configured for the increased amount of processing power.

The benefits of modifying BDFLUSHR vary, depending on the operating system release. In SCO MPX 2.0 with SCO UNIX 3.2v4.0, increasing the value of BDFLUSHR may positively affect the system filesystem performance by decreasing the contention on the buffer cache. In SCO MPX 3.0, increasing the value of BDFLUSHR has a smaller effect on filesystem performance. Decreasing the value of BDFLUSHR from its default of 30 seconds increases the likelihood that both bdflush and an application process will require simultaneous access to the buffer cache.

The Scatter/Gather Feature

Scatter/gather works in the same manner in SCO MPX as it does in SCO UNIX. Please see the Common SCO UNIX Operations chapter for more information on scatter/gather.

On a multiprocessor system, any additional copying of data caused by a disk controller that does not directly support scatter/gather requires additional memory accesses over the high speed memory/CPU bus and reduces the effectiveness of the L2 cache.

mpsar -h

The information reported by mpsar -h is identical to the information reported by sar -h. Please see the Common SCO UNIX Operations chapter for more information.

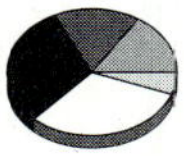

After an additional processor is installed, the number of application processes simultaneously requiring access to the filesystem increases.

If a process is suspended because no temporary work areas or buffer headers are available, then the number of context switches is increased and the start of the disk transfer is delayed. This result lengthens the time required for the filesystem operation. If no buffer headers are available, then values in the omphbufs/s column shown by mpsar -h will be greater than zero.

If the disk adapter cannot be upgraded to one that supports scatter/gather directly, then following the scatter/gather tuning recommendations described in the Common SCO UNIX Operations chapter.

The Copy Buffers Mechanism

SCO MPX compensates for disk adapter restrictions in the same way SCO UNIX does. Please see the Common SCO UNIX Operations chapter for more information.

The additional copying of information to a copy buffer reduces the efficiency of the L2 cache, which also affects performance.

mpsar -B

The information reported by mpsar -B is the same as the information reported by sar -B. Please see the File Read and Write Operation section in the Common SCO UNIX Operations chapter for more information.

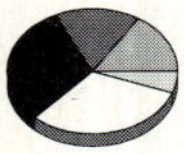

Copying data for filesystem transfers on a multiprocessor system adversely affects not just the filesystem operation performance, but the performance of the rest of the system because of increased CPU/memory bus traffic and increased CPU resource requirements. For optimal multiprocessor system performance, use only disk adapters that can address all memory locations. This rule applies to all devices that are intended for use in a high-performance multiprocessor environment because any additional copying for any device impacts performance.

If a disk adapter with a memory access restriction must be used, then ensure that a sufficient number of copy buffers is configured. Follow the guidelines described in the Common SCO UNIX Operation for tuning the number of copy buffers. With the increased number of processes running as a result of adding the processor, the number of copy buffers required is likely to increase.

Disk adapters with limited addressing capability severely impact the performance of a multiprocessor system.

The Disk Driver, Disk Adapter, and Disks

The disk driver manages the disk adapter hardware so that filesystem data can be transferred to and from the buffer cache to the disk adapter and disks. SCO UNIX and SCO MPX manage disk drivers differently.

In SCO UNIX, when the operating system is ready to transfer data from the buffer cache to the filesystem on the disk, the operating system calls the disk adapter routine xxstrategy() on behalf of the process requesting the transfer to the disk.

Driver multithreading

Drivers can significantly improve throughput on a multiprocessor system by allowing multiple processors to execute the xxstrategy() routine simultaneously. A traditional SCO UNIX driver must be modified in order for multiple processors to execute the xxstrategy() and other support routines simultaneously. This modification is called *multithreading* because the operating system can now execute the driver routines on multiple processors on behalf of multiple processes. Figures 4-8 and 4-9 show how a multithreaded driver reduces the amount of context switching required to add a request to the disk driver list.

If a driver is multithreaded, then any processor can call the xxstrategy() routine to add requests to the list at any time. After xxstrategy() is called, the code pathway for SCO MPX is identical to the code pathway taken in uniprocessor SCO UNIX.

However, if the driver is not multithreaded, then only one processor can add requests to the list at any time. All processes must add requests to the driver's list in turn and must do so only when running on a specific CPU. This restriction results in more context switches to and from the CPU that can add requests to the driver's list.

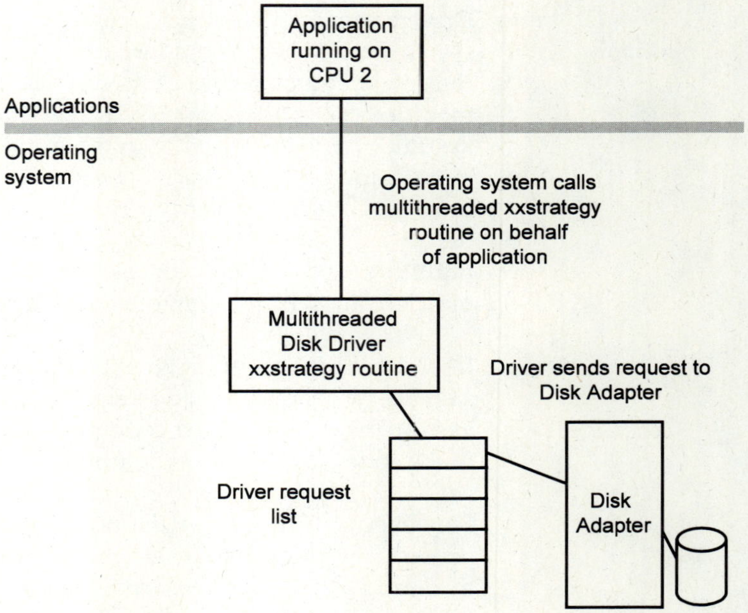

Figure 4-8: When the application is running on CPU 2 and requires some information from the disk, the operating system calls the xxstrategy on behalf of the application. With a multithreaded driver, the request can be added to the driver request list with no additional context switching.

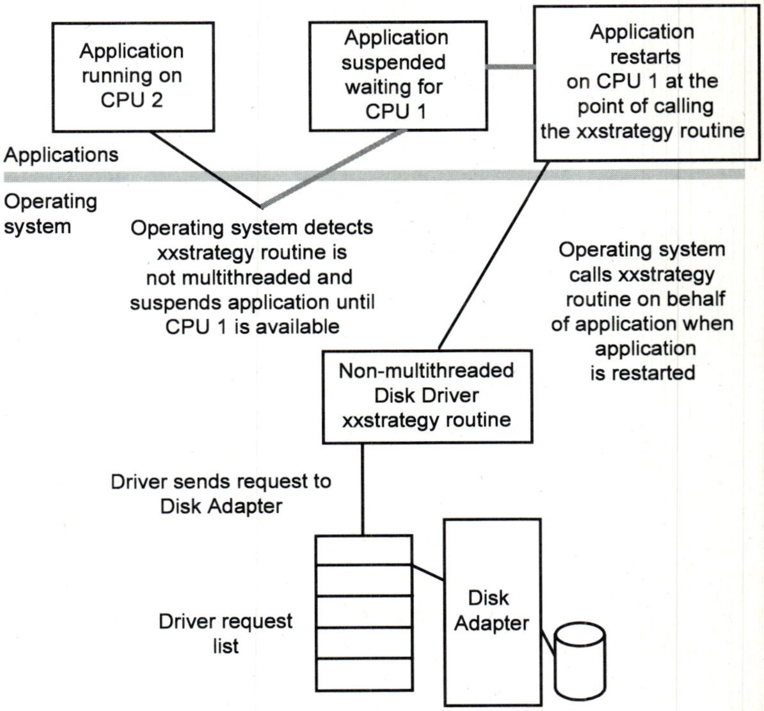

Figure 4-9: When the application running on CPU 2 must retrieve some information from the disk, the operating system calls the xxstrategy routine to add the request to the driver list. The operating system detects that the xxstrategy routine is not multithreaded, and so must schedule the process for execution on CPU 1, because the xxstrategy routine is not safe to execute on CPU 2. The gray line indicates the extra state transitions for the application process from suspended to running on CPU 1, while the black line shows the code execution path. The application cannot resume normal execution until the xxstrategy routine completes, so when the application is restarted on CPU 1, the operating system calls the xxstrategy routine on behalf of the application. The xxstrategy routine adds the request to the driver list. The application encounters extra delay in the completion of the disk request due to the lack of driver multithreading.

For example, if the process is running on the CPU that can add requests to the list, then the pathway taken is the same as in the uniprocessor situation. If the process is not running on the CPU that can add requests to the list, then the process must be suspended and then resume execution on the appropriate processor. This processor change involves two extra context switches and a delay until the appropriate processor is available to add requests to the list.

HINT

If you are using a driver provided with the disk adapter, then check the documentation to see if the driver is multithreaded for SCO MPX. The SCO MPX mpsar Maintenance Supplement supports a new command called mthread to determine whether or not a driver is multithreaded.

Driver request handling

The driver accesses the disk adapter to start the command that executes the data transfer. The driver normally does this by changing values located in special memory locations on the disk adapter. These special memory locations may be known as *registers*. Some multiprocessor architectures allow all processors to access all special device memory locations. Other architectures have restrictions regarding which of these special memory locations are accessible by all processors.

If the process that should start the disk adapter request cannot access the special memory locations, then the processor that can access the special device memory is notified to start the disk adapter request on behalf of the other processor.

After the request is sent to the disk adapter and the disk and the disk has completed the request, an interrupt is sent to the CPU notifying it that the request is complete. The speed at which the interrupts can be serviced by the operating system is dependent on the amount of resource contention occurring on the system. Resource contention may delay the processing of interrupts, thereby adding delays to the operating system notification that the request is complete and delays to the continued execution of the process that is waiting for the request to complete.

The disk adapter, or controller, is the hardware that transfers data between memory and the disk. Some disk adapters are better suited to a multiprocessing environment than others. These adapters often have features that are part of RAID, or Redundant Arrays of Inexpensive Disks. Different combinations of features are available with different levels of RAID. Many of the features are designed for fault tolerance, but some of the features also benefit performance. The combinations are specified in Table 4-4.

RAID level	**Feature**	**Impact on Performance**
0	Data striping: spreading information across multiple disks	Improve performance by allowing parallel disk requests
1	Disk mirroring: data written to one drive is actually written to two drives transparently	Can improve read performance by allowing parallel servicing of read requests
2	Error detection for data striping	No general impact beyond data striping
3	Use two or more data drives and a single parity drive for error detection on data striping	No general impact beyond data striping
4	Match the maximum amount of data transferred to the block size used for striping	No general impact beyond data striping
5	Combines block-level striping of RAID 4 with error recovery in each drive, rather than parity drives	No general impact beyond data striping

Table 4-4: Performance Benefits of RAID Features

The specific performance impact of these features varies considerably among disk adapters. Higher RAID levels are not necessarily supersets of lower RAID levels, so check the hardware documentation for an exact description of what the disk adapter supports.

Additional disk adapter performance features that are optimal for a multi-processor environment are as follows:

- Scatter/gather
- On-board memory caches to avoid delays while waiting for the disk to service the request
- Fast disk request processing that requires minimal CPU time
- 32-bit addressable and capable of doing bus master DMA; that is, DMA transfers can be set up and completed without requiring the primary CPU and no copy buffers are necessary

These high performance disk adapters often have their own processor on the adapter that handles much of the request processing. This special processor frees the primary CPUs and provides more time for the primary CPUs to execute application processes.

To complement the speed of the disk adapter, fast disks should also be configured into the system. The slower the disk, the longer the time required to service the disk request, and the greater the duration of the filesystem operation. A slow disk also increases the likelihood of resource contention because more application processes must wait for the filesystem request to complete. A faster disk reduces resource contention because it can keep up with all the requests made to it, so no processes are kept waiting.

mpsar -d

The information reported by mpsar -d is the same as the information reported by sar -d. Please see the File Read and Write Operation section in the Common SCO UNIX Operations chapter for more details.

cpusar -l The number of times one processor must notify another processor to start a disk request on its behalf can be monitored by looking at the values in the IOcpuints/s column. The values in this column will be greater than zero if the machine has restrictions on which processors can access the special memory locations required to access the disk adapter.

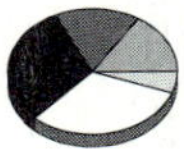

After an additional processor is installed, the amount of disk activity is likely to increase dramatically. This increase results in more contention for the disk resources. Unless the system is correctly tuned, filesystem performance may actually degrade after installation of the additional CPU.

Depending on the filesystem usage patterns after addition of the CPU, another disk adapter and disk subsystem may need to be added in order to share the workload so adequate response time can be maintained.

The length of the disk's queue and the amount of time required to handle the disk requests indicate the ability of the disk subsystem to handle the increased workload. If the values reported by mpsar increase after another processor is added, then the disk subsystem must be reconfigured for optimal performance.

If only some of the disk access times increase, then perhaps rearranging the filesystem data can evenly spread the number of disk requests among all the disks on the system.

If the disk adapter uses a driver that is not multithreaded, then the additional context switching that occurs because of the driver not being multithreaded cannot be tuned away. The most optimal solution is to replace the non-multithreaded driver with one that is multi-threaded.

Filesystem Layout

The same set of considerations, described in the Common SCO UNIX Operations chapter, applies to filesystem layout when SCO MPX is used.

In addition, SCO MPX file read and write performance can be improved if applications are not using the same directory hierarchies. For example, if two processes that are simultaneously running on two different processors both wish to create a file in the directory */usr/application*, one of the processes must wait while the other updates the inode belonging to that directory. If both processes were allowed to change the inode associated with that directory, then the value of the inode would be garbled, since both processes modified it simultaneously.

In extreme cases, many processes may require simultaneous write access to the same directory or file, and because each process must wait its turn for write access to the same directory or file, one or more CPUs may become idle because all the processes on the system are waiting to access this directory or file.

To reduce the likelihood of multiple processes needing the same file or directory at the same time, consider using multiple file systems spread across multiple disks.

If the disk adapter supports grouping together a set of smaller disks into one large virtual disk, then configure the filesystem on this large virtual disk. Because smaller physical disks are servicing the filesystem requests, a greater degree of parallelism in request handling is possible. Greater parallelism increases SCO MPX performance.

Direct Disk Access

The direct disk access interface operates in the same manner in SCO UNIX and SCO MPX. Please refer to the Direct Disk Access section in the Common SCO UNIX Operations chapter for more information.

The primary tuning goals for direct disk access on SCO MPX are as follows:

- Optimize data layout on the disk to reduce resource contention

- Minimize the delay in obtaining the data

- Maximize the number of processes that can simultaneously access the data without incurring any delays

Figure 4-10 summarizes the resources that are described in this section. This diagram is identical to Figure 2-6 and is included here for convenience.

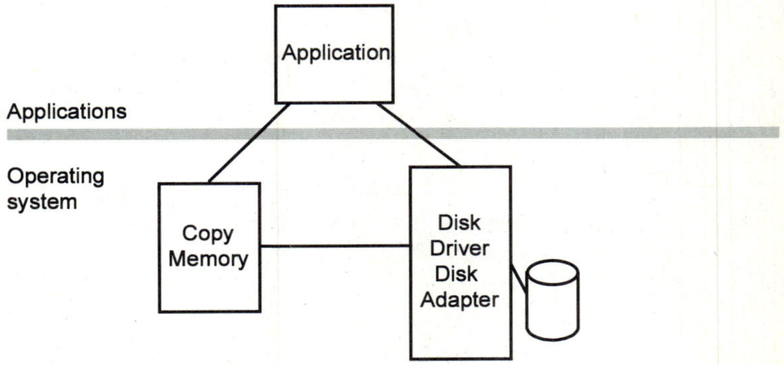

Figure 4-10: The client application uses copy memory only when the disk adapter cannot access storage locations above 16 Mbytes and the client application's data resides above 16 Mbytes. If the disk adapter can access storage locations above 16 Mbytes, then the data flows directly from the client application to the disk driver.

Application Storage and Behavior

The application behavior issues are the same in SCO UNIX and SCO MPX.

The primary resource monitoring tools are those provided by the application. The amount of disk activity must also be monitored, as described in the SCO UNIX Direct Disk Access section.

After installing an additional processor, the amount of contention for the direct disk area increases dramatically because of the greater number of processes that are running. Reconfiguring the application, and possibly the underlying hardware, is required in order for the additional processor to improve system performance.

Depending on the nature of the application, increasing the size of the application storage area may reduce the number of disk requests, thereby minimizing the delay in accessing the data. In general, increase the size of the application storage area until the system starts to page or swap. The database case studies in Chapters 11 and 12 show some examples of the performance improvement possible from increasing the size of the direct disk access area.

Since each direct disk request is passed directly to the disk adapter, tuning the application to make fewer requests results in less contention for the underlying disk resources. Less contention means less waiting on the part of the application processes, thereby decreasing the likelihood that the additional CPUs become idle. If any of the CPUs are idle, then the maximum benefit from the additional processor is not realized. Tuning will improve the performance of the system.

The Copy Memory Mechanism

Copy memory works in the same manner in both SCO UNIX and SCO MPX.

Using disk adapters that cannot access all of the system memory severely limits direct disk access performance in SCO MPX.

mpsar -h The information reported by mpsar -h is the same as the information reported by sar -h. Please see the Direct Disk Access section of the Common SCO UNIX Operations chapter.

Since adding an additional processor is likely to increase the number of disk requests, the optimal solution is to configure only disk adapters that can access all memory in any SCO MPX system.

The Disk Driver , Disk Adapter and Disks

The capacity and configuration of the disk driver, adapter, and disks is critical to optimal direct disk access performance for SCO MPX.

If the application process uses synchronous direct disk access, the application is suspended until the request is serviced by the disk adapter and the application process is notified when the request completes. After the request completes, the operating system changes the state of the process to ready-to-run. The process continues executing when the operating system determines that the ready-to-run process is the most appropriate process to run on a CPU.

If the disk adapter has an on-board read or write cache, then the request may complete before the process is suspended, whereupon the process simply continues executing. When the process continues without suspending, two context switches are avoided and delays due to process scheduling do not occur. Performance of direct disk access is therefore greatly improved with an on-board cache.

AIO

If the application is using asynchronous direct disk access, AIO, then the application sends the request and continues execution. Databases, such as Oracle, often use this mode to achieve maximum transaction throughput and minimize delays. Notifying the application that the request is complete is achieved through a variety of mechanisms, depending on how this mode is configured and what asynchronous support is provided by the disk driver.

HINT:

Always configure AIO when using Oracle Version 7 or Sybase SQL Server System 10 for SCO UNIX and SCO MPX. See the SCO System Administrator's Guide for more information on configuring AIO. The configuration or installation instructions for these products include directions for how to set up the database to use AIO. Both the database and the operating system must be configured to use AIO.

mpsar -b
mpsar -d

The mpsar -b and mpsar -d commands report the same information as the sar -b and sar -d commands. Please see the File Read and Write Operation section of the Common SCO UNIX Operations chapter for more information.

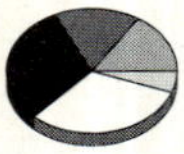

Before adding a CPU, ensure that the system is spending a minimal amount of time idle due to waiting for disk requests to complete. If mpsar/cpusar report %wio and/or %idle values that are consistently more than five, then prior to adding another CPU, configure the system so that both of these values are less than five. The values should be rechecked after the additional CPU is installed to see if additional tuning is required.

For direct disk access, increasing the speed at which disk requests are processed is the most optimal way of reducing %wio and %idle values. To increase the speed, try the following actions:

- Rearrange the data on the disks so that the number of requests to each disk and disk adapter are spread evenly.
- To spread the workload, add another disk adapter and either move some of the disks to the new disk adapter or add more disks to the new adapter. After reconfiguring, ensure that the newly configured disks can handle the load by monitoring the values reported in avwait and avserv after reconfiguration.
- Use disk mirroring to improve the parallelization of disk read requests.
- Use data striping to improve the parallelization of disk read and write requests.
- If possible, install an on-board cache on the disk adapter so that requests access the cache instead of waiting for the disk.

If the amount of %wio and %idle values cannot be reduced to less than five, the potential performance benefits of an additional CPU are reduced. The additional CPU can cause more contention for the already scarce disk resources. The additional CPU is guaranteed to spend some percentage of its time either idle because it is waiting for I/O requests to complete, or idle because no ready-to-run processes are available.

After installing the CPU, monitor the amount of %wio and %idle again and configure the system again if necessary to reduce these values as much as possible.

Data Layout

The guidelines described in the Common SCO UNIX Operations apply to SCO MPX as well. Databases are the most common users of the direct disk access interface; the case studies provide some specific examples of how these rules can be applied.

Serial Connections

Serial connections cover all configurations where serial I/O is used to communicate either to terminals directly connected to the system or to other computers. The resources used by serial I/O under SCO MPX are the same as those described for SCO UNIX.

When connecting terminals to a system running SCO MPX, use intelligent serial adapters rather than non-intelligent serial adapters. The additional processing capacity of the intelligent serial adapters ensures that the amount of additional burden that serial I/O communication places on the system is minimized.

As with disk drivers, intelligent serial adapter drivers may or may not be multithreaded. The same concerns expressed regarding using a non-multithreaded disk driver apply to the use of a non-multithreaded intelligent serial adapter. Check the adapter documentation to determine conclusively if the driver is multithreaded for SCO MPX.

The high rate of transfer supported by most intelligent serial I/O subsystems means that a multithreaded intelligent serial I/O driver should be well matched to the additional processing capacity of the SCO MPX system.

Quick Diagnosis Summary

This section highlights the key monitoring tools and tuning guidelines described in this chapter. This section builds on the quick diagnosis information provided in the SCO UNIX chapter.

CPU usage

To obtain an overall picture of the system, examine CPU usage for all of the CPUs with the tools listed in Table 4-5.

Behavior	Command	Column
Percentage of time the CPU(s) is idle with no ready-to-run processes to execute	mpsar -u and cpusar -u	%idle
Percentage of time the CPU (s) is idle waiting for I/O to complete with no other ready-to-run processes to execute	mpsar -u and cpusar -u	%wio
Percentage of time the CPU(s) spends executing application processes	mpsar -u and cpusar -u	%usr
Percentage of time the CPU(s) spends executing the operating system	mpsar -u and cpusar -u	%sys
Average number of ready-to-run processes during the time interval specified	mpsar -q	runq-sz

Table 4-5: How to Monitor CPU Usage

The CPU usage statistics indicate whether the system has sufficient resources to support the added CPU power, as well as sufficient work to require the added CPU power.

The average number of ready-to-run processes indicates the amount of potential work for the CPUs. When multiple processes run simultaneously, however, resource contention often introduces delay.

After an additional processor is installed, the increased CPU power may cause a resource shortage that prevents the benefit of the added CPU capacity from being fully realized. Use the mpsar and cpusar commands to monitor the resources and determine how to allocate them more efficiently. Remember that a minor resource shortage with one processor can become much worse after another processor is added.

Chapter 5

SCO MPX Case Studies

This chapter contains two case studies illustrating how to tune a multiprocessor system following the seven-step method described in Chapter 1. The first example explores how to identify the conditions under which an additional CPU might benefit performance and then what happens after an additional processor is installed. The second example focuses on understanding the changes to resource usage after an additional CPU is installed.

Calculations and other CPU-intensive application processes show the largest changes in behavior when additional processors are installed. These operations are clearly illustrative of the difference in performance after an additional processor is installed because the number of resources involved in operation completion is limited to the CPU and process scheduling. The more complex file read and write operation is described later in this chapter.

These examples are designed to show how you can analyze the data recorded on the worksheets, draw conclusions regarding resource shortages, and change the resource allocations to increase efficiency and improve performance. Each example uses tools provided on the floppy disk to run the test and collect appropriate resource usage statistics. The appropriate tool from the floppy disk is noted in the example.

The relevant statistics are extracted with another utility and entered into the worksheets that are included at the end of this chapter. The worksheets are provided in the examples as an appendix to show where the data originated. The data presented in the graphs and bar charts in the example description highlights the worksheet data relevant to that particular operation.

Calculation Example

This example shows how to decide an additional CPU should be added to the system. In this example, a set of calculating processes is run on a one, two and four processor machine and the time required for all the processes to complete is measured. The number of calculating processes increases from one in the first series of tests to eight in the last series. This series of tests shows that when the average number of ready-to-run processes is consistently smaller than the number of processors, the installation of an additional processor does not benefit performance.

A CPU-intensive process is any process whose performance is primarily affected by CPU availability and not by the availability of any other resources. For example, if sufficient memory and disk are available to run a database server, then the amount of CPU time becomes a critical factor. Another example of a CPU intensive application process might be a word processing application running on an Open Desktop system. In both of these cases, the availability of the CPU limits the speed of the operation.

This example also shows how some of the process scheduling tunables affect performance of a CPU intensive process.

Step 1. Decide what to improve.

☑ Select the appropriate worksheet for the common operation.

This example shows one way of deciding whether to add an additional CPU to improve the performance of a set of calculating processes running on the system. The SCO UNIX Operating System and SCO MPX tuning worksheets are the appropriate worksheets. The completed worksheets are included at the end of the chapter.

⇩

Step 2. Identify the limited and unlimited resources.

☑ Note any limited resources on the worksheet by marking them with an asterisk (*).

The hardware configuration is as follows:

COMPAQ PROLIANT™ 4000 (4 * Pentium 66 Mhz processors)
64 Mbytes
SMART DRIVE ARRAY™ disk adapter

The machine contains four CPUs, and each test series uses the machine in a one, two and four CPU configuration. No additional hardware is available.

⇩

Step 3. Determine how to measure the operation and test its current performance.

☑ Note the test result on the worksheet in the column marked **Now.**

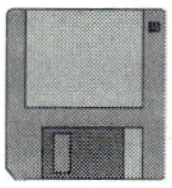

The CPU-intensive sample program used for measuring the operation in this example is included on the floppy disk. The test program is called calcop.

Step 4. Set a realistic performance goal.

☑ Note this on the worksheet in the column marked **Your Goal.**

The goal is to understand under what conditions an additional processor improves performance.

Step 5. Identify the resources to monitor and decide which monitoring tools to use.

☑ The worksheets list the appropriate resources.

When the calcop program runs, it is entirely resident in memory and does not access the disk. The key behaviors to monitor are CPU usage and process scheduling. The program is run with all the sar options to ensure that all the relevant statistics are collected during each test run.

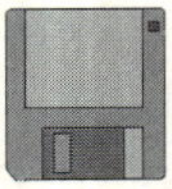

The standard operating system monitoring tools, sar, mpsar and cpusar, are used to monitor operating system and hardware resource usage patterns. The tune2wks, sar2oswks, mpx2wks programs provided on the floppy disk extract the appropriate data for entry into the worksheets.

⇩

Step 6. Run the test with the monitoring tools and monitor the resource usage and record the test results.

☑ Enter the initial values of the tunables and note the resource usage in the column marked **Initial Values**. Note the test results under the column called **Monitoring.**

The series of tests is as follows:

- one calculating process running on one, two and four CPUs (worksheets 5-1 to 5-3)
- two calculating processes running on one, two and four CPUs (worksheets 5-4 to 5-6)
- four calculating processes running on one, two and four CPUs (worksheets 5-7 to 5-9)
- eight calculating processes running on one, two and four CPUs (worksheets 5-10 to 5-12)

Each series starts with a one CPU run and uses that as the reference point to compare the differences after the additional processors are installed. The results of the first test, one calculating process running on one CPU, is equal to 55 seconds.

⇩

Step 7. Decide how to change the resource allocation; rerun the tests and note progress toward the goal. Iterate until either the goal is reached, or until a limited resource is encountered.

☑ Determine whether to increase or decrease the resource/tunable. Note the new tunable values in the column marked **Test #1** and the test results under the column **Res #1.** Use the rest of the columns for the results of subsequent test iterations.

☑ When the goal is reached, implement the new resource allocation.

Test Series #1: One Calculating Process

The test results for one calculating process running on one, two and four CPUs are summarized in Figure 5-1.

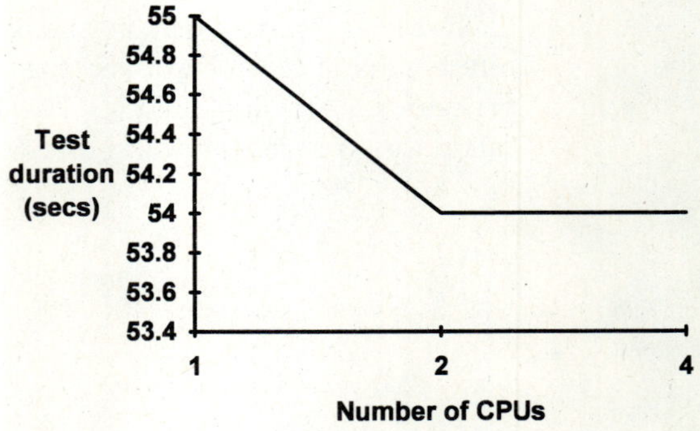

Figure 5-1: Summary of Test Results for One Process

The minor drop in the test duration from 55 to 54 seconds after the second processor is installed can be attributed to the auxiliary CPU executing the mpsar monitoring process. With one processor, the calculating process and the mpsar process must both share the CPU. With two processors, the calculating process and the mpsar process have their own processors and no longer need to share. The usage of the CPUs during part of the test is shown in the Figures 5-2 and 5-3.

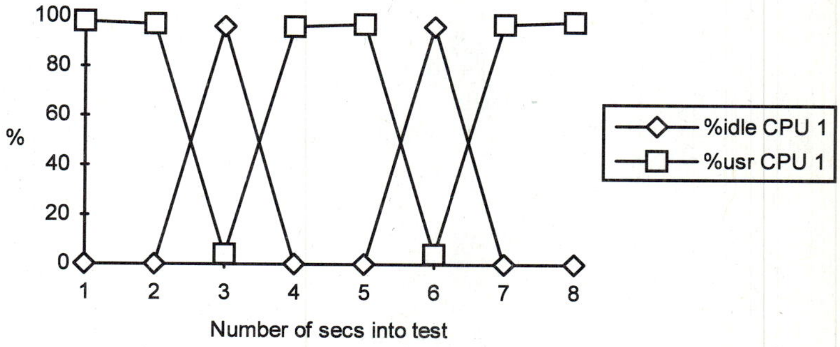

Figure 5-2: %idle and %usr on CPU 1

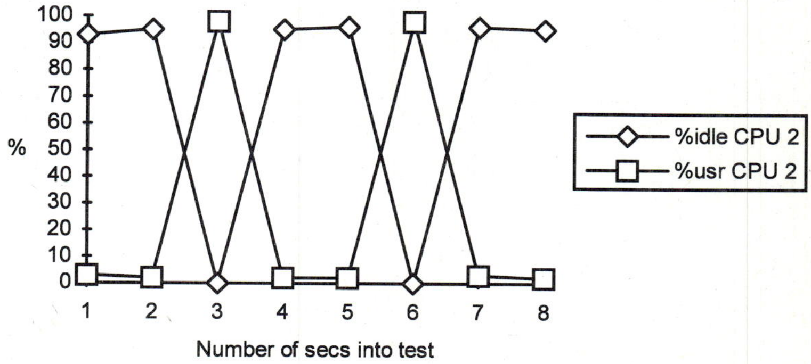

Figure 5-3: %idle and %usr on CPU 2

With two CPUs, the calculating process ran on either CPU 1 or CPU 2. When the test ran on CPU 1, CPU 2 was mostly idle. When the test ran on CPU 2, CPU 1 was mostly idle. The %sys and %wio time were an insignificant percentage of the amount of CPU time and so are not included in this discussion. With four CPUs, the same pattern of %idle and %usr time was observed.

The number of ready-to-run processes is equal to zero during this test. Remember that the runq-sz values reported by mpsar include the idle processes, and since an idle process is assigned to each CPU, the actual number of ready-to-run processes is equal to runq-sz minus the number of CPUs. If you are running the SCO MPX mpsar Maintenance Supplement, then the idle processes are already subtracted out of the runq-sz figures.

The impact of mpsar and cpusar is shown in the data collected for the rate of context switches, pswch/s, and the rate of reading and writing to the buffer cache, lread/s and lwrit/s. The rate of context switches periodically rises above 100. These peaks occur at the same time as the peaks in buffer cache activity. Use the time stamps provided by mpsar/cpusar to match the data patterns. Since the only other ready-to-run application process on the system is mpsar and this process write their data to the filesystem, these peaks in activity are caused by these processes collecting the monitoring data and writing it to files in the filesystem.

The additional CPUs did not significantly reduce the time required to complete the calculating operation because they spent much of their time idle. In general, when the system runs only one calculating process, installing a faster CPU contributes more to performance than adding additional CPUs.

Test Series #2: Two Calculating Processes

The next test runs two float.awk processes instead of one from calcop, on one, two and four processors. Both calculating processes are started simultaneously, and the test waits for both processes to complete before reporting a result. The test results are shown in Figure 5-4.

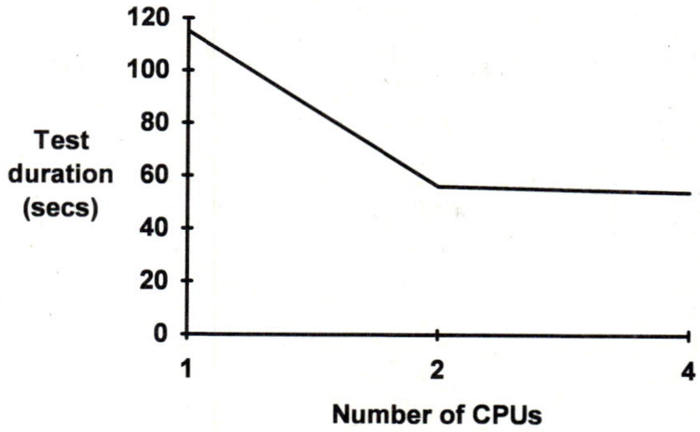

Figure 5-4: Summary of Test Results with Two Processes

After adding the second CPU, the duration of the test decreased by 50%. However, with four CPUs, the test duration did not vary significantly. The slight drop with four CPUs can be attributed to mpsar no longer having to share the two CPUs with the calculating processes. Four CPUs allow the mpsar process and the two calculating processes to each have their own CPU. The CPU usage pattern for the two CPUs is shown in Figures 5-5 and 5-6.

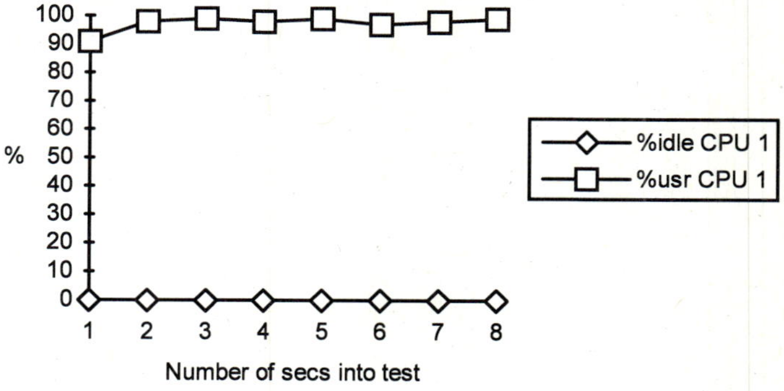

Figure 5-5: %idle and %usr on CPU 1 (Two Processes)

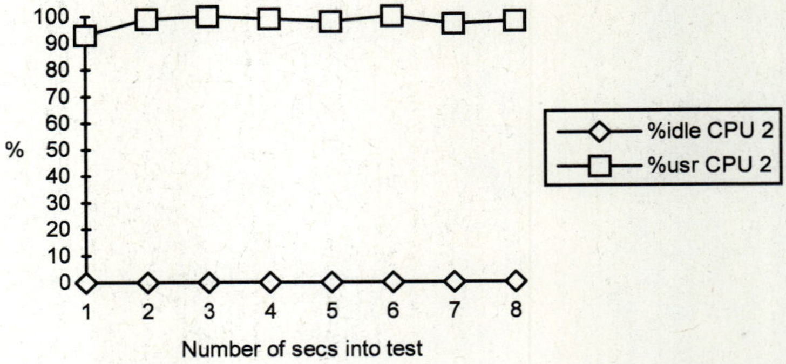

Figure 5-6: %idle and %usr on CPU 2 (Two Processes)

The %idle time for both CPUs is zero for the entire duration of the test as shown in Figures 5-5 and 5-6. Unlike the first series, the %usr time for two CPUs shows greater than 90% CPU utilization for both CPUs. With four CPUs, the alternating %usr and %idle time pattern shown in the first test series with two CPUs can be observed.

The cyclical values observed in the first test series for context switches and buffer cache activity occur in this test. These values can be attributed to the activity of mpsar, and so can be ignored.

The actual number of ready-to-run processes is shown in Figure 5-7. This graph shows that the average number of ready-to-run processes is zero when the number of CPUs is two or more. This statistic correlates with the fact that more than two CPUs have no impact on the test duration. With no ready-to-run processes, the additional CPUs had no work to do, so the additional CPUs could not contribute to a performance increase.

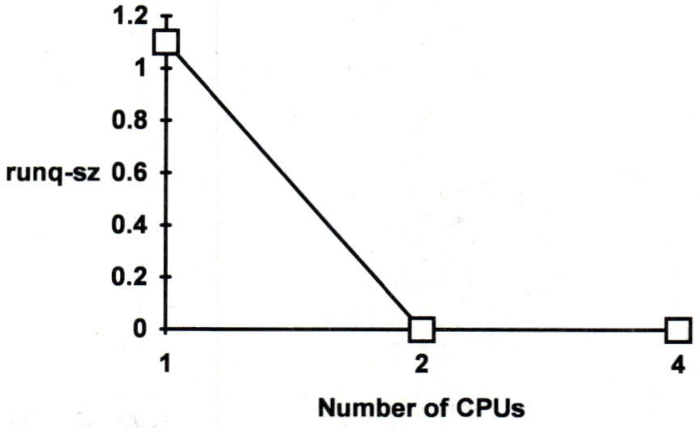

Figure 5-7: Number of Ready-to-Run Processes (Two processes)

Test Series #3: Four Calculating Processes

This test runs four calculating processes on one, two, and four CPUs from calcop. As in test series #2, the test waits for all processes to complete before calculating the duration of the test. The test results are shown in Figure 5-8.

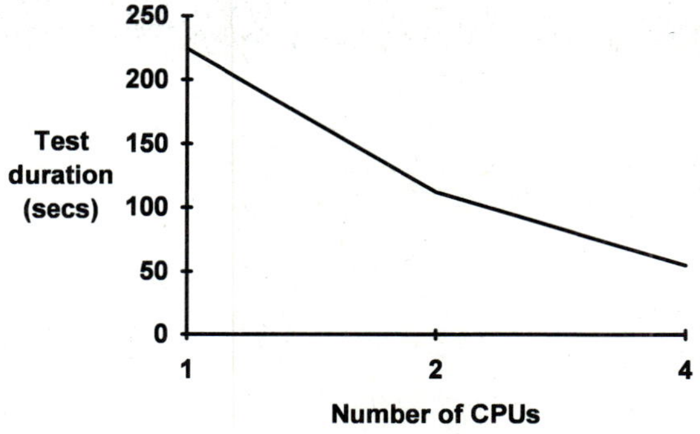

Figure 5-8: Summary of Test Results with Four Processes

With four calculating processes, each processor can run a calculating process, so all processors on the system are used. Each of the calculating processes is independent, so there is no internal application contention that might hinder the execution of each of the calculating process. Since each CPU can run a calculating process, the test duration for four processes on four CPUs is the same as the duration for one calculating process running on one processor.

Only mpsar had to share the CPUs with the calculating processes. With minimal processor sharing, process scheduling has little effect on the duration of the test.

Figure 5-9 shows the actual number of ready-to-run processes during this test.

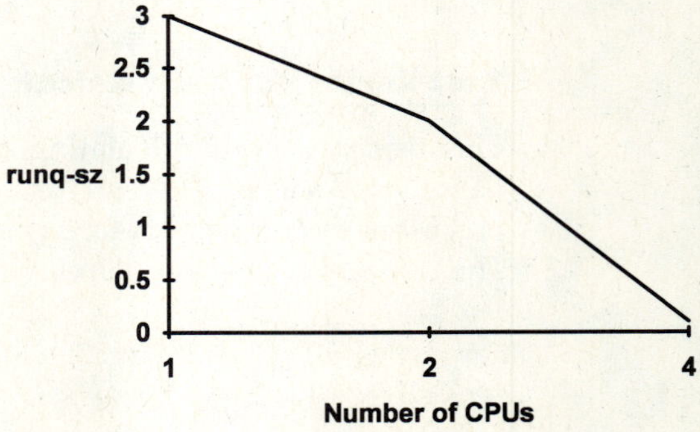

Figure 5-9: Number of Ready-to-Run Processes (Four Processes)

The average number of ready-to-run processes decreases as the number of CPUs increases. This behavior correlates to the decrease in test duration, because more processes can execute simultaneously on more processors. Note that this simultaneous execution is only possible if all the processes are independent. With only four calculating processes, each process no longer has to share the CPU with other processes, so parallel process execution is maximized.

Test Series #4: Eight Calculating Processes

This test series runs eight float.awk processes from the calcop script on one, two and four CPUs. Process scheduling has a greater impact on performance when processes must share the CPU because more ready-to-run processes exist than CPUs to run them. The test results for eight calculating processes are shown in Figure 5-10. The test waits for all eight processes to complete before reporting the test duration.

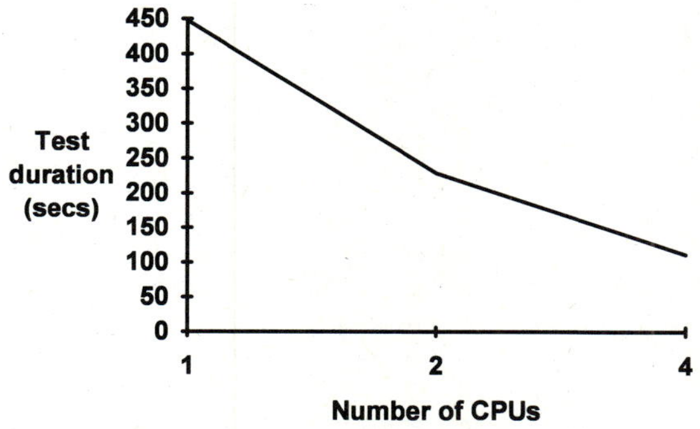

Figure 5-10: Summary of Test Results (Eight Processes)

The test duration with four CPUs is similar to the results observed when two calculating processes are run on one CPU as shown in test series #2. Note the change in scale along the vertical axis in this graph from previous test results.

With only four CPUs, the eight processes must share the CPUs, so some of the processes will run and some will wait. Each calculating process is independent of the other, so when the operating system decides to suspend one process in favor of a waiting process, the suspended process joins the ready-to-run list. The average size of the ready-to-run list is shown in Figure 5-11.

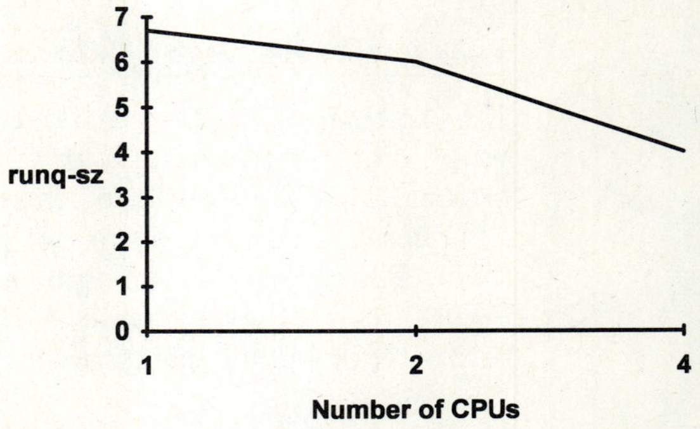

Figure 5-11: Number of Ready-to-Run Processes (Eight Processes)

Once again the duration of the test correlates to the decrease in the size of the ready-to-run list. Since the eight processes must share four CPUs, at any point in time at least four of the processes are waiting to run on the CPUs.

Test Series #5: Scheduling Tunables (loadbalance)

This test series runs the eight calculating processes on four CPUs with different SCO MPX scheduling tunables. Since all of the processes must share the CPU and all of the processes are independent of each other, process scheduling starts to affect the test duration. This set of tests illustrates the behavior of some of the scheduling tunables described in the Process Scheduling section in the Common SCO MPX Operations chapter. These test results are not noted in worksheets because the tunables did not change performance very much.

The first tunable selected is loadbalance, because, in general, setting it to zero reduces the number of context switches. However, setting this to zero can also result in lower priority processes running while higher priority processes wait for CPU access. This behavior may affect the performance of some applications.

Because the test spends a very low percentage of time executing in the operating system, reducing the number of context switches is one of the few ways to increase the amount of time available to the application processes. The test results for a four CPU configuration and an increasing number of calculating processes is shown in Figure 5-12.

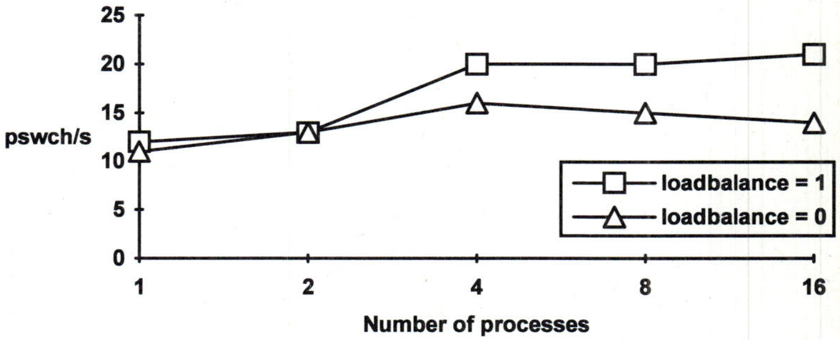

Figure 5-12: Number of Context Switches

As expected, the number of context switches dropped. The more processes executing, the more context switches are avoided. However, the duration of the test did not change as the number of processes increased. The test duration did not change because the time required to execute seven context switches is small compared to the total duration of the test, so the time saved is not measurable. With many more active processes, however, the time saved would possibly be measurable.

Test Series #5: Scheduling Tunables (dopricalc)

The other tunable that could affect the test duration is dopricalc. With dopricalc set to zero, the operating system does not recalculate process priorities when the processes wait for the CPU or when the process runs on the CPU. Figure 5-13 shows the test results for an increasing number of CPUs with dopricalc set to zero and dopricalc set to one.

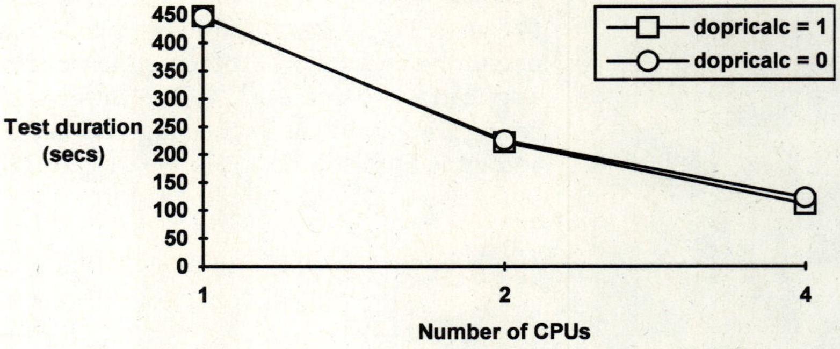

Figure 5-13: Test Results With dopricalc

Figure 5-13 shows that when dopricalc is equal to one, the duration of the test decreases as the number of CPUs increases. The primary reason for this change is shown by the key CPU usage statistics for this test reported for each of the four CPUs. These results are shown in Figure 5-14.

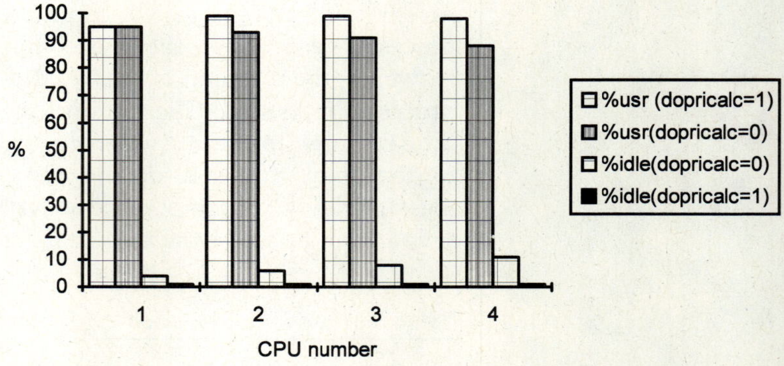

Figure 5-14: %usr and %idle With dopricalc Set to Zero and One

With dopricalc set to one, each CPU spends most of its time executing the calculating processes and very little time idle. This graph also shows that each CPU is equally used when dopricalc is equal to one. With dopricalc set to zero, CPUs 2, 3 and 4 are used much less efficiently than when dopricalc is equal to one. Since the CPUs are used less efficiently, the duration of the test increases when dopricalc is set to zero.

Figure 5-15 shows the number of ready-to-run processes as the number of CPUs increase when dopricalc is set to zero and dopricalc is set to one.

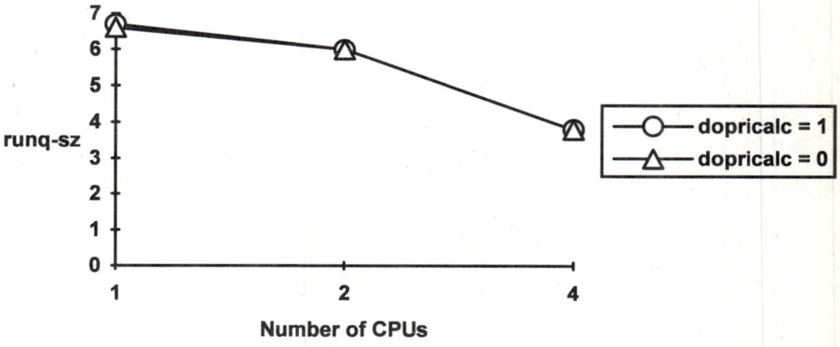

Figure 5-15: Number of Ready-to-Run Processes

This test shows that changing the value of dopricalc has very little effect on the average number of ready-to-run processes. This behavior is expected because the recalculation does not affect the number of ready-to-run processes in this test.

Conclusions

When only a few ready-to-run processes exist, adding CPUs does not reduce the duration of the test. In general, adding CPUs increases performance when the number of actual ready-to-run processes plus the number of running processes is greater than or equal to the number of CPUs. In such cases, when a process is suspended, another ready-to-run process can take its place, so the usage of each CPU is maximized.

This example also shows how independent processes can increase the amount of parallel execution as the number of CPUs increases. If the calculating processes shared one set of formulas that could only be accessed by one process at a time, then only one process at a time could execute on the CPUs and adding more CPUs would not benefit performance. Sharing one set of formulas is only one example of resource contention that can occur on a system when an additional CPU is added. When adding another CPU, the importance of increasing the number of ready-to-run processes by eliminating resource contention when tuning MPX cannot be overemphasized.

File Read and Write Example

This case study explores how an additional CPU can support more users and how the resource usage pattern changes as a result.

The fileop shell script used in this and the SCO UNIX case study is included on the floppy disk. This shell script simulates a number of users executing a combination of simple file read and more complex file read and write operations. The number of users is configurable. Appendix C contains a manual page that describes the fileop script in more detail.

Step 1. Decide what to improve.

☑ Select the appropriate worksheet for the common operation.

This example explores the resource usage changes after an additional processor is installed and more users can be supported. The system tuning is checked to see if any changes need to be made to accommodate the increased capacity of the machine.

The SCO MPX and the SCO UNIX Operating System Tuning worksheets are the appropriate worksheets. The completed worksheets are included at the end of this chapter in Worksheets 5-13 to 5-15.

⇩

Step 2. Identify the limited and unlimited resources.

☑ Note any limited resources on the worksheet by marking them with an asterisk (*).

Additional processors can be installed in the machine. The other hardware components are fixed. The hardware configuration is shown in Figure 5-16. No other hardware is available.

⇩

Step 3. Determine how to measure the operation and test its current performance.

☑ Note the test result on the worksheet in the column marked **Now.**

This example shows the difference in resource usage patterns after an additional CPU is installed and system load is also increased. The first test collects statistics prior to the addition of the second processor, and the second test collects statistics after the addition of the second processor and the increase in system load.

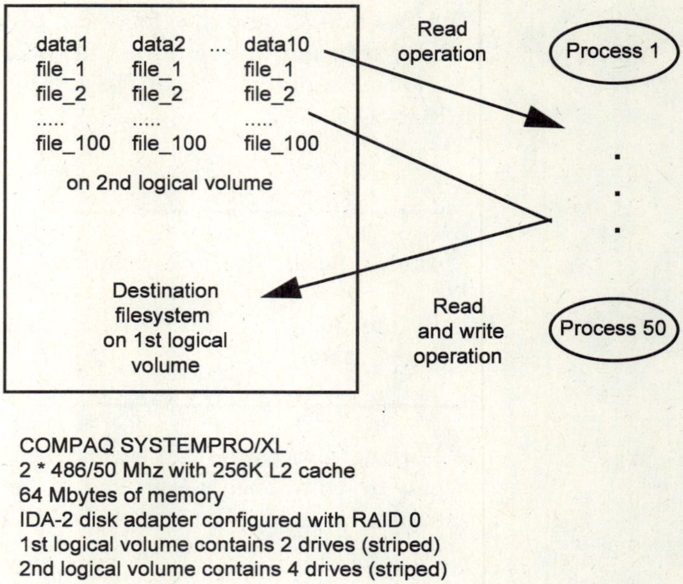

Figure 5-16: Processes 1 through 50 execute a combination of read and read/write operations on files located in the directories data1 through data10. The read operation reads the files from the directories located on the second logical volume. The read and write operation copies files from the second logical volume to the filesystem on the first logical volume. The first logical volume contains the root filesystem.

The fileop shell script is a mixture of typical file read and write operations. The fileop script operates on a previously prepared directory hierarchy created by ctree, also included on the floppy disk. Each process receives a list of 100 files randomly selected by the fileop script. Four read operations are executed for every write operation. Figure 5-16 shows how the data flows during the test.

The following ctree command creates ten directories each containing 100 32 Kbyte files:

```
ctree -f 100 -d 1 -s 32768 -n data1
ctree -f 100 -d 1 -s 32768 -n data2
...
ctree -f 100 -d 1 -s 32768 -n data10
```

The test was first run with 50 processes.

The initial test duration is 450 seconds with one processor and 50 users.

⇩

Step 4. Set a realistic performance goal.

☑ Note this on the worksheet in the column marked **Your Goal.**

The goal is to support close to the same test duration when 100 users are using the system instead of just 50 users.

⇩

Step 5. Identify the resources to monitor and decide which monitoring tools to use.

☑ The worksheets list the appropriate resources.

The standard SCO MPX and Operating System Tuning Worksheets contain all the resources that should be monitored for the filesystem operation.

The fileop script automatically runs sar when the option -sar is specified. The utility sar2oswks extracts the correct data from the sar data files for entry into the worksheet cells. The utility mpx2wks extracts the correct data for entry into the SCO MPX worksheet cells.

⇩

Step 6. Run the test with the monitoring tools and monitor the resource usage and record the test results.

☑ Enter the initial values of the tunables and note the resource usage in the column marked **Initial Values**. Note the test results under the column called **Monitoring.**

With the monitoring tools enabled, the duration of the operation was 480 seconds with 50 processes and one processor. The performance for 50 users is acceptable. Now add a CPU, increase the number of users to 100, and monitor the resource usage changes.

The test now takes 500 seconds. To understand the impact of adding a CPU and increasing the number of users, examine the filesystem resources usage pattern differences. After this examination, the next step is to assess whether any resource allocations need to be changed to accommodate the increase in system activity.

Initial Observations: Two CPU statistics

To understand the differences in resource usage, examine the intermediate storage locations required by the filesystem operation. These intermediate storage locations are described in the Common SCO UNIX Operations and Common SCO MPX Operations chapter.

The first intermediate storage location in the filesystem operation is the namei cache. Figures 5-17 and 5-18 show how the frequency of namei cache requests has increased with more users and an additional CPU, but the increased use has not affected the cache efficiency.

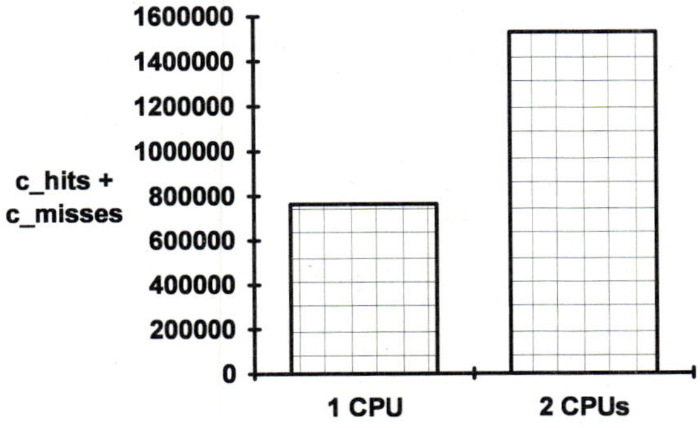

Figure 5-17: Namei Cache Requests for 1 and 2 CPUs

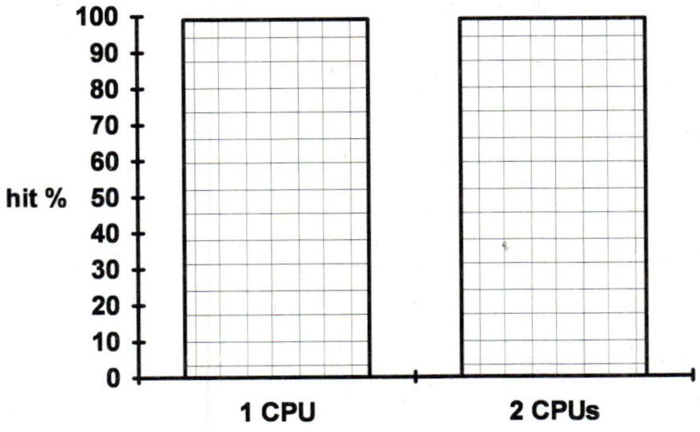

Figure 5-18: Namei Cache Efficiency for 1 and 2 CPUs

Although the namei cache request frequency has more than doubled, the efficiency statistics show that the size of the cache is still optimal for the additional CPU. If the efficiency statistic had decreased, then the values of S5CACHEENTS and S5HASHQS should be increased to restore the original level of cache efficiency.

The maximum number of entries in both the inode and open file table also increased as shown in Figures 5-19 and 5-20.

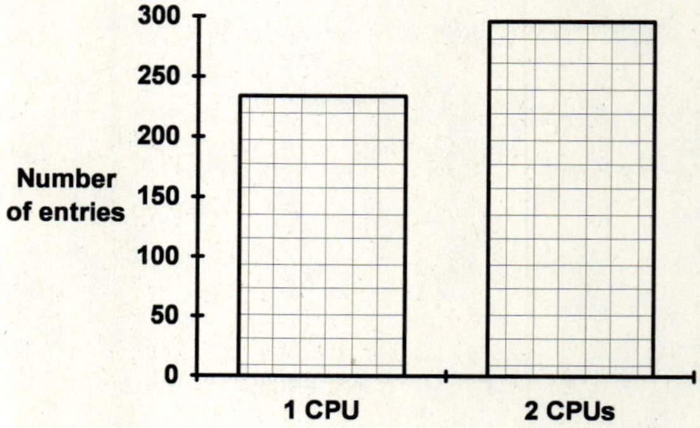

Figure 5-19: Number of Inode Table Entries for 1 and 2 CPUs

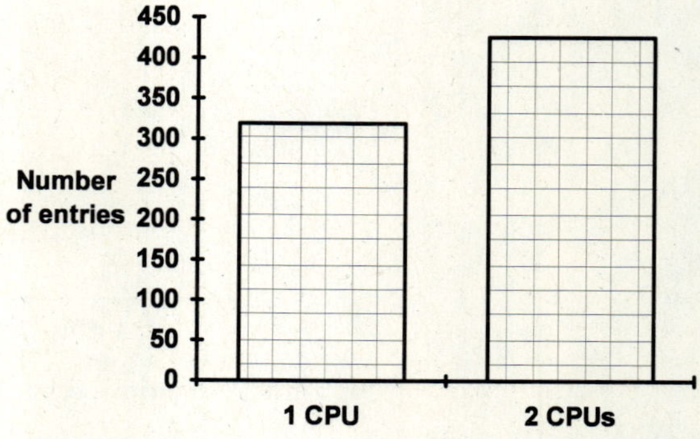

Figure 5-20: Number of Open File Table Entries for 1 and 2 CPUs

This table is not showing the number of times files or inodes are accessed, but the maximum number of occupied table entries. Running a shell script requires opening pipes as well as the files copied as part of the test. Not all operations executed from a shell script require pipes. Each pipe allocates two entries in the open file table and one entry in the inode table. Increasing the number of shell scripts increases the number of pipes, which increases the usage of the tables. The usage did not double because the number of files and inodes used simultaneously did not double. The size of these tables was sufficient to accommodate the increased usage.

The next storage location is the buffer cache. The number of logical reads to the buffer cache and physical reads to the disk because data was not located in the buffer cache increased as shown by Figures 5-21 and 5-22.

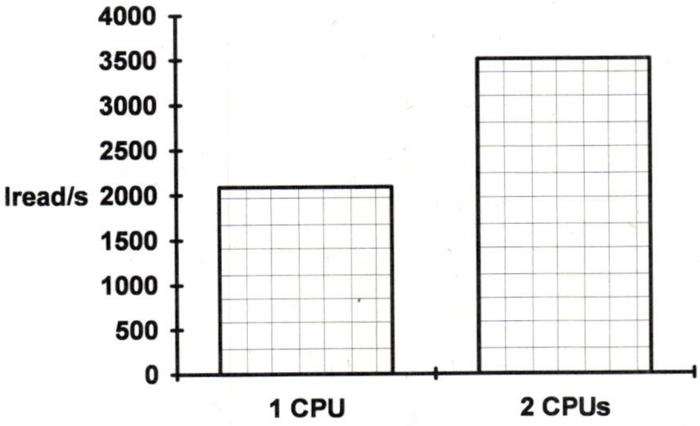

Figure 5-21: lread/s With 1 and 2 CPUs

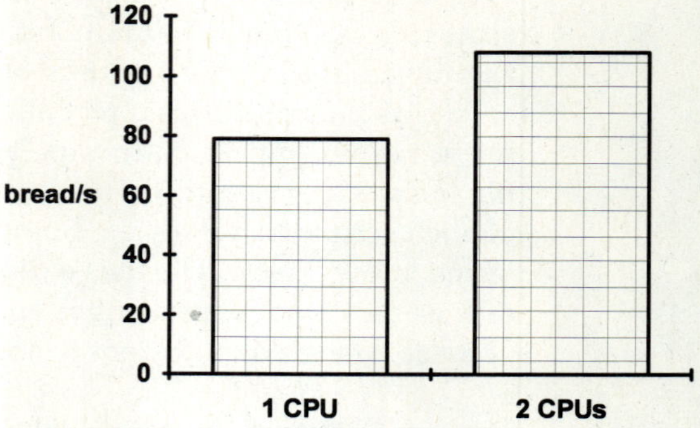

Figure 5-22: bread/s With 1 and 2 CPUs

Even with the increase in the buffer cache activity, the cache efficiency did not change significantly as shown by Figure 5-23.

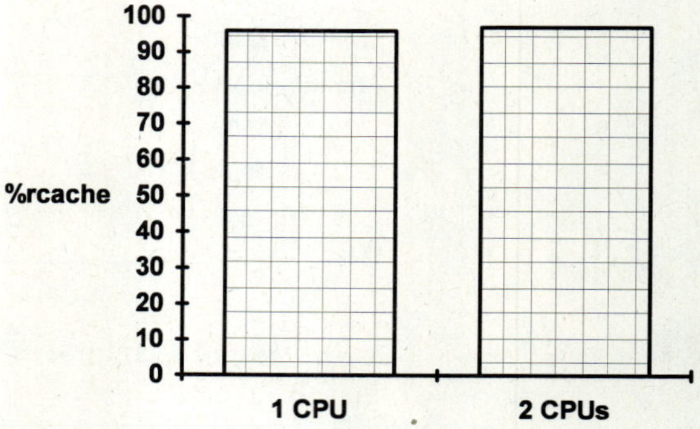

Figure 5-23: %rcache With 1 and 2 CPUs

The IDA-2 disk adapter supports scatter/gather directly in hardware and is capable of addressing memory above 16 Mbytes. No copy buffers and scatter/gather temporary work areas are required for the file operations.

The final storage location is the disk subsystem. The %busy statistic indicates that the disk was 100% busy for both the one and two CPU tests.

The frequency of disk requests handled by the destination filesystem increased from 27 to 43 r+w/s and on the read filesystem increased from 22 to 31 r+w/s. The number of blocks per second handled by both disks also increased from 133 to 224 on the first disk and from 160 to 220. These increases coincide with the increases revealed by the other statistics.

However, on the destination filesystem the avserv time increased from 36 to 266 milliseconds as shown in Figure 5-24.

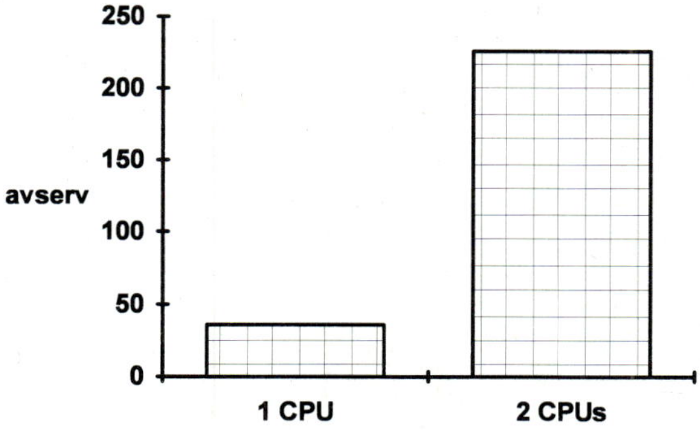

Figure 5-24: avserv With 1 and 2 CPUs

The values reported by mpsar for avserv for the read filesystem also rose from 61 to 87 milliseconds. The avserv time indicates the amount of time required by the disks to service the request.

One possible explanation for the dramatic increase in service time on the destination filesystem is as follows:

- The destination filesystem is the root filesystem. The root filesystem is where all pipe inodes are allocated. Because the fileop test is a shell script that creates many pipes, the frequency of pipe inode creation is higher with 100 users than with 50 users. Inode creation is a synchronous operation that occurs in a special area of the filesystem.

- The destination filesystem is approximately 95% full and is also quite old. The degree of fragmentation is likely to be quite high, so the amount of time required to find free filesystem blocks would also be quite high.

- The amount and frequency of data written to the root filesystem has also increased. Since the inodes are located in a separate area from the filesystem data, the disk heads must frequently travel between the two areas. With more inodes created, and more data written, the frequency of this oscillation is likely to increase, thereby delaying the completion of all write operations while the head travels between the two locations.

These conclusions could be verified by reconfiguring the writes to occur on a separate logical volume from the root filesystem and running the test again. Unlike the example in the SCO UNIX File Operation Case Study, a ramdisk for the pipes is unlikely to provide a significant improvement because the cache on the IDA-2 provides similar performance. Writing to the cache memory on the IDA-2 is equivalent to writing to physical memory on a ramdisk, because the operating system code pathway is the same for both operations.

The CPU usage statistics showed an increase in %wio from 9% to 14%, but a decrease in %sys from 77% to 73%. The idle time has increased slightly from 0% to 1%. The increase in %wio reveals that the amount of time that no ready-to-run processes existed and the processes that were suspended were waiting-on-device-I/O increased.

Examination of the ready-to-run queue compared to %wio at one minute intervals throughout the test confirms that no ready-to-run processes existed. The saravg script extracts interval data so behavior during a test can be examined in more detail. Figures 5-25 and 5-26 shows the relationship between %wio and ready-to-run list size for one CPU. Figures 5-27 and 5-28 show the relationship between %wio and ready-to-run list size for 2 CPUs.

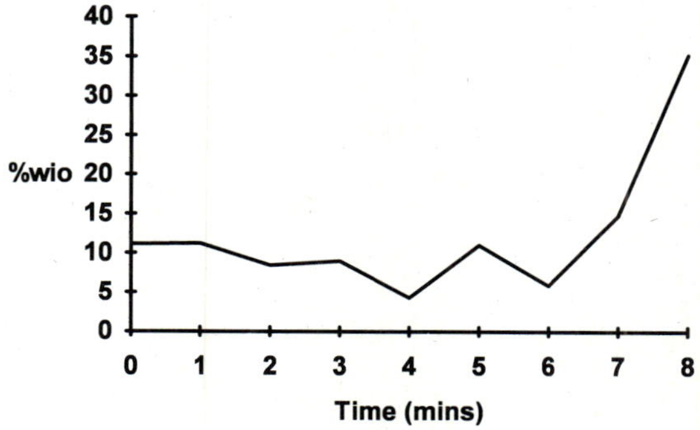

Figure 5-25: %wio for 1 CPU Throughout the Test

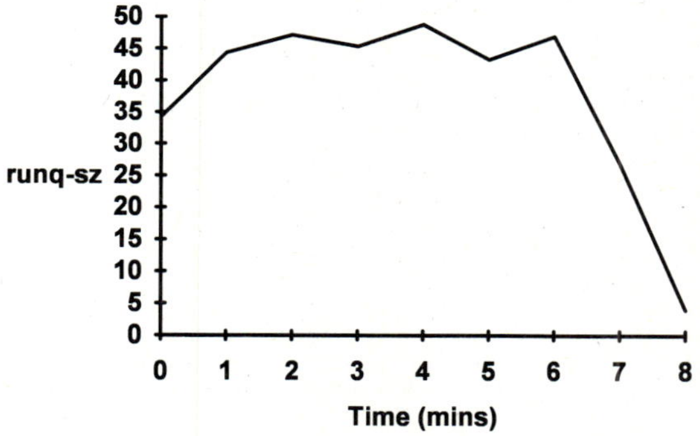

Figure 5-26: Ready-to-run List Size on 1 CPU Throughout the Test

The amount of %wio increases as the size of the ready-to-run list decreases towards the end of the test with just one CPU.

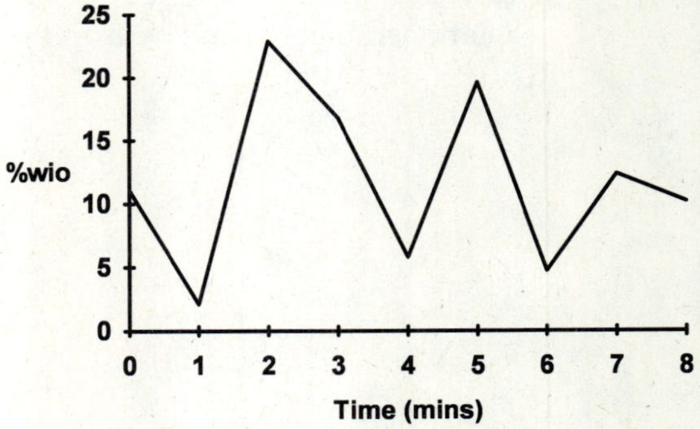

Figure 5-27: %wio for 2 CPUs Throughout the Test

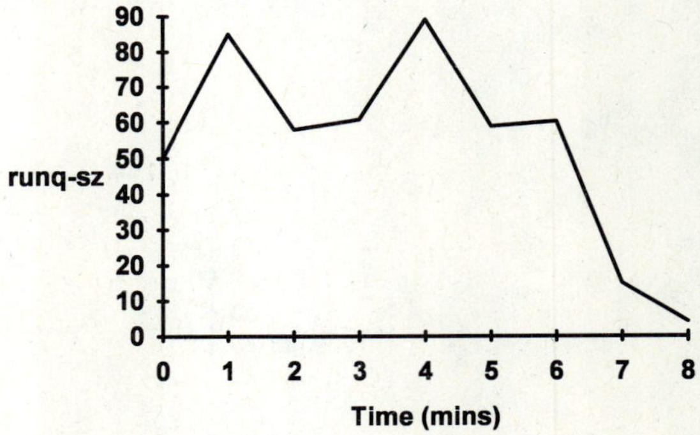

Figure 5-28: Ready-to-run List Size on 2 CPUs Throughout the Test

Figures 5-27 and 5-28 show the relationship between ready-to-run list size and %wio holds after the additional CPU is installed. Once again, when the number of ready-to-run processes decreased, %wio increased because no processes were available for the CPU to run.

One possible way of decreasing %wio is to increase the number of users which should increase the number of ready-to-run processes for the majority of the test duration. After the number of users is increased, the usage patterns for the intermediate storage locations should be checked to ensure that the sizes are still optimal.

The amount of %wio could also be decreased by rearranging the read and destination filesystems as previously described. The filesystem was sufficient for 50 users running on one CPU, but not for 100 users running on two CPUs. Performance may degrade for 100 users unless the filesystem configuration is improved.

If the avserv time decreased, then the number of ready-to-run processes should increase and %wio would decrease. The CPUs would be used more efficiently and the test would either run faster, or more users could be supported without impacting the length of the test.

⇩

Step 7. Decide how to change the resource allocation; rerun the tests and note progress toward the goal. Iterate until either the goal is reached, or until a limited resource is encountered.

☑ Determine whether to increase or decrease the resource/tunable. Note the new tunable values in the column marked **Test #1** and the test results under the column **Res #1.** Use the rest of the columns for the results of subsequent test iterations.

☑ When the goal is reached, implement the new resource allocation.

The test result meets the goal for 100 users. However, the previous analysis shows two areas that could be changed to further increase the efficient use of the additional CPU.

One possible way of decreasing %wio is to increase the number of users which should increase the number of ready-to-run processes for the majority of the test duration. After the number of users is increased, the usage patterns for the intermediate storage locations should be checked to ensure that the sizes are still optimal.

The filesystem was sufficient for 50 users running on one CPU, but not for 100 users running on two CPUs. The amount of %wio could also be decreased by rearranging the read and destination filesystems as previously described. Rearranging the filesystem data should reduce the avserv time and increase the number of ready-to-run processes. The CPUs would be used more efficiently and the test would either run faster, or more users could be supported without impacting the length of the test.

CONCLUSIONS

These tests show how an additional CPU can support a larger number of users. An additional CPU increases the capacity of the system only if ready-to-run processes exist on the system. In both cases, when sufficient numbers of ready-to-run processes are available, the additional CPUs are used effectively and performance increases. To ensure that additional CPUs are used efficiently, the intermediate storage location usage must be re-examined to ensure that the resource allocations are still optimal with the increased workload.

Worksheet 5-1: SCO UNIX Operating System Tuning Worksheet for One Calculating Process

Tunables	Initial Values	2 CPU	4 CPU
*Installed Memory	64Mb		
Application Storage			
GPGSLO, GPGSHI	500 600		
MAXSC, AGEINTERVAL	8 31		
S5CACHEENTS, S5HASHQS	3072 8191		
NFILE	4700		
NINODE, NHINODE	5000 2048		
NBUF, NHBUF	32768 65536		
BDFLUSHR, NAUTOP	30 10		
NCOPYBUF, PLOWBUFS	100 10		
NMPBUF, NMPHEADBUF	16 2048		
NPBUF, DMAABLEBUF	200 64		
SDSKOUT	4		
*Disk Configuration, Data Layout	n/a		
NCLIST	2048		
NPROC, NREGION	3000 6000		
NSCRN, CTBUFSIZ	0 128		
Display adapter, colors	n/a		
Mouse Settings	n/a		
Other Memory Used	n/a		

Worksheet 5-2: SCO UNIX Operating System Tuning Worksheet for One Calculating Process

Resources to Monitor	Initial Values	2 CPU	4 CPU
Free Memory, Free swap	4838 196608	4815 196608	4822 196608
Blocks Swapped in/out	0.0 0.0	0.0 0.0	0.0 0.0
Pages Reclaimed	0.00	0.00	0.00
CPU: %usr, %sys, %wio, %idle	98 2 0 0	51 2 0 47	25 2 0 73
Scheduling: runq-sz, swpq-sz, pswch/s	0 0 9	0 0 12	0 0 12
Namei Cache	91%	92%	92%
File Table, Inode Table	55 0 75 0	58 0 77 0	60 0 78 0
Buffer Cache %rcache Reads: bread/s lread/s Writes: bwrit/s, lwrit/s	99 0 30 3 31	99 0 41 3 52	99 0 50 4 68
Scatter/Gather: mpbuf/s, ompb/s, mphbuf/s, omphbufs/s	0 0 2 0	0 0 3 0	0 0 4 0
Copy Buffers	n/a	n/a	n/a
Direct Disk Requests	n/a	n/a	n/a
Copy Memory	n/a	n/a	n/a
Sdsk Request Blocks	n/a	n/a	n/a
Disk Driver : %busy avque, r+w/s, blks/s, avwait, avserv	n/a	n/a	n/a

Now	Your Goal	Monitoring	2 CPU	4 CPU
55	55	55	54	54

Worksheet 5-3: SCO MPX Tuning Worksheet for One Calculating Process

Tunables	**Initial Values**	**2 CPU**	**4 CPU**
*Number of CPUs	1	2	4
loadbalance	1		
preemptive	1		
dopricalc	1		
primove	10		
cache_affinity	1		
Resources to Monitor	**Initial Values**	**2 CPU**	**4 CPU**
CPU 1: %usr, %sys, %wio, %idle		55 2 0 43	51 2 0 37
CPU 2: %usr, %sys, %wio, %idle		46 2 0 51	0 0 0 100
CPU 3: %usr, %sys, %wio, %idle			41 4 0 55
CPU 4: %usr, %sys, %wio, %idle			0 1 0 99
CPU 1 InterCPU interrupts		1.33 3.02 0.00	1.20 2.33 0.00
CPU 2 InterCPU interrupts		3.02 1.33 0.00	0.02 0.00 0.00
CPU 3 InterCPU interrupts			0.77 0.86 0.00
CPU 4 InterCPU Interrupts			2.11 0.90 0.00

Now	**Your Goal**	**Monitoring**	**2 CPU**	**4 CPU**

Worksheet 5-4: SCO UNIX Operating System Tuning Worksheet for Two Calculating Processes

Tunables	Initial Values	2 CPU	4 CPU
*Installed Memory	64Mb		
Application Storage			
GPGSLO, GPGSHI	500 600		
MAXSC, AGEINTERVAL	8 31		
S5CACHEENTS, S5HASHQS	3072 8191		
NFILE	4700		
NINODE, NHINODE	5000 2048		
NBUF, NHBUF	32768 65536		
BDFLUSHR, NAUTOP	30 10		
NCOPYBUF, PLOWBUFS	100 10		
NMPBUF, NMPHEADBUF	16 2048		
NPBUF, DMAABLEBUF	200 64		
SDSKOUT	4		
*Disk Configuration, Data Layout	n/a		
NCLIST	2048		
NPROC, NREGION	3000 6000		
NSCRN, CTBUFSIZ	0 128		
Display adapter, colors	n/a		
Mouse Settings	n/a		

Worksheet 5-5: SCO UNIX Operating System Tuning Worksheet for Two Calculating Processes

Resources to Monitor	**Initial Values**	**2 CPU**	**4 CPU**
Free Memory, Free swap	4707 196608	4785 196608	4753 196608
Blocks Swapped in/out	0 0	0 0	0 0
Pages Reclaimed	0.00	0.00	0.00
CPU: %usr, %sys, %wio, %idle	97 3 0 0	97 2 0 1	50 2 0 48
Scheduling: runq-sz, swpq-sz, pswch/s	1.1 0 11	0.0 0 15	0.0 0 13
Namei Cache	91%	92%	92%
File Table, Inode Table	66 0 78 0	59 0 77 0	62 0 80 0
Buffer Cache %rcache Reads: bread/s lread/s Writes: bwrit/s, lwrit/s	99 0 39 3 43	99 0 40 3 51	99 0 48 3 68
Scatter/Gather: mpbuf/s, ompb/s, mphbuf/s, omphbufs/s	0 0 2 0	0 0 3 0	0 0 3 0
Copy Buffers	n/a	n/a	n/a
Direct Disk Requests	n/a	n/a	n/a
Copy Memory	n/a	n/a	n/a
Sdsk Request Blocks	n/a	n/a	n/a
Disk Driver : %busy avque, r+w/s, blks/s, avwait, avserv	n/a	n/a	n/a

Now	**Your Goal**	**Monitoring**	**2 CPU**	**4 CPU**
115	55	115	56	54

Worksheet 5-6: SCO MPX Tuning Worksheet for Two Calculating Processes

Tunables	**Initial Values**	**2 CPU**	**4 CPU**
*Number of CPUs	1	2	4
loadbalance	1		
preemptive	1		
dopricalc	1		
primove	10		
cache_affinity	1		
Resources to Monitor	**Initial Values**	**2 CPU**	**4 CPU**
CPU 1: %usr, %sys, %wio, %idle		96 3 0 1	45 2 1 52
CPU 2: %usr, %sys, %wio, %idle		98 1 0 1	1 1 0 97
CPU 3: %usr, %sys, %wio, %idle			97 0 0 3
CPU 4: %usr, %sys, %wio, %idle			58 3 0 39
CPU 1 InterCPU interrupts		4.55 2.93 0.00	1.64 2.73 0.00
CPU 2 InterCPU interrupts		2.93 4.55 0.00	0.26 1.38 0.00
CPU 3 InterCPU interrupts			0.49 0.58 0.00
CPU 4 InterCPU Interrupts			2.93 0.63 0.00

Now	**Your Goal**	**Monitoring**	**2 CPU**	**4 CPU**

Worksheet 5-7: SCO UNIX Operating System Tuning Worksheet for Four Calculating Processes

Tunables	Initial Values	2 CPU	4 CPU
*Installed Memory	64Mb		
Application Storage			
GPGSLO, GPGSHI	500 600		
MAXSC, AGEINTERVAL	8 31		
S5CACHEENTS, S5HASHQS	3072 8191		
NFILE	4700		
NINODE, NHINODE	5000 2048		
NBUF, NHBUF	32768 65536		
BDFLUSHR, NAUTOP	30 10		
NCOPYBUF, PLOWBUFS	100 10		
NMPBUF, NMPHEADBUF	16 2048		
NPBUF, DMAABLEBUF	200 64		
SDSKOUT	4		
*Disk Configuration, Data Layout	n/a		
NCLIST	2048		
NPROC, NREGION	3000 6000		
NSCRN, CTBUFSIZ	0 128		
Display adapter, colors	n/a		
Mouse Settings	n/a		
Other Memory Used	n/a		

Worksheet 5-8: SCO UNIX Operating System Tuning Worksheet for Four Calculating Processes

Resources to Monitor	Initial Values	2 CPU	4 CPU
Free Memory, Free swap	4739 196608	4721 196608	4690 196608
Blocks Swapped in/out	0.0 0.0	0.0 0.0	0.0 0.0
Pages Reclaimed	0.00	0.00	0.00
CPU: %usr, %sys, %wio, %idle	98 2 0 0	97 2 0 1	98 1 0 1
Scheduling: runq-sz, swpq-sz, pswch/s	3.0 0 9	2.0 0 16	0.1 0 20
Namei Cache	92%	92%	92%
File Table, Inode Table	64 0 80 0	62 0 78 0	63 0 80 0
Buffer Cache %rcache Reads: bread/s lread/s Writes: bwrit/s, lwrit/s	99 0 33 2 30	99 0 41 3 51	99 0 50 3 66
Scatter/Gather: mpbuf/s, ompb/s, mphbuf/s, omphbufs/s	0 0 2 0	0 0 3 0	0 0 3 0
Copy Buffers	n/a	n/a	n/a
Direct Disk Requests	n/a	n/a	n/a
Copy Memory	n/a	n/a	n/a
Sdsk Request Blocks	n/a	n/a	n/a
Disk Driver : %busy avque, r+w/s, blks/s, avwait, avserv	n/a	n/a	n/a

Now	Your Goal	Monitoring	2 CPU	4 CPU
224	55	224	112	55

Worksheet 5-9: SCO MPX Tuning Worksheet for Four Calculating Processes

Tunables	**Initial Values**	**2 CPU**	**4 CPU**
*Number of CPUs	1	2	4
loadbalance	1		
preemptive	1		
dopricalc	1		
primove	10		
cache_affinity	1		
Resources to Monitor	**Initial Values**	**2 CPU**	**4 CPU**
CPU 1: %usr, %sys, %wio, %idle		96 3 0 1	94 4 0 2
CPU 2: %usr, %sys, %wio, %idle		99 1 0 1	99 0 0 1
CPU 3: %usr, %sys, %wio, %idle			99 0 0 1
CPU 4: %usr, %sys, %wio, %idle			99 1 0 0
CPU 1 InterCPU interrupts		5.02 3.00 0	5.25 3.74 0
CPU 2 InterCPU interrupts		3.00 5.02 0	1.17 3.26 0
CPU 3 InterCPU interrupts			0.7 1.37 0
CPU 4 InterCPU Interrupts			2.37 1.78 0

Now	**Monitoring**	**Your Goal**	**2 CPU**	**4 CPU**

Worksheet 5-10: SCO Operating System Tuning Worksheet for Eight Calculating Processes

Tunables	Initial Values	2 CPU	4 CPU
*Installed Memory	64Mb		
Application Storage			
GPGSLO, GPGSHI	500 600		
MAXSC, AGEINTERVAL	8 31		
S5CACHEENTS, S5HASHQS	3072 8191		
NFILE	4700		
NINODE, NHINODE	5000 2048		
NBUF, NHBUF	32768 65536		
BDFLUSHR, NAUTOP	30 10		
NCOPYBUF, PLOWBUFS	100 10		
NMPBUF, NMPHEADBUF	16 2048		
NPBUF, DMAABLEBUF	200 64		
SDSKOUT	4		
*Disk Configuration, Data Layout	n/a		
NCLIST	2048		
NPROC, NREGION	3000 6000		
NSCRN, CTBUFSIZ	0 128		
Display adapter, colors	n/a		
Mouse Settings	n/a		
Other Memory Used	n/a		

Worksheet 5-11: SCO UNIX Operating System Tuning Worksheet for Eight Calculating Processes

Resources to Monitor	Initial Values	2 CPU	4 CPU
Free Memory, Free swap	4644 196608	4575 196608	4564 196608
Blocks Swapped in/out	0.0 0.0	0.0 0.0	0.0 0.0
Pages Reclaimed	0.00	0.00	0.00
CPU: %usr, %sys, %wio, %idle	98 2 0 0	98 2 0 0	98 1 0 1
Scheduling: runq-sz, swpq-sz, pswch/s	6.7 0 8	6.0 0 17	4.0 0 20
Namei Cache	91%	92%	92%
File Table, Inode Table	65 0 77 0	64 0 77 0	69 0 81 0
Buffer Cache %rcache Reads: bread/s lread/s Writes: bwrit/s, lwrit/s	100 0 31 2 30	98 1 46 3 51	100 0 45 3 63
Scatter/Gather: mpbuf/s, ompb/s, mphbuf/s, omphbufs/s	0 0 2 0	0 0 2 0	0 0 3 0
Copy Buffers	0 0	0 0	0 0
Direct Disk Requests	0 0	0 0	0 0
Copy Memory	0 0	0 0	0 0
Sdsk Request Blocks	n/a	n/a	n/a
Disk Driver : %busy avque, r+w/s, blks/s, avwait, avserv	n/a	n/a	n/a

Now	Your Goal	Monitoring	2 CPU	4 CPU
448	55	448	229	111

Worksheet 5-12: SCO MPX Tuning Worksheet for Eight Calculating Processes

Tunables	Initial Values	2 CPU	4 CPU
*Number of CPUs	1	2	4
loadbalance	1		
preemptive	1		
dopricalc	1		
primove	10		
cache_affinity	1		
Resources to Monitor	**Initial Values**	**2 CPU**	**4 CPU**
CPU 1: %usr, %sys, %wio,%idle		96 4 0 0	95 5 0 1
CPU 2: %usr, %sys, %wio,%idle		100 0 0 0	99 0 0 1
CPU 3: %usr, %sys, %wio,%idle			99 0 0 1
CPU 4: %usr, %sys, %wio,%idle			98 1 0 1
CPU 1 InterCPU interrupts		4.62 3.73 0.00	5.24 3.78 0.00
CPU 2 InterCPU interrupts		3.73 4.62 0.00	1.60 3.45 0.00
CPU 3 InterCPU interrupts			1.07 2.11 0.00
CPU 4 InterCPU Interrupts			3.14 1.70 0.00

Now	Monitoring	Your Goal	2 CPU	4 CPU

Worksheet 5-13: SCO UNIX Operating System Tuning Worksheet for the File Operation

Tunables	Initial Values	2 CPU
*Installed Memory	64Mb	
Application Storage	n/a	
GPGSLO, GPGSHI	200 300	
MAXSC, AGEINTERVAL	8 31	
S5CACHEENTS, S5HASHQS	3072 8191	
NFILE	3000	
NINODE, NHINODE	2500 2048	
NBUF, NHBUF	32640 32768	
BDFLUSHR, NAUTOP	30 10	
NCOPYBUF, PLOWBUFS	100 10	
NMPBUF, NMPHEADBUF	16 2048	
NPBUF, DMAABLEBUF	200 64	
SDSKOUT	4	
*Disk Configuration, Data Layout	RAID 0	
NCLIST	2048	
NPROC, NREGION	800 2400	
NSCRN, CTBUFSIZ	0 128	
Display adapter, colors	n/a	
Mouse Settings	n/a	
Other Memory Used	n/a	

Worksheet 5-14: SCO UNIX Operating System Tuning worksheet for the File Operation

Resources to Monitor	**Initial Values**	**2 CPU**
Free Memory, Free swap	2561 65536	1289 65536
Blocks Swapped in/out	0.0 0.0	0.0 0.0
Pages Reclaimed	0	0
CPU: %usr, %sys, %wio, %idle	13 77 9 0	12 73 14 1
Scheduling: runq-sz, swpq-sz, pswch/s	42.0 0 119	65.0 0 266
Namei Cache	99%	99%
File Table, Inode Table	319 0 234 0	426 0 296 0
Buffer Cache %rcache Reads: bread/s lread/s Writes: bwrit/s, lwrit/s	96 79 2090 68 562	97 108 3505 114 767
Scatter/Gather: mpbuf/s, ompb/s, mphbuf/s, omphbufs/s	0 0 21 0	0 0 30 0
Copy Buffers	0 0	0 0
Direct Disk Requests	0 0	0 0
Copy Memory	0 0	0 0
Sdsk Request Blocks		
Disk Driver : %busy avque, r+w/s, blks/s, avwait, avserv	100 2 27 133 17 36	100 2 43 224 22 266
ida-1	100 2 22 160 7 61	100 3 31 220 19 87

Now	**Your Goal**	**Monitoring**	**2 CPU**
450	450	486	500

Worksheet 5-15: SCO MPX Tuning Worksheet for the File Operation

Tunables	**Initial Values**	**2 CPU**
*Number of CPUs	1	2
loadbalance		0
preemptive		0
dopricalc		0
primove		10
cache_affinity		0
Resources to Monitor	**Initial Values**	**2 CPU**
CPU 1: %usr, %sys, %wio, %idle		12 73 14 1
CPU 2: %usr, %sys, %wio, %idle		13 73 14 0
CPU 3: %usr, %sys, %wio, %idle		
CPU 4: %usr, %sys, %wio, %idle		
CPU 1 InterCPU interrupts		
CPU 2 InterCPU interrupts		
CPU 3 InterCPU interrupts		
CPU 4 InterCPU Interrupts		

Now	**Monitoring**	**Your Goal**	**2 CPU**

Chapter 6

Common Open Desktop Operations

This chapter describes typical operations that are executed on an Open Desktop system. An Open Desktop system interacts closely with the user, so display update and keyboard/mouse response are important aspects of Open Desktop system performance. Much of this chapter is devoted to the keyboard echo and display update operation.

The common theme underlying the Open Desktop operations is the shortage of available memory. The mechanisms that SCO UNIX uses to compensate for memory shortages are discussed at the beginning of this chapter. Because Open Desktop applications tend to be large and the amount of memory in an Open Desktop system tends to be small, optimizing system memory usage is key to successful Open Desktop tuning. This goal underlies most of the resource interactions and tuning recommendations for these common operations. Many of the tuning recommendations described in this chapter apply to any SCO UNIX or SCO MPX system that experiences a memory shortage.

The display update and keyboard/mouse response operation affects Open Desktop users because the responsiveness of the system to key presses and mouse movements is critical to efficient system use. This section describes all of the interactions that occur, the resources that are used, and possible changes to the resource usage patterns. Chapter 7 contains a case study illustrating the impact of a memory shortage and the effects of adding additional memory on a display update operation.

A Word about Monitoring Tools

The Open Desktop monitoring tools are the same as the SCO UNIX monitoring tools. In addition to the tools described in the Common SCO UNIX Operations chapter, a new tool for monitoring memory management is introduced in this chapter. This new tool is called vmstat(C) and is described in more detail in the on-line manual pages.

The vmstat command provides a snapshot of the system paging activity information differently from sar or mpsar. The sar command provides frequency-oriented information, such as requests per second, while vmstat provides absolute statistics, such as total number of requests. The vmstat command provides many of the same statistics, but not in a frequency-oriented manner. Only the statistics that are different from those reported by sar are discussed in this chapter.

The units of the values reported by the different options of the monitoring tools vary. In some cases, the values are reported in units of 512-bytes, and in other cases in units of 1 Kbyte or 4 Kbytes. When comparing statistics between the monitoring tools, check that the units are compatible before drawing any conclusions.

How SCO UNIX Manages Memory

Since SCO UNIX is the underlying operating system in Open Desktop, this discussion of memory management applies to SCO UNIX, SCO MPX, Open Desktop and Open Server. A majority of this discussion applies to SCO UNIX, SCO MPX and Open Desktop operating system releases prior to release 3.0.

An application uses memory for three purposes: *instructions*, *stack*, and *data*. The instructions are the binary encoding of the CPU commands used to complete the application operations. The stack area provides a temporary work space where the application and the operating system keep track of what functions the application has called. The application temporarily stores information in the data area that it requires to complete operations.

SCO UNIX provides applications with more memory than the physical amount of memory present in the machine with a mechanism called *virtual memory*. In order for the application to use the memory, a virtual memory location must be associated with a physical memory location. The operating system initializes this association when the application starts running.

NREGION

Virtual memory is divided into 4 Kbyte sections known as *pages*. The operating system manages these pages with a data structure called a *region*. When the operating system boots, it allocates the total number of region data structures. The total number of regions is determined by the value of NREGION.

page fault

When the application begins executing, the application instructions stored in the filesystem are copied into memory as the instructions are needed. The mechanism by which necessary pages are copied into memory when the application first starts is known as a *page fault*. Page faults also occur for the following reasons:

- when the operating system copies a page from the swap device
- when the application first modifies a page so that an application-specific copy of the page is required to store the application information. This mechanism is known as *copy-on-write*.
- when the application first accesses a byte in virtual memory and no physical memory has been allocated to store that byte

The operating system stores the virtual memory pages either in physical memory or in a special disk partition known as a *swap area*. Only pages that are not copied from the filesystem are stored in the swap area. If all of the applications have enough memory, the operating system does not use the swap area.

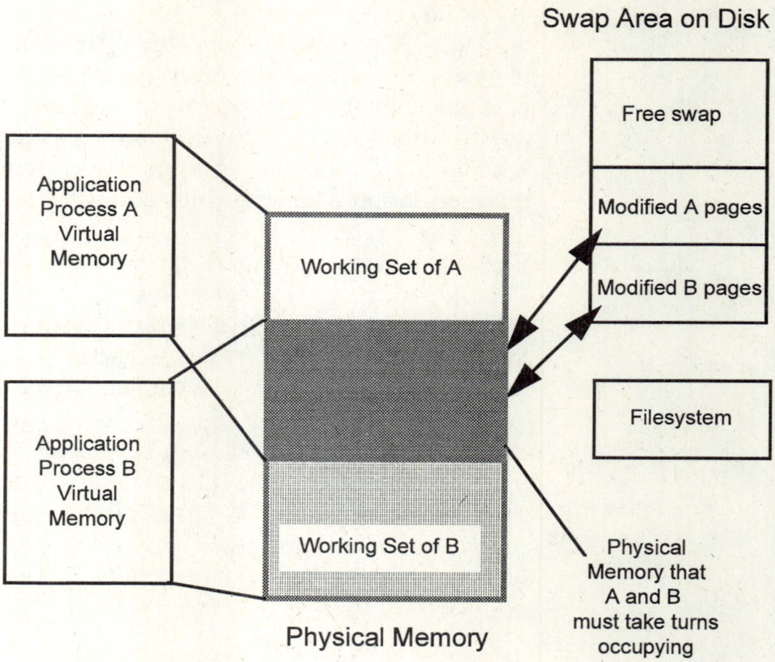

Figure 6-1: Application processes A and B require more memory than is currently available. A and B must take turns accessing some of the memory in order for both of them to run. The pages of the application that are frequently accessed and left in memory are called the working set. The working sets of A and B are represented by the two pairs of shaded areas called working set of A and working set of B. The working sets remain resident unless more memory is needed. The working set of A and B are not necessarily physically contiguous.

When the system starts to run short of physical memory, the operating system makes more memory available by transferring the information contained in pages from physical memory to the swap area on the disk. Only the modified pages, such as those comprising application data space, are transferred to the swap device. This operation frees physical memory for other uses. However, moving data from memory to the disk consumes more CPU and disk resources, thereby adversely impacting system performance.

SCO UNIX has two methods for moving data from physical memory to the disk. These methods are known as *paging* and *swapping*. Figure 6-1 shows the relationships between physical memory, virtual memory and the swap areas.

Paging

When the operating system begins paging, it transfers pages to the swap area that have not been accessed recently. This transfer operation is known as *paging out*. Paging also involves transferring pages from the swap area to memory when they are required by the application. This operation is known as *paging in*. Paging in and out are transparent to the application. The operating system uses direct disk access to transfer pages to and from the swap device. When the pages are copied to memory from the swap device, direct disk access control blocks are allocated.

Application response times may be reduced when paging is occurring, because the CPU is busy moving data from memory to the disk instead of executing the application. The amount of data travelling between the disk and memory also increases, and the usage of all the resources associated with copying data to and from the disks is increased.

The operating system determines the pages that have not been used recently with the *page table* feature of the Intel i386 and later microprocessors. Page tables describe the layout of the application's memory and provide a bookkeeping mechanism for memory usage statistics. When a page is accessed, a *referenced* bit is set in the entry corresponding to that page in a data structure known as the *page table entry*.

AGEINTERVAL

Before the operating system starts paging, the operating system scans all of the application page table entries and resets the referenced bits. If the bit is set when the scan occurs again, the operating system knows the page is accessed frequently, and so is not a candidate for transfer to the swap area. The frequency of the memory scan is controlled by the tunable parameter AGEINTERVAL.

A frequently accessed page is a member of that application's *working set*. The operating system tries to keep the working set of the application resident in memory as its best attempt at maintaining adequate performance even when the system has insufficient memory. Therefore, members of the application's working set are not transferred to the disk unless the need for physical memory is acute.

The operating system scans memory only when the amount of free memory is less than 5 * GPGSLO. Aging stops when the amount of free memory in the system is greater than or equal to the value of GPGSLO * 10. For example, if GPGSLO is 25, then the operating system starts to age pages when the amount of free memory is equal to 125 pages. Aging stops when the amount of free memory is equal to 250 pages. Five is the current default value for the multiplier that determines the start of aging.

Increasing AGEINTERVAL reduces the scanning frequency, while decreasing AGEINTERVAL increases the frequency. Although increasing AGEINTERVAL means the operating system spends less time scanning memory, the accuracy of the application's working set is also reduced, since the information as to which pages are accessed frequently is not updated regularly. The accuracy of this information affects the efficiency of paging, since pages that are accessed very frequently are treated the same as pages that are only occasionally accessed. In the worst case, frequently accessed pages are paged out before infrequently accessed pages because they are both marked as part of the working set.

If the working set is resident in memory, then the application can complete its operations without the operating system transferring pages from the disk to memory. When the use of the application changes, the members of the working set usually change because different parts of the application are required to complete the new operation.

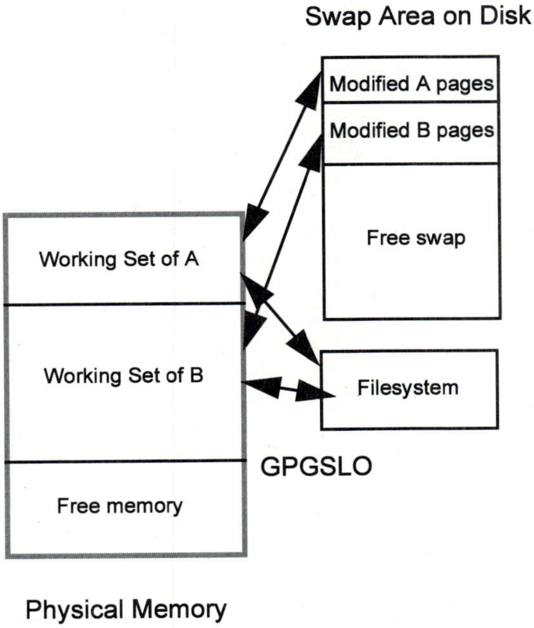

Figure 6-2: When vhand begins, only GPGSLO number of pages are free. The swap device also contains a large amount of free space.

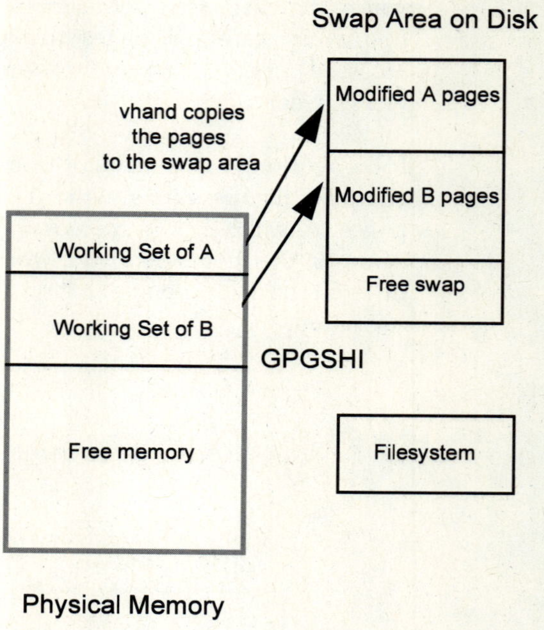

Figure 6-3: The system process vhand reduces the working sets of A and B until GPGSHI number of pages are free. The modified pages are transferred to the swap device. The filesystem pages are discarded because they can be retrieved from the filesystem when needed by the application process.

The change in the working set may cause some paging activity, and a delay may be observed. For example, a change in application usage might be moving from entering text in a word processing application to spell checking the entire document. On a system with a memory shortage, paging occurs until the new working set for the word processor spell checking functions are established.

vhand A system process known as *vhand* scans all of the regions currently in use looking for pages that have not been accessed recently. Figure 6-2 and 6-2 show the relationship between GPGSLO, GPGSHI and vhand.

GPGSLO, GPGSHI

The tunable parameters GPGSLO and GPGSHI are thresholds that control the start and end of vhand execution. The vhand process begins to execute when either of the following events occur:

- The amount of free memory reaches GPGSLO
- A clock tick occurs and any process is waiting to allocate memory (the B state displayed by ps -el in the S column)

The vhand process stops executing when either of the following events occurs:

- A single pass through all the working sets of the applications is complete
- The amount of free memory reaches GPGSHI

If the amount of free memory does not reach GPGSHI after the first pass through memory, then vhand is suspended until the next clock tick. When the next clock tick occurs, vhand makes another pass through the working sets. The minimum number of pages reclaimed by vhand is equal to GPGSHI minus GPGSLO.

The system process vhand determines which pages to transfer by first selecting those that have the least impact on application performance. The operating system maintains two lists of pages to be reclaimed as follows:

- Those that are stored in the filesystem and so do not need to be transferred to the swap area because these pages can be retrieved from the filesystem when needed
- Those that must be transferred to the swap area

Pages that are stored in the filesystem are reclaimed before pages that must be transferred to the swap area.

After the operating system reclaims the page, the operating system invalidates the page table entry for that page. Invalid pages are added to the end of a list known as the *page free list.* When the operating system allocates memory to applications, the operating system takes pages from the front of the list. This list is managed so the same pages can be obtained should they be needed by the application before they are reallocated to a different application or allocated to the same application for a different purpose.

Because the operating system suspends the application while this paging activity occurs, the performance of the application is impacted by the shortage of memory.

Swapping

When paging does not reclaim the amount of memory required by the applications, the operating system frees memory by swapping. Swapping involves the selection of much larger areas of memory for transfer to the swap area. When the data used for managing a process is moved to the disk, the process is said to be *swapped out.* The operating system cannot execute the process until its data is moved back into memory, or *swapped in.* When a system swaps, large amounts of data are copied to and from the disk. Response time is reduced because the operating system uses resources for swapping rather than for completing application operations.

sched

Swapping is managed by a system process known as *sched.* The sched process is suspended until an application requests more memory than is currently available.

When the application requests more memory than is currently available, it is suspended and marked as needing memory. This state is noted with a B in the S column of the ps -el display for that process. The operating system then executes the sched process so it can begin swapping processes until enough free memory is available to satisfy the requirements of the process in the needing-memory state.

Figures 6-4 and 6-5 show the state of the swap area and physical memory before and after sched has swapped out a process because another process needed memory.

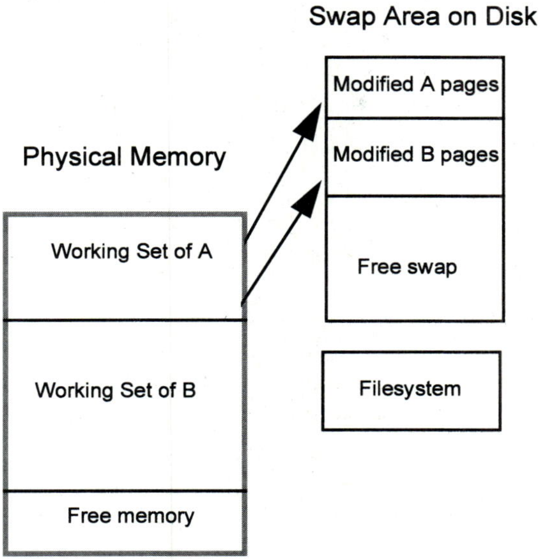

Figure 6-4: Application process B is running on the CPU and requests more memory than is currently available. The system process sched starts to free memory to satisfy the memory request. While sched is attempting to free memory, process B is marked as needing-memory.

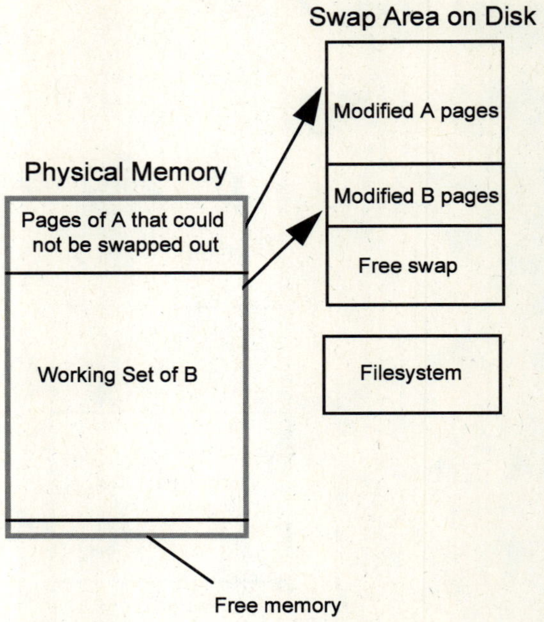

Figure 6-5: The system process sched has finished swapping out application process A. The amount of free memory and the amount of free swap have both decreased. The swap space is now occupied by part of process A, and more physical memory is occupied by process B. The state of process B is now running on the processor.

The sched process first selects candidates for swapping out that are currently suspended waiting for resources, or ones that have a lower priority than the applications currently executing. More memory may still be required after swapping out these applications. If more memory is still necessary, the sched process selects lower priority applications that are waiting for the CPU.

The sched process only swaps a lower priority process if it has been located in memory for at least two seconds. The sched process also executes periodically and assesses whether to change the swapped processes by swapping some processes in and others out.

When a process is swapped out, as many of the memory pages associated with that process as are necessary to alleviate the memory shortage are transferred to the disk. Occasionally, the operating system is restricted in the pages it can copy to the disk. Swapping a process releases more memory than paging, and also consumes more disk and CPU resources, because of the increased amount of information travelling between the disk and CPU.

MAXSC

The configurable variable MAXSC states the number of pages that can be transferred to the disk in one paging operation. The higher the value, the larger the disk transfer size. This variable allows the system administrator to increase the efficiency of disk adapters that operates more optimally with fewer large requests than with more small requests. The documentation for the disk adapter may provide some information on whether large requests are more optimal. The value of MAXSC must not be modified for releases of Open Desktop prior to Open Desktop 3.0 and releases of SCO UNIX prior to 3.2v4.2.

When the operating system moves data between the physical memory and the swap device, additional CPU and disk resources are used. Moving data between the physical memory and the swap device lengthens the response time for most operations. Paging and swapping can be frustrating to watch, because much disk activity occurs, but the application display does not change. Even with all the disk activity, the application cannot complete the operation because it is waiting for memory.

The effect of paging and swapping on system performance can be determined by monitoring the number of processes that are affected and the amount of additional resources that are consumed when the system is paging and/or swapping.

Table 6-1 summarizes the commands used to monitor resources used by paging and swapping. Table 6-1 is presented in the order that the paging and swapping statistics should be examined. When monitoring SCO MPX, use mpsar in place of sar to monitor each of these behaviors.

Behavior	Command	Column
The amount of free swap space measured in 512-byte blocks	swap -l	free
The amount of free memory in pages	sar -r	freemem
Number of pages that are reclaimed by vhand or sched per second	sar -p	rclm/s
Average number of processes that are swapped out	sar -q	swpq-sz
Percentage of time during the interval that at least one process has been swapped out	sar -q	%swpocc
The number of disk transfers used for copying data from disk to memory per second	sar -w	swpin/s
Total number of 512-byte blocks copied from swap area to memory per second	sar -w	bswin/s
The number of disk transfers used for copying data from memory to disk per second	sar -w	swpot/s
Total number of 512-byte blocks copied from memory to swap area per second	sar -w	bswot/s

Table 6-1: Paging and Swapping Statistics

Behavior	Command	Column
Total number of processes swapped out	vmstat -s	Success in swapping out a process
Total number of processes that have failed to be swapped in	vmstat -s	Fail in swapping in a process
Total number of times processes swapped in	vmstat -s	Success in swapping in a process
Amount of CPU time consumed by vhand	ps -el	vhand: TIME
Amount of CPU time consumed by sched	ps -el	sched: TIME
Average number of pages transferred from the filesystem per second	sar -p	pgfil/s

Table 6-1(Continued): Paging and Swapping Statistics

swap -l The value displayed in the blocks column is the total amount of free swap space. This value is displayed in units of 512-bytes. The following equation describes the total amount of swap space used:

$$\frac{(blocks\_column - free\_column)}{2} = swap\_space\_used(1\ Kbyte\ units)$$

This value provides an approximation to the amount of additional memory needed to stop paging and swapping.

sar -r The sar -r command reports the average amount of free memory in the freemem column. This value is reported in units of 4 Kbytes.

sar -p The rate that pages are being freed by either sched or vhand is shown by the rclm/s column displayed by sar -p. This column shows the average number of pages that are reclaimed by vhand and sched per second. The higher the value, the more actively vhand or sched free pages. When this value is zero, neither paging nor swapping are occurring.

sar -q The column swpq-sz shows the average number of processes swapped out during the time interval specified when sar was invoked. The higher this value, the greater the amount of resources used by sched to overcome the memory shortage. The amount of CPU time accumulated by the sched process can be found by using ps -el and looking at the TIME column. If the system has somehow reached an equilibrium in terms of memory needs, then swapping may no longer be necessary and the amount of time accumulated by sched stops increasing.

The %swpocc column indicates the percentage of time one or more processes are swapped out during the time interval specified in sar. If the value is 100%, then at least one process is always swapped out, but not necessarily the same process over that time period. The value is a percentage occupancy measurement and does not accumulate statistics for individual processes. A value of 50% indicates that for half of the interval specified, at least one process was swapped out.

The number of processes that are affected by swapping is shown by the percentage of time that at least one process is swapped out and by the average number of processes that are swapped out. If at least one process, not necessarily the same one, is swapped out all the time, then overall application performance is affected because additional resources are used to swap processes in and out of memory.

sar -w The sar -w command shows the amount of disk activity consumed by paging and swapping. The swpin/s value indicates the number of disk transfers occurring per second for copying data from the disk to memory. The larger the value, the greater the amount of disk activity.

The bswin/s column shows the average number of 512-byte blocks copied from the swap area on disk to memory per second. The average number of disk blocks sent with each disk request can be calculated with the following equation:

$$\frac{bwin/s}{swpin/s} = average\_number\_of\_blocks\_per\_disk\_request$$

The greater the ratio, the more blocks are transferred to the disk for each paging or swapping disk request. The lower the ratio, the fewer blocks are transferred for each request, and the disk usage is less than optimal. The number of blocks per disk request is dependent on the memory usage pattern and is not configurable.

The values reported in the columns swpot/s and bswot/s are similar to these reported in bswin/s and swpin/s, except the values account for disk transfers for copying pages to the swap area instead of from the disk to the swap area. The value of bswot/s is reported in units of 512-byte blocks. The equation described above also applies to calculating the average number of blocks per disk request for copying pages to the swap area.

vmstat -s

The vmstat -s command provides cumulative information rather than the frequency-oriented information reported by sar. The total number of processes that have been successfully swapped out is displayed in the row corresponding to "success in swapping out."

Attempts to swap a process in fail when severe memory shortages exist. The total number of times that the operating system attempted to swap a process in, but for some reason the attempt failed, is displayed in the row corresponding to the "fail in swapping in a process."

The total number of times the operating system successfully swapped a process in is shown in the row corresponding to the "success in swapping in a process."

sar -p

The sar -p command shows the average number of pages that are paged in from the filesystem per second in the pgfil/s column. This value is reported in units of 4 Kbytes.

HINT :

The total amount of disk activity attributable to paging and swapping per second is shown by the following equation:

$$(\mathit{pgfil/s})*8 + \mathit{bswin/s} + \mathit{bswot/s} = \mathit{total\_disk\_activity}\ (512\text{-byte blocks})$$

Memory is used most efficiently when the maximum amount of memory is available to the applications that are active on the system.

The steps to achieve efficient memory usage are as follows:

1. Run the active applications and see how much memory is required by calculating the amount of swap space used with the equation for swap -l. Continue to free memory or add memory until swap space usage is minimized. Free all memory not actively used by the applications or the operating system. Appendix B contains suggestions for saving memory.

2. If a memory shortage remains, tune paging to regulate the frequency and intensity of disk activity. This step has a marginal effect on performance since paging must still occur to alleviate the memory shortage.

Tuning AGEINTERVAL is unlikely to give rise to improved performance if the system is already paging, because a majority of the resources are consumed by the paging activity and not by the operating system bookkeeping. With a higher frequency of aging, more CPU time is consumed for bookkeeping, but the working set definition is generally more accurate because the information is updated regularly.

The values of GPGSLO and GPGSHI control the frequency and aggressiveness of the background memory reclamation process. The optimal settings for GPGSLO and GPGSHI depends on the memory usage patterns of the system and whether the users want vhand to run constantly and reclaim small amounts of memory, or infrequently, but reclaiming large amounts of memory.

The greater the difference between these two variables, the more pages are trimmed from the working set of each process. Conversely, the smaller the difference between these two variables, the less the working sets are trimmed and the lower the amount of reclaimed free memory after vhand executes.

Changing the values of GPGSLO and GPGSHI does not solve the underlying memory shortage. Instead, changing these values allows the system administrator to change how the operating system attempts to compensate for the memory shortage.

Whether a system does start to swap depends on the memory usage pattern of the applications. If the application makes small and infrequent requests for additional memory, paging may provide sufficient free memory for those requests to be satisfied. If the application makes large and frequent requests for memory, the likelihood of swapping increases. Changing the pattern of application usage may decrease the chance of swapping.

Swapping may actually benefit the performance of some common operations by ensuring that only the processes that are running and require memory are occupying memory. For example, a *getty* process runs for each console multiscreen. If the X server is configured to run on a single console screen, the other getty processes running for the other multiscreens are typically not executed. Eventually, these unused processes are swapped out, thereby leaving memory for those processes that are actually running.

If the common operation uses only a few processes that are small enough to remain fully resident after all the unnecessary processes have been swapped out, then system performance may be identical to one with a larger amount of memory that has not undergone swapping. Such a scenario is infrequent, as X windows and Motif™ applications tend to be quite complex, sometimes involving multiple large processes. The likelihood of having sufficient memory left over to run the active applications after swapping unused processes is small.

Mouse and Keyboard Response Display Update

Moving the mouse and typing at the keyboard cause changes to the display on the computer screen. How quickly the computer screen responds to mouse movements and key presses often determines the productivity of the time spent with the computer system.

Updating the display after typing or moving the mouse involves a number of different resources and intermediate storage locations. This common operation description starts at the keyboard and mouse and traces the operations that are required to transform that key press or mouse movement into an event that causes the display to be updated. The interactions of these intermediate storage locations are shown in Figure 6-6.

The Mouse, Keyboard and Event Driver

Key presses and mouse movements generate interrupts that are handled by special purpose device drivers in the operating system. These device drivers process the interrupts and pass the events to a central input device driver called the *event driver*. The event driver passes the information regarding keyboard and mouse inputs, or any other type of input device, to the X server in a format that the X server recognizes.

After the mouse is moved, the X server updates the screen location of the cursor. Changing the location of the mouse cursor in response to a mouse movement is a form of updating the display. Because Open Desktop supports many different mouse types and related types of input devices, a number of configurable variables are provided to customize the input device behavior.

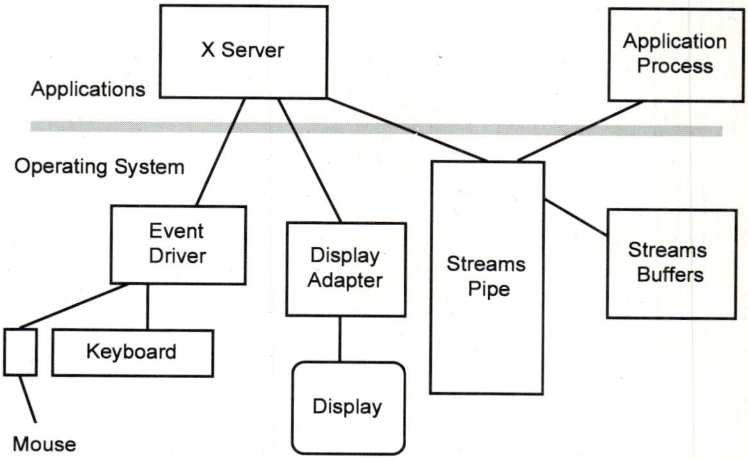

Figure 6-6: After the user moves the mouse or types a key, the mouse and keyboard drivers send events to the event driver. The X server reads these events and sends them to the appropriate application process via the streams pipe mechanism. Based on this event, the application process decides what to change on the display and sends the instructions to the X server over the streams pipe. The X server manipulates the display adapter to change the display.

kbm_poll, kbm_poll_max

The value of kbm_poll and kbm_poll_max control the smoothness of the keyboard mouse cursor motion. This variable only changes the behavior of the keyboard mouse. If the keyboard mouse cursor motion is not smooth, then increase the value of kbm_poll in */etc/conf/pack.d/kbmouse/space.c.* Increasing the values of kbm_poll and kbm_poll_max causes the mouse driver to read the mouse motion information more frequently. This increased frequency smooths the mouse motion on faster systems by ensuring that all the mouse events are read by the operating system and none are inadvertently missed. On machines with 66 MHz CPUs, the value of kbm_poll_max can be increased to a maximum of the default value plus 1000.

SENSITIVITY Mouse sensitivity is the distance the mouse must move before a motion event is recognized. The sensitivity is adjusted by modifying the variable SENSITIVITY in */usr/lib/event/devices* that corresponds to the mouse type used. The mouse type associated with each multiscreen is listed in */usr/lib/events/ttys*. The X server must be restarted in order for the change in sensitivity to take effect. Reducing the value of SENSITIVITY means the mouse must be moved a greater distance in order for a motion to be detected. Increasing the value means the mouse must be moved a shorter distance in order for the movement to be detected.

The scomouse(X) utility can be used to set mouse behavior within an Open Desktop session. All values set with scomouse(X) take priority over existing default values. Both sensitivity and acceleration can be set with scomouse(X). *Acceleration* defines how the sensitivity of the mouse changes when the mouse is moved a small or a large amount.

No monitoring tools are available to monitor mouse and keyboard behavior.

The CPU is required for responding to interrupts from the keyboard and mouse devices and for converting the data to a form the X server understands. If the CPU is not available to handle these interrupts, then delays in mouse cursor update and keyboard echo may be experienced. Increase the availability of the CPU with the recommendations provided in the calculations section of the Common SCO UNIX Operations chapter. Minimizing paging and swapping activity also increases CPU availability.

The X Server

The X server is a special application process that manages the screen. The X server reads the events from the event driver and then distributes them to the applications running on the Open Desktop system. While the X server updates the display or processes other events, any new events generated by key presses or mouse movements remain in the X server queue until the server has completed processing the events previously received.

Before the X server can process an event, the working set of the X server that manipulates events must be in memory. If parts of the X server are paged out, then these pages are transferred from the swap area or the filesystem to memory before event processing can continue. Paging is another source of delay in the time between when a key is pressed and when the display is updated in response to that key.

The amount of processing that the X server must do on the keyboard or mouse events varies. For example, if the user is changing the current input focus, the X server may need to send an event to the application currently owning that window notifying it that the window has been lost. The X server must also send another event to the application owning the new window notifying it that the window has been obtained. However, if only the mouse cursor position has changed, the cursor location is updated and the next event can be processed.

Because the X server is an application process, the same tools used to monitor application processes can be used to monitor the X server. Table 6-2 shows how to monitor application resource usage.

Behavior	**Command**	**Column**
The amount of CPU time used by the process	ps -el	TIME
The amount of memory used by the process	ps -el	SZ
State of the process	ps -el	S
Number of ready-to-run processes	sar -q	runq-sz

Table 6-2: How to Monitor Application Resource Usage

These statistics are described in more detail in the Common SCO UNIX Operations chapter.

The X server shares the CPU resource with all the other applications and with the operating system. Paging, swapping, or other CPU-consuming operations can cause the X server to wait for the CPU to become available before the X server can continue processing events. This delay lengthens the time required to update the display, thereby affecting system responsiveness.

When Open Desktop is running on a system with a memory shortage, the first key press or mouse motion may cause disk activity and a delay in the response to the input events After a few keys are typed, however, these additional keys cause no disk activity and the delay is reduced considerably. If this situation occurs, the operating system is responding to the shortage of memory by changing the working set of pages when the key was first pressed. After the system determines the new working set, then no disk transfers from the swap area are required to continue handling keystrokes.

Streams and Stream Pipes

After the X server has processed the key, the key press event travels to the application. Since multiple windows could be open on the screen, the application that receives the key press is determined by which window is the currently active window. Information travels between the X server and the application when both processes are running on the same machine using a mechanism called a *stream pipe*.

When the X server is running on a different machine than the client application, the X server uses a similar mechanism to read events from the network, except the messages travel over the network rather than locally. See the Monitoring Client/Server Connections chapter for more information on these types of connections.

A stream pipe is similar to a standard SCO UNIX pipe(S), except the underlying transfer mechanism uses streams instead of the filesystem.

Streams is a message-oriented communication pathway between two processes. The message data is stored in buffers. The CPU copies the data from the application to the streams buffer and then from the streams buffer to the X server. If the CPU is busy executing other operations, then a delay in this message transfer may occur. See the Monitoring Client/Server Connections chapter for more information on streams.

When an application must draw on the display managed by the X server, the application constructs a streams message for the X server in a format that the X server recognizes. The X server reads the message after the message has travelled through the stream pipe. Applications also use stream pipes when communicating with the X server after the application decides what parts of its window needs to be updated as a result of the new input information.

Table 6-3 summarizes how to monitor streams usage when TCP/IP is installed.

Behavior	**Command**	**Column/row**
Number of queues configured	netstat -m	config/queues
Number of queues in use	netstat -m	alloc/queues
Number of queues free	netstat -m	free/queues
Total number queues allocated since the operating system booted	netstat -m	total/queues
Maximum number of queues allocated since the operating system booted	netstat -m	max/queues

Table 6-3: How to Monitor Streams Usage

Behavior	Command	Column/row
Number of queue allocation failures since the operating system booted	netstat -m	fail/queues
Number of "class 0" or 4 byte streams buffers configured	netstat -m	config/class 0, 4 bytes
Number of 4 byte streams buffers allocated	netstat -m	alloc/class 0, 4 bytes
Number of unallocated 4 byte streams buffers	netstat -m	free/class 0, 4 bytes
Total number of 4 byte streams buffers allocated since the operating system booted	netstat -m	total/class 0, 4 bytes
Maximum number of 4 byte streams buffers allocated since the operating system booted	netstat -m	max/class 0, 4 bytes
Number of failures to allocate 4 byte streams buffers since the operating system booted	netstat -m	fail/class 0, 4 bytes

Table 6-3 (Continued): How to Monitor Streams Usage

netstat -m netstat -m is described in more detail in the Monitoring Client/Server Connections chapter.

crash If TCP/IP is not installed on the system, then use crash(ADM) with the strstat option to view streams usage information. The information displayed by crash is identical to the information displayed by netstat -m, except only the size is noted instead of both class and size. The total amount of memory is also not displayed.

The X server generally uses 64- and 128-byte messages, so always check these to ensure that the supply is sufficient. However, other types of buffers may also be used, so all sizes of buffers should be monitored.

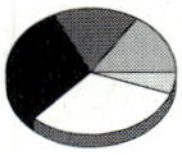

Monitoring streams usage over time is important to efficient communication between the X server and the applications. If the X server must wait for an appropriately sized streams buffer to become available, then the time required for the display to be updated is increased. See the Monitoring Client/Server Connections chapter for more information on allocating streams.

The memory used by the stream pipe mechanism is not subject to paging or swapping. Reducing paging/swapping activity affects the efficiency of this mechanism only from the standpoint of freeing the CPU to copy the data from the streams buffers to the appropriate location in the X server or the application.

Application Behavior

When the application receives the keyboard or mouse movement information from the X server, the application determines how to update its window. The part of the application responsible for determining the changes must be resident in memory in order for these decisions to be made. If the working set that is resident in memory does not include the correct pages, then additional pages must be transferred from the swap area or from the filesystem. This transfer adds delay to the handling of key press events or mouse movements.

If memory is in short supply and the operating system has swapped out the application, the operating system transfers the necessary pages from the swap area and the filesystem to memory. Because insufficient memory is available to hold the necessary pages, the operating system frees some physical memory by transferring other applications that are currently in memory out to the swap area. When enough memory is available, the operating system copies the target application to memory.

Because Open Desktop applications tend to occupy large amounts of memory, such a swapping operation may take some time and generate a large amount of disk activity. If such disk activity occurs in response to the key presses, then the target application has very likely been swapped out and now must be transferred back to memory before it can continue executing.

After the application decides how to update its window, the application sends messages via stream pipes to the X server telling the X server what to draw in order to update the application window.

The same monitoring tools described in the X server section can be used to monitor the application.

With some Open Desktop applications, the amount of memory needed for the application binary can be greater than 8 Mbytes. The memory needed for the application binary is a fixed size and cannot be changed. The amount of additional memory required by the application after it starts running may be configurable, so check the application documentation for variables that can be changed to modify the amount of additional memory needed by the application.

Many Open Desktop applications use shared libraries of frequently accessed functions. A shared library allows multiple applications to simultaneously access the same set of commonly accessed function. Shared libraries use memory more efficiently than static libraries, because static libraries require a copy of the commonly accessed functions to be included with each application using the functions. Since both the Motif™ and Xlib shared libraries are quite large, applications that use the shared libraries save a considerable amount of memory when multiple applications are used. Shared libraries for Xlib and Motif are not provided with Open Desktop releases 1.0 and 1.1. To save memory, consider upgrading any applications that are compiled with these early releases to applications that are compiled on Open Desktop 2.0 or later.

The Display Adapter and Display

The X server updates the display by manipulating the display adapter hardware. These display adapters are also known as graphics adapters or video adapters. The speed at which the screen can be updated has a great impact on the time required for the system to respond to mouse movements and keystrokes.

Some display adapters are equipped with processors that can move and manipulate information on the display without requiring the CPU. Others require the CPU to complete all the necessary actions to update the display.

frame buffer

Most adapters provide an area of memory that represents the information actually visible on the screen. Generally this memory is modified by either the graphics adaptor processor or the CPU before the contents are redisplayed on the screen. This memory is often called the *frame buffer*.

If the CPU modifies this memory then the new information to be displayed is transferred from physical memory to the frame buffer across the system bus. Depending on the capabilities of the graphics adapter, the CPU may be required to execute this transfer operation. Otherwise, the CPU must wait for this transfer to complete before proceeding with other operations. If the system bus is of high capacity, then the information can travel very quickly. Some hardware manufacturers provide different versions of their adapters suitable for different types of system buses. For example, the Compaq QVision™ adapter is available in both ISA and EISA versions.

Local Bus

Some hardware platforms provide what is known as a *local bus*. An example of a local bus is the Peripheral Component Interface (PCI). A local bus provides a fast and direct bus between a graphics adapter and the CPU. Because display adapters often require large data transfers, they are nearly always the first adapter attached to a local bus. Such a hardware feature greatly improves the speed at which the display is updated.

VRAM

The hardware on the display adapter also affects the speed with which the CPU can write information to the adapter's memory. An adapter can use memory called Video Random Access Memory, VRAM. With VRAM, the CPU and the graphics hardware can simultaneously access the frame buffer. This type of memory is sometimes referred to as *dual-ported memory* because two hardware functions can access the memory simultaneously. Adapters with Dynamic Random Access Memory, DRAM, do not support simultaneous access, so the CPU waits to access the memory while the graphics hardware accesses the video memory.

Since large amounts of information are often transferred between physical memory and the frame buffer, the speed at which data can be moved to the display hardware is critical to rapid display update. If the adapter supports 256 colors, then one byte per pixel is transferred. If a 400 x 400 pixel image is updated, then 400 * 400, or 160,000, bytes must be transferred to the graphics hardware. If only 16 colors are used, then two pixels fit into one byte, which means only half the amount of data must be transferred.

In some cases applications automatically scale their output to take into account the size of the physical display. With a higher resolution display mode, for example 1024 x 768 instead of 800 x 600, more pixels need to be updated to ensure the image on the display is of a fixed size. In such cases, use a lower display resolution and use mkdev(ADM) graphics to change the current system settings.

xpyinfo(X)

Determine the number of colors that are supported by the X server with the xpyinfo(X) command. The line that reads depth of root window states how many planes are supported; the number of colors is two raised to the power of this value as shown by the following equation:

$$2**(depth\_of\_root\_window) = number\_of\_colors$$

For example, if depth of root window equals one, then the number of colors supported is two, because two to the power of one equals two. If a four is displayed, then the X server supports 16 colors because two to the power of four equals 16. If that many colors are not necessary, try selecting a smaller number of colors with mkdev graphics and reconfiguring the display adapter. Reducing the number of colors may improve the performance of updating the display.

No monitoring tools are provided with Open Desktop to monitor the display adapter and display. Check the hardware documentation for any additional tools that may be provided.

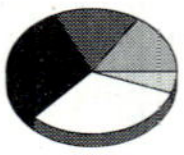

If the system is not paging and not performing any other activity at the time of the display update, then one solution to reducing the time taken by the display update operation is to purchase a graphics adapter with more capabilities and higher speed. Always check that the adapter is supported by Open Desktop or is provided with an Open Desktop driver.

One way of determining the speed of the display adapter is to start a single window and move the window around on the screen with the mouse. Do this test when no other applications are running. The first time the window is moved, the update may take some time because some paging may occur to replenish the working set of the application. If the window is moved again, then additional paging should not be necessary. The system display adapter may be slowing down the display update operation if the redrawing required to update the window from top to the bottom is observable.

Verify that the correct graphics driver is configured for the adapter installed in the system. Using the correct graphics driver is important for maximum performance of the graphics hardware. Examine the current graphics driver assigned to each multiscreen by reading the file */usr/lib/grafinfo/grafdev*. If the driver specified does not precisely match the graphics hardware installed, use mkdev graphics to see if a more appropriate driver is available. If so, then change the assignment of graphics drivers using mkdev graphics.

Quick Diagnosis Summary

Memory shortage is often a cause of delay in display update and other operations executed in Open Desktop. How to monitor key aspects of memory usage is summarized in Table 6-4. When monitoring SCO MPX, use mpsar in place of sar to monitor each of these behaviors. Suggestions for making more memory available are included in Appendix B.

Behavior	Command	Column
The amount of free swap space measured in 512-byte blocks	swap -l	free
The amount of free memory in pages	sar -r	freemem
Number of pages that are freed by vhand or sched per second	sar -p	rclm/s
Average number of processes that are swapped out	sar -q	swpq-sz
Total number of 512-byte blocks copied from disk swap area to memory per second	sar -w	bswin/s
Total number of 512-byte blocks copied from memory to disk swap area per second	sar -w	bswot/s

Table 6-4: Paging and Swapping Statistics

The X server is similar to any other application process and so must share resources, such as memory and CPU, with all the other application processes running on the system. Adequate X server performance relies on the system having a sufficient amount of memory to hold the X server and enough CPU time to allow the X server to process all of the events and deliver them to the application processes.

Chapter 7

Open Desktop Case Study

This chapter contains a case study illustrating the effects of memory shortages on performance of display updates. This case uses the seven-step method to understand the resource usage patterns and find the optimal resource allocation.

Completed worksheets are included at the end of this chapter as a sort of appendix to show how to analyze the data and draw conclusions regarding resource shortages.

> **Step 1.** Decide what to improve.
>
> ☑ Select the appropriate worksheet for the common operation.

The speed at which the display is updated is too slow and makes interacting with the system frustrating. The worksheet selected is shown in Worksheets 7-1 and 7-2 at the end of this chapter.

⇩

> **Step 2.** Identify the limited and unlimited resources.
>
> ☑ Note any limited resources on the worksheet by marking them with an asterisk (*).

The initial assumption is that all hardware is limited, but if the memory shortage is so severe that additional hardware resources are necessary, then buying more hardware will be considered.

The current hardware configuration is as follows:

1 486/25 MHz CPU
8 Mbytes of Memory
Cirrus 5422 Graphics Adapter, Non-intelligent
1 wd1007 Disk Adapter with 1 ESDI Disk

⇩

Step 3. Determine how to measure the operation and test its current performance.

☑ Note the test result on the worksheet in the column marked **Now.**

The command xrefresh(X) redraws the display without requiring any additional keyboard input. This command isolates the behavior that needs to be measured. The xrefresh(X) command is executed multiple times from a shell script to lengthen the test and reduce the error in measurement.

The odtop program included on the floppy disk automatically runs this test and collects the statistics with sar.

⇩

Step 4. Set a realistic performance goal.

☑ Note this on the worksheet in the column marked **Your Goal.**

The initial goal is to reduce the duration of the test by 50%, to approximately 12.5 seconds. Because upgrading hardware is a possibility for increasing performance, this goal seems realistic.

Worksheets 7-1 and 7-2 show the completed worksheets for this series of tests.

⇩

> **Step 5.** Identify the resources to monitor and decide which monitoring tools to use.
>
> ☑ The worksheets list the appropriate resources.

The resources to be monitored are shown in the worksheet in Worksheet 7-2.

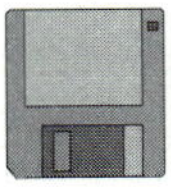

The standard operating system monitoring tool, sar, is used to monitor operating system and hardware resource usage patterns. The odtop program includes a framework for running the test and collecting data. The resource usage data is extracted using the tool sar2oswks.

⇩

> **Step 6.** Run the test with the monitoring tools and monitor the resource usage and record the test results.
>
> ☑ Enter the initial values of the tunables and note the resource usage in the column marked **Initial Values**. Note the test results under the column called **Monitoring.**

The results of this test are shown in Worksheet 7-2.

Initial Observations

Some conclusions can be drawn regarding the memory usage patterns during the initial test. These conclusions are as follows:

- The values reported for rclm/s, as noted in the Pages Reclaimed worksheet cell, and freeswp, as noted in the Free Swap worksheet cell, show that the system is paging to compensate for a memory shortage. No processes were swapped out as indicated by %swpocc equal to zero, so sched was not running.

- The values reported by freemem are consistently less than GPGSLO, so vhand cannot reclaim pages as fast as those pages are consumed

Figure 7-1 shows how free memory fluctuates during the test. This interval data was extracted using the saravg utility provided on the floppy disk.

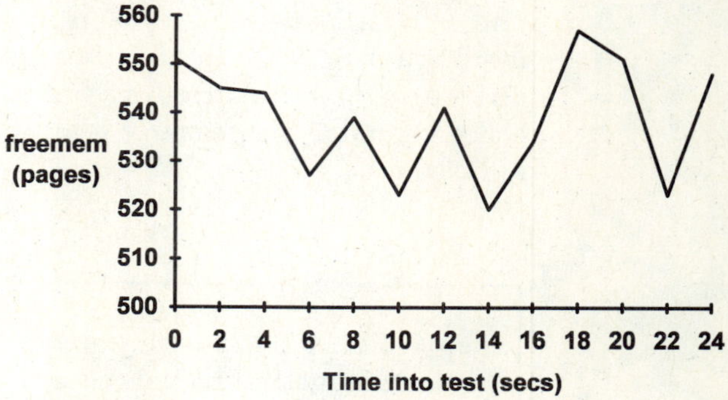

Figure 7-1: Fluctuations in Free Memory Throughout Test

Figure 7-1 shows that free memory does change during the test, but for most of the test, free memory is less than 550, which is the current value of GPGSLO. Since free memory is less than 550, vhand is unable to free pages quickly enough to keep up with the demand for memory to run the applications. If vhand could free memory quickly enough, then vhand would run until the amount of free memory reached GPGSHI. Figure 7-2 provides further evidence that memory was reclaimed throughout the test because the number of rclm/s is always greater than zero.

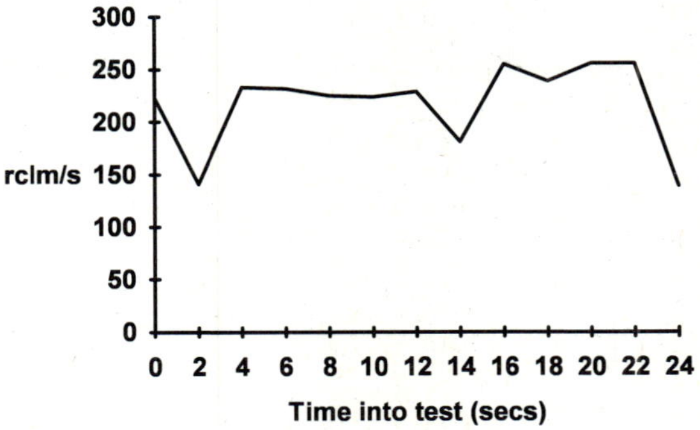

Figure 7-2: Frequency of Reclaiming Pages During the Test

The approximate amount of additional memory required can be calculated with the following equation:

$$\frac{blocks\_column - free\_column}{2}$$

and, in this case, is equal to:

$$\frac{47104 - 35477}{2} = 5813\ Kbytes$$

Appendix B suggests ways in which memory can be freed. This appendix reveals that no feasible method in the table can free the required amount of memory.

The average number of blks/s handled by the disk is 700 with an avserv time of 32 milliseconds. Each disk request also spends an average of 33 milliseconds waiting on the driver's list before being serviced by the disk. Considering that the disk adapter is not full 32-bit or Bus Master DMA capable, 700 blks/s is a large number of blocks per second for this particular disk subsystem to handle. This particular disk adapter uses programmed I/O, so requires the CPU to handle the data transfer associated with each request.

With the length of time required to process the disk transfers, the processes are likely to be waiting for disk transfers to complete. Performance can possibly be improved by decreasing the amount of disk traffic. An average of six filesystem physical reads, bread/s, and three filesystem physical writes, bwrit/s, occurred per second. Since the test requires only a minimal amount of interaction with the disk, most of the disk activity must arise from paging.

This conclusion is confirmed by examining the rate of reclamation and number of blocks paged out. The values of rclm/s in Figure 7-2 show that on average 200 pages are reclaimed by sched and vhand per second. The average number of 512-byte blocks paged out per second is equal to 657. The disk activity must be caused by paging. A quick check through the statistics not included on the worksheet also shows that value of %swpocc is equal to zero, so sched is not running. The disk activity must be caused solely by vhand.

The amount of CPU time available to the applications, %usr, in this test is 48%, while 23% of the CPU time is spent executing the operating system, as indicated by %sys. Nearly 28% of the CPU time is spent waiting-for-device-I/O to complete, so the amount of disk activity is preventing the efficient use of the CPU. Increasing the amount of CPU time available to execute the test should improve performance, and one way of increasing the amount of CPU time available is to decrease the amount of paging.

⇩

Step 7. Decide how to change the resource allocation; rerun the tests and note progress toward the goal. Iterate until either the goal is reached, or until a limited resource is encountered.

☑ Determine whether to increase or decrease the resource/tunable. Note the new tunable values in the column marked **Test #1** and the test results under the column **Res #1.** Use the rest of the columns for the results of subsequent test iterations.

☑ When the goal is reached, implement the new resource allocation.

Test #1: Reduce GPGSLO and GPGSHI

The first set of resource allocation changes are to see what happens when the memory shortage is artificially alleviated by adjusting the start of vhand execution. The values of GPGSHI and GPGSLO are reduced to 32 and 16, respectively, so the level of free memory must be extremely low before paging occurs. Reducing these variables to such low levels is only a temporary test to help understand what the performance benefit might be if sufficient memory were available on the system.

Changing GPGSHI and GPGSLO does not permanently alleviate the memory shortage, because 16 pages of free memory may cause sched to start swapping processes out in order to satisfy application requests for more memory.

The operating system is reconfigured and the test run again. The test duration decreases to 17 and is noted in Worksheet 7-2. The duration of the test is still too long, however, so more analysis is required.

Examine the memory usage statistics again. The values reported by rclm/s are much lower than in the first test. Although performance has improved, the amount of free memory still falls below the current value of GPGSLO. When this happens, vhand will start to reclaim memory and rclm/s will be greater than zero. Figure 7-3 shows how rclm/s changed over the duration of the test.

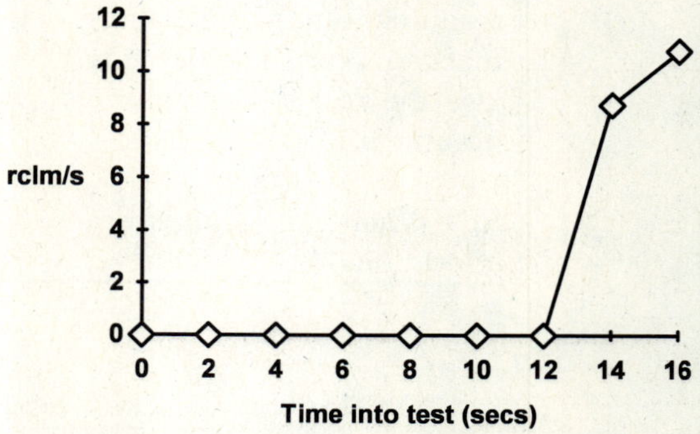

Figure 7-3: Changes in rclm/s For the Test Run

Although the level of rclm/s is on the average lower than in the previous tests, the amount of memory is still not sufficient to accommodate all the applications. No swapping occurred because swpq-sz is equal to zero and %swpocc is also equal to zero. Figure 7-4 shows how free memory fluctuated during the test.

For most of the test, the level of free memory remained above GPGSLO, so vhand would not be running. Since vhand was not running, the amount of disk activity caused by paging should have decreased. The average amount of disk activity has decreased from 700 blks/s to 136 blks/s. The average time required to service the disk request has decreased from 32 to 22 milliseconds, so the disk is better able to service the reduced amount of traffic.

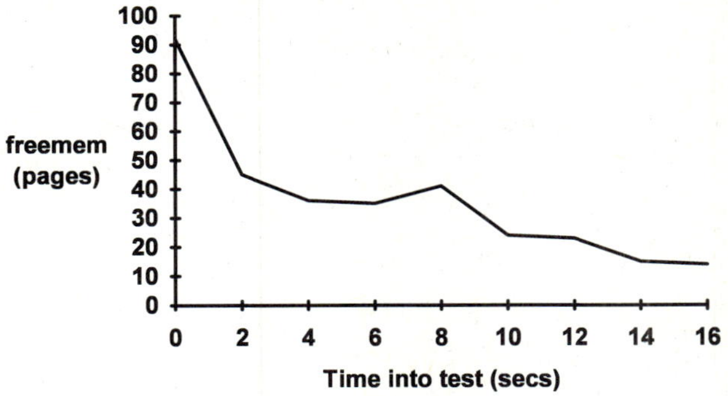

Figure 7-4: Levels of Free Memory During the Test

The decrease in paging activity has increased the availability of the CPU for application execution, as shown by the increase in %usr from 48% to 56%. The amount of %sys time has decreased from 23% to 15%, but the %wio time has increased slightly, from 28% to 29%.

However, the test is still too long, and %wio is still too high for efficient CPU usage. Since most of the disk activity is still caused by paging, the memory shortage that is causing paging to occur must be alleviated. To alleviate the memory shortage, either more memory must be added, or the usage of the existing memory must be reduced.

The amount of swap space used during this test is equal to:

$$\frac{47104 - 39102}{2} = 4001\,Kbytes$$

Because the decrease in paging improved performance, installing a sufficient amount of additional memory should improve performance.

Test #2: Add Four Mbytes

Having shown that performance of the display update is improved when paging is eliminated, add four Mbytes of physical memory to the machine. Restore the original values of GPGSLO and GPGSHI, so that the system runs at a level of free memory that reduces the risk of swapping.

Run the test again. The duration of the test is now 14 seconds and is noted in Worksheet 7-2. Examine the memory usage statistics to see what has changed. No pages are now reclaimed because rclm/s is equal to zero.

For most of the test, the level of free memory remained above GPGSLO, so vhand would not be running. Since vhand was not running, the amount of disk activity caused by paging should have decreased. The average number of blks/s is now equal to 19 blks/s rather than 136 blks/s as shown in the previous test. The disk response times have also improved, because avserv has gone from 22 to 19.

Some swap space has been used. A closer examination of the sar statistics show that the swap space usage stayed constant during the test, so the swap space was used prior to starting the test. Paging or swapping prior to the test indicates a memory shortage still exists and perhaps performance could be improved by adding more memory.

The amount of CPU time available to run the X server and other user applications has increased. The amount of %usr is now up to 74% and %wio is down to 7%. The increase in CPU time helps explain why the performance of the test increased.

Test #3: Add Four More Mbytes

Since installing memory caused an improvement, perhaps an additional four Mbytes will cause a further increase. Install an additional 4 Mbytes of memory and run the test again.

The new test results are noted in Worksheet 7-3. The test duration has not changed.

Examine the memory usage statistics to see why the test result did not change. The value of rclm/s is still equal to zero. The statistics show that for the first time, no swap space was used either prior to running the test or during the test. The amount of free memory is equal to 845 pages, which is well above GPGSLO, so the risk of vhand running is minimal.

The additional memory is not required for increased performance, and so could be removed and installed somewhere where it would benefit performance.

Test #4: Reconfigure X Server

Now that paging is completely eliminated, check the other resource usage patterns for possible shortages that could be limiting performance. Over 80% of the CPU time is spent executing user applications and only 3% of the time is spent %wio. No other shortages are occurring on the system.

Because most of the time is now spent executing user applications, the tuning options are limited. One possible source of performance improvement is to modify the number of colors used by the X server. Fewer colors require less data to be transferred when the display is updated, and so could improve the responsiveness of screen update.

Reconfigure the X server to use 16 colors.

The test now takes 11 seconds, so reducing the amount of data transferred to the display has improved the responsiveness of the system. The amount of %usr and %sys time has not changed significantly.

A faster graphics adapter may benefit performance by reducing the amount of time required to update the screen with 16 or a larger number of colors.

Conclusions

This example shows what a dramatic difference sufficient memory makes to the display update operation. Artificially setting the values of GPGSLO and GPGSHI is one way of predicting the effect on performance of eliminating paging. Setting these values to their extreme low points is not feasible for the long term because applications still need memory and instead of paging, the operating system will swap applications in order to free memory.

This example also shows the impact of paging on the ability of the disk to provide adequate response times. When the level of paging decreases, the disk can service the other requests more efficiently. Paging and swapping affect the amount of CPU time available to applications by increasing %sys and possibly increasing %wio as a result of greater disk activity.

Worksheet 7-1: SCO UNIX Operating System Tuning Worksheet (part 1)

Tunables	Initial Values	Test #1	Test #2	Test #3	Test #4
Installed Memory	8 Mbytes	8 Mbytes	12 Mbytes	16 Mbytes	16 Mbytes
Application Storage	n/a				
GPGSLO, GPGSHI	550 600	16 32	550 600		
MAXSC, AGEINTERVAL	8 31				
S5CACHEENTS, S5HASHQS	256 61				
NFILE	200				
NINODE, NHINODE	400 128				
NBUF, NHBUF	100 128				
BDFLUSHR, NAUTOP	30 10				
NCOPYBUF, PLOWBUFS	0 10				
NMPBUF, NMPHEADBUF	0 16				
NPBUF, DMAABLEBUF	40 4				
SDSKOUT	n/a				
Disk Configuration, Data Layout	1 ESDI disk				
NCLIST	120				
NPROC, NREGION	100 330				
NSCRN, CTBUFSIZ	0 n/a				
Display adapter, colors	256	256	256	256	16
Mouse Settings	default				

Worksheet 7-2: SCO UNIX Operating System Tuning Worksheet (part 2)

Resources to Monitor	Initial Values	Test #1	Test #2	Test #3	Test #4
Free Memory, Free swap	537 35477	40 39102	660 41176	845 47104	794 47104
Blocks Swapped in/out	10.6 657.4	11.7 18.9	0.0 0.0	0.0 0.0	0.0 0.0
Pages Reclaimed	200.67	3.02	0.00	0.00	0.00
CPU: %usr, %sys, %wio, %idle	48 23 28 0	56 15 29 0	74 18 7 0	81 16 3 0	80 17 3 0
Scheduling: runq-sz, swpq-sz, pswch/s	1.3 0 63	1.0 0 63	1.0 0 47	1.2 0 49	1.1 0 54
Namei Cache	97%	97%	97%	97%	98%
File Table, Inode Table	141 0 153 0	134 0 148 0	135 0 1480	136 0 148 0	124 0 137 0
Buffer Cache %rcache Reads: bread/s lread/s Writes: bwrit/s, lwrit/s	93 6 85 3 28	87 17 124 4 33	97 4 134 4 38	96 5 134 5 38	99 2 160 6 45
Scatter/Gather: mpbuf/s, ompb/s, mphbuf/s, omphbufs/s	1 0 2 0	9 0 2 0	0 0 2 0	0 0 2 0	1 0 3 0
Copy Buffers	0 0	0 0	0 0	0 0	0 0
Direct Disk Requests	1 0	2 0	0 0	0 0	0 0
Copy Memory	0 0	0 0	0 0	0 0	0 0
Sdsk Request Blocks	n/a	n/a	n/a	n/a	n/a
Disk Driver : %busy avque, r+w/s, blks/s, avwait, avserv	70 2 22 700 33 32	51 2 23 136 22 22	15 2 8 19 20 19	19 3 10 25 39 20	13 7 8 24 40 17

Now	Your Goal	Monitoring	Res #1	Res #2	Res #3	Res #4
22	12	25	17	14	14	11

Chapter 8

Monitoring Client/Server Connections

This chapter describes the resource interactions and intermediate storage locations that are used when a client machine communicates with a server over a network.

This chapter starts out describing how the processes that manage the connection between the client and the server application use resources and how to monitor those resource usage patterns. The next section discusses the underlying mechanisms that allow the two processes on different machines to communicate over the network. Because the availability of the CPU is often the limiting factor in network operation performance, most of the recommendations for tuning the client and the server involve increasing CPU availability.

The Common Client/Server Operations chapter describes specific operations that are executed in a networking environment using the infrastructure described in this chapter. The NFS distributed computing filesystem from Sun Microsystems is discussed in the Common Client/Server Operations chapter. The Remote File Access Case Studies chapter contains two remote file access case studies. Chapters 9 and 10 assume an understanding of the material presented in this chapter.

Networking tuning is more difficult because the resources on more than one machine must be optimized. Sufficient CPU, memory and network resources must be available for the connection management, transmission mechanisms and applications to run optimally in a client/server environment.

A Word About Monitoring Tools

The SCO UNIX and SCO MPX monitoring tools, sar(ADM), mpsar(MP), and cpusar(MP) are used and referred to in this chapter. In all places where sar is mentioned, mpsar and/or cpusar could also be used, although these multiprocessor tools may not be explicitly mentioned.

New tools introduced in this chapter are:

- llistat(ADM)
- netstat(TC)
- nfsstat(NADM)
- rpcinfo(NADM)
- traceroute(ADMN)

These commands are described in more detail in various system administrator's manuals that accompany the SCO products. The exact location of the descriptions varies, depending on the release of the product that is installed. This chapter refers to the documents and on-line information that is provided with Open Desktop 3.0, Open Server 3.0, SCO UNIX Release 3.2.4v2 and SCO MPX 3.0.

When A Client Is Connected To A Server

Client, Server

In this book, *client* refers to the machine or process that requests access to another machine or process in order to complete an operation. *Server* refers to the machine or process that provides that access and the corresponding service that allows the client to complete the operation.

Local, Remote

The term *local* describes any action that can be completed without accessing another machine. *Local* is also used to describe information located on the same machine as the application process accessing it. *Remote* describes any action that requires access to another machine. *Remote* is also used to describe information or application execution that is located on another machine.

When a client is connected to a server, optimal resource allocation becomes more complex. When an operation executes on only one machine, resources must be monitored and tuned only on that machine. When machines are connected with a network and the completion of the operation relies on cooperation between the client and server, the duration of the operation is equal to the sum of the following actions:

- the duration of the client portion of the operation
- the duration of the server portion
- the time for the necessary information to travel between the client and server machines

In this more complex environment, tuning requires monitoring and allocating the resources on the client and the server to minimize the duration of their respective portions of the operation. In addition, the resources required for data transmission over the network must be monitored and optimally allocated. When allocating resources, the goals are as follows:

- To ensure that the network transmissions occur as efficiently as possible. Maximum efficiency implies sufficient streams resources and no errors or retransmissions caused by defective or inefficient hardware.

- To maximize the availability of the CPU on both the client and the server, since many of the client/server operations require the CPU.

No matter how quickly the client and the server complete their portions of the operation, inefficient network transmissions can add significant delay to the time required to complete the operation. Inefficient network transmission can also provide clues to hidden resource shortages or mismatched hardware capabilities.

Once the network transmissions are as efficient as possible, begin allocating resources on the client and the server. If the client takes a long time to send requests to the server and a long time to process requests from the server, then no matter how fast the server responds to those requests, performance is limited by the ability of the client to process the responses from the server and not by the ability of the server to complete those requests. Conversely, if the server is experiencing resource shortages, then no matter how optimally tuned the client might be, the server is limiting performance. In most cases, determining whether the client or the server is causing the delay is difficult, so an analysis of both sets of resources usage patterns must often be done to assess where the resource shortages are most extreme.

Figure 8-1 shows the pathway of data travelling from the application on the client to the application on the server. The next sections describe what happens during this journey from the perspective of the client and the server.

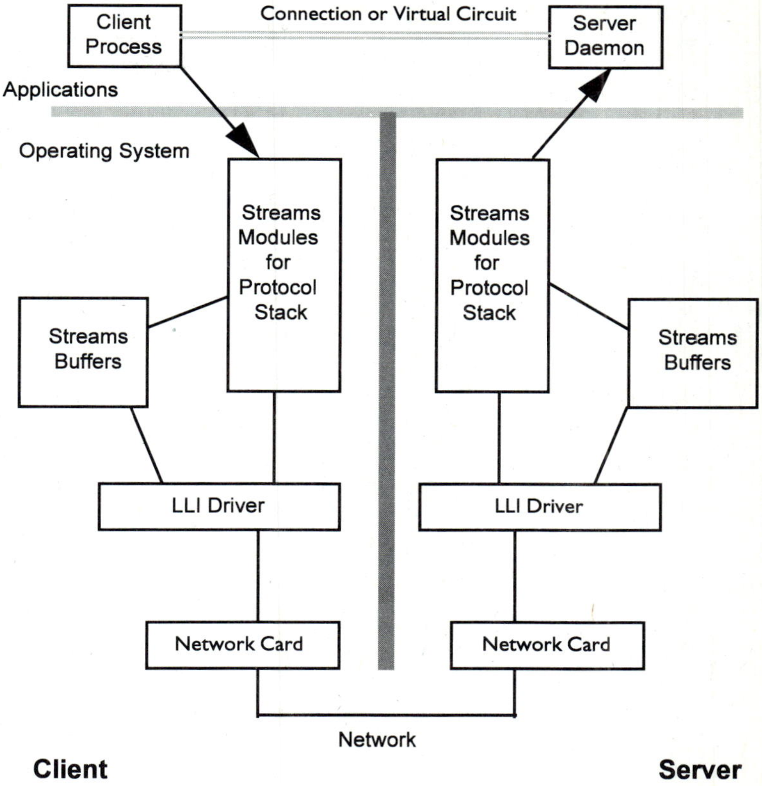

Figure 8-1: Summary of client/server interaction. In order for a client application to access a remote server, the client and the server must establish a connection over the network. After the connection is established, requests and information pass between them using the underlying network protocol. The protocol might be TCP/IP, UDP, or IPX/SPX. These network protocols use streams buffers to hold the data while packaging it for transmission across the network and for decoding the information when it arrives from the network. Streams buffers provide the mechanism for data to travel from the protocol stack to the LLI driver. The LLI driver manages the network card. The network card sends and receives the network packets.

THE CLIENT

The client initiates the communication to the server by sending a message to the server application. The *protocol* defines the way a message is packaged by the client, addressed to the server, sent over the network, then unpackaged by the server and delivered to the server application. A protocol must be supported on both the client and the server in order for them to successfully communicate. A protocol can be considered a series of specialized processing layers that handle the packaging and un-packaging of messages.

Connection-oriented Service

Client and server applications can communicate in either a *connection* or *connectionless* manner. The underlying protocol must support the type of communication the applications will use. Connection-oriented communication means that a dedicated pathway is set up between the client and the server. This pathway exists until one or the other destroys it. This dedicated pathway is called a *virtual circuit* because it resembles an electrical circuit in that it is a link between the client and the server; however, instead of being a physical connection, the link is set up and maintained by the networking software. Many virtual circuits can use the same underlying network subsystem.

The highest layer of the network protocol guarantees that the information travels between the application processes in a specific order, and that any missing messages are re-sent by the sender. This type of connection is called a *reliable* connection. The Transport Connection Protocol (TCP) explicitly acknowledges each message received by the server. The acknowledgment means that the every message sent by the client results in another message from the server confirming receipt of the message. TCP implements an optimization called *windowing* that allows the receiver to acknowledge a group of requests instead of each one individually. If the server does not acknowledge the message or set of messages in a specific period of time, then the client resends the message.

Connectionless service

Connectionless, or *datagram,* service does not require a dedicated link for client and server communication The User Datagram Protocol (UDP) is the datagram service provided as part of the TCP/IP package. Applications use this type of service when reliability and order in the delivery and receipt of messages is not required. Such a service is often used when only one message needs to be sent to the client and the server in order to complete the operation and no acknowledgment from the server is required. Applications also use this service when the application provides the reliability features.

Protocols support either connection-oriented or connection-less service. Table 8-1 summarizes the type of services provided by the protocols supported in Open Desktop 3.0.

Protocol	Type of Service
TCP/IP	connection-oriented
UDP	connection-less
IPX	connection-less
SPX	connection-oriented

Table 8-1: Types of services provided by Open Desktop and Open Server 3.0.

Both client and server operations can be monitored with the monitoring tools described in the product chapters. In general, the same guidelines for tuning a stand-alone system apply to a client or server system attached to a network. However, when monitoring the distribution of CPU time with sar -u, be aware of the following:

- The %wio value does not include the time waiting for the network transmissions to complete, but does still include the percentage of time the CPU was idle while waiting for disk i/o to complete.

- The %sys time includes the percentage of time spent processing streams and all other network-related operating system processing. The values for %sys are generally much higher when the system is using networking.

- Depending on how many other application processes are running on the system, %idle can give an indication as to the amount of time spent waiting for the network transmissions to complete. The most extreme case is when all processes on the client are waiting for network transmissions to complete. The most common case is that at least one process on the client is waiting for network traffic at any time, so %idle cannot be relied on to indicate whether delays on the network are delaying operation completion.

The normal tuning guidelines for a stand-alone system, increasing %usr time and decreasing %sys time, do not always apply to network systems. The difference arises because %sys may increase after the CPU is freed to handle more incoming or outgoing network messages. An increase in the available CPU time may result in greater application throughput because more network messages are processed. The guidelines regarding reducing %wio and %idle still apply, since a CPU that is idle because of waiting for any reason is not doing any productive work.

The Server

This section describes what happens on the server when a connection is established and messages are sent between the client and the server. The server network interface card must first receive the message and then the streams protocol stack must unpack it and send it to a special application process that runs on the server. This special process sets up the connection and then either implements the service itself, or sends the message to the application process that will provide the service to the client.

Receiving the Message

The network interface card driver determines that the frame is addressed to this machine by matching the network address of the packet with the network address of the card. After a match is detected, the network card generates an interrupt; then the Link Layer Interface driver copies the packet from the card to a streams buffer. The LLI driver sends the buffer up the stream for unpacking by the protocol streams modules. The LLI driver is described in more detail later in this chapter.

If the sender uses TCP, the messages are explicitly acknowledged by the server protocol stack sending a special packet back to the sending machine. No acknowledgment is made at the network interface card level. After the streams modules comprising the protocol stack have processed the packets and reconstructed the sender's message, the final streams module passes the reconstructed message to the application.

After the return message is packaged for network transmission, the return message is sent over the network to the client. The CPU is required for all of the message handling. If the CPU is not available, then the message is delayed waiting until the CPU is available.

Server Daemons

Network services have special processes called *daemons* that wait for messages from clients wishing to establish a connection on the server. Other daemons handle datagram-style communication. These daemons are application processes just like any other application process and so must share the same resources, such as memory and CPU, with all the other applications running on the server. Additional information on these special processes can be found in the SCO Open Desktop System Administrator's Manual.

cpd — *cpd* is used by SCO TCP/IP to check that no two machines on the network are using the same serial number. cpd runs occasionally on both clients and servers, so it accumulates CPU time.

inetd — *inetd* listens for connection requests from clients. When a connection request is recognized, inetd generates the appropriate server process to act on that connection. The file */etc/services* lists all the services and the *inetd.conf* lists the configuration information for those services that the inetd process is able to provide to remote systems. inetd runs on both the client and the server when requests are received, otherwise it is suspended waiting for requests. If sufficient resources are not available to run this process, then clients wishing to connect to the server will experience delay.

ldsocket — *ldsocket* initializes the special streams module that supports the socket-style interface. ldsocket runs on both clients and servers. After the sockets are set up, ldsocket exits and so should not appear in a ps(C) listing.

routed — *routed* manages routing information. When routed starts, packets are sent to all other hosts. Each host responds and the sender updates its routing information according to the responses received. This process runs frequently on both clients and servers. If sufficient resources are not available to run routed, then routing information may become out of date and packet journey time may be adversely affected.

rusersd — *rusersd* recognizes requests from the rusers command. rusersd runs on both clients and servers, but is normally used on the clients. This process is suspended until an rusers request is received.

rwalld — *rwalld* recognizes requests from the rwall command. *rwalld* runs on both clients and servers, but is normally used on the clients. *rwalld* is suspended until an rwall request is received.

slink — *slink* constructs the protocol stack used by TCP/IP by connecting the streams modules implementing parts of the TCP/IP protocol. slink runs on both clients and servers. After building the protocol stack, slink is indefinitely suspended and so should not accumulate CPU time after building the protocol stack.

strerr

strerr writes the error messages generated by the streams log driver to files in the */usr/adm/streams* directory. strerr runs on both clients and servers and only accumulates CPU time when error messages occur.

syslogd

syslogd writes messages to the log file specified by */etc/syslog.conf.* This process runs occasionally on both clients and servers and accumulates CPU time.

telnetd, rlogind

telnetd and *rlogind* are daemon processes that are started by inetd when a request for remote server access via telnet or rlogin is received.

Because the daemon processes are just like any other application process, the daemon processes share system resources, such as the CPU, memory and disk, with all the other application processes on the system. These daemon processes have no special priority access to resources. Ensuring that sufficient resources are available for these processes is important to server performance.

The same tools used on the client for monitoring the protocol and network efficiency can be used on the server.

The primary goals for server tuning are as follows:

- Maximize network efficiency and optimize streams resource usage
- Maximize the availability of the CPU
- Maximize efficient use of other resources used by the server applications

Recommendations for tuning the server to meet these goals are provided in this and the other product chapters.

Remember that increasing the amount of CPU time available for handling messages may increase %sys rather than reduce it. If the server can handle more client requests because of increased system efficiency and availability of CPU time, then the number of network messages processed by the server will increase, and %sys will increase as a result. Because this behavior is the opposite of what is expected on a system without networking and so could be misinterpreted, the increased capacity of the server should be corroborated through performance testing to prove that the server is actually more efficient.

The hardware configuration of the server must be sufficient to provide adequate response to all of the clients. As the number and types of network clients grow with the increased usage the computer system, servers often experience severe resource shortages that adversely impact performance. Frequent monitoring of resource usage patterns is therefore a useful tool to detect these resource shortages before they become severe.

TCP/IP, UDP

Transmission Control Protocol (TCP) allows applications to communicate over a network by means of virtual circuits. User Datagram Protocol (UDP) provides a connectionless client/server communication service. Internet Protocol (IP) specifies how packets are addressed when they travel on the network between the sender and the receiver. Both UDP and TCP messages use the Internet Protocol to specify the format of packets.

TCP and UDP differ in the amount of processing that is done on the incoming and outgoing messages before they are sent to the application processes. Because TCP ensures a reliable, ordered communication service over the virtual circuit, before messages are transmitted over the network, the virtual circuit and sequencing information must be added to the message.

The server decodes this information and, if the messages are received out of order, holds the messages until all the expected messages are received. If an error occurs when a message in the sequence is received, then the server notifies the client so it can resend the message. The TCP protocol stack on the server explicitly acknowledges how many of the messages have been received, so the TCP protocol stack on the client knows exactly where to begin retransmission.

A message sent over UDP does not require the sequencing or virtual circuit information to be added to the message.

The network protocol address specifying the location of the server must be also added to the message. When using either UDP or TCP, the format of the address is defined by the Internet Protocol. Internet Control Message Protocol (ICMP) is another protocol that allows messages to be passed back and forth between gateways. Gateways are discussed in the Network Layout section of this chapter.

A *packet* or *frame* is a message that has been processed and is ready to be sent over the network. The words *frame* and *packet* are often used interchangeably.

A more detailed description of TCP/IP and UDP can be found in the book *Internetworking with TCP/IP: Principles, Protocols and Architecture* by *Douglas Comer* (ISBN: 0-13-470188-7).

Despite the differences between UDP and TCP, the same tools are used to monitor both of them. Table 8-2 summarizes the monitoring commands. Some of the commands monitor resource usage and others provide helpful information in the diagnosis of network traffic and error conditions.

Behavior	Command	Column
Services Accessing Network Connections	netstat -a	Local Address, Foreign Address, port & final column
Status of Network Connection Services	netstat -a	(state)
Amount of data, in bytes, packaged by the connection service but waiting to be sent over the network	netstat -a	Send-Q
Amount of data, in bytes, received over the connection and waiting to be processed by the connection service	netstat -a	Recv-Q
Protocol being used by connection service	netstat -a	Proto
Protocol errors	netstat -s	Relevant rows

Table 8-2: Connection Monitoring Tools

netstat -a

The connection services currently used by a system can be displayed with netstat -a. The column Local Address shows the services available on the system and those services that are in use. For example, machine_name.shell is the connection used by rcp. If multiple processes use a service, then the column contains multiple entries. If the shell service is not in use, then the value displayed is *.shell. If the service is in use, then the name machine_name.shell is shown. When the connection is in use, the column Foreign Address shows the name of the destination system.

Some of the services displayed are defined in the */etc/services* file. However, some of the entries shown correspond to applications and other networking products that make connections between machines without accessing the information in */etc/services*.

The status of any connection is displayed in the (state) column. Connections that are available, but not currently in use, are labeled LISTEN, because the system is waiting to see if a connection needs to be made. Connections that have been made are shown as ESTABLISHED. Other values may be shown in this column for some services.

For an established connection, the Send-Q column shows how many bytes of data have been processed by the connection service but not yet sent across the network. The Recv-Q column shows the number of bytes of data that have been received from the network but have not yet been processed by the connection service. Messages waiting to be processed are stored in a stream buffer. For a connection service that is not currently in use, then the value in this column is equal to zero.

HINT:

The values shown in both the Send-Q and Recv-Q columns often oscillate between zero and other values. This oscillation is because netstat(NADM) reads data from the network subsystem in order to display information and processing of that information is in progress while netstat executes. The interim state of the netstat messages causes the values to vary. If the values displayed in the either the Send-Q or Recv-Q columns increase, then the CPU is not available to process the messages, and stream buffers usage may increase because of CPU unavailability.

The Proto column shows the protocol used by the connection service. This information, given in */etc/services*, cannot be tuned or otherwise modified. The protocol is determined by the implementation of the service, for example, TCP or UDP.

netstat -s

The values reported by netstat -s show the number of errors that are encountered when the messages are processed by each of the network protocols. The information shown indicates the reliability of the network and the network interface card. If any rows corresponding to error information are greater than zero, then the reliability of the network may be affecting performance. When the client and server are using a connection-oriented protocol, the sending machine retransmits any messages that contain errors.

If the error is encountered in a packet in the middle of a series of sequenced packets that comprise a message, the message cannot be assembled from the packets until all of the packets are received error-free. The packets containing errors must be re-sent by the sending machine, and then received and processed by the destination machine. Once this occurs, the packets can be assembled into a message and sent to the application process. The retransmission causes delays and adds to the amount of CPU time required to transmit the message. Figure 8-2 shows the interactions between the client and the server when an error occurs during transmission.

With TCP, the values in the rows named "discarded for bad checksums," "discarded for bad head offset fields," and "discarded because packet too short" show how many times packets are ignored because the information received in the packets did not comply with the TCP protocol. In an efficient network, these values are equal to zero.

If the values are greater than zero, then errors are affecting the efficiency of the network because packets must be retransmitted. The percentage of errors occurring can be determined by dividing the total number of packets containing errors by the total number of packets sent. The total number of packets sent is displayed by the netstat -s command in the packets received row of the TCP section.

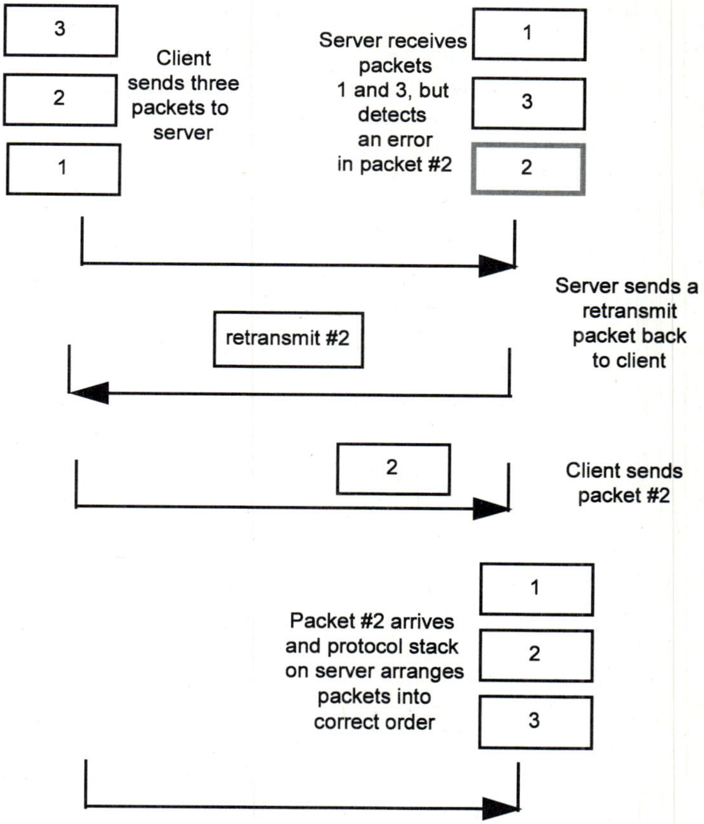

Figure 8-2: The client sends three packets to the server. The server receives packets #1 and #3, but packet #2 has an error. The server notifies the client to re-send packet #2. The client resends the packet and the server receives the packet and orders the packets into the correct sequence for the application. Because the detection of the error, the handling of the retransmission and the sequencing of the packets occur in the protocol stack, additional CPU and streams buffers resources are used than if no errors occurred.

The value for retransmit timeouts shows the number of times the acknowledgment for a packet was not received by the sender of the packet. The value in the row may be greater than zero for these reasons:

- The packet may have become corrupted during transmission
- The packet may have been lost during transmission
- The acknowledgment was not received within the specified time limit

The time limit value cannot be changed by the system administrator because TCP automatically adapts the value to the network characteristics. When network usage patterns change, the values shown in the retransmit timeouts column may change as well.

When the client and server communicate via UDP, the rows containing error information are named "incomplete headers," "bad data length fields," and "bad checksums." If any of these columns show values greater than zero, the efficiency of the network is lower than it could be, and performance is affected.

The rows containing error information for IP are "bad header checksums," "with size smaller than minimum," "with data size < data length," "with header length < data size," "with data length < header length." TCP and UDP both use IP, so the number of errors encountered by IP may affect the performance of TCP and UDP. The greater the number of errors, the less efficient the network. A large number of errors may indicate defective network interface hardware at some network location.

The primary tuning guideline for efficient network connections is to reduce the number of packet/message retransmissions caused by errors. Before reallocating any resources used by TCP/IP, always check the efficiency of the network by looking at the error rates detected by TCP/IP. The cost of retransmitting packets is high, so the greater the error rate, the lower the efficiency of the network.

The values reported by netstat -s can be used to identify the reasons for the errors. Identify the causes of errors with the following actions:

- Determining the protocols used by the connection service
- Looking for errors in the rows that apply to that protocol

The protocols used by the common operations are explicitly stated in the common operation descriptions.

If the value of re-transmit timeouts always increases no matter how the network is configured, then the physical connections may be at fault, and all network connections should be checked for poor installation. The network connections can be checked by disconnecting and reconnecting the network to the network card and re-inserting the network interface card into its slot in the machine.

Some tuning changes, such as reducing the percentage of errors, that would normally reduce the amount of %sys time actually cause it to increase. The reason for the increase is that the CPU may have previously been busy resending packets rather than handling new packets. The increased efficiency of the CPU means that it can handle more new packets, thereby increasing application performance.

IPX/SPX

The IPX/SPX protocol supports Internetwork Packet Exchange (IPX) and Sequenced Packet Exchange(SPX) protocols. SPX provides a connection-oriented service, and IPX provides a connectionless datagram service. Applications access these interfaces by calling procedures that are defined as part of the Transport Layer Interface (TLI). Novell Virtual Terminal (NVT) protocol service is also available. SPX, IPX and NVT are implemented as streams modules. Both SPX and NVT use the message service of IPX. IPX is the streams module that connects to the LLI driver that controls the network interface card.

SPX is similar to TCP in that both are connection-oriented services that provide explicit acknowledgment for each packet sent across the network. SPX differs from TCP in that one packet is sent and an acknowledgment must be received before another packet is sent. TCP supports the sending of multiple packets before an acknowledgment is sent.

IPX is similar to UDP except the packet size is limited to 500 bytes, although Ethernet supports packets of up to 1500 bytes.

Services are broadcast over the network by a Service Advertising Protocol, SAP. Services include file server, print server, gateway server and application server. SAP provides a mechanism for systems to describe the services they are providing to the network. When the system initializes, the available services are broadcast to the network, and when the system is turned off, the closure of those services is also broadcast. SAP relies on IPX because the broadcast messages do not require an acknowledgment. Clients use the information provided by the SAP to determine which nodes they can access for a given service.

The special listener process that manages SAP is called sapd. Every minute, this process sends a message to all the other machines on the network notifying these machines of the services that are available. As the size of the network increases, these messages can generate a lot of network traffic. The broadcast messages do not travel across gateways or routers. Any new service information is generally transmitted to other networks that are connected to the gateway or router.

The following section describes the daemon processes that run on an IPX/SPX server.

npsd — *npsd* assembles and initializes the NetWare®protocol stack. Once the protocol stack is initialized, any files that might have been opened during the initialization process remain open and the process is suspended indefinitely. This daemon is similar to the slink process in TCP/IP.

nvtd — *nvtd* establishes a connection between the host and clients using the NVT protocol. When a client makes a connection to the server, the nvtd process allocates a pseudo-tty and generates a login connection for the client to use. The nvtd process is only active when making connections and is normally suspended otherwise. nvtd is similar to the telnetd in TCP/IP.

sapd — *sapd* maintains a list of the services provided by the server. A client looking for a service asks this special process which services are supported on that server. The sapd process acts as a router helping clients locate the appropriate services. The sapd process broadcasts its list of services to all of the nodes on the network once every minute. This interval is not tunable.

xechod — *xechod* listens for nping(PADM) messages and returns the appropriate packets to the client that issues the nping. xechod is suspended until an nping message is received. Unlike the other daemons in this list, the xechod process runs on both the client and the server.

Since IPX/SPX uses conventional LLI network drivers, the llistat command can be used to monitor the network. Special IPX/SPX monitoring commands are summarized in Table 8-3.

Behavior	Command	Column
Number of times a packet travels through a router to reach the network described by NET	drouter	NET, HOPS
Estimated amount of time to reach the network	drouter	TIME
Destination machine on destination network	drouter	NODE
Time for packet to travel to destination	nping	time is displayed in milliseconds
Send/Receive packets between machines via IPX	throw/catch	
Obtain IPX/SPX configuration information	getlan	

Table 8-3: Special IPX/SPX Monitoring Commands

drouter The drouter command displays the packet routing information. The value displayed in the NET column is the network number for which the rest of the data is displayed. The value shown in the HOPS column shows the number of times a packet has travelled through a router to reach the network specified by the value in NET. The value shown in TIME is an estimate of the number of clock ticks (100ths of a second) required to reach the network described in NET. The NODE column displays the target host on the network.

nping The command nping provides information similar to the ping command in TCP/IP. The time taken per packet is displayed in milliseconds. This value provides an indication of the travel time between the client and the server.

catch, throw

Although they are not directly related to monitoring, the commands throw(PADM) and catch(PADM) are useful because they can be used to construct a test case where data is sent from one machine to another with the IPX datagram protocol. The throw command reads data from standard input, stdin, and sends the data to the specified host. The command waits for a response from the server. The catch command reads data from the network and sends an acknowledgment to the system that originally sent the message.

getlan

IPX/SPX configuration information is provided by the getlan(PADM) command. The information displayed by this command is not directly relevant to resource usage monitoring.

Since IPX/SPX are implemented as streams modules, sufficient streams resources must be available to handle all of the network traffic generated by the clients and the servers.

Some tunable variables are defined in */etc/conf/pack.d/spx/spx_tune.h* and */etc/conf/pack.d/nvt/nvt_tune.h*. These variables are described in more detail in the SCO IPX/SPX Administrator's Guide and Reference. These tunable variables do not normally affect performance and are best left untouched.

As with all other listener processes, the server must be configured with sufficient resources to ensure these listener processes run frequently enough to service their clients.

STREAMS

The network subsystem uses an intermediate storage location called *streams buffers* while processing the network messages and packets. All of the network protocols discussed in this chapter use streams modules to transform the messages into packets on the sending machine and to unpack and combine the packets into messages on the receiving machine.

Streams module

A *streams module* is an operating system program that can be inserted into a particular data travel pathway. These streams modules can be chained together so they operate on the information in a specified order. This chain of modules, plus some special modules, is called a *stream*. A streams buffer contains the information to be processed by the streams modules. In the context of networking, the phrase *downstream* means the information travels from the application to the network interface card; the phrase *upstream* means the information travels from the network interface card to the application. A protocol such as TCP is implemented using a series of streams modules that are known as the *TCP protocol stack*.

The protocol stack allocates the most appropriate size of streams buffer for the message. The streams are constructed when the operating system initializes, depending on the network protocols, modules and network interface cards configured into the system.

An example of the processing that occurs on a stream is the conversion of network addresses. Network addresses at the IP level are different from the physical addresses that are used by the packets on the network. A special streams module is located between the IP layer and the LLI driver to decode the IP address and convert it to a physical address. As the messages travels downstream, the IP address is converted to an address appropriate for the network.

The information that the application sends is copied from the application storage area to a streams buffer. The information is then processed by the appropriate streams modules associated with the connection service and network protocol specified by the application.

After protocol processing, the data continues down the stream to the Link Layer Interface driver. The Link Layer Interface driver manages the network interface card that connects the computer to the network.

When the LLI driver receives the information in the streams buffers, it copies the information onto the network.

At the destination, when the LLI driver receives the packet, the network card driver copies the data received from the network into a streams buffer. The driver then passes the buffer up the stream for unpacking by the protocol modules. Once all the packets of a message are received, the message is then passed to the application.

The CPU executes all streams processing. Therefore, the availability of the CPU determines the time required for packet/message handling as the information flows along the stream.

NSTREAM

The number of streams supported by the operating system is set by the value of NSTREAM. If NSTREAM is not large enough to support all the services required, then some of the network or X windows services may not be available. If the operating system cannot allocate a stream, the operating system prints the following message:

```
CONFIG: stropenX - Out of streams (NSTREAM = Y
exceeded)
```

where Y is the current value of NSTREAM. The value of NSTREAM affects the availability of services and only impacts performance indirectly.

NQUEUE

The total number of streams modules supported by the system is determined by the value of NQUEUE. Like the value of NSTREAM, the value of NQUEUE does not directly affect performance.

The netstat -m command can display current values of NSTREAM and NQUEUE. The line beginning with the word streams displays the current setting of NSTREAM and the line beginning with the word "queues" is the current value of NQUEUE.

NBLK4 - NBLK4096

The number of each size of streams buffers allocated by the operating system is determined by a series of configurable variables: NBLK4, NBLK16, NBLK64, NBLK128, NBLK256, NBLK512, NBLK1024, NBLK2048 and NBLK4096. Each size is configured separately. When a buffer of one size is not available, a buffer of the next larger size is allocated. If a buffer of the next size is not available, the protocol stack aborts the processing of the message and executes error recovery.

The application is affected by the shortage of streams buffers in one of the following ways:

- The application is suspended until a streams buffer becomes available
- The application fails in a way that makes diagnosing the true cause of the error quite difficult
- The application generates an error message that allows diagnosis of the underlying resource shortage

For example, a 14-byte message is normally stored in a 16-byte streams buffer. If no 16-byte streams buffers are available, then a 64-byte buffer is used. If no 64-byte buffers are available, then the request fails, and an error message is returned to the requesting application. Because of the allocation of larger buffers, a shortage of a smaller buffers can cause a shortage of larger buffers, thereby causing an inefficient memory usage pattern. In some cases, applications cannot continue until a buffer is available. In these cases, the lack of streams buffers causes an even longer delay to operation completion.

Streams messages are managed according to a priority mechanism. With this mechanism, a request may fail even if the appropriate-sized buffer is available because that buffer is reserved for a higher priority message. Requests for streams buffers are prioritized into three categories: low, medium and high. The percentage of buffers reserved for a particular priority is configurable with two variables: STRLOFRAC and STRMEDFRAC.

STRLOFRAC

The value of STRLOFRAC indicates the percentage of buffers that can be used to satisfy a low priority request. For example, if NBLK64 is set to 100 and STRLOFRAC is set to 95, then 95 64-byte buffers can be used for low priority messages. If all 95 are in use, then the next low priority request will fail, even though five buffers are free.

STRMEDFRAC

The value of STRMEDFRAC indicates the percentage of buffers that can be used to satisfy a medium-level priority request. The value of STRMEDFRAC should be between STRLOFRAC and 100.

A high priority request is always satisfied if a free buffer of either the appropriate size, or the next size up, is available.

When a request for a streams buffer fails, a loss of functionality usually occurs. Unfortunately, this loss of functionality does not always occur in an obvious way. Therefore, the importance of having sufficient streams buffers cannot be overstated.

Other configurable variables relating to streams, such as NMUXLINK, NSTRPUSH, STRMSGSZ and STRCTLSZ do not directly affect performance. The values of NSTREVENT and MAXSEPGCNT affect the amount of memory used by streams. In most cases, these should be left at their default values, as the amount of memory used is not significant. See the Open Desktop System Administrator's Manual for more information on these variables.

Flow Control

The list of messages to be processed by a streams module may grow to a specified length. When the list achieves this size, flow control is asserted and further attempts to write to the stream cause the operating system to suspend the application process doing the writing until the list is shorter. Flow control is a mechanism that controls the size of the message list by suspending all requesting processes when the list is full and then allowing them to resume when the list empties. Although flow control affects performance, flow control is not directly configurable.

Flow control affects application performance because the application may be suspended if the message queue cannot be emptied as fast as the application processes send requests. The availability of the CPU and the ability of the network interface card to send requests impact the speed at which the queue of messages can be emptied. Figures 8-3 and 8-4 show how flow control affects streams resource usage.

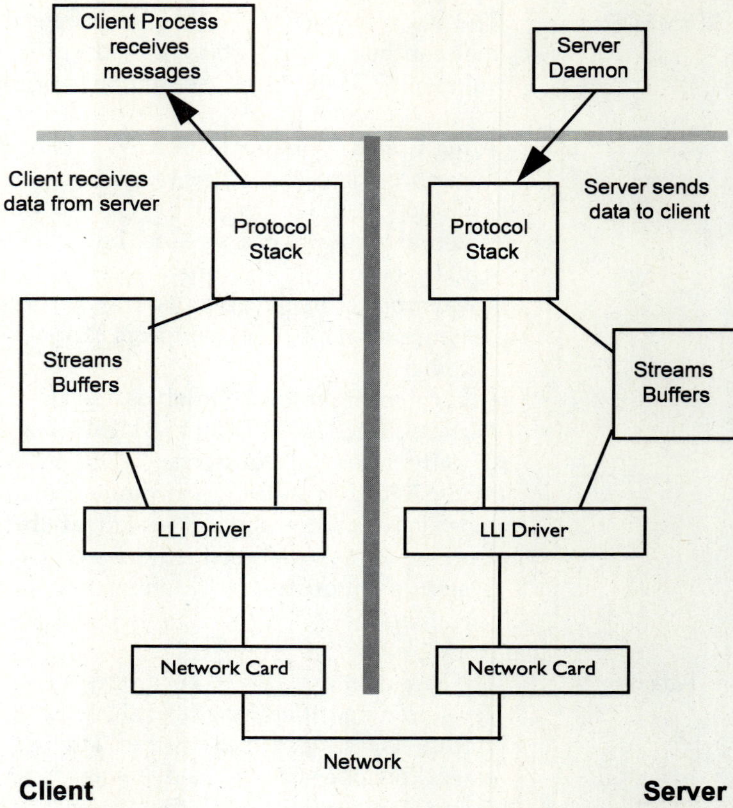

Figure 8-3: The server sends messages to the client until the client can no longer receive them. The protocol stack detects the size of the message list has approached the limit, and sends a flow control message to the server machine.

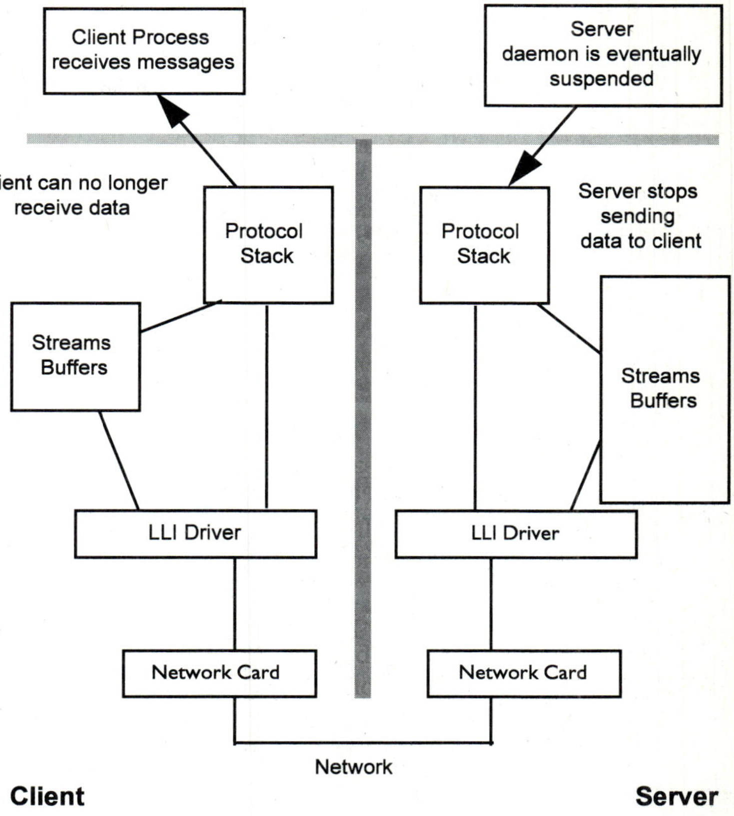

Figure 8-4: The server machine receives the flow control message and eventually suspends the server daemon that is generating the messages. The number of streams buffers used on the server increases because the messages cannot be sent.

Flow control also affects application processes receiving data from the stream. If the application process does not read the data frequently enough, the incoming streams queue can fill up, thereby causing a flow control message to be sent to the sending machine. The sending machine then suspends all writing activity until the receiving machine is ready to receive messages once again.

Sufficient resources on the receiving machine must therefore be available to ensure that the application processes reading data from the network run frequently enough to avoid streams backlogs.

HINT:

The command netstat -i shows the number of packets that are sent and received by a system. If the values reported by this command rises in bursts, then check the application documentation to see if the application can be configured to use the network with a more consistent activity level. Steady traffic requires a smaller number of streams buffers and is less likely to cause flow control to occur.

Table 8-4 summarizes the commands that monitor streams usage.

Behavior	**Command**	**Column/row**
Number of queues configured	netstat -m	config/queues
Number of queues currently used	netstat -m	alloc/queues
Number of queues free	netstat -m	free/queues
Total number queues allocated since the operating system booted	netstat -m	total/queues
Maximum number of queues allocated since the operating system booted	netstat -m	max/queues
Number of queue allocation failures since the operating system booted	netstat -m	fail/queues

Table 8-4: Streams Monitoring Commands

Behavior	Command	Column/row
Number of "class 0" or 4-byte streams buffers configured	netstat -m	config/class 0, 4 bytes
Number of "class 0" streams buffers allocated	netstat -m	alloc/class 0, 4 bytes
Number of unallocated "class 0" streams buffers	netstat -m	free/class 0, 4 bytes
Total number of "class 0" streams buffers allocated since the operating system booted	netstat -m	total/class 0, 4 bytes
Maximum number of "class 0" streams buffers allocated since the operating system booted	netstat -m	max/class 0, 4 bytes
Number of failures to allocate "class 0" streams buffers since the operating system booted	netstat -m	fail/class 0, 4 bytes

Table 8-4 (Continued): Streams Monitoring Commands

netstat -m

The usage statistics for each size buffer are displayed. The class label also denotes the size of the buffer. For example, class 0 denotes 4-byte buffers and class 1 denotes 16-byte buffers. The rest of the rows displayed by netstat -m report information on the streams buffers of other sizes. netstat -m also displays the following information:

```
total configured streams memory: xx KB
streams memory in use: yy KB
maximum streams memory used: zz KB
```

where xx, yy, and zz are equal to the amounts of memory used.

The command netstat -m is useful because it provides all the relevant streams buffer and memory usage information in one place in a straightforward manner as shown in the table. If any of the values shown in the fail column are greater than zero, then a streams shortage has occurred.

Before reallocating any memory on either the server or the client, ensure that a sufficient number of streams buffers are available to support the number of messages. All failures to allocate streams buffers must be eliminated before reallocating memory for any other use. Lack of streams buffers causes a number of side effects, including the following:

- Inefficient memory usage because larger streams buffers are allocated when smaller ones would be sufficient

- Higher network traffic because message retransmission results in an overall larger number of frames, but fewer messages successfully completed

- More CPU usage due to increased network traffic because of the retransmissions

- Difficult to diagnose application failures

The symptom of insufficient streams may actually hide an underlying problem with the network interface card, the configuration of the protocol, or the availability of the CPU to process messages. Because insufficient streams is often a symptom of an underlying problem, increasing the number of streams does not always improve performance.

Packets waiting to be sent are kept in streams buffers until the network card can send them. If the network card sends packets at a slower rate than the applications generate them, then flow control will be invoked and the usage of streams buffers will increase. Increasing the number of streams buffers does not actually improve performance, because the messages must still wait until the network card can send them. Instead, increasing the number of streams buffers decreases the possibility of network and application errors. Increasing the number of streams buffers does not solve the inability of the network card to send messages fast enough.

Incoming packets are stored in streams buffers awaiting unpacking by the server protocol stack. If the CPU is unavailable to process these incoming packets, then the streams buffers usage increases and flow control may be invoked. As above, increasing the number of streams buffers decreases the likelihood of buffers running out, but does not increase the availability of the CPU. Likewise, increasing the number of streams buffers does not reduce the duration of the operation, because the lack of CPU time is what is actually causing the delay. Increasing the number of streams buffers does decrease the number of packet retransmissions and does increase the efficiency of the network.

Remember that failure to allocate a buffer of a given size causes a buffer of the next larger size to be allocated. For example, if allocation failures are reported on 16 and 64-byte buffers, then raise the number of 16-byte buffers until no more allocation failures occur on this size before increasing the number of 64-byte buffers. Increasing just the 16-byte buffers may solve both the 16-byte and 64-byte allocation failures, thereby allocating memory more efficiently than increasing both size of buffers.

Increasing the number of smaller size buffers may eliminate the errors encountered when allocating both the smaller and the larger size buffers. Only when a sufficient number of streams buffers are consistently available for all sizes should the allocation of other resources be considered.

If increasing the number of streams buffers causes the server to either page or swap, then increasing the amount of memory available to the server is critical to reasonable performance. Paging and swapping decrease the amount of CPU time available to process network messages, and the streams buffers may run out again because the CPU is busy paging and swapping instead of processing network messages.

Use the techniques described in the Open Desktop chapter to determine the amount of free memory available and whether paging and swapping are occurring. If paging or swapping are occurring, then either reduce current memory usage as suggested in Appendix B, or install additional memory.

The Link Layer Interface Driver, Network Card And Network

The *Link Layer Interface driver* is the last streams module in the stream. The last module in the stream is known as the *streams driver*. The LLI driver manages the network interface card that connects the machine to the network.

Each driver is written specifically for the hardware it manages. Because network vary in their capabilities, each driver and network card combination impacts performance differently.

Table 8-5 summarizes some of the capabilities of network interface cards and how they impact the time required to transmit data.

Feature	Impact on Transmission Time
8-bit, 16-bit, 32-bit wide data path for system bus access	The wider the data path, the shorter the transmission time because more data can be sent in parallel.
Bus master DMA, preferably 32-bit so all memory is accessible	Reduces transmission time because the CPU is not necessary to copy data from the streams buffer to the network card. If all the memory is accessible, then transmission time is reduced because streams buffer can be copied directly to network interface card. If the streams buffer is not directly addressable by network interface card, then streams buffer must be copied to an intermediate location that is accessible by the card.
Amount of memory on card	In general, the more memory the card has, the shorter the transmission time.

Table 8-5: Features of Network Interface Cards

If the network card cannot transmit packets as fast as the protocol stack generates packets, then streams buffer usage increases because the packets waiting to be transmitted are stored in the streams buffers. If the network interface card cannot receive packets as fast as the packets are sent over the network, then retransmission of packets may be necessary, and network efficiency is decreased.

Since servers tend to receive packets from multiple clients, a higher capacity network interface card may need to be installed on the server to keep up with the network traffic. For example, the server may require a 32-bit bus master EISA network interface card, whereas the clients may use lower capacity 16-bit or 8-bit cards.

Some network interface cards can access the streams buffer directly and transmit the information contained in it without copying it into an intermediate storage location. Other cards require the CPU to copy the information to memory on the card itself before transmitting the information over the network. Reducing the amount of CPU time required for transmission of data minimizes delays due to the lack of CPU availability and increases the availability of the CPU for other operations. Reducing the amount of CPU time required for network transmissions is essential to good server performance.

A network interface card that cannot keep up with the frequency of packets can cause additional network traffic because packets must be re-sent, thereby reducing the efficiency of the network. Because the bookkeeping for tracking the packets that have been acknowledged is executed in a higher layer in the protocol stack, resending a packet starts in the higher protocol layers. The cost of packet retransmission is high because the packet must be packaged up and sent over the network again. In general, when a network card is busy handling one packet, all other packets intended for that machine are ignored until the card completes the handling of that packet.

The Network

The network is the physical connection between the machines. The term *network* is also used to describe the collection of machines attached to the physical connection that transmits the data.

The time taken for packets to travel across the network depends on the following factors:

- The network technology used
- The amount of network traffic
- The layout of the network, or the *topology*

The first two are discussed in this section and the topology is discussed in the Network Layout section. Only the technologies supported in Open Desktop are discussed in this section.

Ethernet

Ethernet supports data transfer rates up to a maximum of 10 Mbits/second. This transfer rate does not take into account any packet processing at either the source or destination. With packet processing at either end of the transmission, the actual data rate is somewhat lower than the theoretical maximum.

When a packet of data is transmitted across Ethernet, all of the *transceivers* physically connected to that network receive the transmission. A transceiver is the physical device that connects the network card to the network. The network interface card is responsible for deciding which packets are actually addressed to the computer. The Ethernet hardware protocol is known as CSMA/CD, or Carrier Sense Multiple Access with Collision Detection.

When multiple machines attempt to access the network at the same time, a collision occurs, and both machines stop their transfers. After a random delay, each machine restarts its transfer. If another collision occurs, then the delay is increased exponentially, and the machine tries again. Each time a collision occurs, both machines increase their respective delays exponentially until the transfer is complete.

After the first collision, additional collisions for that particular packet of information are avoided because of the random delay before the machine tries to send the packet again. Figures 8-5 to 8-7 show how the random delay affects packet transmissions.

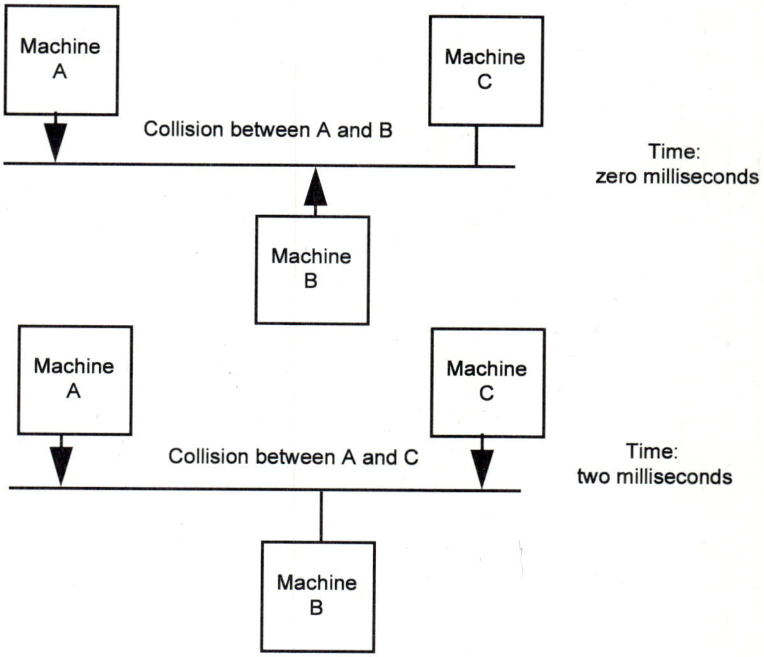

Figure 8-5: When machine A and machine B attempt to simultaneously transmit a message, a collision occurs. Machine A calculates a random delay of two milliseconds and machine B calculates a random delay of three milliseconds. After the delay, machine A still cannot transmit a message because machine C also wants to send a message. Both machine A and machine C calculate their respective delays and retransmit at the appropriate time.

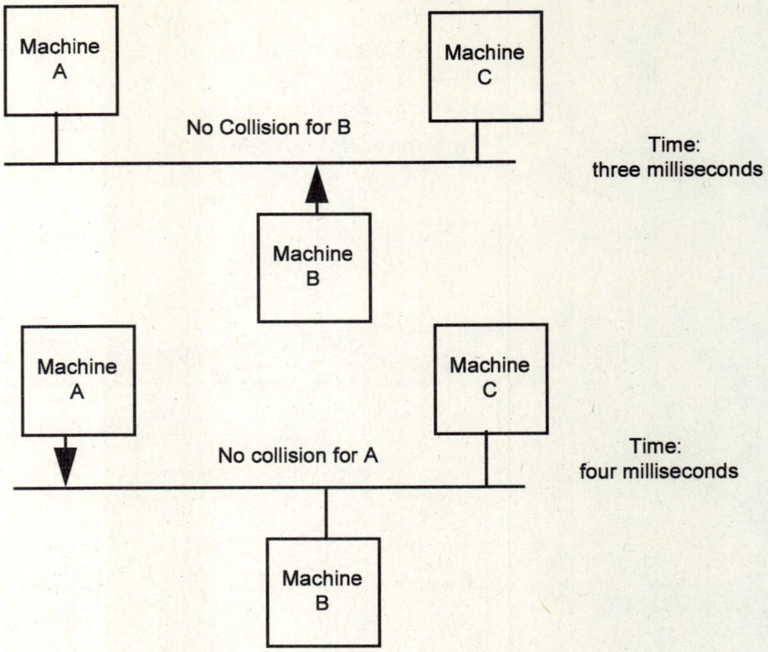

Figure 8-6: Machine A and B can now transmit the message with no collisions occurring.

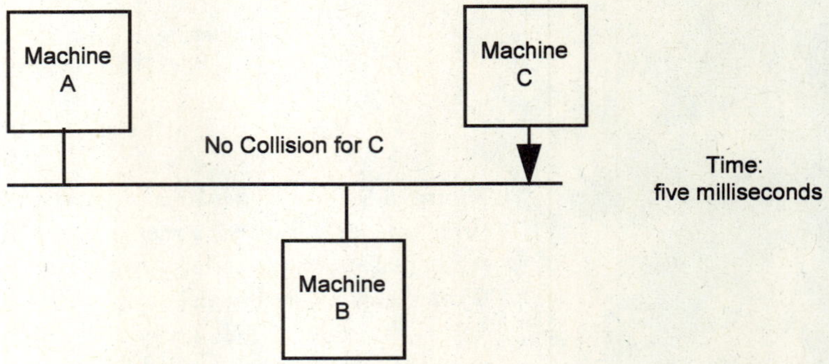

Figure 8-7: Machine C can now transmit the message with no collisions. Because of the random delay recalculation, the likelihood of another collision occurring is greatly reduced, and delays due to collisions are normally minimal.

The higher the level of collisions on the network, the greater the percentage of transfers impacted by the delay caused by the collision. The transfer rate achieved from client to server is always lower than the fundamental value provided by the hardware, for example, 10 Mbits/sec, because of the protocol processing and collisions.

Table 8-6 summarizes how to monitor the LLI driver, network interface card and network usage. The first group of entries describes how to determine the amount of network traffic; the second group describes how to determine the number of errors. Calculating percentages based on the total number of errors and the total number of packets sent gives an indication of the efficiency of the network.

Behavior	**Command**	**Column**
Name of network interface card	netconfig	chains display
Reset LLI driver statistics to 0	llistat -c	none
Number of packets received	netstat -i	Ipkts, Address, Name
Number of packets sent	netstat -i	Opkts, Address, Name
Number of collisions	netstat -i	Collis
Number of incoming frame errors	netstat -i	Ierrs
Number of outgoing frame errors	netstat -i	Oerrs
Number of bytes that can be sent in one transmission	netstat -i	Mtu
Name of the adapter	netstat -i	Network

Table 8-6: How To Monitor the LLI Driver, Network Interface Card and Network Usage

Behavior	Command	Column
Number of bytes transmitted by the network interface card	llistat -l	Transmitted Octets
Number of frames sent	llistat -l	Frames Transmitted
Number of network interface card interrupts	llistat -l	Device Interrupts
Number of interrupts generated when no frames to be processed	llistat -l	Spurious Interrupts
Number of times frames had to be resent	llistat -l	Total Collisions, Frames Involved in a Collision, Out of Frame Collisions, Frames Dropped due to Excessive Collisions
Number of times frames had to be re-sent because of no streams buffers	llistat -l	Frames Dropped due to No Streams
Which streams buffers ran out	netstat -m	fail, and all streams buffer size rows
Number of times frames dropped because device-specific resources ran out	llistat -l	Frames Dropped due to No Resources

Table 8-6 (Continued): How To Monitor the LLI Driver, Network Interface Card and Network Usage.

netconfig The name of the network interface card is an argument to some of these monitoring tools. The name is the value used when configuring the network subsystem with netconfig(ADM). Use the chains display to determine the network card used for the protocol being monitored. The netconfig also displays the different network protocols and network cards that are configured in the system. Please see the Open Server System Administrator's Guide for more information.

llistat -c

Before running any test operation that uses llistat to monitor network traffic, clear the accumulated statistics by executing the following command:

```
llistat -c network_card_name
```

where network_card_name is the name of the network card from netconfig. Only the superuser can run this command.

netstat -i

The Ipkts and Opkts columns displayed by netstat -i show the number of packets that have been received (Input packets) and sent (Output packets) for each network interface card used by this machine. The Address column shows the name corresponding to that address. This name is found by either matching the network address to a name in the */etc/hosts* file or by querying the network name server, if the name is controlled by the name server. See the Open Desktop System Administrator's Guide for a discussion of name servers.

The values displayed are the actual number of packets transmitted or received, instead of a frequency, such as number of packets transmitted per second. The values are updated each time packets are sent or received.

The Collis column displays the absolute number of collisions experienced by this network interface card. On a typical Ethernet network, some small number of collisions is inevitable. The percentage of collisions can be obtained with the following equation:

$$\frac{Collis}{Opkts} * 100 = percentage\_of\_outgoing\_collisions$$

The number of errors encountered when receiving incoming or sending outgoing frames is shown by the Ierrs and Oerrs columns.

The Name column shows the name of the adapter that is being used for that network address. The number of the adapter is appended to the name of the adapter. For example, the e3b0 is the first adapter using the e3B driver. The loopback driver is shown as lo0.

The Mtu column shows the number of bytes that can be sent in one packet for transmission. Ethernet adapters show a maximum value of 1500 because the maximum size of an Ethernet frame is 12,000 bits. 12,000 bits divided by 8 bits per byte is equal to 1500 bytes.

The Network column identifies the network to which the adapter is attached. The network is obtained by matching the IP address with the values in */etc/networks*. For example, if the IP address is A.B.C.D and there is an entry in */etc/networks* for A.B, and this matching entry has the name called "accountsystem" then "accountsystem" is the name that is displayed.

To obtain correct values for the test, run netstat once at the beginning and once at the end of the test operation. The difference in the values is the number of packets sent/received during the operation.

HINT:

The net2wks utility provided on the floppy automatically computes the correct resource usage statistics when given files containing netstat -i data from before and after the test.

llistat -l

The llistat command provides information specific to a network interface card. Not all drivers collect statistics for all of the information reported by llistat, so some columns may be equal to zero because that statistic is not collected by that driver. Other drivers may collect additional statistics beyond those described here. See the hardware documentation for specific details for statistics not described here.

If more than one network interface card is configured, then llistat should be invoked with an explicit name for the card rather than relying on the default card chosen by llistat. The name of the network interface card is the value used when the network subsystem is configured with netconfig. Use netconfig at any time to see the different network protocols and network cards that are used. See the Open Desktop System Administrator's Manual for more information on netconfig.

The column Transmitted Octets displays the number of bytes transmitted by the network card. The value provides a measure of the amount of data the system running the llistat command transmits to the network.

The Frames Transmitted value shows the number of times information was passed from the network driver to the network interface card for transmission across the network. The values reported by netstat -i and llistat -i are the same. The values reported by netstat -s are different in that they are divided into the different protocols.

In many cases, when the network card receives a frame, the network card generates an interrupt notifying the driver that a frame has arrived. The number of interrupts generated by the network card is shown in the column Device Interrupts.

The number of interrupts generated that did not involve the receipt of a frame is shown in the Spurious Interrupts column. This value is normally equal to zero. Some drivers show the number of interrupts equal to the number of spurious interrupts. In such cases, both of these values should be ignored.

The values shown in the Total Collisions, Frames Involved in a Collision, Out of Frame Collisions, and Frames Dropped due to Excessive Collisions columns show how many times network collisions caused frames to be resent.

The percentage of frames affected by collisions can be determined with the following equation:

$$\frac{Total\_Collisions}{Frames\_Transmitted} * 100 = Percentage\_Frames\_Affected\_by\_Collisions$$

This percentage shows the number of frames affected by collisions and gives an indication of network efficiency.

The value in the column Frames Dropped due to No Streams shows how many times frames could be not taken off the network because no streams buffers were available to store the incoming messages. Use netstat -m to see which streams buffers ran out.

The value in the column Frames Dropped due to No Resources shows the number of times frames could not be taken off the network because some resource in the driver was exhausted. The resources vary, depending on the network card. For example, the wdn network interface driver uses this column to report when a packet could not be received because the wdn network card was busy handling another packet.

The primary goals of tuning the network are as follows:

- Eliminate streams allocations errors
- Reduce collisions and retransmissions

Before changing any resource allocation, determine the efficiency of the network by checking for errors when sending or receiving packets and whether a sufficient number of streams buffers are available.

If llistat displays a value greater than zero in the column Frames Dropped due to No Streams, use netstat -m to check which streams buffer size ran out. Increase the number of buffers according to the recommendations provided in the Streams section of this chapter.

If the values displayed in the Ierrs or Oerrs columns always increase when running the test operation, then check the physical network connections and network card for possible hardware defects. Network interface cards vary significantly, so always check the documentation provided with the network card(s) for any tunable options.

TCPWINDOW

If the network interface card has a large, for example 32 Kbyte buffer, try increasing the *TCPWINDOW* variable in the file */etc/conf/pack.d/tcp/space.c*. Increasing the value of *TCPWINDOW* increases the amount of information which may be transferred in one network transmission.

Setting the value of tcp_round_mss equal to zero may increase the performance of network interface cards with larger buffers. This variable is located in */etc/conf/pack.d/tcp/space.c.* With a value of zero, the size of the transfer is not shortened to the nearest 1 Kbyte value. Any size of transfer can then be sent.

Use llistat -l and check the columns Total Collisions, Frames Involved in a Collision, Out of Frame Collisions, and Frames Dropped due to Excessive Collisions. The values in these columns should be equal to zero unless the network is heavily loaded. If the percentage of collisions is greater than 5%, then either the network is being used heavily or there is a problem with one or more connections. Collisions affect the duration of the test operation by introducing delay due to network traffic. The collision values reported by llistat refers only to affected output packets.

If the network is heavily loaded, then, if possible, repeat the test measurement when the network is not heavily used to see how much the duration of the operation is impacted by the heavy network traffic. If the time taken by the test operation decreases, reconfiguring the network to reduce the number of errors can improve performance. See the Network Layout section for more information on reconfiguring the network. However, if the time taken by the test operation does not change by more than 10%, then proceed with tuning both the client and the server.

If the time taken by the test operation falls when the amount of network traffic is lower, consider changing the topology of the network to increase its efficiency and reduce the number of collisions. When the network is heavily used, the most effective technique is to change the topology of the network. The method varies with the different protocols. Please see the Network Layout section for more information on reconfiguring the network.

Network Layout

Network efficiency is also determined by the layout of the machines on the network and the route that frames take on the journey from the source to destination machine.

The physical limitations of Ethernet must first be overcome, and then the network layout can be analyzed for possible ways in which collisions could be reduced. The amount of flexibility in the layout depends on the requirements of the network user community; those needs must be taken into account when modifying the layout for increased efficiency.

Repeaters

Because of physical constraints, one section of thick Ethernet coaxial cable can extend to a maximum of 500 meters. Thin coaxial cable can only extend to 185 meters, but suppliers generally provide products that allow longer lengths to be configured. Adding two repeaters extends the cable length to 1500 meters. Multiple repeaters can connect up to five segments, but only three of those segments can be populated with computers; the others must be empty. The empty segments are used only for extending the cable length. Any Ethernet configuration must comply with the Ethernet standard described in the following document: Local Area Network - CSMA/CD Access Method and Physical Layer Specification, American National Standard, ANSI/IEEE Std. 802.3.

When frames are sent, they are received by all the transceivers physically connected to the network, so extending the length of the cable results in longer journey times for the information travelling between machines.

The repeater rejuvenates the electronic signals that comprise a frame so the signal is strong enough to sustain another 500 meter journey.

Bridges

Since networks often need to be longer than 1500 meters, different Ethernet sections can be connected together using a bridge. These different sections are called *subnets*. The term subnet refers to a smaller section of a larger network. A bridge transmits from one subnet to another. Unlike a repeater, the frames are taken from the first network section and reconstructed and retransmitted on the second network, instead of being electronically recharged.
Since the frames are read and retransmitted by the bridge, the journey time for the frames is increased by travel through the bridge. The time required for the frame to travel over the bridge is greater than the time required to travel through a repeater. No other parts of the network are affected by this transfer when the bridge passes packets of data to the destination network section.

Gateways

Two separate networks can be connected by a computer configured as a gateway. The gateway machine is connected to both networks and is configured so that the gateway is separately addressable by all machines connected to each of the attached networks. Figure 8-8 shows a gateway connecting two subnets. A gateway looks at the frame addresses of frames found on network A and transfers frames addressed for network B to network B. The gateway also looks for frames addressed for network B that are travelling on network A and transfers those packets to network B.

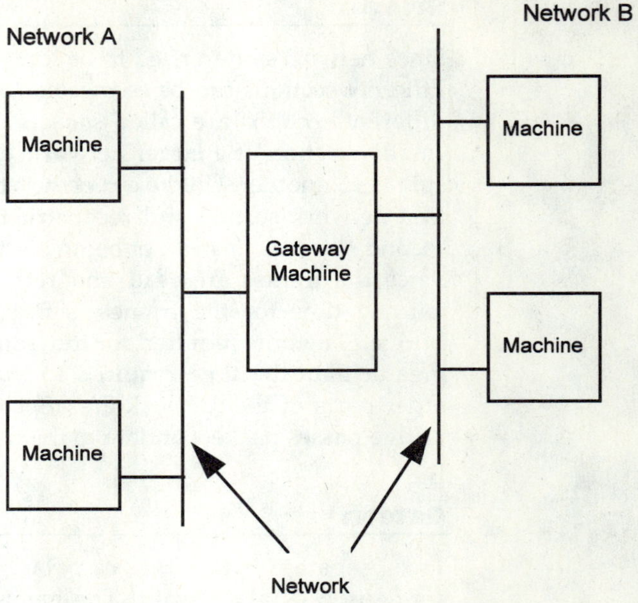

Figure 8-8: A Gateway Machine Connecting Two Networks

Each packet sent on the network carries information, known as *time-to-live*, stating how much longer the packet is valid. This value is reduced when packets pass through a gateway. When this value reaches zero, the packet is discarded and information is sent to the packet source, stating that the time for the particular route was exceeded.

tcp_ttl, udp_ttl

For TCP, the time-to-live value is given by the value of tcp_ttl in */etc/conf/pack.d/tcp/space.c*. Modifying the value affects how far a packet can travel. For UDP, the value is given by udp_ttl in */etc/conf/pack.d/udp/space.c*.

Routing

When dividing the network into subnets, servers and clients should be, where possible, on the same subnet to avoid frequent delays in the client/server communication.

As the network grows in size and complexity, the routing of frames becomes a greater factor in the information journey time. For simple networks with no sub-nets, frame routing cannot be reduced. If the frame travels between gateways and bridges to arrive at its destination, the selection of those gateways and bridges can affect the journey time. The route a packet takes over the network is selected automatically, and so cannot be tuned.

Table 8-7 summarizes how to monitor the journey of the packet.

Behavior	**Command**	**Column**
Routing	netstat -r	Destination/ Gateway/Use
Routing	traceroute	All rows

Table 8-7: Commands For Monitoring the Journey of a Packet

netstat -r

The command netstat -r shows the gateway that is used when a message is transmitted to a particular system or network. The Destination column shows one of the following:

- the destination network address
- the system name retrieved from */etc/hosts*
- a system name retrieved from a name server

The gateway column specifies the gateway associated with that network address. The information provided by netstat -r does not change unless the network topology changes, because the information is defined when the network is configured.

traceroute

The traceroute command provides a list of all the network addresses that are used during the packet's journey from the sender to the receiver. The duration of each section of the journey from the sender to the received is displayed in milliseconds

Because this command displays the actual route taken by a packet, comparisons between different routes can be made. If the route taken by packets can change without any intervention, then the values shown by traceroute may change when traceroute is executed multiple times.

Over time, a network layout that might have provided sufficient throughput with a small number machines installed may no longer be appropriate with a larger number of machines.

Bridges and gateways help reduce the number of collisions because the same number of machines can be connected to the network, but they are connected to separate parts of the network, thereby decreasing the likelihood of collision. Each subnet of the overall network has fewer machines directly connected to it, so fewer collisions occur.

If the network already contains multiple smaller networks, use netstat -r to check the routes that are taken by the packets. Confirm the precise route taken by packets going from the client to the server to ensure that it is optimal by using traceroute.

Even though computers might be located on separate network sections, information can still travel between them through bridges and gateways. The number of collisions occurring on the network must be balanced with the additional amount of time required to travel over a bridge or gateway to decide what the optimal network layout should be.

Whether a bridge is used to improve network performance depends on the frame travel patterns for that network. For example, if one server is providing a service for one group of clients and another server is providing service for a different group clients, then performance might be improved by connecting each server to all of its respective clients with two subnets. The resulting configuration is one server and its clients on one subnet and another server and its clients on the other subnet. A bridge could then connect the two subnets so any communication that might have occurred prior to the division into subnets can still occur.

Quick Diagnosis Summary

This section highlights the key monitoring tools and tuning guidelines described in this chapter.

Network Efficiency

The primary behaviors that should be monitored to diagnose network efficiency are summarized in Table 8-8.

Behavior	Command	Column
Streams usage	netstat -m	fail column for each buffer size
Number of times frames had to be re-sent because of no streams buffers	llistat -l	Frames Dropped due to No Streams
Protocol errors	netstat -s	Rows that apply to the protocol in use
Number of packets transmitted and received	netstat -i	Ipkts, Opkts, Address, Name
Number of collisions	netstat -i	Collis
Number of incoming/outgoing errors	netstat -i	Ierrs, Oerrs
Number of times frames had to be re-sent	llistat -l	Total Collisions, Frames Involved In a Collisions, Out of Frame Collisions, Frames Dropped due to Excessive Collisions

Table 8-8: Key Behaviors For Diagnosing Network Efficiency

The primary tuning guidelines for maximizing network efficiency are as follows:

- Eliminate streams errors
- Eliminate network errors, such as retransmission errors
- Minimize collisions by reorganizing network layout
- Maximize CPU time for processing streams messages

Chapter 9

Common Client/Server Operations

The common operations described in this chapter are remote server access and remote file access. The remote server access operation covers situations where users access servers and run applications directly on the server. This type of access is also known as *remote login*. The remote file read and write operation describes the resources that are used to support clients accessing files located on other machines. This chapter builds on the information provided in Chapter 8. Chapter 10 includes two network tuning examples.

A Word About Monitoring Tools

As in the previous chapter, the SCO UNIX and SCO MPX monitoring tools, sar, mpsar, and cpusar are used and referred to in this chapter. In all places where sar is mentioned, mpsar and/or cpusar could also be used, although these multiprocessor tools may not be explicitly mentioned.

One new tool, nfsstat(NADM), is introduced in this chapter. This command is described in more detail in the SCO Open Desktop/SCO Open Server System Administrator's Guide.

Remote Server Access

The simplest way to reach information on another machine is through *remote server access* with a special type of login process. This special login process allows a user or client to access information on the remote machine exactly as if the client were accessing the information locally through a normal login. Once the user gains access to the server machine, the user can execute applications on the server. The application process updates the client display with the appropriate information via the special login process. Executing applications on a server machine while logged in from a client machine is known as *remote application execution.* Figure 9-1 shows a sample remote login access configuration.

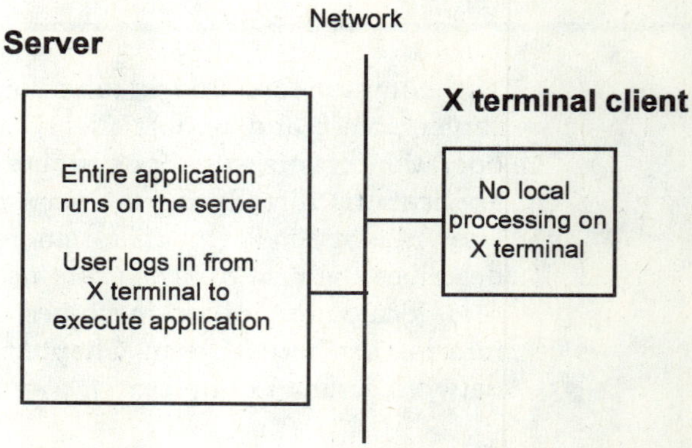

Figure 9-1: The X terminal client has no local processing capacity beyond running the embedded X server, so all of the applications that the user wants to run must be executed on the server. The display update involves the application sending the new display information to the X terminal over the network.

Because the application process actually executes on the server, optimizing remote application execution via the remote login mechanism is similar to optimizing local application execution. Additional consideration must be made for optimizing the resources required for transmitting information between the client and the server.

Two common mechanisms for accessing server machines are X terminals and Open Desktop client workstations. X terminals support only local running of the X server. All other application execution occurs on the server. Open Desktop client workstations are more flexible, because part of an application can run on the client and part can run on the server. Such a split is possible only if the application is constructed with a *client/server* architecture. If the application does not have a client/server architecture, then the application either runs completely on the client or completely on the server. Figure 9-2 shows a client/server configuration.

Database applications intended for network use are commonly constructed with separate but cooperating client and server application processes that communicate via TCP/IP. Some other types of applications, such as word processing applications, require only a single process and so can be run either on the Open Desktop client workstation or on the Open Desktop server with the remote login mechanism. Even if the Open Desktop client workstation actually executes the application process, the files manipulated by the application can be located on the server. This type of remote file access is discussed in the Remote File Access section of this chapter.

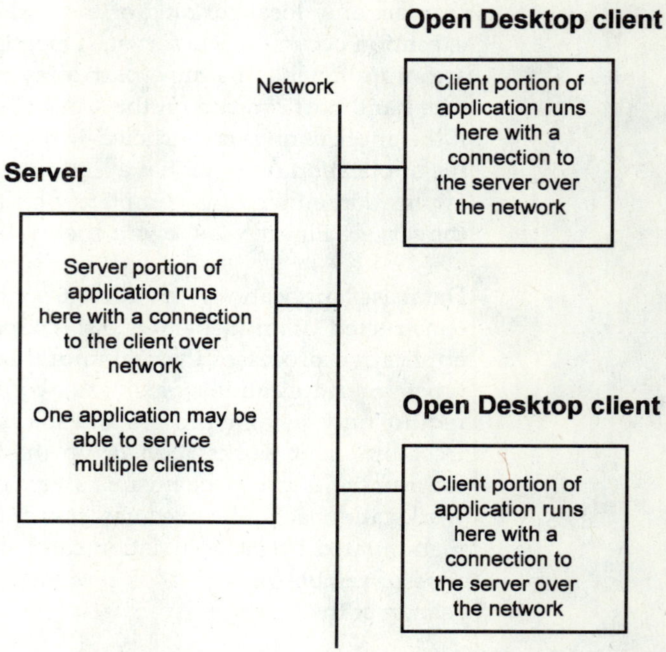

Figure 9-2: The server runs one part of the application while the clients run the other part. Both the client and the server portions must cooperate in order to complete the operation. Unlike the X terminal scenario presented previously, the Open Desktop clients here have local processing capacity and so can run applications that do not access the server. In these configurations, both the client and the server must be tuned for optimal performance. If the application is not client/server, then the Open Desktop client may also use the remote login facility to execute the application remotely, similar to the X terminal configuration. A client with local processing capacity is more flexible than one without, but that flexibility may not be necessary in the particular computer environment.

X Terminal Display Update

X terminals are specially constructed devices that support only the running of an X server. The X server is responsible for managing the screen, the mouse, and the keyboard attached to the X terminal. A typical X terminal might be connected to a server and have multiple windows displaying information from different applications.

A user running an application can connect to the server system and execute the application on that server machine. The application running on the server then sends messages to the X server via TCP/IP, instructing the X server how to update the X terminal display. The packets are packaged by the server and then unpackaged by the X terminal.

In order for the X terminal user to run applications on the server, a connection between the X terminal and the server must be established. This connection is typically made by a remote login process, such as scologin(X), rlogin(TC), or telnet(TC). Please see the Open Desktop System Administrator's Guide for more information on how to configure these mechanisms.

After the connection is made, the user starts the application and the application process sends messages to the X terminal to update the appropriate window on the X terminal screen with the application display information. As the user interacts with the application, more messages notifying the application process on the server of key press events and mouse movements are sent over TCP/IP. In response to these events, the application sends messages to the X terminal instructing the X server managing the screen how to update the application window. This interaction is described in more detail in the Common Open Desktop Operations chapter.

The messages that travel between the X terminal and the application process on the server use the TCP/IP protocol and require all of the streams resources and processing described in the previous chapter.

The capacity and performance of X terminals vary greatly. Some X terminals have specially designed hardware to increase the speed of drawing. Others contain more conventional general purpose CPUs. CPUs of different speeds are also available.

The amount of memory installed in an X terminal also affects the speed at which the windows on the screen can be updated. An X server performance optimization requiring additional memory is known as *backing store*. When a window, or part of a window, is covered by another window, the part of the window that is covered can be stored by the X server in the X terminal memory. After the covered window is uncovered, the newly exposed window is then redrawn using the information in the X terminal memory rather than retrieving the information over the network from the server machine.

The backing store feature makes interacting with the server system appear more responsive and reduces the number of messages between the X terminal and the server machine. The reduction in message traffic may result in an actual increase in server performance, because network traffic processing requires the CPU; less time spent processing messages means the CPU is available for application execution.

When the packets are received by the X terminal, the appropriate actions are taken, for example a line is drawn.

The time required to update the display is composed of the following increments:

- The time required to send the key presses or mouse movements to the server over the network

- The time required for the application process to complete its operation and decide how to update the application window

- The time required for the messages to be sent instructing the X server how to update the application's window

- The time required for X terminal to update the window

All four of these time intervals must be monitored in order to understand how to optimize the resource allocation on the server and reduce the time required for the display update operation.

The resource usage pattern of the application process running on the server should be monitored with the mechanisms described for the appropriate common operation. Please refer to the common operations in the product chapters for more information.

Monitoring the network is described in the TCP/IP section in the previous chapter.

Some X terminal manufacturers provide monitoring tools to facilitate understanding how the X terminal resources are used. The tools might monitor the amount of memory used, and the usage of the network by the X terminal. See the X terminal documentation for more information.

Use the following method to optimize X terminal display update performance:

- Maximize network efficiency by eliminating errors and streams buffers shortages
- Increase the application performance on the server by increasing CPU availability
- Eliminate any other resource shortages that occur when running the application on the server

The first step in optimizing X terminal display update performance is to ensure that the network usage is efficient. See the Monitoring Client/Server Connections chapter for more information on how to increase network efficiency.

Once a sufficient number of streams are available, tuning the server to increase the speed of the application is the next step. The goal of tuning is to free the CPU by eliminating paging and swapping and by decreasing the search time required to access information. More free CPU time means more time to execute both the application and the streams modules that process network messages. For more details on server tuning recommendations, please see the appropriate product chapters.

Balancing the resource requirements of all the applications running on the server is often required. In some cases, balancing may involve installing additional hardware on the server system in order for it to adequately service all of the clients.

The information provided by netstat -a is useful for determining which network services are used by the clients accessing the server. Should netstat -a show that other services are in use at the same time, then try monitoring the display update operation when fewer clients are using the server. With fewer clients accessing the server, isolating the resources used by the operation under scrutiny is easier.

If the server still cannot adequately service all of the clients, then consider sharing the workload of the server with other servers on the network. Assigning users to particular servers for specific operations is one way of dividing the work among two or more servers. This mechanism increases performance only if the servers chosen have sufficient resources to adequately support all of the clients. If the new servers become overloaded, then spreading the workload has achieved no overall performance gain.

In this situation, installing additional hardware is the most efficient way of improving the response time for the users on the client machines. See the appropriate product chapter for the server environment for recommendations on what kinds of situations are best improved by hardware upgrades, for example, memory, disk or CPU.

Consider purchasing a higher capacity X terminal if the following combination of circumstances occurs:

- The network has a low number of collisions and no streams or other network errors

- The server has sufficient resources to run the application process, but the display update is still too slow

Since all other causes of display update delays are resolved, then purchasing a higher capacity X terminal is the only way to significantly affect the performance of display update.

Open Desktop Display Update

An Open Desktop client is more flexible than an X terminal because the user can run application processes:

- On the server, so the client behaves like an X terminal, as shown in Figure 9-1

- On the client, but with information from the server

- Partly on the client and the server, with information from either or both, as shown in Figure 9-2

The first configuration is similar to the X terminal remote login situation described previously, except that instead of using the X terminal monitoring tools for tuning, use the tools and methods recommended in the Common Open Desktop and SCO UNIX Operations chapters to tune the client. The server tuning rules are the same as those for X terminal Remote Server Access and are described in more detail in the previous section. Because an Open Desktop environment is very flexible, tuning can improve the responsiveness and usability of the system.

The second case is similar to those described in the Open Desktop chapter. Both the resources used for remote access to the information and the resources used by the application process in completing the operation must be optimized. If the user acquires the information for the application process by copying it from the server to the client, then commands such as rcp can be used. The duration of the operation is equal to the sum of the following actions:

- The time required for the information to be transferred to the client
- The time required for the application to complete its operation on the information.

Mechanisms for transferring information between the client and server are discussed in the Remote File Access section of this chapter.

If the user accesses the information for the application via a remotely mounted filesystem, then the application must access the information over the network rather than reaching it directly on the same machine. The duration of an operation in this configuration is equal to the sum of the following actions:

- The time required for the application to establish a connection with the server and retrieve the necessary information
- The time required for the application to complete its operation on the information

This sequence of actions can occur many times during the operation, because the application may require more information than that which can be retrieved in a single network transmission. Mechanisms for accessing information on remote filesystems are discussed in the Remote File Access section of this chapter.

The third case is the most complex. The client part of the application cooperates and communicates with the server part of the application, and tuning of all the resources involved in this cooperative effort must be done in order to achieve optimal performance. In this case, the duration of the operation is equal to the sum of the following actions:

- The time required to execute the client portion of the operation
- The time required to transmit information between the client and the server

- The time required to execute the server portion of the operation

This sequence of actions may occur many times during an operation. The tuning required for this situation is a combination of the following steps:

- Making sufficient resources available to the client and server application portions executing on their respective hardware/software configurations

- Making sufficient resources available so the network data transmission time is minimized

In most network configurations, a combination of one or more of these methods of accessing data and applications will exist. Such complexity makes tuning more difficult, but not impossible.

The client and server are monitored using the tools and methods defined in the appropriate product chapters. The network and streams resources can be monitored using the tools described in the Monitoring Client/Server Connections chapter.

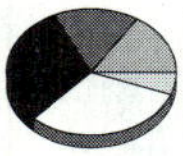

The steps for tuning any of the above configurations are as follows:

- Ensure that the network is running efficiently with no streams buffers allocation failures, no network errors and a minimum number of collisions and re-transmissions

- Increase the availability of the CPU on both the client and server and ensure that no resource shortages occur

After allocating sufficient streams buffers and reducing the network error rate, begin examining the resource usage patterns on the client and the server.

The primary goal of client tuning for the display update operation is increasing the amount of CPU time available. For example, if the client cannot respond to requests from the server to update the display because of a memory shortage, then no matter how fast the server sends requests, the client cannot process them, so the client is the primary factor delaying the completion of the operation. See the Open Desktop chapter for further recommendations on tuning the Open Desktop client for the display update operation.

In many cases, the display update on the client occurs in parallel to the operations executing on the server system. If the server is deciding on the information to be displayed then the client may be able to update the display faster than the server can generate the information to be displayed.

HINT:

In an environment where multiple clients access the server, the server is generally the slower of the client/server pair. The machine with the greater %idle and %wio values is generally the slower of the pair and should be tuned first.

After the resources on the first machine are optimally allocated, the performance of the display update on the second machine may be improved by further tuning. For example, the increased responsiveness of the properly tuned machine may inadvertently cause a resource shortage, such as streams buffers, on the other machine, and this resource shortage must be fixed in order for the display update time to be minimized. The configuration of the first machine may also need to be revisited after the second machine is tuned, in case the additional speed of the second machine inadvertently causes a resource shortage on the first machine.

Remember that performance tuning can be done in small steps over a long period of time and so revisiting the tuning of either the client or the server can be postponed unless the resource shortage on either the client or server is severe.

REMOTE FILE ACCESS OPERATIONS

Remote file access is accomplished either by copying the files from the server to the client or by accessing them remotely over the network.
The rcp command copies files from one machine to another. The files can then be accessed on the local machine without requiring further network messages. The primary tuning goal for file transfer commands is to minimize the time for the information to travel between the client and the server by maximizing the amount of CPU time available to send the data from the client to the server.

The NFS environment allows users to access files located on the server using the same mechanisms as if the files are located on the same machine. Since all the files remain on the remote machine, every time the client wants to access the remote files, messages must be sent over the network between the client and the server. Here again, the primary tuning objective is to maximize CPU availability so that the time required for the client and server portions of the file access operation and the network transmissions is minimized.

TRANSFERRING FILES WITH RCP

The rcp command copies files to and from machines on the network. The rcp command relies on the TCP/IP connection service for communication between the client and the server. Figure 9-3 shows the location of files before and after using the rcp command.

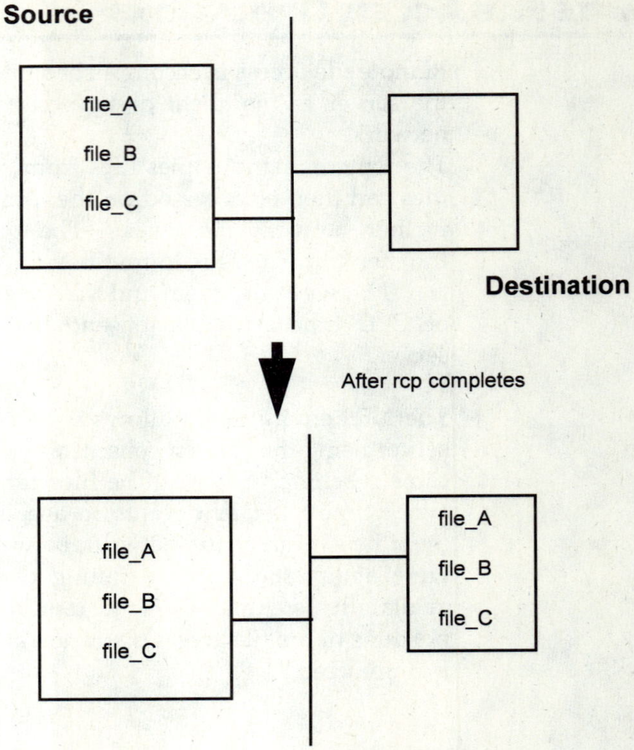

Figure 9-3: The files are originally located only on the source machine. During the execution of the rcp command, the machine which originally stored the files executes a file read operation to transfer the files over the network. The machine that is receiving the files executes a file write operation in order to store the files in its filesystem. After the rcp command completes, the files are located on both the source and destination machines. The destination machine can now access the files locally without having to access the source over the network.

When the user starts rcp, a connection is established between the two machines via TCP. This connection provides a reliable, ordered flow of data between the client and the server. Messages sent by the source application process are divided into packets and sent over the network. When these packets are received by the destination, the TCP protocol orders the packets into the correct sequence and delivers the reconstructed message to the application process. Ordered packets ensure that no file corruption occurs, because the individual messages do not contain any information about where the data should be placed in the file.

The rcp client application uses resources, such as the buffer cache, just like any other process accessing the filesystem running on the source and destination machines.

After the client/server connection is established, rcp passes the information down the stream to the network interface card, which then sends the frame over the network to the destination. The destination receives the packets, checks them for errors, orders them into the correct sequence and passes them to the application process. Both the source and destination machine use streams buffers to store the information as it is packaged and unpackaged by the protocol stack.

In addition to the resources used for the client/server connection, rcp uses the same resources as the cp(C) command executing locally on the client. When either rcp or cp must access files, the namei cache is used to map the filename to the inode. The inode table contains the inodes that are currently open by the application processes, and the buffer cache temporarily stores the filesystem data copied from the disk. The disk is accessed in the same fashion when the files are either read by cp to transfer to another location in the filesystem or read by rcp to transfer to the destination..

When cp transfers files between locations on the filesystem, both the file read and write operations occur on the same system. When rcp transfers files, the source executes the file read part of the operation and the destination executes the file write part of the operation. The two machines should be tuned with the part of the application they execute in mind.

Figure 9-4 shows the locations of the source and destination portions of the file transfer operation.

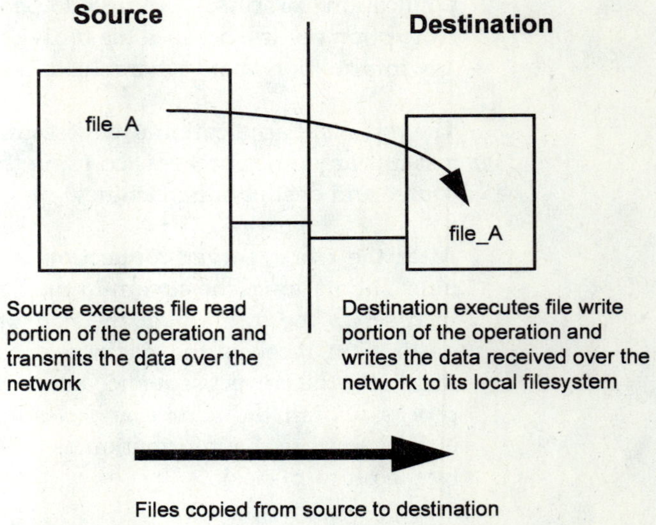

Figure 9-4: The files are copied to the destination from the source.

When all the transfers between the source and destination are complete, the connection is broken and the rcp client and server application processes terminate.

inetd The inetd(ADMN) daemon is a special process on the server that waits for client requests from applications such as rcp. The rcp client application specifies the type of service required with a special number, called a *port*. The inetd process manages all client requests arriving for connections to this service. The ports are defined in the file */etc/services*.

When the daemon receives the client rcp request, inetd makes a copy of itself and assigns the new process, called a *shell server*, to manage the connection for this rcp request. The shell server runs the generic remote command mechanism called *rcmd*. The rcmd mechanism starts the rcp server process and then sets up a standard inter-process communication mechanism to transfer the information between rcp and the shell server, which then communicates to the rcp client process over TCP/IP.

Further network messages from the client arrive at the server and are unpackaged by the streams protocol stack. All messages require streams buffers so they can be transformed from frames into messages for the rcp server application process.

The source and destination part of the operation are monitored as described in the File Read and Write Operations section of the appropriate operating system chapter. The connections are monitored as described in the Monitoring Client/Server Connections chapter.

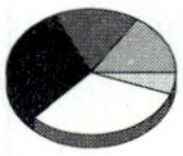

The steps for tuning the rcp operation are as follows:

- Ensure that the network is running efficiently with no streams buffer allocation failures on either the client or the server, no network errors, and a minimum number of collisions and re-transmissions

- Optimize the file read and/or write operation on the source and destination

Use the recommendations in the Monitoring Client/Server Connections chapter to tune network efficiency and streams buffers.

The machine that is transmitting the files uses many of the same resources that it would use during a local file read operation. The machine that is receiving the files uses many of the same resources it would use during a local file write operation. Tuning rcp involves maximizing network connection efficiency and then tuning the client and the server for file read and write operations.

Remember that using rcp involves a considerable amount of connection set-up, and that overhead is fixed no matter how much data is transferred. The capacity for changing the duration of the transfer time is limited by the amount of time required to set up the connection between the client and the server. Connection set-up time can be decreased with greater network efficiency, but not dramatically.

HINT:

If the %idle time of the client is greater than zero and the rcp is the only application process running on the client, then the server is causing the client to wait for the operation to complete, and so the server should be tuned first. This rule works in reverse only if the server is serving only that one client, because %idle is rarely greater than zero when the server serves multiple clients.

If the server and the client are executing only rcp operations, then the value shown by %wio is the percentage of time spent waiting for disk transfers, and %idle is the time spent waiting for network transfers. The value shown by %idle is also the time either the client or the server spends waiting for the other to complete its portion of the operation. For example, when the client copies files to the server, the value of %idle is the percentage of time the client spends waiting for the information to be transferred to the server and for the server to complete writing the files.

If a memory shortage on either the server or client is causing the disk shortage because of paging or swapping, then follow the recommendations for alleviating memory shortages described in the Common Open Desktop Operations chapter and Appendix B.

Remote File Access In The NFS Environment

The NFS environment allows clients to access a filesystem located on another machine. Once the client has established a connection with the remote machine, or mounted the remote filesystem, the client can access the files as if the files were physically located on the client machine.

The underlying communication between the client and server machines is accomplished via TCP/IP. Unlike rcp, the files are not copied to the destination, but instead remain on the server.

As described in the Common SCO UNIX Operations chapter, the following events occur when an application process reads a file on a local system:

- The filename is mapped to an inode using the namei cache and an entry is added to the open file table

- If the file data is in the buffer cache, then the data is returned to the application process

- If the file data is not in the buffer cache, then the information is retrieved from the disk and a copy of it stored in the buffer cache and then returned to the application

If the files that the application process wish to read are located on an NFS server, then, in addition to all of the above, the data must be retrieved from the remote server by transferring the information from the server to the client using special NFS processes. Figure 9-5 shows how the processes interact to access data on the server.

On a local system, the following events occur when the client processes wishes to write a file:

- The client writes the information to the buffer cache and then continues execution

- At some point in the future, the system process bdflush writes all of the modified buffers to the disk

For a write operation in the NFS environment, the first step also includes transferring the information to the NFS server. Rather than relying on delayed write and bdflush, the NFS server synchronously writes the file on the server on behalf of the client application. The client resumes normal execution after writing the information to the local buffer cache, and then special NFS processes guarantee that the data is written to the server.

Because accessing a remote filesystem requires the cooperation of the client and the server and communication between the two, tuning remote filesystem access consists of optimizing all parts of the total operation as follows:

- the client side of the operation
- the data transmission time
- the server filesystem access

This sequence of actions may occur many times during a particular file read or write operation. Tuning NFS clients and servers follows the same principles of maximizing network efficiency and CPU availability on both the client and the server that are presented throughout this and the previous chapters.

The Client

The application process accesses local and remote files with the same mechanisms. The remote filesystem containing the desired file can be either automatically mounted the first time the application accesses the file or it can be explicitly mounted by the system administrator prior to the application needing the file. The mount point describes the type of filesystem that contains the file. For example, with the file */mnt/letter.doc,* the directory */mnt* contains information that specifies the NFS environment must be used to access the *letter.doc* file.

The *automounter* provides a mechanism for automatically mounting remote filesystems on the client. This process listens for mount requests on the client. Using the automounter does not affect the speed at which the files can be accessed. The only consideration with the automounter is that it is a special listener process that consumes resources and deciding whether to use it depends on the available resources and how important the added convenience is to system maintenance.

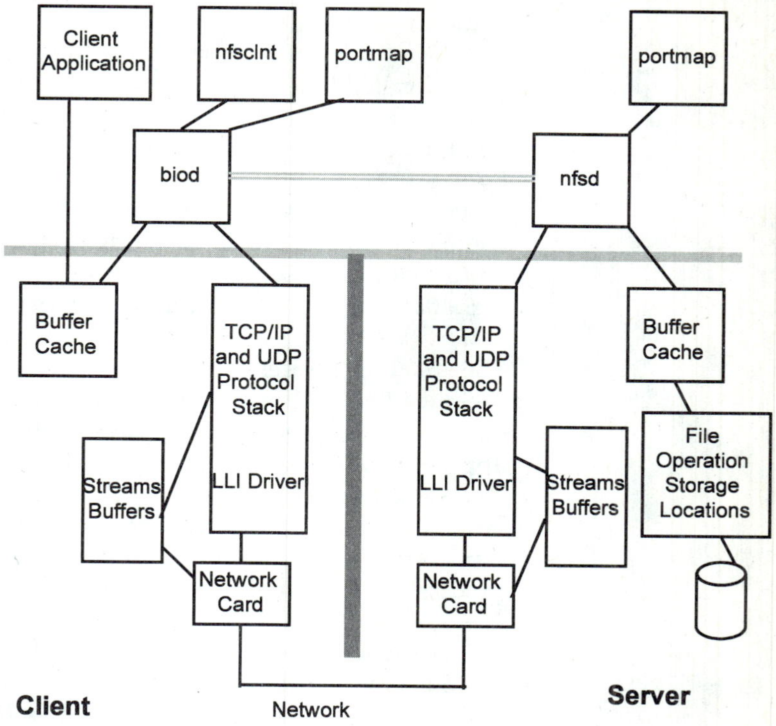

Figure 9-5: This diagram shows the processes that are involved in a remote file access operation using the NFS environment.

When the application wishes to access the remote file, the filename is mapped to an inode in the namei cache. Tuning the namei cache typically has very little effect on the duration of the remote file operation because the filename mapping is such a small portion of the overall time required to read or write the remote filesystem data. Once the filename is mapped, the client buffer cache is searched to locate the file information. When the file information is re-used by applications, the client is more likely to find the data in the buffer cache, so tuning filename mapping can reduce the operation duration, because the information is not retrieved over the network.

biod If the file information is not found in the buffer cache, then the NFS client sends a request for the information to the special NFS process called *biod*.

The biod process retrieves the information from the remote server by executing a remote procedure call on the server. The biod process is suspended until the read operation on the server completes and the data is received from the server. A client system can run multiple biod processes to increase the number of simultaneous requests for remote filesystem information.

The biod processes improve performance because they can optimize file read operations by reading more than just what the client has requested. This feature is called *read-ahead* and benefits applications that are accessing files in a sequential fashion. The biod processes also collect write requests and send them as one large request. Because a larger amount of filesystem data is transferred for the same network overhead, the network processing resources are used more efficiently.

The sequence of steps that occurs on the client for a remote file write operation is similar to a local write operation. The filename is mapped to an inode and the information is written to the local buffer cache.

In addition, the biod process keeps track of what buffers have been written to files on the remote file system and sends them to the server. When buffers are written by the bdflush system process or reused, they are passed to the biod process. The biod process can group these requests using a mechanism similar to the operating system scatter/gather feature to improve performance. This transfer is also accomplished via a remote procedure call. The biod process is suspended until the file write has completed on the server and an acknowledgment has been received by the client.

When all the biod processes are suspended waiting for requests, a mechanism that allows one file write at a time to be sent to the server is used. This one-by-one mechanism is much slower than the biod process because no grouping of write requests and no read-ahead occurs. Having a sufficient number of biod processes is essential for optimal read and write performance.

Each remote procedure call operation requires a special identifier and two special processes to manage the request called nfsclnt(NADM) and portmap(NADM).

nfsclnt, portmap

The nfsclnt process manages the special identifiers for each remote procedure call request and the client communicates with the server portmap daemon. The number of special identifiers is the maximum number of simultaneous requests that can be in progress at any one time.

HINT:

The number of special identifiers can be found using the ps(C) command. Run ps -el and examine the entry corresponding to nfsclnt. The number after the name "nfsclnt" is the maximum number of simultaneous requests allowed. If ps shows multiple nfsclnt processes, then add all the numbers shown to find the maximum number of simultaneous requests allowed.

The remote procedure call uses UDP because each request from the client to the server is independent and contains all the filesystem information necessary to complete the operation. The sequencing and reliability of TCP is therefore not necessary. The UDP messages still require all the protocol processing in the stream associated with transmitting data over the network. Streams buffers are used as intermediate storage locations for these messages.

The Server

An NFS system server administrator makes specific filesystems available to NFS clients by adding the names of the filesystems to the */etc/exports* file. When the server receives the frame from the client, it stores the incoming packets in streams buffers for the incoming streams modules. After the incoming protocol stack has unpacked the message, the message is reconstructed and sent to the special NFS server listener process called nfsd(NADM).

nfsd

Each nfsd process can process a single request at a time, so when all of the processes are busy, any incoming requests are held in streams buffers until an nfsd process is available. If nfsd cannot keep up with the number of incoming filesystem read and write requests, then the number of streams buffers simultaneously in use will increase.

Remember that the daemon processes, such as nfsd and biod, are normal application processes and must share CPU and disk resources with all the other processes on the system. The duration of the remote read or write operation is affected by any shortage of resources that affects the ability of these daemon processes to complete their portion of the file read and write operation.

The nfsd process running on the server actually executes the file read and write operation on behalf of the client. When the read operation on the server is completed, the UDP streams modules package the information and send it back to the client.

For data integrity, all write operations are satisfied by writing the information to the disk instead of relying on the bdflush delayed write mechanism. Changing the size of the buffer cache on the server does not have much impact on the duration of the remote file write operation. Because of the synchronous nature of the file write operation, file writes in the NFS environment take significantly longer than local filesystem write operations.

If the buffer cache on the client contains copies of file information that is modified on the server by either another client or the server, the entry in the client's buffer cache is invalidated. This procedure ensures filesystem data integrity. Before the client accesses file data in the local buffer cache, NFS makes a remote procedure call to the server to see if the data in the client buffer cache is still valid. If the buffer is no longer valid because some other client has written information to that file, then the buffer on the client is marked as invalid and the up-to-date data is retrieved from the server.

NFS Daemons

The NFS daemons running on the client and the server are described in the following section.

automount — *automount(NADM)* monitors requests to access directories. When a remote directory is accessed, automount determines whether to silently mount the necessary remote filesystem. The automount daemon runs on both the client and the server and is suspended until a directory access is detected.

biod — The *biod* process runs on the client and handles requests for remote file system access. Under normal circumstances this process runs on the client frequently, so the NFS environment performance is severely compromised if insufficient resources are available on the client to run it. Although biod exists on the server, it will be suspended.

lckclnt — The *lckclnt(NADM)* process manages special identifiers for remote procedure calls involving locking. The lckclnt process is suspended indefinitely and exists on both the client and the server.

lockd — The *lockd(NADM)* process handles local and remote file locking requests. The client locking request is detected by lockd running on the client and is passed to the lockd process running on the server with a remote procedure call. The lockd process is suspended unless the client is using file locking. A lockd process exists on both the client and the server.

mountd — The *mountd(NADM)* process completes remote procedure call requests to mount server filesystems on behalf of clients. Normally, mountd runs only on the server and is suspended until a mount request is received.

nfsclnt The *nfsclnt(NADM)* process manages special identifiers used for remote procedure calls. The nfsclnt process is suspended indefinitely and is found on both clients and servers.

nfsd The *nfsd(NADM)* process runs on the server and handles all NFS system client requests. A server may run multiple nfsd processes. Because nfsd runs frequently, server performance is severely compromised if insufficient resources are available on the server to run it.

pcnfsd The *pcnfsd(NADM)* process provides remote procedure call services for machines running the DOS version of the NFS environment. The pcnfsd process runs only on the server and runs frequently only if clients are using the DOS version of NFS. The consequences of insufficient resources for this process are the same as for portmap.

portmap The *portmap(NADM)* process allows a client to request that a particular port be used for the remote procedure call executed on behalf of an application. The portmap process runs frequently and on all client and server machines that are running the NFS environment. If sufficient resources are not available to run portmap, then the ability of NFS to respond to client requests is adversely affected.

statd This process provides crash and recovery functionality for NFS file locking services. This process is suspended unless file locking is used and exists on both the client and the server.

All of these processes share resources, such as CPU and memory, with all of the other applications running on the machine. For good performance, sufficient resources must be available for the active daemons to run.

Use the mechanisms described in the Monitoring Client/Server chapter section for monitoring the network and the mechanisms described in the File Read and Write Operations for the operating system running on the client and the server. The NFS specific monitoring tools are described in Table 9-1.

Behavior	Command	Column
Number of remote procedure calls from client to server	nfsstat -cr	calls
Number of failed client-to-server procedure calls	nfsstat -cr	badcalls
Number of client message retransmissions	nfsstat -cr	retrans
Number of remote procedure calls from server to client	nfsstat -sr	calls
Number of failed server to client procedure calls	nfsstat -sr	badcalls
Number of times a client handle is needed	nfsstat -c	nclget
Number of times a process is suspended waiting for a client handle	nfsstat -c	nclsleep
Number of different types of remote procedure call executed by the client	nfsstat -cn	all
Number of different types of remoe procedure calls executed by the NFS server	nfsstat -sn	all
Connections used by NFS	netstat -a	Local Address
Amount of CPU time consumed by client and server daemons	ps -el	the TIME column for the rows corresponding to the daemons

Table 9-1: NFS Monitoring Commands

nfsstat -cr — The nfsstat -cr command displays a calls column that reports the total number of remote procedure calls made by the client to the server. The number of failed remote procedure calls is shown by the column badcalls. The retrans column displayed by nfsstat -cr shows the number of times a network message had to be retransmitted because some network error occurred.

The nclget column shows the number of times a client handle has been requested by a process for a remote procedure call. The nclsleep column shows the number of times the client handles have run out and caused the requesting process to be suspended due to the insufficient number of client handles.

nfsstat -sr — The command nfsstat -sr displays the same information as nfsstat -cr, except the numbers are for those calls received, rather than sent, by the server. Both nfsstat -cr and nfsstat -sr provide the total number of remote procedure calls sent and received by the machine.

nfsstat -cn — The values in the columns displayed by nfsstat -cn show the total number of calls for each type of procedure executed and the percentage of the total that the procedure represents. For example, if the total number of calls is equal to 100, and 30 of those calls were read calls, then the entry for read is 30 because 30% of the calls are read calls.

nfsstat -sn — The nfsstat -sn command displays the same information, except the numbers are for those calls received, rather than sent, by the server.

ps -el — The ps -el command provides a complete listing of all the processes that are running on the client system. Check the amount of CPU time that the biod processes are consuming. Ensure that at least one nfsclnt process is running and check the maximum number of simultaneous requests that are configured by looking at the number following the name of the nfsclnt process.

netstat -a — Some of the entries in netstat -a can be traced with the additional information provided by rpcinfo -p. The number shown in the port column maps to the numbers in the Local Address column of netstat -a. To complete the mapping, use only the numbers after the first period(.). For example, if rpcinfo shows the number 1035 then look for entries of either the form "*.1035", or "sysname.1035" in the netstat output. The final, untitled, column of the rpcinfo -p display shows which NFS process is using the service.

The steps involved in tuning remote file access using NFS are as follows:

- Ensure that the network usage is efficient by eliminating streams buffer allocation failures and network retransmission errors.

- Tune the client and the server so that sufficient resources are available for the NFS daemons to complete their portion of the file operation with minimum delay.

The techniques for determining the efficiency of network usage are described in the Monitoring Client/Server Connections chapter.

If the retransmissions and badcalls values displayed by nfsstat increase during each test operation, one or both, of the network interface cards may have difficulty keeping up with the messages sent across the network. The size of the transfer used by NFS can be reduced in an attempt to stop overloading the network card. The following command can be used to reduce the size to 1 Kbyte:

```
mount -f NFS  rsize=1024, wsize=1024,
svr_name:/svr_directory cli_mnt_pt
```

where svr_name is the name of the server, svr_directory is the name of the directory on the server where the remote filesystem is located, and cli_mnt_pt is the mount point for the remote filesystem on the client. More information can be found in the SCO Open Desktop/SCO Open Server System Administrator's Guide.

Another solution to retransmission errors is to upgrade the network interface card to one with a higher capacity.

If nclsleep is greater than zero, increase the number of client handles by restarting nfsclnt with a larger number of handles. Try doubling the current number of handles available and see if nclsleep becomes zero.

Only after all network errors and re-transmissions have been eliminated should attention be focussed on tuning the client and the server.

The types of procedure calls indicate the proportion of read versus write operations. These proportions can help determine which portion of the file operation to tune on the client and the server. More read operations mean the read portion of the file operation should be tuned first; more write operations mean the write portion of the operation should be tuned first.

HINT:

In an environment where multiple NFS clients are accessing the NFS server, the server is usually the machine with one or more resource shortages. In addition, the usage pattern of an NFS server is typically a greater number of read operations than write operations. In such cases, tuning the buffer cache may benefit performance. Use the buffer cache monitoring tools described in the Common SCO UNIX Operations chapter to determine the usage pattern.

If the number of write operations is less than or equal to the number of read operations, then the primary goal of server tuning is to maximize the throughput of the disk subsystem and to increase the availability of the CPU. Since NFS file server writes are synchronous, tuning the buffer cache minimally affects performance.

If the number of read operations is less than or equal to the number of write operations then the primary goal of server tuning is to increase the availability of the CPU and to minimize disk activity.

If isolating the client and the server is possible so that only one client is accessing the server and only one test operation is running, then run the test operation and check the amount of %idle and %wio time on both the client and the server. If the amount of %idle time on the client is greater than 5%, then the client is waiting for the server, and the server definitely needs to be tuned until %idle on the client is equal to 5%.

Using a disk adapter with an on-board cache can provide large performance improvements for an NFS server because the time required for a synchronous disk write is greatly reduced. If a disk adapter with an on-board cache is not available, then copying files to the client and then running the application can result in quicker filesystem access than accessing the files remotely. This solution is especially applicable if the application operates on very large files.

If many clients are using the server, then increasing the number of special nfsd processes may improve the server's ability to respond to NFS filesystem requests. Since incoming requests are queued if an nfsd process is not available, a shortage of these processes can cause a streams shortage, which then results in inefficient network usage. The availability of the CPU to execute these nfsd processes is also critical to rapid server response. More nfsd processes mean more disk activity, and so the capacity of the disk subsystem may need to be increased in order to adequately service these additional NFS processes.

Tuning the namei cache has less effect in an NFS client/server environment than in a local environment. In addition, the optimal size for an application data storage area when using NFS may be different to that used when the application is accessing a local filesystem. The optimal size changes because the data travels further to reach the application and if the application can store the data in its own storage area, then the application can continue without waiting for the remote filesystem access to complete. Please refer to the appropriate product chapter for additional filesystem tuning recommendations.

Tuning the client involves ensuring that resource shortages are not inhibiting the execution of the biod processes.

If the client system supports multiple users, all of whom are using remote filesystems, performance may be improved by increasing the number of simultaneously running biod processes. Provided the client has sufficient amounts of underlying hardware to support the additional processes, increasing the number of biod processes allows more requests to be in progress simultaneously. Without a sufficient number of biod processes, the client will not execute read-ahead and not join write requests.

The maximum number of special remote procedure call identifiers managed by nfsclnt may also need to be increased to support the additional biod processes. See the SCO Open Desktop System Administrator's Guide for more information on configuring the number of biod processes.

HINT:

If ps -el shows that the biod processes never accumulate CPU time even after many NFS file transfers have taken place, then follow the instructions in the section "Programs are hung" in the SCO Open Desktop Administrators Guide.

If the client executes more file read than write operations, then increase the size of the buffer cache until a memory shortage occurs.

If the client executes more writes than reads, or if the read pattern is such that the buffer cache hit rate does not increase even after increasing the size of the cache, then tuning the buffer cache is unlikely to improve performance. When the size of the buffer cache is increased and the number of remote procedure calls executed by the client does not fall, then the buffer cache is not causing a delay to the filesystem operation. If the system has a memory shortage, decreasing the buffer cache may be the more optimal solution.

Please refer to the appropriate product chapter for additional diagnosis and tuning recommendations.

Each time a significant tuning change is made to either the client or the server, the other should be checked to see if a further adjustment must be made to further enhance performance.

Quick Diagnosis Summary

This section highlights the key monitoring tools and tuning guidelines described in this chapter. The information in this section can be used as a future reference and builds on the information presented in this and the preceding chapters.

Remote Server Access

In addition to the networking behaviors described in the Monitoring Client/Server Connections chapter, the primary behaviors that should be monitored to tune remote server access are summarized in Table 9-2.

Behavior	Command	Column
Resource usage pattern of the application running on the server	ps -el	SZ
CPU usage on server	sar/mpsar/ cpusar -u	%sys, %usr, %idle and %wio
Paging activity on server	sar/mpsar -p	rclm/s
Swapping activity on server	sar/mpsar -w	bswot/s, bswin/s
X terminal resource usage	X terminal specific	X terminal specific

Table 9-2: Key Behaviors For Remote Server Access

The primary tuning guidelines for increasing remote server access performance are as follows:

- Eliminate streams errors
- Eliminate network errors, such as retransmission errors
- Minimize collisions by reorganizing network layout
- Maximize CPU time for processing streams messages
- Provide sufficient resources for the applications running on the server

Remote File Access

In addition to the networking behavior described in the Monitoring Client/Server Connections chapter, the primary behaviors that should be monitored for remote file access are summarized in Table 9-3.

Behavior	Command	Column
Resource usage pattern of the application running on the server	ps -el	SZ
CPU usage on server	sar/mpsar/ cpusar -u	%sys, %usr, %idle and %wio
Paging activity on server	sar/ mpsar -p	rclm/s
Swapping activity on server	sar/ mpsar -w	bswot/s, bswin/s
Buffer cache activity on client and server	sar -b	all columns
Disk activity on client and server	sar -d	all columns
X terminal resource usage	X terminal specific	X terminal specific

Table 9-3: Key Behaviors For Remote File Access

The primary tuning guidelines for maximizing remote file access performance are as follows:

- Eliminate streams errors
- Eliminate network errors, such as retransmission errors

- Minimize collisions by reorganizing network layout
- Maximize CPU time for processing streams messages, including eliminating, where possible, all paging and swapping activity
- Tune the part of the filesystem operation that is running on the client and the server for the given operation
- Ensure that the server has sufficient disk speed and capacity to cope with the synchronous write activity generated by NFS

Chapter 10

Remote File Access Case Studies

These two examples show how to tune two different methods of remote file access using the seven step method. The first example uses the rcp command to read files from the server and the second example uses the NFS environment to access files on a remote server. The relationships between the overhead involved in setting up a connection and discovering the limits to how the system can be tuned are explored. This chapter assumes some familiarity with the material presented in the Common SCO UNIX Operations, Monitoring Client/Server Connections and Common Client/Server Operations chapters.

These examples are designed to show how you can analyze the data recorded on the worksheets to assess the efficiency of the network and how much time the client and the server are contributing to the duration of the operation. Both examples use the tools provided on the floppy disk to run the test and collect appropriate resource usage statistics for the client and server machines as well as the network. The relevant statistics for each worksheet can be extracted with the utilities provided on the disk so you are not overwhelmed with the large amount of data gathered in a networked environment. The worksheets are provided in both examples as a sort of appendix to show where the data originated. The data presented in the graphs and bar charts in the example description highlights the worksheet data relevant to that particular operation.

Remote File Access Using RCP

This example shows how to tune a combination of simple read operations over the network and more complex read and write operations. The test uses the rcpop script that is included on the floppy disk.

The rcpop script starts 10 processes, each of which reads and write files stored on the server filesystem. When the process reads information, it copies the data from the server with rcp. When the process writes information, it reads the data from the server with rcp and stores it in a temporary file on the client, and then copies the file back to the server. The ratio of reads to writes is approximately four to one.

Step 1. Decide what to improve.

☑ Select the appropriate worksheet for the common operation.

This example explores whether the file read and write operation in this configuration can be improved. The client and the server are running SCO UNIX and they are connected via ethernet. The appropriate worksheets are included at the end of this chapter in Worksheets 10-1 to 10-8.

⇩

Step 2. Identify the limited and unlimited resources.

☑ Note any limited resources on the worksheet by marking them with an asterisk (*).

The hardware configuration is fixed except for the possibility of upgrading the network card in the client. The hardware configuration is shown in Figure 10-1.

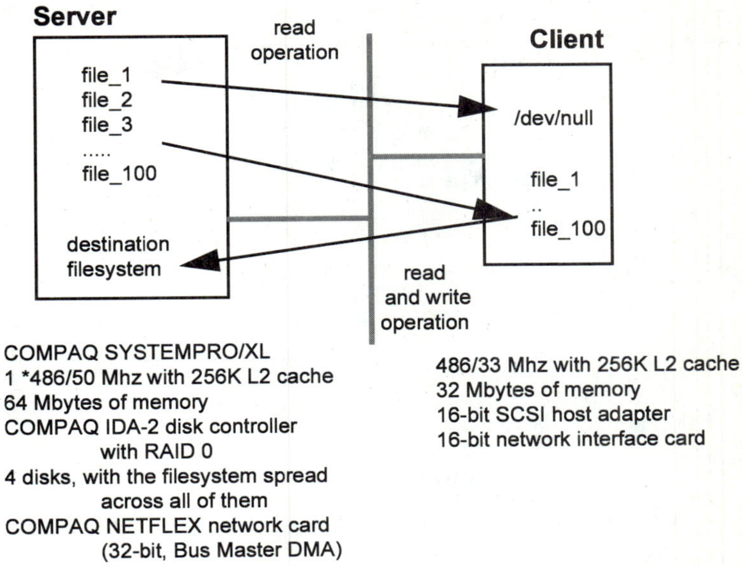

Figure 10-1: For the read operation, the files are copied with rcp from the server to the client. For the read and write operation, the files are copied from the server to the client, and then copied back to the server.

⇩

Step 3. Determine how to measure the operation and test its current performance.

☑ Note the test result on the worksheet in the column marked **Now.**

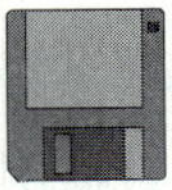

The rcpop script is a mixture of typical file read and write operations. The script operates on a directory hierarchy created by ctree, also included on the floppy disk. Each process receives a list of 100 files on which to execute file operations in a ratio of approximately four reads for every write. These files are randomly selected by the rcpop script.

The following command lines show how the ctree utility is used to create a directory hierarchy on the server containing 800 8 Kbyte files as follows:

```
ctree -d 4 -f 100 -n dataarea -s 8192
```

When the rcpop script is invoked, the test directory must be specified with the -testdir option. In this case, dataarea is the name of the test data area. Figure 10-1 shows how the files move from the client to the server.

The test duration with monitoring disabled is equal to 1011 seconds.

⇩

Step 4. Set a realistic performance goal.

☑ Note this on the worksheet in the column marked **Your Goal.**

The goal is to reduce the operation duration by 25%. An additional goal is to further understand whether the hardware configuration is affecting performance of file read and write operations over the network.

⇩

Step 5. Identify the resources to monitor and decide which monitoring tools to use.

☑ The worksheets list the appropriate resources.

The standard SCO UNIX, SCO MPX and Network tuning worksheets define the resources that should be monitored.

The utilities, sar2oswks, sar2mpxwks, and net2wks, are used to process the sar data collected on the client and the server into a form appropriate for entering into the worksheets. The shell script tune2wks extracts the correct tunables for the first part of each of the worksheets. All of these utilities are included on the floppy disk. Appendix C contains manual pages that describe these utilities.

⇩

> **Step 6.** Run the test with the monitoring tools and monitor the resource usage and record the test results.
>
> ☑ Enter the initial values of the tunables and note the resource usage in the column marked **Initial Values**. Note the test results under the column called **Monitoring.**

The rcpop script automatically calls the appropriate monitoring tools when the -sar option is specified. The duration of the test increased to 1122 seconds. This increase is the result of both rcpop and sar competing for filesystem resources.

Initial Observations

The tuning guidelines for rcp suggest checking the network efficiency first, and then focussing on tuning the appropriate read and/or write portion of the operation on the client. The first statistics to examine are those relating to the efficiency of the network.

The networking statistics show that the percentage of errors on input is 3.8%. This value is computed with the following equation:

$$\left(\frac{number\_of\_errors}{total\_number\_of\_packets}\right) * 100$$

The current value of this equation is equal to:

$$\left(\frac{864}{22456}\right) * 100 = 3.8\%$$

The values for this equation are obtained from Worksheet 10-6. Considering that only two machines are active on the network, this percentage is higher than expected. However, the client network card is a 16-bit ISA card, while the server network card is 32-bit EISA bus master DMA card. The ISA card may not be able to keep up with the responsiveness of the EISA card. The ISA card should be considered for an upgrade as a possible pathway to improving performance.

No collisions occur during the test. No collisions are expected because only two machines are using the network and the probability of collision is low.

To collect some more information, the netstat -a command was run at intermittent intervals on the server while the test was running. On the server, a large number of bytes are queued waiting for transmission over TCP/IP, as shown by the netstat -a command. This observation implies that the client cannot keep up with the transmissions from the server.

The CPU is required to handle messages. The CPU usage statistics on the client and the server show a high percentage of idle time. The client is spending 71% of its time idle, and the server is spending 86% of its time idle. Neither the client nor the server are able to saturate their CPU resources.

These statistics show that both the client and server have sufficient CPU power to package the streams messages and prepare them for transmission to the client, but the client cannot keep up with the messages sent by the server. Because the client CPU spends a high percentage of its time idle, these statistics corroborate the theory presented earlier that the network interface card is not fast enough to keep up with the server. More tests are necessary to prove this theory.

The client is spending 22% of its time executing in the operating system and network subsystem, and just 3% of the time executing applications. The server, however, is spending only 11% of its time executing in the operating system, and just 2% of the time executing applications.

No swapping or paging has occurred, so no memory shortage exists.

The ready-to-run queue statistics for the client show an average size of 3.2. This value indicates that over the duration of the test, on average at least three processes were ready-to-run. This number is an average, and the number does fluctuate during the test run. Since the test runs 10 processes, excluding sar, the rest of the processes must have been suspended waiting for access to a resource. Performance could possibly be improved by reducing the amount of time the processes were suspended. Reducing this suspension time should increase CPU usage and reduce %idle time.

The CPUs on both the client and the server are idle because no ready-to-run processes are available for them to execute. For a majority of the test, the processes are not suspended waiting for disk activity to complete because %wio is less than 5% on both machines. The processes are probably suspended waiting for the network communication to complete.

On the client, ps -el shows the processes are waiting on addresses (WCHAN) within the operating system. However, decoding these addresses is difficult without an operating system debugger or source code. More circumstantial information may be available from examining the other statistics.

The client and server machines are executing both the file read and write operations, so the intermediate storage location usage for both parts of the operation must be examined. The statistics for the filesystem operation on the client show close to optimal values as follows:

- The namei cache shows a 99% hit rate

- The open file and inode tables show no overflows
- The buffer cache efficiency statistics show a 100% read hit rate
- The scatter/gather control blocks and buffers are not running out
- The number of copy buffers is also sufficient
- The disk statistics show that the disk averages only 17 blocks per second with the disk busy only 17% on average for the duration of the test

The statistics for the filesystem operation on the server show slightly less than optimal values as follows:

- The namei cache shows an 94% hit rate
- The open file and inode tables show no overflows
- The buffer cache efficiency statistics show a 98% read hit rate
- The scatter/gather control blocks and buffers are not running out
- The number of copy buffers is also sufficient
- The disk statistics show that the root disk is handling 27 blocks per second with the disk busy only 49% of the time. The second disk, containing the script itself, is handling 10 blocks per second and is only 14% busy on average for the duration of the test.

None of these filesystem statistics point to the source of the delay and the idle time. Because the conclusions as to which resources to modify are not obvious, some tests were run with a smaller amount of data to see how the resource usage patterns change.

⇩

Step 7. Decide how to change the resource allocation; rerun the tests and note progress toward the goal. Iterate until either the goal is reached, or until a limited resource is encountered.

☑ Determine whether to increase or decrease the resource/tunable. Note the new tunable values in the column marked **Test #1** and the test results under the column **Res #1.** Use the rest of the columns for the results of subsequent test iterations.

☑ When the goal is reached, implement the new resource allocation.

Test #1: 4 Kbyte Files

After deleting the original 8 Kbyte files, a new server directory hierarchy containing smaller files was created with the following command:

```
ctree -d 4 -f 100 -n dataarea -s 4096
```

The files are now 4 Kbytes each.

The test duration is now 1084 seconds, so no major difference was encountered by halving the amount of data. The number of octets sent across the network by the client has fallen from 3,506,303 to 2,234,698, but this new value is not half of the previous one. The number of packets sent by the client has also fallen from 22,494 to 18,351, but also not by half. The expected behavior would be a reduction in the network traffic by half because the amount of data is reduced by half.

The CPU, buffer cache and disk usage have changed minimally from the initial test.

The lack of change in statistics in proportion to the amount of data sent across the network seems to indicate some fixed overhead that may be preventing performance of this operation from increasing dramatically.

Another test with still less data is set up to see if the boundaries of this fixed overhead can be determined.

Test #2: 2 Kbyte Files

After deleting the 4 Kbyte files, a new directory hierarchy was created containing 2 Kbyte files with the following command:

```
ctree -d 4 -f 100 -n dataarea -s 2048
```

The duration of the test is now 946 seconds.

The efficiency of the network has increased because the number of errors and collisions has dropped. The number of octets and packets sent across the network has also dropped, but once again not by the expected amount.

Another test with even less data is set up to continue the search for boundaries.

Test #3: 1 Kbyte Files

After deleting the 2 Kbyte files, another directory hierarchy was created containing 1 Kbyte files using the following command:

```
ctree -d 4 -f 100 -n dataarea -s 1024
```

The duration of the test has fallen to 913 seconds. Figure 10-2 summarizes the changes in the test duration up to this point.

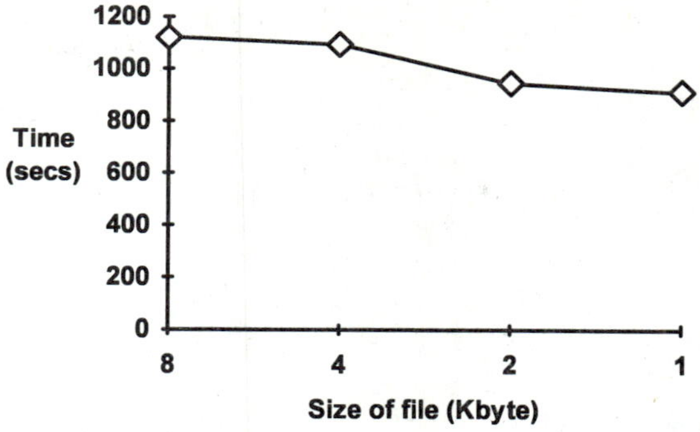

Figure 10-2: Changes in Test Duration Versus Size of File Transfers

The number of packets and octets has once again fallen, but not by half. Figure 10-3 shows the number of octets received by the client and Figure 10-4 shows the number of octets transmitted by the client.

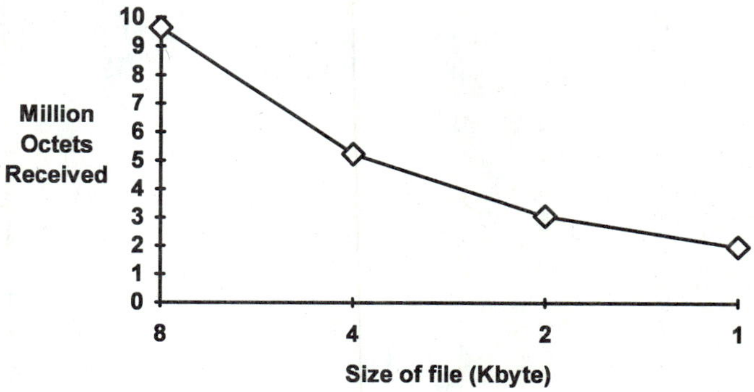

Figure 10-3: Number of Octets Received by Client

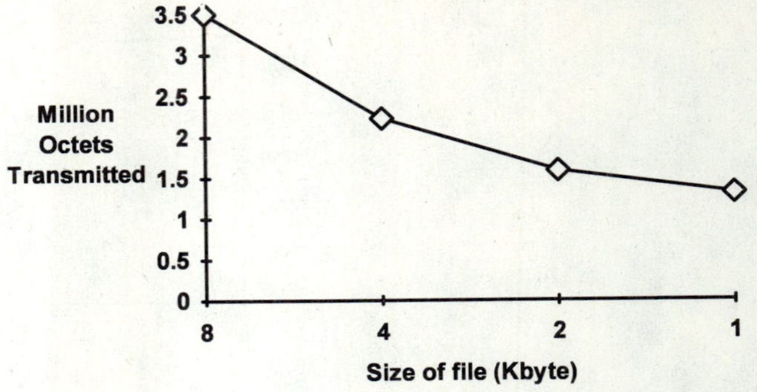

Figure 10-4: Number of Octets Transmitted by Client

These two graphs show that as the size of the file transfer is increased, the number of octets transmitted and received also increases. When the file size is greater than four Kbytes, the number of octets increases proportionately. When the file size is less than four Kbytes, however, the number of octets does not change proportionately.

The number of packets sent and received also shows a similar relationship, as shown by Figure 10-5.

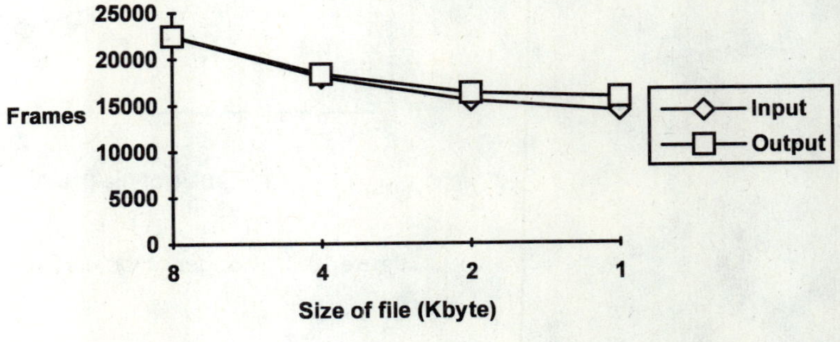

Figure 10-5: Number of Client Packets Received and Transmitted

The network efficiency, CPU and filesystem statistics did not change dramatically for any of the tests.

Test #4: Upgrade Client Network Card

Conventional tuning seems unable to significantly alter the test duration. No resource shortages appear to be stopping performance from improving. In the initial observations, some comments about the inability of the client network card to keep up with the server were noted. For the final test, a 32-bit bus master network card was installed in the client and tested.

The new card was installed and the 8 Kbyte tests were run once again. The test duration fell from 1120 to 960 seconds. The amount of network traffic fell, as shown by Figure 10-6.

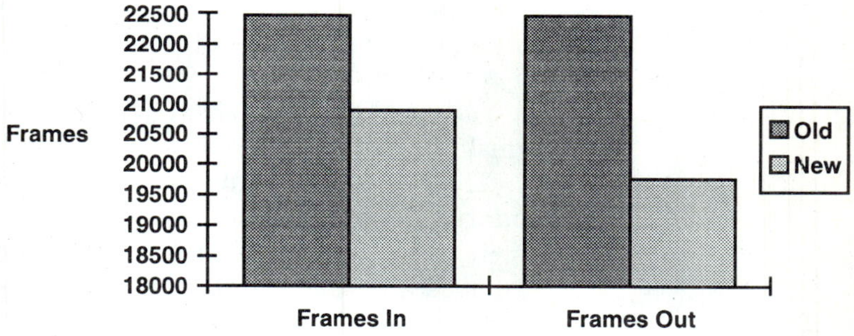

Figure 10-6: Comparison Between Number of Frames Transmitted and Received with Old and New Network Cards Installed on Client

The upgraded client network interface card has also decreased the number of frames handled by the server. This statistic is shown in Figure 10-7.

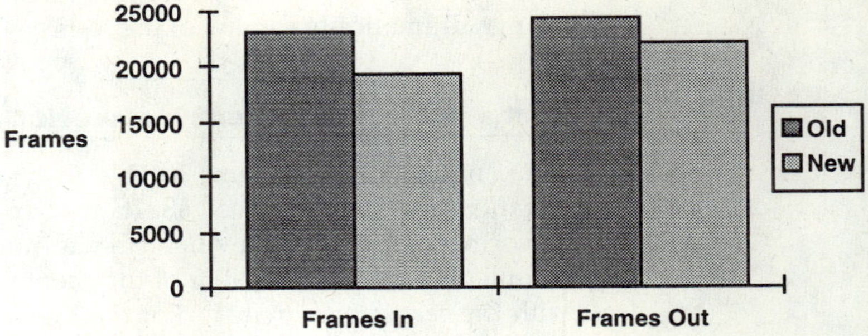

Figure 10-7: Comparison Between Number of Frames Sent and Received

In addition, the client input packet error rate has decreased from 864 to zero. The number of collisions has decreased from 87 to eight. The network is much more efficient as a result of fewer errors and the decrease in collisions.

The %idle time on the client has decreased from 71% for the original test to 59%. The %sys time has increased from 22% to 33%. The decrease in %idle time has resulted in an increase in the amount of time the CPU spent executing the operating system. This increase in %sys time often occurs when tuning network systems because the operating system processes the messages in a shorter period of time, so it must spend more time on average executing in the operating system.

The server CPU statistics have not changed.

To confirm the final improvement, the test was repeated, but without monitoring. The final test result was 820 seconds. The replacement network card has improved the performance of the test by 19%.

Conclusions

As shown by this case study, a network card that is mismatched with the capacities of the client and the server can cause delay. A network card matched to the capabilities of the system and the amount of network traffic increases the efficiency of both the client and the server. This case study shows how systematic analysis of the data and an understanding of the resources involved in remote file access and connection management, plus an element of good guessing based on understanding that data, can isolate the underlying resource that is limiting performance.

Despite the hardware upgrade, the goal in this example was not reached. An explanation for this lies in the way in which the file operations are set up with rcp.

Each time the rcp command is executed, a connection must be established between the client and the server using inetd. Connection establishment requires packets to be transferred between the client and the server. This connection setup overhead is a fixed cost of using rcp to transfer files. The number of additional packets sent between the client and the server is determined by the amount of data that is transferred between the machines.

When rcp is used to copy lots of small files, such as in this example, the connection establishment overhead becomes a significant contributor to the time taken by the entire operation. A more efficient remote file access mechanism should therefore be chosen in order to significantly change the performance of the operation.

The combination of a more efficient remote file access mechanism and upgraded network card should reduce the duration of the test to meet the original goal.

Remote File Access With The NFS Environment

This example also uses a shell script that executes a combination of simple read and more complex read and write operations.

The nfsop shell script copies the files to the client and also copies the files to a temporary filesystem on the server. The nfsop shell script is included on the floppy disk.

> **Step 1.** Decide what to improve.
>
> ☑ Select the appropriate worksheet for the common operation.

This example explores whether the file read and write operation in this configuration can be improved.

The completed client SCO UNIX worksheets are shown in Worksheets 10-9 through 10-14 at the end of this chapter. The completed client Networking worksheets are shown in Worksheets 10-15 through 10-18. The completed server SCO UNIX worksheets are shown in Worksheets 10-19 through 10-23. The completed server Networking worksheets are shown in Worksheets 10-24 through 10-27.

⇩

> **Step 2.** Identify the limited and unlimited resources.
>
> ☑ Note any limited resources on the worksheet by marking them with an asterisk (*).

The hardware configuration is fixed and is shown in Figure 10-8.

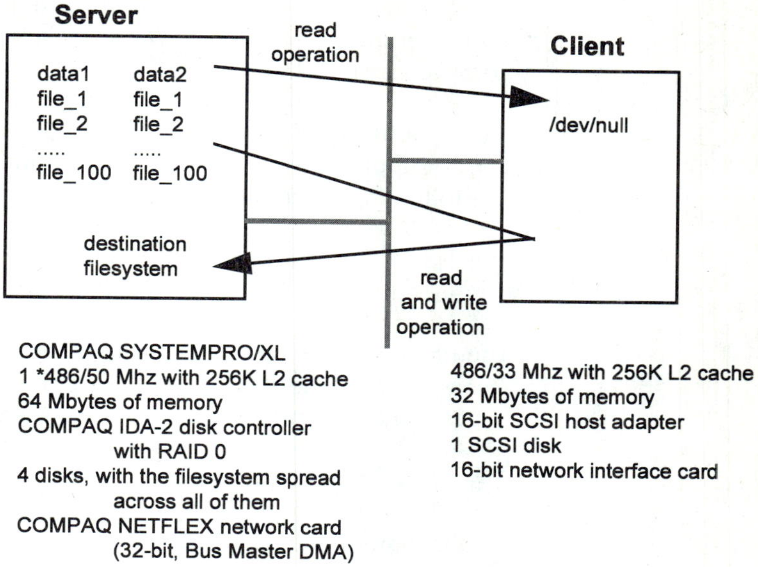

Figure 10-8: The read operation copies the file from the server to /dev/null. The read and write operation copies the file from the remotely mounted filesystem on the server to a temporary file also located on the server.

⇩

Step 3. Determine how to measure the operation and test its current performance.

☑ Note the test result on the worksheet in the column marked **Now.**

As in the previous example, each process executes read and write operations on a list of 100 files randomly selected by nfsop. These files are located in a directory hierarchy created by ctree. Each process executes approximately four read operations for every write operation. To simulate more than one user, the shell script waits for all 10 processes to complete, and then displays the duration of the operation.

The ctree utility is used to create two directory hierarchies, called data1 and data2, on the server each containing 100 32 Kbyte files. The following command creates this directory tree:

```
ctree -f 100 -d 1 -s 32768 -n data1
ctree -f 100 -d 1 -s 32768 -n data2
```

The nfsop script displays the time taken to complete the file read and write operation. The script also allows a directory hierarchy to be used again in order to keep the test environment as similar as possible between different test runs. Figure 10-8 shows how the files move between the two machines.

Unfortunately, some problems were encountered while attempting to gather the initial test results. Most of these problems were caused by resource shortages, as shown in the following sections. These descriptions provide a useful insight into how resource shortages can affect the functioning of applications as well as their performance.

First Try: Streams Shortage

During the first attempt, the client system displayed the following message on the console:

```
WARNING: NFS server sysname not responding, still
trying
```

A few minutes later the test had still not completed. An attempt to access the filesystem on the server with cd failed because the cd command did not complete. Another attempt to get status of the remote filesystem using df -v also failed because that command also did not return. Because the nfsop tests had not completed, the statistics that are normally gathered automatically were not available, and so the information had to be examined manually to determine what might be causing the problem.

The server streams buffer usage, as shown by netstat -m, showed no streams buffer shortages on the server. Examining the server data revealed only 523 remote procedure calls. Considering 10 processes on the client were attempting to access over 100 files, each of length 32 Kbytes, at least 1000, and more likely many more, remote procedure calls would have been expected.

The client's nfsstat statistics showed only 56 remote procedure calls executed, with 16 badcalls, 80 re-transmits and 96 timeouts. The netstat -m information showed streams buffer shortages at size 2048 and 4096. The 2048 size buffers experienced 147 failures, while the 4096 size buffers had 137 failures.

Both of these buffer allocations were doubled, the operating system re-booted, and the test run again.

Second Try: Streams Shortage

Once again both the 2048 and 4096 size buffers were in short supply and the message:

```
WARNING: NFS server sysname not responding, still
trying
```

appeared on the client console.

The NBLK2048 and NBLK4096 tunables were doubled again, the operating system re-booted, and the test run once more.

Third Try: Increase RPC Client Handles

The warning message appeared once again on the client's console, but no streams shortages were observed.

However, the remote procedure call statistics still revealed some inefficient resource usage with only 64 calls completing, 48 re-transmits, and 56 timeouts. The value of nclsleep is 23, which suggests that processes were suspended waiting for an NFS client handle. Excessive delays in waiting for client handles mean the remote procedure call communication is inefficient. The number of client handles must be increased to overcome this inefficiency. Although 2315 input packets had been received, 17 errors had occurred. The cause of these errors is not apparent at this time, but the cause of the sleeping on client handles is apparent, so the latter is addressed first.

Restarted nfsclnt with 16 client handles rather than the standard eight client handles. The next message to appear on the console was:

```
WARNING: NFS server servername ok
```

This message indicates that the server is now accessible. However, 16 handles may not be sufficient for all 10 processes to run without waiting for handles, so the number of handles was increased to 24 permanently by modifying the */etc/rc2.d/N89nfs* script.

The system was rebooted to ensure that it was in a known state and the test run again.

Fourth Try: Increase Number of nfsd Processes

The NFS server failure message appeared once again. Running nfsstat on the server showed the client was not issuing any new requests to the server. A simple cd test to access the remotely mounted filesystem showed that the server and client could communicate successfully. This was corroborated by the following message on the client's console:

```
WARNING: NFS server servername ok
```

However, the test processes were accumulating very little CPU time on the client, as shown by running ps -el and examining relevant TIME columns. Unlike the third try, nclsleep was equal to zero, so no process on the client had to wait for a client handle.

Because there are very few tools that can help determine exactly what is going wrong with the server daemons, at this point, a good guess seems to be the most logical path forward.

Increasing the number of simultaneous client requests may require a similar increase in the capacity of the server to handle those client requests. The processes that service client requests are called nfsd, and the default number of them is four. With 24 client handles, increasing the number of nfsd processes available to service these clients seems like a logical next step.

The number of nfsd was increased to 24.

Fifth Try: Simplify Test Case

To guarantee a known state, the client was rebooted and the test run again with the increased number of nfsd processes. The NFS server error messages re-appeared, so the problem had not been solved.

Instead of continuing on this path which seemed to be going nowhere, a simpler path was chosen. This simpler path involved setting up a simpler test and examining the resulting data manually rather than automatically.

Throughout all of these attempts, llistat was reporting errors on incoming packets. The first simple test was to mount the remote filesystem and then run several processes that continually listed the directory contents. This simple test showed no errors.

A more complex test was set up that involved executing the following shell script from within the remotely mounted filesystem:

```
#!/bin/sh
for i in `ls`
do
cp $i /dev/null
done
```

When this script was run, the llistat command reported errors in received packets. After only 89 input frames had been received, 3 errors had occurred. This error rate is unexpectedly high, and so the networking hardware was checked to see if it was contributing to the inefficient network.

The hardware was checked as follows:

- The network connection was disconnected and reconnected (no change)
- A different network connection was used (no change)
- The machine was opened and the installation of the boards was verified (no change)

In all cases, the errors continued and no change in behavior was seen. At this point, another good guess was necessary to move forward.

Considering that the increase in network activity generated by the second simple test caused the errors, but the first simple test did not, perhaps the size of the NFS transfers is too large for the client network card. The remote filesystem was mounted once again, but this time with the rsize and wsize options set to 1024 with the following command:

```
mount -f NFS  rsize=1024, wsize=1024,
svr_name:/svr_directory cli_mnt_pt
```

where *svr_name* was set to the name of the server, *svr_directory* is equal to the directory on the server and *cli_mnt_pt* is the client mount point.

The first and second simple tests were run again, and this time no errors occurred.

The nfsop script was also run, and it successfully completed with no errors. The server was rebooted with the default number of nfsd processes so that the performance testing could be started at a known point. The number of client handles, however, was left at 24, because in previous tests processes were clearly impacted by a lack of client handles.

The initial results without monitoring were in the range of 406 to 414 seconds.

⇩

Step 4. Set a realistic performance goal.

☑ Note this on the worksheet in the column marked **Your Goal.**

The goal is to reduce the operation duration by 50%. An additional goal is to further understand whether the hardware configuration is affecting performance of the remote file access operations.

⇩

Step 5. Identify the resources to monitor and decide which monitoring tools to use.

☑ The worksheets list the appropriate resources.

The standard SCO UNIX and Network tuning worksheets define the resources that should be monitored.

The utilities, sar2oswks and net2wks, are used to process the sar data collected on the client and the server into a form appropriate for entering into the worksheets. All of these utilities are included on the floppy disk. Appendix C contains manual pages that describe these utilities.

⇩

Step 6. Run the test with the monitoring tools and monitor the resource usage and record the test results.

☑ Enter the initial values of the tunables and note the resource usage in the column marked **Initial Values**. Note the test results under the column called **Monitoring.**

Unfortunately, some problems were also encountered in running the tests with monitoring enabled.

Monitoring Run #1

The first monitoring run failed when the client produced the error message:

```
./nfsop.1: fork failed - too many processes
```

This error message may be caused by variety of resource shortages, including too low a value for MAXUP and not enough memory. Since the default value of MAXUP is equal to 25 on the client and the shell script starts more than 25 processes including the monitoring tools, the value of MAXUP was increased to 50.

The test ran successfully with MAXUP set to 50.

Initial Observations

The data from the first successful monitoring test run is shown in Worksheets at the end of the chapter. through 10-27. None of the previous tests produced sufficient information to warrant entering it into worksheets. The essential resource usage data is highlighted in the following descriptions.

Remote file access tuning when using the NFS environment involves ensuring that the network is efficient and then tuning the appropriate read and write file operations on the client and server.

The network statistics now show no streams shortages on either the client or the server. These shortages were fixed while debugging the test environment. However, the network is not at maximum efficiency because collisions are occurring on the client. Collisions are surprising considering only these two machines are running on the network. The client is also reporting errors with input packets, while the server reports none. As seen in the previous example, these errors may be a reflection of the inability of the network card to keep up with the server network card in this test. Upgrading the network card on the client may be one path towards increased network efficiency and improved performance.

The remote procedure call statistics shows that during the test 551 calls had to be retransmitted from the client. The percentage of calls that were retransmitted can be calculated with the following equation:

$$(\frac{retrans}{total\_calls}) * 100 = percentage\_calls\_affected$$

With the values for retrans and total calls from the worksheet, approximately 1.5% of the total number of remote procedure calls executed by the client. The server experienced no remote procedure call errors. The input packet errors and the retrans errors indicate some inefficiency on the client.

The availability of the CPU on both the client and the server determines how quickly they can process outgoing and incoming network packets. The client CPU statistics indicate that an average of 85% of the time is spent executing operating system code. The CPU is spending only 11% of its time idle, either idle with no processes to run (6%), or idle waiting for I/O (5%) to complete. The high percentage of %sys time could possibly be caused by the retransmission and input packet errors and could possibly be reduced if the network were more efficient.

The server, on average, is also spending 55% of its time executing operating system code. The server has a much higher idle percentage, especially in %wio, which is up to 19%. However, the %wio statistic indicates that the system is idle because some processes are waiting for I/O transfers to complete. Reducing %wio is one pathway to follow to increase performance on the server.

Neither the client nor the server are experiencing a memory shortage since no paging or swapping is occurring.

The filesystem statistics for the client show the following resource usage patterns:

- Namei cache hit rate is 99%
- Open file and inode table have sufficient space
- Buffer cache read hit rate is 95%
- Number of copy buffers, scatter gather and Sdsk control blocks are sufficient
- The disk activity is minimal

The filesystem statistics on the server show the following resource usage patterns:

- Namei cache hit rate is 90% (could be increased)
- Open file and inode table have sufficient space
- Buffer cache read hit rate is 97%
- Number of copy buffers, scatter gather and Sdsk control blocks are sufficient
- The disks are quite active, but that is to be expected since the NFS environment executes all write operations synchronously and the test is executing a considerable number of write operations

These statistics do not show any drastic resource shortages. Network traffic could be reduced by increasing the size of the client buffer cache because more of the application file data could be stored in the client buffer cache rather than in the server. The performance increase is limited by the amount of data that is re-used. In the nfsop test, a percentage of the data is reused, so increasing the buffer cache should have some positive impact.

The server namei cache efficiency statistic could also be increased. The server has a sufficient amount of memory to facilitate increasing the namei cache to its maximum size of 4096 entries.

⇩

Step 7. Decide how to change the resource allocation; rerun the tests and note progress toward the goal. Iterate until either the goal is reached, or until a limited resource is encountered.

☑ Determine whether to increase or decrease the resource/tunable. Note the new tunable values in the column marked **Test #1** and the test results under the column **Res #1.** Use the rest of the columns for the results of subsequent test iterations.

☑ When the goal is reached, implement the new resource allocation.

Tests #1-8: Increase Client Buffer Cache from 2 Mbytes to 9 Mbytes

To assess the relationship between the network traffic and the size of the client buffer cache, a series of tests where the client buffer cache was increased are run. The server namei cache is also increased, but no other tunables on the server are changed.

Both machines are rebooted and the test run again.

First check whether the efficiency of the namei cache has increased. The hit % is still equal to 90%, so the namei modification on the server has not increased the cache efficiency. The size could be further increased by overriding the maximum value, but before undertaking such an action some consideration needs to be given as to why a cache of 4096 entries is still generating a hit rate of only 90%.

The test consists of 10 processes accessing 100 randomly selected files from a list of 200. Because the server is not executing any other operations during the test, a cache of 4096 entries should be capable of providing a hit rate in excess of 95%.

However, before the namei cache can record a hit, the entry must be present in the cache. The first time a file is accessed, a miss is counted. The next time the file is accessed, a hit is counted. The cache must contain entries before a hit can be recorded, so there will be a delay before the cache becomes effective.

Figure 10-9, produced with saravg, shows how the hit rate varies through the test. The saravg utility is also included on the floppy disk.

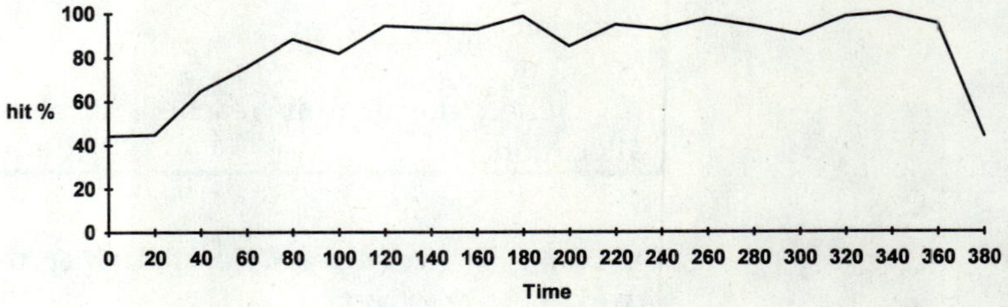

Figure 10-9: Namei Cache Hit Rate During the Test

The namei cache is saving disk accesses, but because the average measured by sar at the end of the test includes the period of time while the cache was filling, the reported average is lower than one might expect. Further increases in the namei cache size will not lead to improvements in the cache efficiency. At the moment, no further tuning on the server is indicated.

On the client, the test duration decreased up until the client buffer cache size was equal to nine Mbytes, as shown by Figure 10-10.

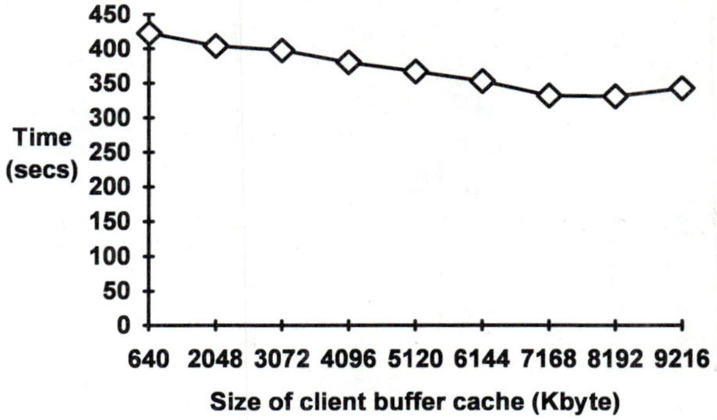

Figure 10-10: Size of Client Buffer Cache Plotted Against Duration of Test

The number of packets transferred between the client and the server has decreased as the buffer cache has increased up until the cache reached nine Mbytes. This decrease is shown in Figure 10-11.

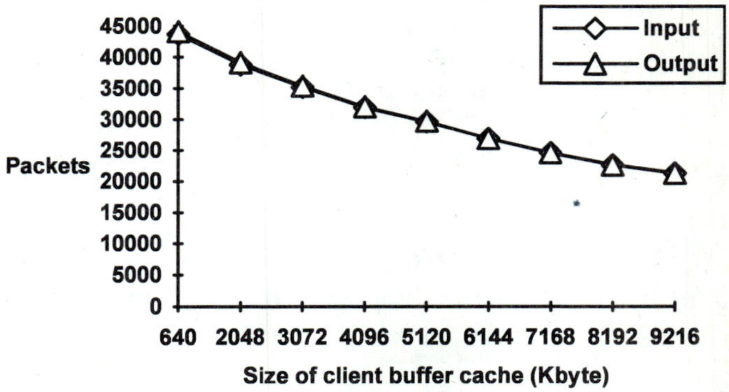

Figure 10-11: Number of Packets Sent and Received by Client

Each increase in the buffer cache size reduces the number of packets sent over the network. However, as the buffer cache grows, the proportion of the network traffic reduction is smaller.

Each increase in the buffer cache size is responsible for a smaller reduction in network traffic.

The number of remote procedure calls has also dropped. Increasing the buffer cache size has changed the way in which the client uses the server. Figure 10-12 shows the total number of remote procedure calls as the buffer cache increases.

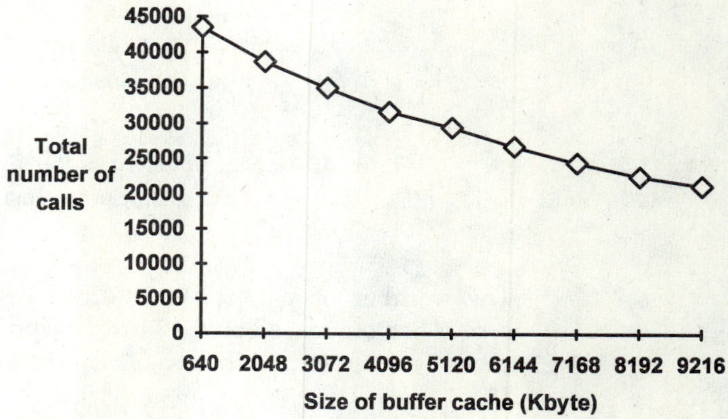

Figure 10-12: Total Number of Remote Procedure Calls

The number of retransmitted calls is less than 0.3%. The amount of time the client spent executing the operating system increased to a maximum of 91% at 7 Mbytes, and was always in excess of 85%.

The remote procedure call statistics can be examined more closely by looking at read and write calls. Figures 10-13 and 10-14 show the total number of read and write remote procedure calls.

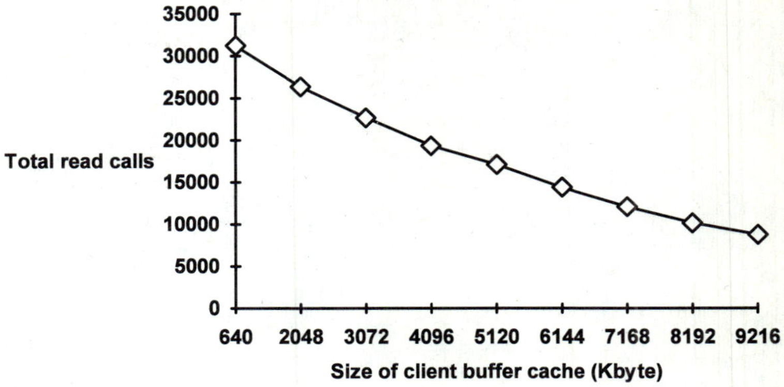

Figure 10-13: Total Number of Read Remote Procedure Calls

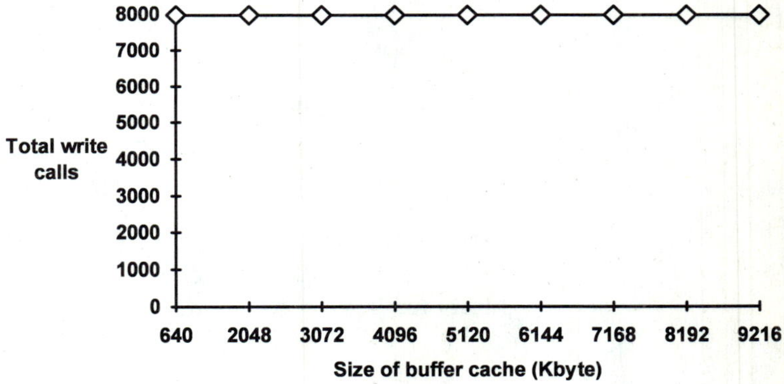

Figure 10-14: Total Number of Write Remote Procedure Calls

Figure 10-14 shows that the number of write remote procedure calls is independent of the size of the buffer cache. One of the reasons performance does not improve linearly when increasing the buffer cache on the client is because the percentage of write remote procedure calls increases as a proportion of total remote procedure calls.

The read remote procedure calls decrease as a percentage of the total. Figure 10-15 shows how the percentage of the two types of calls changes as the size of the buffer cache increases.

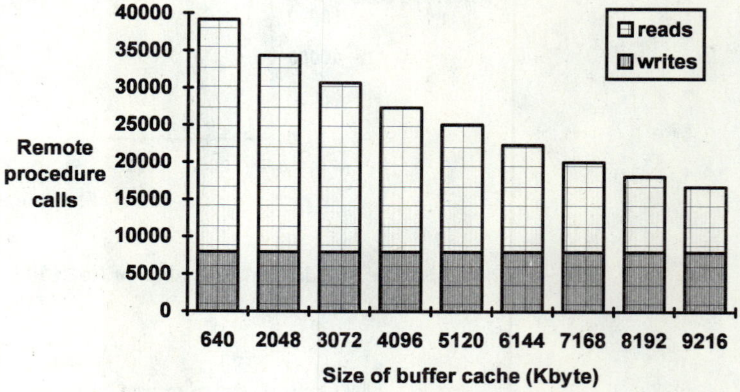

Figure 10-15: Percentage of Read Remote Procedure Calls and Write Remote Procedure Calls

Since the amount of data that must be written during the test is independent of the buffer cache size, the number of write operations is also constant. The duration of the write remote procedure call becomes a more significant part of the overall test duration as the size of the client buffer cache increases. Since write operations in the NFS system are synchronous, increasing the size of the client or server buffer cache will have minimal positive impact on performance.

The buffer cache efficiency on the client reaches 99% at eight Mbytes, so this appears to be the optimal size for this test environment.

The network efficiency when the cache is equal to eight Mbytes is still less than optimal, however. The number of collisions is equal to 293, which is greater than the original value of 182, while the percentage of input packets that have errors is less than 0.2%, which is less than the original percentage of 0.7%. With no resource shortages, such as streams or CPU, preventing the packets from being processed correctly, upgrading the network card is the only option left to improve the network efficiency.

However, upgrading is not an option at this point, so this level of efficiency must be sufficient.

With an eight Mbyte buffer cache, the client is optimally tuned considering the hardware limitations. The server statistics should now be examined to see if additional performance could be obatined.

With no errors, no collisions and no streams allocation failures, the network statistics on the server show no areas where tuning is needed. The next area to examine is the CPU usage. With the client buffer cache equal to eight Mbytes, the CPU on the server spends 29% of its time %idle and 20% of its time %wio. Since the read operations are now being serviced primarily by the client and server buffer cache, the speed of the write operations should be examined.

Since NFS writes all of its data synchronously to the filesystem, improving the performance of synchronous writes should benefit all the clients using the NFS system to access this server. Increasing the buffer cache does not improve the performance of synchronous writes. No other resources that are involved in the write operation are in short supply, so increasing them will not improve performance.

With only an average of 37 writes, as indicated by bwrit/s, occurring per second, the potential performance increase is limited. If the number of writes was much greater, then the potential for performance improvement is much higher.

One way of improving synchronous writes is to improve the speed of the disk adapter and disks in servicing the write requests. Some disk adapters support built-in memory that allows write requests to be made to the memory and then written to the disks at some point in the future. These *caching disk adapters* can be quite useful in server machines that run databases and/or the NFS environment because they improve the speed of the disk write operation. The duration of the disk write is reduced because the application processes do not wait for the write to access the disk because the data is written to the built-in memory rather than the disk. The data in the built-in memory is written at some later point so information is not lost.

Test #9: Install Disk Cache

This test does not change any tunables and instead requires the special cache memory on the disk adapter to be enabled. The duration of the test is now 321 seconds, a reduction of 10 seconds.

The average time required by the disk to service the write requests, as indicated by avserv, reduced from 15 milliseconds to 7 milliseconds. Even though the time required for the disk to service the write requests decreased by half, with only an average of 40 writes per second, the percentage test improvement of 19% is expected.

In addition, when the disk adapter uses a cache, the processes spend much less time waiting for the I/O requests to complete. The time saved benefits all file write operations in the NFS environment. The remainder of the time saved turns into idle time because no other applications are currently accessing the server. Under normal circumstances, this time would be used because multiple clients would be accessing the files over the NFS environment simultaneously.

Conclusions

These two examples show that tuning in a network configuration is not always straightforward. Understanding the overheads involved in some network operations can help you decide what the optimal configuration and layout for the system data and applications. Remote file access may be appropriate in some circumstances, but in others, the overhead involved may cost more than keeping local copies of the data.

A complete understanding of what the system is supposed to be doing helps in understanding and isolating the areas that need to be tuned for optimal performance. Such an understanding also helps when no obvious path forward exists, and so a good guess can often reveal some very useful information that can lead to solving the underlying resource shortage.

Worksheet 10-1: rcp Client SCO UNIX Tuning Worksheet (part 1)

Tunables	Initial Values	Test #1	Test #2	Test #3	Test #4
Installed Memory	64Mb				
Application Storage	n/a				
GPGSLO, GPGSHI	25 40				
MAXSC, AGEINTERVAL	8 31				
S5CACHEENTS, S5HASHQS	256 61				
NFILE	350				
NINODE, NHINODE	450 512				
NBUF, NHBUF	8192 4096				
BDFLUSHR, NAUTOUP	30 10				
NCOPYBUF, PLOWBUFS	100 30				
NMPBUF, NMPHEADBUF	0 100				
NPBUF, DMAABLEBUF	40 16				
SDSKOUT	4				
Disk Configuration, Data Layout					
NCLIST	120				
NPROC, NREGION	100 300				
NSCRN, CTBUFSIZ	0 128				
Display adapter, colors	n/a				
Other Memory Used	n/a				

Worksheet 10-2: rcp Client SCO UNIX Tuning Worksheet (part 2)

Resources to Monitor	Initial Values	Test #1	Test #2	Test #3	Test #4
Free Memory, Free swap	11971 196608	12007 196608	12015 196608	12011 196608	11992 196608
Blocks Swapped in/out	0.0 0.0	0.0 0.0	0.0 0.0	0.0 0.0	0.0 0.0
Pages Reclaimed	0.00	0.00	0.00	0.00	0.0 0.0
CPU: %usr, %sys, %wio, %idle	3 22 3 71	3 21 3 73	4 23 2 72	4 23 1 72	5 33 3 59
Scheduling: runq-sz, swpq-sz, pswch/s	3.2 0 31	3.2 0 33	4.4 0 33	5.6 0 36	6.5 0 31
Namei Cache	99%	99%	99%	99%	99%
File Table, Inode Table	123 0 130 0	123 0 131 0	123 0 128 0	124 0 129 0	124 0 128 0
Buffer Cache %rcache Reads: bread/s lread/s Writes: bwrit/s, lwrit/s	100 0 158 8 60	100 0 160 7 59	100 0 177 7 63	100 0 179 7 63	100 0 182 9 65
Scatter/Gather: mpbuf/s, ompb/s, mphbuf/s, omphbufs/s	0 0 1 0	0 0 1 0	0 0 1 0	0 0 1 0	0 0 1 0
Copy Buffers	0 0	0 0	0 0	0 0	0 0
Direct Disk Access	0 0	0 0	0 0	0 0	0 0
Copy Memory	0 0	0 0	0 0	0 0	0 0
Sdsk Request Blocks	4.59 0.00	4.59 0.00	4.92 0.00	4.81 0.00	4.60 0
Disk Driver : %busy avque, r+w/s, blks/s, avwait, avserv	13 4 5 17 84 29	13 4 5 15 74 28	12 3 5 15 53 25	11 3 5 15 36 23	19 4 5 19 89 35

Now	Your Goal	Monitoring	Res #1	Res #2	Res #3	Res #4
1011	900	1122	1084	946	913	960

Worksheet 10-3: rcp Server SCO UNIX Worksheet (part 1)

Tunables	Initial Values	Test #1	Test #2	Test #3	Test #4
Installed Memory	64Mb				
Application Storage					
GPGSLO, GPGSHI	200 300				
MAXSC, AGEINTERVAL	8 31				
S5CACHEENTS, S5HASHQS	4096 8191				
NFILE	3000				
NINODE, NHINODE	2500 2048				
NBUF, NHBUF	32640 32768				
BDFLUSHR, NAUTOUP	30 10				
NCOPYBUF, PLOWBUFS	100 10				
NMPBUF, NMPHEADBUF	16 2048				
NPBUF, DMAABLEBUF	40 64				
SDSKOUT	4				
Disk Configuration, Data Layout	IDA-2 4 disks				
NCLIST	2048				
NPROC, NREGION	800 2400				
NSCRN, CTBUFSIZ	0 128				
Display adapter, colors					
Mouse Settings					
Other Memory Used					

Worksheet 10-4: rcp Server SCO UNIX Tuning Worksheet (part 2)

Resources to Monitor	Initial Values	Test #1	Test #2	Test #3	Test #4
Free Memory, Free swap	3930 65536	3935 65536	3957 65536	3956 65536	3959 65536
Blocks Swapped in/out	0.0 0.0	0.0 0.0	0.0 0.0	0.0 0.0	0.0 0.0
Pages Reclaimed	0.00	0.00	0.00	0.00	0.00
CPU: %usr, %sys, %wio, %idle	2 11 1 86	2 11 1 86	2 11 1 86	2 11 1 86	3 11 2 84
Scheduling: runq-sz, swpq-sz, pswch/s	2.2 0 115	2.2 0 114	2.2 0 133	2.2 0 138	2.0 0 110
Namei Cache	94%	94%	94%	94%	93%
File Table, Inode Table	177 0 189 0	177 0 189 0	177 0 189 0	177 0 189 0	178 0 189 0
Buffer Cache %rcache Reads: bread/s lread/s Writes: bwrit/s, lwrit/s	98 5 270 14 69	99 3 273 13 68	99 2 294 13 71	100 1 299 13 72	98 7 332 10 97
Scatter/Gather:	0 0 4 0	0 0 4 0	0 0 3 0	0 0 3 0	0 0 1 0
Copy Buffers	0 0	0 0	0 0	0 0	0 0
Direct Disk Access	0 0	0 0	0 0	0 0	0 0
Copy Memory	0 0	0 0	0 0	0 0	0 0
Sdsk Request Blocks	0.00 0.00	0.00 0.00	0.00 0.00	0.00 0.00	0.00 0.00
Disk Driver 1: %busy avque, r+w/s, blks/s, avwait, avserv	49 1 5 27 2 90	44 1 5 26 1 85	44 1 5 24 2 87	37 1 5 24 1 71	50 1 6 30 2 89
Disk Driver 2: %busy avque, r+w/s, blks/s, avwait, avserv	14 1 2 10 4 61	13 1 2 6 5 64	13 1 2 5 8 61	10 1 1 4 4 67	16 1 3 11 4 63

Now	Your Goal	Monitoring	Res #1	Res #2	Res #3	Res #4
1011	900	1122	1084	946	913	960

Worksheet 10-5: rcp Client Network and Streams Tuning Worksheet (part 1)

Tunables	Initial Values	Test #1	Test #2	Test #3	Test #4
NBLK4, NBLK16	296 296				
NBLK64, NBLK128	296 392				
NBLK256, NBLK512	200 88				
NBLK1024, NBLK2048	52 208				
NBLK4096	48				
NQUEUE, NSTREAM	864 160				
STRLOFRAC, STRMEDFRAC	95 97				
nfsd, biod, nfsclnt, lckclnt	n/a				
TCPWINDOW, tcp_round_mss	4*1024 1				
tcp_ttl, udp_ttl	60 30				

Worksheet 10-6: rcp Client Network Tuning Worksheet (part 2)

Resources to Monitor	**Initial Values**	**Test #1**	**Test #2**	**Test #3**	**Test #4**
Streams	no failures	no failures	no failures	no failures	no failures
Input Packets/errors	22456 864	17797 592	15466 19	14344 0	20875 0
Output Packets/errors	22494 0	18351 0	16296 0	15804 0	19774 0
Collisions	87	198	40	46	8
Octets Received	9643144	5244357	3063902	1981520	9374917
Octets Transmitted	3506303	2234698	1597177	1313169	2935046
NIC Interrupts	40453	32962	30009	28554	19676
RPC calls: total calls, badcalls, retrans, badxid, timeout, wait, newcred	0 0 0 0 0 0 0	0 0 0 0 0 0 0	0 0 0 0 0 0 0	0 0 0 0 0 0 0	0 0 0 0 0 0 0
nclget, nclsleep	0 0	0 0	0 0	0 0	0 0
RPC calls: null, getattr, setattr, root, lookup, readlink, read, wrcache, write, create, remove, rename, link, symlink, mkdir, rmdir, readdir, fsstat	0 0 0 0 0 0 0 0 0 0 0 0 0 0 0 0 0 0	0 0 0 0 0 0 0 0 0 0 0 0 0 0 0 0 0 0	0 0 0 0 0 0 0 0 0 0 0 0 0 0 0 0 0 0	0 0 0 0 0 0 0 0 0 0 0 0 0 0 0 0 0 0	0 0 0 0 0 0 0 0 0 0 0 0 0 0 0 0 0 0
Network Topology					
Protocol Errors	n/a	n/a	n/a	n/a	n/a

Now	**Your Goal**	**Monitoring**	**Res #1**	**Res #2**	**Res #3**	**Res #4**
1011	900	1122	1084	946	913	960

Worksheet 10-7: rcp Server Network and Streams Tuning Worksheet (part 1)

Tunables	Initial Values	Test #1	Test #2	Test #3	Test #4
NBLK4, NBLK16	1300 652				
NBLK64, NBLK128	768 872				
NBLK256, NBLK512	548 324				
NBLK1024, NBLK2048	107 180				
NBLK4096	41				
NQUEUE, NSTREAM	1424 292				
STRLOFRAC, STRMEDFRAC	95 97				
nfsd, biod, nfsclnt, lckclnt	n/a				
TCPWINDOW, tcp_round_mss	4*1024 1				
tcp_ttl, udp_ttl	60 30				

Worksheet 10-8: rcp Server Network and Streams Tuning Worksheet (part 2)

Resources to Monitor	Initial Values	Test #1	Test #2	Test #3	Test #4
Streams	no failures	no failures	no failures	no failures	no failures
Input Packets/errors	22922 0	18768 0	16679 0	16155 0	19801 0
Output Packets/errors	23603 0	18492 0	15222 0	14108 0	20897 0
Collisions	0	0	0	0	8
Octets Received	3636296	2363059	1717360	1430027	3297588
Octets Transmitted	10601837	5808099	2753238	1670213	9321179
NIC Interrupts	22917	18761	16676	16142	19791
RPC calls: total calls, badcalls, retrans, badxid, timeout, wait, newcred	0 0 0 0 0 0 0	0 0 0 0 0 0 0	0 0 0 0 0 0 0	0 0 0 0 0 0 0	0 0 0 0 0 0 0
nclget, nclsleep	0 0	0 0	0 0	0 0	0 0
RPC calls: null, getattr, setattr, root, lookup, readlink, read, wrcache, write, create, remove, rename, link, symlink, mkdir, rmdir, readdir, fsstat	0 0 0 0 0 0 0 0 0 0 0 0 0 0 0 0 0 0	0 0 0 0 0 0 0 0 0 0 0 0 0 0 0 0 0 0	0 0 0 0 0 0 0 0 0 0 0 0 0 0 0 0 0 0	0 0 0 0 0 0 0 0 0 0 0 0 0 0 0 0 0 0	0 0 0 0 0 0 0 0 0 0 0 0 0 0 0 0 0 0
Network Topology					
CPU time used by daemons					

Now	Your Goal	Monitoring	Res #1	Res #2	Res #3	Res #4
1011	900	1122	1084	946	913	960

Worksheet 10-9: NFS Client SCO UNIX Tuning Worksheet (part 1)

Tunables	Initial Values	Test #1	Test #2	Test #3	Test #4
Installed Memory	64Mb				
Application Storage	n/a				
GPGSLO, GPGSHI	25 40				
MAXSC, AGEINTERVAL	8 31				
S5CACHEENTS, S5HASHQS	256 61				
NFILE	350				
NINODE, NHINODE	450 512				
NBUF, NHBUF	640 512	2048 2048	3192 2048	4096 2048	5120 4096
BDFLUSHR, NAUTOUP	30 10				
NCOPYBUF, PLOWBUFS	100 30				
NMPBUF, NMPHEADBUF	0 100				
NPBUF, DMAABLEBUF	40 16				
SDSKOUT	4				
Disk Configuration, Data Layout	1 SCSI disk				
NCLIST	120				
NPROC, NREGION	100 300				
NSCRN, CTBUFSIZ	0 128				
Display adapter, colors	n/a				

Worksheet 10-10: NFS Client SCO UNIX Tuning Worksheet (part 2)

Resources to Monitor	Initial Values	Test #1	Test #2	Test #3	Test #4
Free Memory, Free swap	13744 196608	13404 196608	13100 196608	12857 196608	12579 196608
Blocks Swapped in/out	0.0 0.0	0.0 0.0	0.0 0.0	0.0 0.0	0.0 0.0
Pages Reclaimed	0.00	0.00	0.00	0.00	0.00
CPU: %usr, %sys, %wio, %idle	4 85 5 6	4 86 5 4	4 85 4 6	4 87 4 5	5 89 3 3
Scheduling: runq-sz, swpq-sz, pswch/s	8.7 0 173	8.9 0 163	8.6 0 153	8.9 0 151	8.8 0 146
Namei Cache	99%	99%	99%	99%	99%
File Table, Inode Table	170 0 201 0	180 0 206 0	180 0 207 0	180 0 206 0	173 0 201 0
Buffer Cache %rcache Reads: bread/s lread/s Writes: bwrit/s, lwrit/s	95 14 277 24 81	95 14 293 25 84	96 12 298 25 86	97 11 313 26 90	97 10 323 27 92
Scatter/Gather: mpbuf/s, ompb/s, mphbuf/s, omphbufs/s	0 0 1 0	0 0 1 0	0 0 1 0	0 0 1 0	0 0 1 0
Copy Buffers	0 0	0 0	0 0	0 0	0 0
Direct Disk Access	0 0	0 0	0 0	0 0	0 0
Copy Memory	0 0	0 0	0 0	0 0	0 0
Sdsk Request Blocks	3.73 0.00	5.00 0.00	4.87 0.00	4.26 0.00	4.09 0.00
Disk Driver : %busy avque, r+w/s, blks/s, avwait, avserv	8 1 4 13 1 22	9 1 5 16 5 18	9 1 5 16 9 19	10 2 4 15 18 23	9 2 4 14 14 23

Now	Your Goal	Monitoring	Res #1	Res #2	Res #3	Res #4
409-414	205	423	404	398	380	367

Worksheet 10-11: NFS Client SCO UNIX Tuning Worksheet (part 1)

Tunables	Initial Values	Test #5	Test #6	Test #7	Test #8
Installed Memory	64Mb				
Application Storage	n/a				
GPGSLO, GPGSHI	25 40				
MAXSC, AGEINTERVAL	8 31				
S5CACHEENTS, S5HASHQS	256 61				
NFILE	350				
NINODE, NHINODE	450 512				
NBUF, NHBUF		6144 4096	7168 4096	8192 4096	9216 8192
BDFLUSHR, NAUTOUP	30 10				
NCOPYBUF, PLOWBUFS	100 30				
NMPBUF, NMPHEADBUF	0 100				
NPBUF, DMAABLEBUF	40 16				
SDSKOUT	4				
Disk Configuration, Data Layout	1 SCSI disk				
NCLIST	120				
NPROC, NREGION	100 300				
NSCRN, CTBUFSIZ	0 128				
Display adapter, colors	n/a				
Mouse Settings	n/a				

Worksheet 10-12: NFS Client SCO UNIX Tuning Worksheet (part 2)

Resources to Monitor	Initial Values	Test #5	Test #6	Test #7	Test #8
Free Memory, Free swap		12314 196608	12036 196608	11746 196608	11453 196608
Blocks Swapped in/out		0.0 0.0	0.0 0.0	0.0 0.0	0.0 0.0
Pages Reclaimed		0.00	0.00	0.00	0.00
CPU: %usr, %sys, %wio, %idle		5 89 3 3	5 91 2 2	6 88 3 3	5 84 5 6
Scheduling: runq-sz, swpq-sz, pswch/s		8.8 0 142	9.1 0 141	9.0 0 133	8.7 0 122
Namei Cache		99%	99%	99%	99%
File Table, Inode Table		177 0 205 0	171 0 200 0	179 0 205 0	177 0 205 0
Buffer Cache %rcache Reads: bread/s lread/s Writes: bwrit/s, lwrit/s		97 9 337 28 96	98 8 359 30 102	99 7 499 30 98	98 7 350 29 99
Scatter/Gather: mpbuf/s, ompb/s, mphbuf/s, omphbufs/s		0 0 1 0	0 0 1 0	0 0 1 0	0 0 1 0
Copy Buffers		0 0	0 0	1 0	6 0
Direct Disk Access		0 0	0 0	0 0	0 0
Copy Memory		0 0	0 0	0 0	0 0
Sdsk Request Blocks		4.17 0.00	4.67 0.00	4.14 0.00	4.71 0.00
Disk Driver : %busy avque, r+w/s, blks/s, avwait, avserv		10 2 4 14 20 23	10 2 5 15 17 21	9 1 4 15 9 21	11 2 5 16 21 23

Now	Your Goal	Monitoring	Res #1	Res #2	Res #3	Res #4
			353	332	331	343

Worksheet 10-13: NFS Client SCO UNIX Tuning Worksheet (part 1)

Tunables	Initial Values	Test #9	Test #10	Test #11	Test #12
Installed Memory		64Mb			
Application Storage		n/a			
GPGSLO, GPGSHI		25 40			
MAXSC, AGEINTERVAL		8 31			
S5CACHEENTS, S5HASHQS		256 61			
NFILE		350			
NINODE, NHINODE		450 512			
NBUF, NHBUF		8192 4096			
BDFLUSHR, NAUTOUP		30 10			
NCOPYBUF, PLOWBUFS		100 30			
NMPBUF, NMPHEADBUF		0 100			
NPBUF, DMAABLEBUF		40 16			
SDSKOUT		4			
Disk Configuration, Data Layout		1 SCSI disk			
NCLIST		120			
NPROC, NREGION		100 300			
NSCRN, CTBUFSIZ		0 128			
Display adapter, colors					
Other Memory Used					

Worksheet 10-14: NFS Client SCO UNIX Tuning Worksheet (part 2)

Resources to Monitor	Initial Values	Test #9	Test #10	Test #11	Test #12
Free Memory, Free swap		11716 196608			
Blocks Swapped in/out		0.0 0.0			
Pages Reclaimed		0.00			
CPU: %usr, %sys, %wio, %idle		5 92 2 1			
Scheduling: runq-sz, swpq-sz, pswch/s		10.1 0 42			
Namei Cache		99%			
File Table, Inode Table		173 0 203 0			
Buffer Cache %rcache Reads: bread/s lread/s Writes: bwrit/s, lwrit/s		98 8 376 31 107			
Scatter/Gather: mpbuf/s, ompb/s, mphbuf/s, omphbufs/s		0 0 1 0			
Copy Buffers		0 0			
Direct Disk Access		0 0			
Copy Memory		0 0			
Sdsk Request Blocks		4.95 0.00			
Disk Driver : %busy avque, r+w/s, blks/s, avwait, avserv		9 2 5 16 12 19			

Now	Your Goal	Monitoring	Res #9	Res #10	Res #11	Res #12
			321			

Worksheet 10-15: NFS Client Network Tuning Worksheet (part 1). This Worksheet Did Not Change for Tests #1-#9.

Tunables	Initial Values	Test #1	Test #2	Test #3	Test #4
NBLK4, NBLK16	296 296				
NBLK64, NBLK128	296 392				
NBLK256, NBLK512	200 88				
NBLK1024, NBLK2048	52 208				
NBLK4096	48				
NQUEUE, NSTREAM	864 160				
STRLOFRAC, STRMEDFRAC	95 97				
nfsd, biod, nfsclnt, lckclnt	4 4 24 4				
TCPWINDOW, tcp_round_mss	4096 1				
tcp_ttl, udp_ttl	60 30				

Worksheet 10-16: NFS Client Network Tuning Worksheet (part 2)

Resources to Monitor	Initial Values	Test #1	Test #2	Test #3	Test #4
Streams	no failures	no failures	no failures	no failures	no failures
Input Packets/errors	43679 329	38827 258	35185 193	31871 131	29600 112
Output Packets/errors	44103 0	39136 0	35385 0	31986 0	29669 0
Collisions	182	105	574	103	93
Octets Received	36337192	30953687	26897878	23186632	20691766
Octets Transmitted	15243887	14442709	13840851	13288065	12912847
NIC Interrupts	77922	69436	63300	57007	52865
RPC calls: total calls, badcalls, retrans, badxid, timeout, wait, newcred	43500 0 551 0 551 0 0	38658 0 426 0 426 0 0	35005 0 328 0 328 0 0	31690 0 244 0 244 0 0	29429 0 188 0 188 0 0
nclget, nclsleep	43500 0	38658 0	35005 0	31690 0	29429 0
RPC calls: null, getattr, setattr, root, lookup, readlink, read, wrcache, write, create, remove, rename, link, symlink, mkdir, rmdir, readdir, fsstat	0 1328 249 0 2746 0 31209 0 7968 0 0 0 0 0 0 0 0 0	0 1326 249 0 2753 0 26362 0 7968 0 0 0 0 0 0 0 0 0	0 1326 249 0 2751 0 22711 0 7968 0 0 0 0 0 0 0 0 0	0 1354 249 0 2747 0 19372 0 7968 0 0 0 0 0 0 0 0 0	0 1345 249 0 2748 0 17119 0 7968 0 0 0 0 0 0 0 0 0
Network Topology					

Now	Your Goal	Monitoring	Res #1	Res #2	Res #3	Res #4

Worksheet 10-17: NFS Client NetworkTuning Worksheet (part 2)

Resources to Monitor	Initial Values	Test #5	Test #6	Test #7	Test #8
Streams		no failures	no failures	no failures	no failures
Input Packets/errors		26877 74	24551 49	22647 41	21332 35
Output Packets/errors		26857 0	24518 0	22581 0	21258 0
Collisions		78	81	293	70
Octets Received		17628425	15069373	12921461	11424688
Octets Transmitted		12449893	12074321	11772788	11560497
NIC Interrupts		48221	44251	41460	39282
RPC calls: total calls, badcalls, retrans, badxid, timeout, wait, newcred		26699 0 105 0 105 0 0	24389 0 77 0 77 0 0	22478 0 66 0 66 0 0	21154 0 52 0 52 0 0
nclget, nclsleep		26699 0	24389 0	22478 0	21154 0
RPC calls: null, getattr, setattr, root, lookup, readlink, read, wrcache, write, create, remove, rename, link, symlink, mkdir, rmdir, readdir, fsstat		0 1353 249 0 2753 0 14376 0 7968 0 0 0 0 0 0 0 0 0	0 1345 249 0 2747 0 12080 0 7968 0 0 0 0 0 0 0 0 0	0 1353 249 0 2757 0 10151 0 7968 0 0 0 0 0 0 0 0 0	0 1408 249 0 2752 0 8777 0 7968 0 0 0 0 0 0 0 0 0
Network Topology					

Now	Your Goal	Monitoring	Res #5	Res #6	Res #7	Res #8

Worksheet 10-18: NFS Client NetworkTuning Worksheet (part 2)

Resources to Monitor	Initial Values	Test #9	Test #10	Test #11	Test #12
Streams		no failures			
Input Packets/errors		22590 17			
Output Packets/errors		22494 0			
Collisions		94			
Octets Received		12880237			
Octets Transmitted		11758767			
NIC Interrupts		40965			
RPC calls: total calls, badcalls, retrans, badxid, timeout, wait, newcred		22404 0 37 0 37 0 0			
nclget, nclsleep		22404 0			
RPC calls: null, getattr, setattr, root, lookup, readlink, read, wrcache, write, create, remove, rename, link, symlink, mkdir, rmdir, readdir, fsstat		0 1331 249 0 2746 0 10110 0 7968 0 0 0 0 0 0 0 0 0			
Network Topology					

Now	Your Goal	Monitoring	Res #9	Res #10	Res #11	Res #12

Worksheet 10-19: NFS Server SCO UNIX Tuning Worksheet (part 1) This worksheet did not change for Tests #2-#8.

Tunables	Initial Values	Test #1	Test #2	Test #3	Test #4
Installed Memory	64Mb				
Application Storage	n/a				
GPGSLO, GPGSHI	200 300				
MAXSC, AGEINTERVAL	8 31				
S5CACHEENTS, S5HASHQS	3072 8191	4096 8191			
NFILE	3000				
NINODE, NHINODE	2500 2048				
NBUF, NHBUF	32640 32768				
BDFLUSHR, NAUTOUP	30 10				
NCOPYBUF, PLOWBUFS	100 10				
NMPBUF, NMPHEADBUF	16 2048				
NPBUF, DMAABLEBUF	200 64				
SDSKOUT	4				
Disk Configuration, Data Layout	RAID 0				
NCLIST	2048				
NPROC, NREGION	800 2400				
NSCRN, CTBUFSIZ	0 128				
Display adapter, colors	n/a				

Worksheet 10-20: NFS Server SCO UNIX Tuning Worksheet (part 2)

Resources to Monitor	Initial Values	Test #1	Test #2	Test #3	Test #4
Free Memory, Free swap	3316 65536	3305 65536	3306 65536	3306 65536	3305 65536
Blocks Swapped in/out	0.0 0.0	0.0 0.0	0.0 0.0	0.0 0.0	0.0 0.0
Pages Reclaimed	0.00	0.00	0.00	0.00	0.00
CPU: %usr, %sys, %wio, %idle	1 55 19 26	1 54 21 25	0 55 20 25	1 56 21 22	0 55 22 22
Scheduling: runq-sz, swpq-sz, pswch/s	2.1 0 349	2.1 0 321	2.2 0 290	2.3 0 274	2.0 0 260
Namei Cache	90%	90%	89%	90%	89%
File Table, Inode Table	187 0 200 0	187 0 200 0	187 0 200 0	187 0 200 0	189 0 199 0
Buffer Cache %rcache Reads: bread/s lread/s Writes: bwrit/s, lwrit/s	97 22 646 36 186	96 24 626 37 182	96 23 620 38 176	96 24 623 39 175	96 23 611 40 174
Scatter/Gather	0 0 4 0	0 0 3 0	0 0 3 0	0 0 3 0	0 0 3 0
Copy Buffers	0 0	0 0	0 0	0 0	0 0
Direct Disk Access	0 0	0 0	0 0	0 0	0 0
Copy Memory	0 0	0 0	0 0	0 0	0 0
Sdsk Request Blocks	0.00 0.00	0.00 0.00	0.00 0.00	0.00 0.00	0.00 0.00
Disk Driver : %busy avque, r+w/s, blks/s, avwait, avserv (ida-0)	7 1 7 18 0 11	9 1 8 20 0 11	9 1 7 19 0 12	10 1 7 20 0 13	6 1 6 16 0 11
ida-1	59 1 38 98 0 15	60 1 39 101 0 15	62 1 40 103 0 16	64 1 41 107 0 15	65 1 42 110 0 15

Worksheet 10-21: NFS Server SCO UNIX Tuning Worksheet (part 2)

Resources to Monitor	Initial Values	Test #5	Test #6	Test #7	Test #8
Free Memory, Free swap		3306 65536	3305 65536	3307 65536	3304 65536
Blocks Swapped in/out		0.0 0.0	0.0 0.0	0.0 0.0	0.0 0.0
Pages Reclaimed		0.00	0.00	0.00	0.00
CPU: %usr, %sys, %wio, %idle		1 54 23 22	1 54 24 22	1 49 20 29	0 53 19 28
Scheduling: runq-sz, swpq-sz, pswch/s		2.0 0 247	2.1 0 234	2.0 0 208	2.1 0 190
Namei Cache		90%	89%	89%	90%
File Table, Inode Table		188 0 201 0	187 0 200 0	187 0 200 0	186 0 198 0
Buffer Cache %rcache Reads: bread/s lread/s Writes: bwrit/s, lwrit/s		96 25 594 40 168	96 25 582 41 164	96 23 524 37 147	96 21 549 37 145
Scatter/Gather		0 0 3 0	0 0 4 0	0 0 3 0	0 0 3 0
Copy Buffers		0 0	0 0	0 0	0 0
Direct Disk Access		0 0	0 0	0 0	0 0
Copy Memory		0 0	0 0	0 0	0 0
Sdsk Request Blocks		0.00 0.00	0.00 0.00	0.00 0.00	0.00 0.00
Disk Driver : %busy avque, r+w/s, blks/s, avwait, avserv (ida-0)		8 1 8 21 0 10	8 1 8 21 0 10	8 1 7 20 0 11	7 1 6 16 0 13
ida-1		64 1 42 109 0 15	65 1 43 111 0 15	58 1 39 100 0 15	58 1 39 100 0 15

Worksheet 10-22: NFS Server SCO UNIX Tuning Worksheet (part 1)

Tunables	Initial Values	Test #9	Test #10	Test #11	Test #12
Installed Memory	64Mb				
Application Storage	n/a				
GPGSLO, GPGSHI	200 300				
MAXSC, AGEINTERVAL	8 31				
S5CACHEENTS, S5HASHQS	3072 8191				
NFILE	3000				
NINODE, NHINODE	2500 2048				
NBUF, NHBUF	32640 32768				
BDFLUSHR, NAUTOUP	30 10				
NCOPYBUF, PLOWBUFS	100 10				
NMPBUF, NMPHEADBUF	16 2048				
NPBUF, DMAABLEBUF	200 64				
SDSKOUT	4				
Disk Configuration, Data Layout	RAID 0	enable cache			
NCLIST	2048				
NPROC, NREGION	800 2400				
NSCRN, CTBUFSIZ	0 128				
Display adapter, colors					

Worksheet 10-23: NFS Server SCO UNIX Tuning Worksheet (part 2)

Resources to Monitor	Initial Values	Test #9	Test #10	Test #11	Test #12
Free Memory, Free swap		3301 65536			
Blocks Swapped in/out		0.0 0.0			
Pages Reclaimed		0.00			
CPU: %usr, %sys, %wio, %idle		1 56 8 36			
Scheduling: runq-sz, swpq-sz, pswch/s		2.4 0 242			
Namei Cache		89%			
File Table, Inode Table		183 0 196 0			
Buffer Cache %rcache Reads: bread/s lread/s Writes: bwrit/s, lwrit/s		97 19 580 41 163			
Scatter/Gather		0 0 3 0			
Copy Buffers		0 0			
Direct Disk Access		0 0			
Copy Memory		0 0			
Sdsk Request Blocks		0.00 0.00			
Disk Driver : %busy avque, r+w/s, blks/s, avwait, avserv (ida-0)		3 1 1 7 0 10			
ida-1		28 1 43 112 0 7			

Worksheet 10-24: NFS Server Network Tuning Worksheet (part 1). After the initial debugging, these values did not change for Tests #1-#9.

Tunables	Initial Values	Test #1	Test #2	Test #3	Test #4
NBLK4, NBLK16	1300 652				
NBLK64, NBLK128	768 872				
NBLK256, NBLK512	548 324				
NBLK1024, NBLK2048	107 180				
NBLK4096	41				
NQUEUE, NSTREAM	1424 292				
STRLOFRAC, STRMEDFRAC	95 97				
nfsd, biod, nfsclnt, lckclnt	4 4 8 4				
TCPWINDOW, tcp_round_mss	4096 1				
tcp_ttl, udp_ttl	60 30				

Worksheet 10-25: NFS Server Network Tuning Worksheet (part 2)

Resources to Monitor	Initial Values	Test #1	Test #2	Test #3	Test #4
Streams	no failures	no failures	no failures	no failures	no failures
Input Packets/errors	45126 0	40105 0	36343 0	32912 0	30573 0
Output Packets/errors	45008 0	39996 0	36226 0	32793 0	30463 0
Collisions	0	2	2	0	0
Octets Received	15325942	14520032	13918168	13362242	12984754
Octets Transmitted	36259141	30819987	26731728	22975461	20484622
NIC Interrupts	45123	40103	36341	32911	30572
RPC calls: total calls, badcalls, retrans, badxid, timeout, wait, newcred	44051 0 0 0 0 0 0	39084 0 0 0 0 0 0	35333 0 0 0 0 0 0	31934 0 0 0 0 0 0	29617 0 0 0 0 0 0
nclget, nclsleep	0 0	0 0	0 0	0 0	0 0
RPC calls: null, getattr, setattr, root, lookup, readlink, read, wrcache, write, create, remove, rename, link, symlink, mkdir, rmdir, readdir, fsstat	0 1345 249 0 2769 0 31638 0 8050 0 0 0 0 0 0 0 0 0	0 1339 249 0 2777 0 26685 0 8034 0 0 0 0 0 0 0 0 0	0 1332 249 0 2766 0 22961 0 8025 0 0 0 0 0 0 0 0 0	0 1362 249 0 2761 0 19552 0 8010 0 0 0 0 0 0 0 0 0	0 1347 249 0 2757 0 17263 0 8001 0 0 0 0 0 0 0 0 0
Network Topology					
Protocol Errors					
CPU time used by daemons					

Worksheet 10-26: NFS Server Network Tuning Worksheet (part 2)

Resources to Monitor	Initial Values	Test #5	Test #6	Test #7	Test #8
Streams		no failures	no failures	no failures	no failures
Input Packets/errors		27758 0	25395 0	23562 0	22215 0
Output Packets/errors		27644 0	25293 0	23440 0	22099 0
Collisions		4	0	4	2
Octets Received		12522120	12144242	11851182	11636780
Octets Transmitted		17383268	14833939	12717949	11211820
NIC Interrupts		27756	25394	23562	22212
RPC calls: total calls, badcalls, retrans, badxid, timeout, wait, newcred		26804 0 0 0 0 0 0	24466 0 0 0 0 0 0	22544 0 0 0 0 0 0	21206 0 0 0 0 0 0
nclget, nclsleep		0 0	0 0	0 0	0 0
RPC calls: null, getattr, setattr, root, lookup, readlink, read, wrcache, write, create, remove, rename, link, symlink, mkdir, rmdir, readdir, fsstat		0 1354 249 0 2759 0 14459 0 7983 0 0 0 0 0 0 0 0 0	0 1347 249 0 2750 0 12143 0 7977 0 0 0 0 0 0 0 0 0	0 1353 249 0 2757 0 10205 0 7980 0 0 0 0 0 0 0 0 0	0 1408 249 0 2754 0 8816 0 7979 0 0 0 0 0 0 0 0 0
Network Topology					

Worksheet 10-27: NFS Server Network Tuning Worksheet (part 2)

Resources to Monitor	Initial Values	Test #9	Test #10	Test #11	Test #12
Streams		no failures			
Input Packets/errors		23394 0			
Output Packets/errors		23265 0			
Collisions		6			
Octets Received		11832976			
Octets Transmitted		12623854			
NIC Interrupts		23393			
RPC calls: total calls, badcalls, retrans, badxid, timeout, wait, newcred		22441 0 0 0 0 0 0			
nclget, nclsleep		0 0			
RPC calls: null, getattr, setattr, root, lookup, readlink, read, wrcache, write, create, remove, rename, link, symlink, mkdir, rmdir, readdir, fsstat		0 1332 250 0 2748 0 10130 0 7981 0 0 0 0 0 0 0 0 0			
Network Topology					
Protocol Errors					
CPU time used by daemons					

Chapter 11

Oracle Case Studies

These two examples highlight some key Oracle Version 7, SCO UNIX and SCO MPX tuning issues. The first case study focuses on installing an Oracle system and determining the optimal sizes for key Oracle data structures. The second case study examines how to isolate the cause of a performance degradation after a database has been reconfigured. Both cases use the seven-step method and tuning worksheets as the framework for data collection and resource usage analysis.

Both cases assume a familiarity with the common operation technical background and performance tuning concepts presented in this book as well as the layout and configuration issues described at the start of this chapter. These cases also assume a familiarity with Oracle terms, such as *db_block_buffers*, *two-task* and *checkpoint*. Please see appropriate Oracle manuals for more information on these and other terms used in the case study.

Oracle Layout

For an optimally tuned and configured Oracle database, the CPU, memory and disk resources must be optimally allocated. The operating system must also be configured to provide the Oracle application with the maximum amount of hardware resources.

The first resource to consider is the CPU. The amount of CPU time available to Oracle should be maximized by following the guidelines presented in the previous chapters. An optimally tuned Oracle system that does not use the network should report a %usr time between 70% and 80% and a %sys time between 20% and 30%, with %wio and %idle less than 5%. If the Oracle system uses the network then the ratio should be closer to 50%/50%, with %wio and %idle less than 5%. If the reported CPU usage is significantly different from these ratios, then analyze the resource usage patterns to determine what is causing the larger values of %sys, %idle or %wio.

post-wait driver

Configuring Oracle and SCO UNIX/SCO MPX to use the *post-wait driver* will also increase CPU efficiency. When the system is running SCO MPX, further efficiency increases can be realized by configuring the scheduling variables as follows:

- loadbalance = 0
- preemptive = 0
- cache_affinity = 0
- dopricalc = 0

These variables are set to zero because Oracle performs most optimally when its server processes determine when they should relinquish the CPU. Setting these four variables to zero gives the Oracle processes the maximum amount of time on the CPU.

The next resource to consider is the amount of memory available to the Oracle database and the operating system. For optimal performance, Oracle should be configured to use the direct disk access interface and asynchronous I/O, or AIO. Both Oracle and the operating system must be configured to use these features. When Oracle is configured to use the filesystem, both Oracle and the operating system buffer data, and this double-buffering is an added overhead to every transaction. Direct disk access and AIO avoid this overhead, thereby increasing performance.

db_block_buffers

When asynchronous direct disk transfers are used, the number of db_block_buffers directly affects the amount of disk activity generated by Oracle. As long as the records retrieved from the database are re-used, increase the number of db_block_buffers until the system starts to page or swap, then gradually decrease the number of db_block_buffers until the system stops paging and swapping. The application will then have the largest intermediate storage location possible without compromising performance by causing a memory shortage. When Oracle is the primary application running on the system, the size of many operating system data structures, such as the buffer cache, can be reduced to increase the amount of memory available to Oracle.

The amount of data written during a checkpoint is affected by the number of db_block_buffers. The disk subsystem chosen should be able to handle the volume of disk activity generated by a checkpoint without compromising the performance of other transactions.

With the amount of CPU time and memory available to Oracle at a maximum, design the database and the disk subsystem layout for minimum delay with the following principles:

- Place the redo logs on a separate set of disks, mirrored for reliability if necessary. The redo log disks are unique in that the database writes to these disks only in a sequential fashion. Since disks run at their quickest when writing data sequentially without disruption, separating the logs from the other random access activity is optimal for performance.

- Spread the database records across as many disks as feasible.

The specific application of these guidelines depends on the structure of the database and the pattern of record access. Ways to monitor disk usage and how to decide where to move the data are described in these examples. The importance of good database layout cannot be over-stated, because the time spent in designing an optimal layout for a particular disk subsystem is more than compensated for by the additional performance realized.

Oracle Installation Example

This example describes how to configure and tune an Oracle system to meet a set of performance requirements. The situation is described, and then the seven-step method is used to analyze the resource usage pattern achieve the specified performance goal.

Situation Summary

The application is a set of parcel-tracking devices connected by a variety of mechanisms to a central Oracle database. The database contains parcel information, such as identification number, source and destination addresses, and current location. When a new parcel is received, an identification number is assigned to it, and the database record for this parcel is initialized. When the parcel passes through a distribution center, the current location is updated. Customers can telephone their local distribution center to find out the exact location of their parcel.

The most common database transaction is an update to the current location of the parcel in the parcel information.

There are at most 150,000 parcels active in the database at any one time.

The performance requirements are based on the amount of time required to process 50,000 parcels at a particular distribution center. The average number of parcels processed during peak periods was determined, including adding a worst case estimate for the number of customer enquiries. Maintaining adequate response time during peak periods is essential to the commercial needs of the business, since the speed at which parcels are processed is the critical factor determining the capacity of the business.

Flexibility is a key requirement for the choice of hardware and software for the distribution center because the business is expected to grow.

The Seven Steps

Step 1. Decide what to improve.

☑ Select the appropriate worksheet for the common operation.

The time-critical operation is the basic transaction of querying the database and updating the location of the parcel. Queries for the location of the parcel are also time-critical, because customers are waiting for answers while the database is retrieving the information.

The worksheets for SCO UNIX, SCO MPX, and Oracle are shown in Worksheets 11-1 through 11-5 at the end of this chapter. The relevant data from these worksheets is highlighted throughout this example.

⇩

Step 2. Identify the limited and unlimited resources.

☑ Note any limited resources on the worksheet by marking them with an asterisk (*).

Although the ideal situation is unlimited budgets with unlimited hardware, a more realistic scenario is one with some limitations. In this case, the limitations are the amount of memory and the number of disks attached to the fast disk subsystem with caching disk controller. Step 7 will show whether additional CPUs, memory and disks are required to meet the performance requirement.

Figure 11-1 shows the hardware environment.

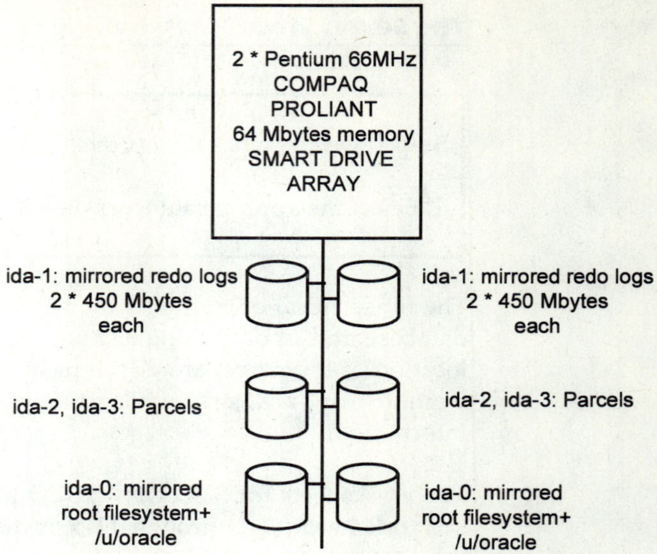

Figure 11-1: The redo logs are installed on two mirrored disks and are configured as 2*450 Mbyte divisions. The mirroring provides data reliability. The parcel data is spread across two disks. The root filesystem and */u/oracle* filesystem are also installed on a pair of mirrored disks. The second CPU is enabled in Test #4.

The AIO driver and post-wait driver are configured into Oracle following the instructions described in the Oracle For SCO UNIX Installation and Configuration Guide. These drivers are also configured into the operating system. When AIO was configured, the following entry was added to the */usr/lib/aiomemlock* file:

```
oracle 50441648
```

With this large value, the AIO driver pre-allocates up to 48 Mbytes of memory for asynchronous direct disk transfers. This value is large enough to avoid further reconfiguration as the number of db_block_buffers changes through this series of tests.

⇩

Step 3. Determine how to measure the operation and test its current performance.

☑ Note the test result on the worksheet in the column marked **Now.**

The test is a set of multiple processes that read and update the parcel information.

The test is run on the current installation with one processor and the result is 1031 seconds, which is just over 17 minutes. The test results were slightly erratic, but the difference between the longest and shortest duration was less than 1%, so the test is sufficiently stable for this tuning exercise.

⇩

Step 4. Set a realistic performance goal.

☑ Note this on the worksheet in the column marked **Your Goal.**

The time necessary to process 50,000 parcels needs to be less than eight minutes. The test is much simpler than the combination of applications that normally runs on the system, so the performance goal is quite aggressive to ensure that sufficient spare capacity is available when the system is run under normal conditions.

After the system is installed, further monitoring of the system may reveal other resources that need to be tuned to compensate for the other applications that run intermittently on the system. Because parcel-tracking is the primary use of the system, the database will be optimally tuned, and the other applications will be accommodated as necessary.

⇩

Step 5. Identify the resources to monitor and decide which monitoring tools to use.

☑ The worksheets list the appropriate resources.

The operating system resources to monitor are identified on the SCO UNIX and SCO MPX Tuning worksheets. The key Oracle resources are identified on the Oracle Tuning worksheet.

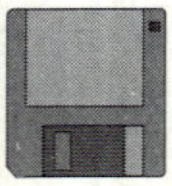

The sar, cpusar, and mpsar commands are used to monitor the operating system resources. The data is extracted with the sar2wks and mpx2wks scripts. The oraclestat script extracts the correct Oracle statistics from the dynamic performance tables described in the Oracle RDBMS Database Administrator's Guide Volume III. The sar2wks, mpx2wks and oraclestat scripts are included on the floppy disk.

⇩

Step 6. Run the test with the monitoring tools and monitor the resource usage and record the test results.

☑ Enter the initial values of the tunables and note the resource usage in the column marked **Initial Values**. Note the test results under the column called **Monitoring.**

The test result with the monitoring tools enabled was not significantly different from the original result of close to 17 minutes. The results are noted in Worksheet 11-2.

Initial Observations

The key Oracle resources are CPU availability, memory (for the db_block_buffers), and disk throughput, so examine these resources first.

The CPU statistics show that %wio was equal to 54% and %idle was equal to 1%. Over half of the CPU resource is not used, because no ready-to-run processes are available. Since the suspended processes are waiting-on-device-I/O, a resource shortage in the I/O subsystem must exist. Only 28% of the time was spent executing Oracle and the test program, and 16% of the time was spent executing the operating system. The optimal %usr and %sys ratio is 80% to 20%, so the current ratio can be improved considerably.

The amount of free memory (from freemem) is given by the following equation:

*8975 * 4 = 35,900 Kbytes*

At no point during the test does a memory shortage occur, as indicated by the values reported by the paging and swapping statistics. The number of pages reclaimed per second (rclm/s) and the number of processes on the swap queue (swpq-sz) are both equal to zero.

The intermediate storage locations and resources necessary to complete a transaction with the direct disk access interface are as follows:

- application-specific
- copy memory
- disk driver, adapter and disks

Oracle supports an intermediate storage location called the Oracle *cache*. This intermediate storage location is where the data for the direct disk transfers is located. The size of the Oracle direct disk access area is configured with db_block_buffers.

The current size is given by the following equation:

$$1000 * 2 = 2{,}000 \text{ Kbytes}$$

where 1000 is the current value of db_block_buffers specified in two Kbyte units.

The disk adapter can access all memory, so no copy memory is used.

The frequency of direct disk access read and write requests per second is equal to 124, as reported by pbuf/s.

Figure 11-2 shows the number of 512-byte blks/s handled by each logical volume. Referring to the original hardware configuration, the ida-0 logical volume contains the root filesystem and the ida-1 logical volume contains the redo logs. The ida-2 and ida-3 logical volumes contain the database records.

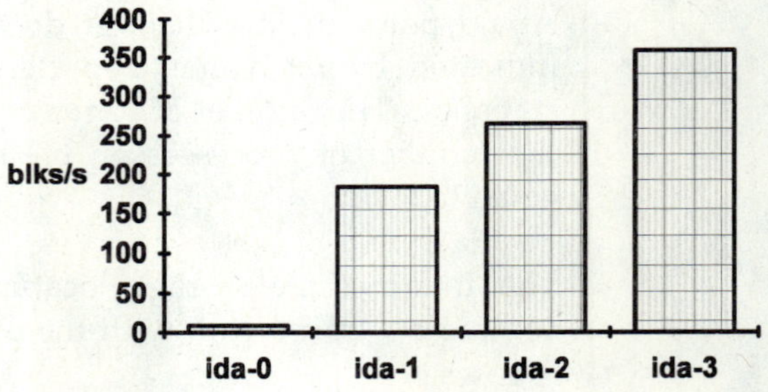

Figure 11-2: The blks/s for Each Logical Volume

Figure 11-3 shows the avserv time for all four logical volumes.

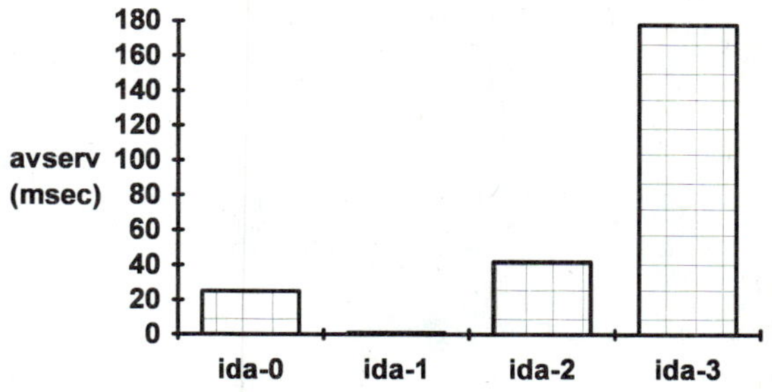

Figure 11-3: The avserv Time for Each Logical Volume

Figures 11-2 and 11-3 show that the ida-3 database volume is much busier than the ida-2 database volume and that both of the database volumes are busier than either the redo log or the root filesystem logical volume. The level of activity for the redo log depends on how quickly each transaction completes, so this disk will be underutilized if other resource shortages prevent transactions from completing as quickly as possible.

Despite the level of disk activity, the requests are not held up in the driver because avque is close to zero. In this situation, the avserv time is the key indicator of the ability of the disks to handle the number of requests.

Some filesystem use is expected because Oracle clients and shadow processes communicate via pipes. Examining the resource usage pattern for the filesystem intermediate storage locations shows that these resources are allocated optimally. The resource usage pattern for the filesystem resources are noted in Worksheet 11-2.

Returning to the database to find a source of delay, we see that the number of checkpoints is equal to zero, so these are not causing the unequal disk activity and affecting the duration of the test.

Because the Oracle cache is designed to reduce disk activity, the amount of disk activity can be reduced by increasing the number of db_block_buffers. Performance should increase when the number of direct disk transfers is reduced.

⇩

Step 7. Decide how to change the resource allocation; rerun the tests and note progress toward the goal. Iterate until either the goal is reached, or until a limited resource is encountered.

☑ Determine whether to increase or decrease the resource/tunable. Note the new tunable values in the column marked **Test #1** and the test results under the column **Res #1.** Use the rest of the columns for the results of subsequent test iterations.

☑ When the goal is reached, implement the new resource allocation.

Test #1: Increase db_block_buffers to 10,000

The amount of free memory is 35 Mbytes. Increasing the number of db_block_buffers to 10,000 leaves sufficient free memory and provides a good reference point for determining any further increases. 10,000 db_block_buffers occupy 20 Mbytes of memory.

The time taken to complete 50,000 transactions has fallen from 1029 to 493 seconds.

The CPU utilization is much closer to the ideal ratio. The amount of time spent executing Oracle is equal to 74%, and %sys time is equal to 26%. %wio and %idle are equal to zero.

The system has not started to page or swap.

The frequency of direct disk access requests has not changed significantly. Because a larger Oracle buffer cache can store more information, the number of reads from the database logical volumes decreases. However, the log writer must write to the log each time a transaction completes.

The length of the test is shorter, so the frequency of transactions has risen, and that increase requires the log writer to write more frequently. Increased log activity may explain why the frequency of direct disk access requests has not changed.

Figures 11-4 shows the number of 512-byte blks/s handled by each logical volume for this test. Figure 11-5 shows the avserv time for each logical volume for this test configuration.

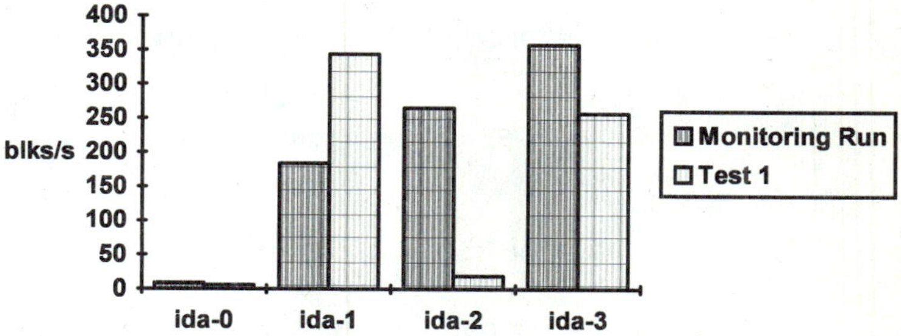

Figure 11-4: The blks/s for Each Logical Volume for the Initial Configuration and Test #1

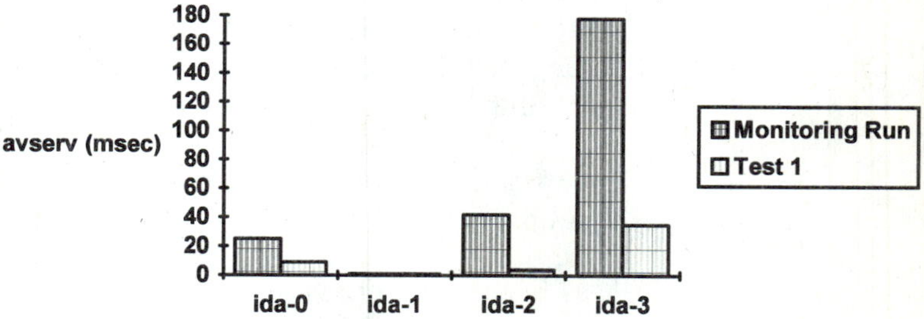

Figure 11-5: The avserv Time for Each Logical Volume for the Monitoring Run and Test #1

The amount of activity on ida-1 confirms the increased activity of the log writer because of the higher transaction frequency. The decrease in activity on ida-1 and ida-2 confirms that increasing the number of db_block_buffers reduces the amount of disk activity. The disk activity that remains is serviced quicker than with a lower value of db_block_buffers, possibly due to the disk heads needing to travel a shorter distance on average.

Considering that almost 15 Mbytes of free memory are still available, another attempt at raising the number of db_block_buffers should yield even better performance.

Test #2: Increase db_block_buffers to 16,500

Increase the value of db_block_buffers by 6500 (13 Mbytes total increase), so the total size of db_block_buffers is 16,500 or 33 Mbytes.

Run the test again and record the resource usage patterns.

The amount of free swap has decreased, so some paging or swapping has occurred. The number of pages reclaimed per second, as indicated by rclm/s, is also greater than zero, with some sar intervals showing an average of 33 pages per second. The 0.21 noted in the worksheet is the average over the entire duration of the test. Considering that the system will also support other applications, the memory shortage will only become more acute, so decreasing the number of db_block_buffers until no paging occurs should be an optimal configuration for a system that will run more than just Oracle.

The amount of swap space used is given by the following equation:

$$\frac{196608 - 191941}{2 * 1024} = 2.27\,Mbytes$$

This equation is described in more detail in the Common Open Desktop Operations chapter.

Reducing db_block_buffers by this much (between 1000 and 1500) would leave the amount of free memory hovering around GPGSLO, so paging might still occur if other applications are also running. Reducing db_block_buffers by 2500 leaves some spare memory for other applications and should still provide a performance benefit over the previous value of 10,000 buffers.

Test #3: Decrease db_block_buffers to 14,000

Set db_block_buffers to 14,000 and run the test again.

The test result is equal to the previous test result, and no paging or swapping occurred, so the performance goal has been achieved.

The CPU statistics show that the CPU is fully utilized, because %wio and %idle are both equal to zero. The ratio of %usr to %sys time is equal to 74% to 26%, which is within the acceptable range.

The disk statistics show that the database logical volumes are still quite busy. Spreading the database records over more disks would yield a performance improvement, but since no more disks can be added, this resource usage pattern will remain unchanged.

With close to 100% CPU usage or a consistently high number of ready-to-run processes, an additional processor might improve performance. Before an additional processor is added, the number of ready-to-run processes, as specified by runq-sz, is checked to ensure that processes exist for the additional CPU to run. The statistics show an average ready-to-run list length of 11.1, so an additional CPU would have work to do.

Test #4: Install an Additional CPU

Configure the additional processor, install SCO MPX, and set the following SCO MPX scheduler variables to zero: loadbalance, preemptive, dopricalc and cache_affinity. Run the test again.

The test duration has reduced again, this time to 260 seconds. This result surpasses the original goal.

A quick check through the resources shows how adding the processor has changed the usage pattern.

Both CPUs spend less than 5% of their time either %idle or %wio, although the total amount of time the CPU spends idle (%idle plus %wio) is greater than 5%. The %usr to %sys ratio is close to optimal, with a ratio of 69% to 23% on the first CPU and 70% to 23% on the second CPU.

The amount of free memory has increased slightly. The average amount of %sys time is 23%, and the average amount of %usr time is 70%. The average amount of %wio time has increased to 4%, along with %idle of 1%. The frequency of direct disk reads is the same, but the frequency of writes has decreased from 53 to 44 per second. This decrease cannot be readily explained.

The number of direct disk access requests has decreased to an average of 64 per second.

As expected, the disk subsystem shows an overall increase in activity. Figure 11-6 summarizes the changes in avserv; Figure 11-7 summarizes the changes in blks/s between one and two CPUs.

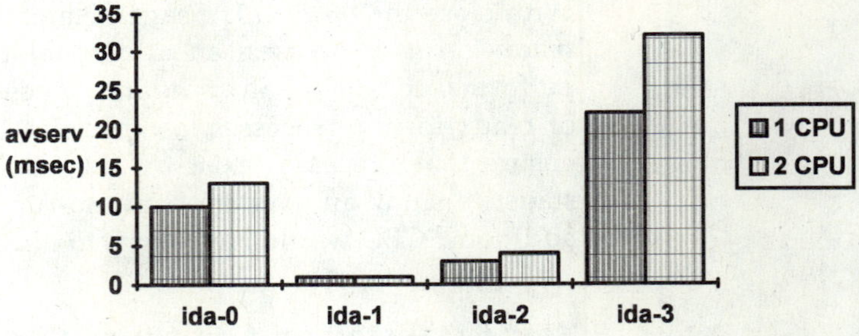

Figure 11-6: Changes in avserv for One and Two CPU Tests

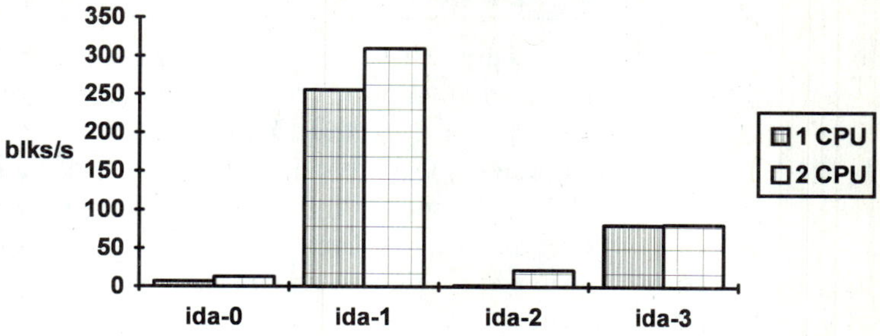

Figure 11-7: Changes in blks/s for One and Two CPU Tests

Although the logical volume containing the redo logs is the busiest volume, the disks can keep up because the avserv time is close to one millisecond. One explanation for why the disk can maintain its speed is that writes to the redo logs are sequential, the most optimal pattern of disk head travel. Because the disk head travel pattern is sequential, isolating the logs on their own disks gives the best performance.

To maximize the use of the second CPU, the layout of the database records must be changed so that workload for ida-3 is spread to more disks. This rearrangement should reduce %wio and %idle and reduce %sys so it is closer to the ideal value of 20%.

However, no additional disks are available, so the existing configuration must be maintained. The performance benefit of the additional CPU leaves sufficient spare capacity for the other applications that will run intermittently, so the second CPU will remain installed.

Conclusion

Increasing the size of the Oracle intermediate storage location reduces the amount of disk activity and dramatically improves the performance of the Oracle installation. One of the key Oracle tunables is db_block_buffers. The value of db_block_buffers should be set as large as the amount of memory allows. If paging or swapping occurs, reduce the value of db_block_buffers until paging and swapping cease.

The layout of the database is also critical to performance. This example showed how the increase in performance affected the frequency of requests to the logical volume containing the redo log. The sequential nature of the disk head travel is very efficient, and so the redo logs should be installed on separate disks to maintain this efficient disk usage pattern. Although performance once again improved with the additional CPU, the current database layout is not efficient enough to maximize the use of the additional CPU. Reconfiguring the database tables to include one or more additional disks will improve the utilization of the additional CPU.

Oracle Reconfiguration Example

This example shows how to use the seven step method to isolate an unexpected performance drop after the database was reconfigured.

Situation Summary

The situation is the same parcel-tracking system as described in the previous example. However, in this case the database was reconfigured from the original size of 150,000 records to 300,000 records. The other difference was the configuration of the redo logs. In the first example, the two redo logs were each equal to 450 Mbytes. In this example, both redo logs are equal to 50 Mbytes.

The Seven Steps

Step 1. Decide what to improve.

☑ Select the appropriate worksheet for the common operation.

The database size needed to increase because more parcels were travelling through the system. Unfortunately, after the reconfiguration, the performance of the time-critical operations decreased dramatically.

The SCO UNIX, SCO MPX and Oracle resource usage statistics for this example are shown in Worksheets 11-6 through 11-10.

⇩

Step 2. Identify the limited and unlimited resources.

☑ Note any limited resources on the worksheet by marking them with an asterisk (*).

The hardware environment is shown in Figure 11-8. The software configuration is the same as in the previous example.

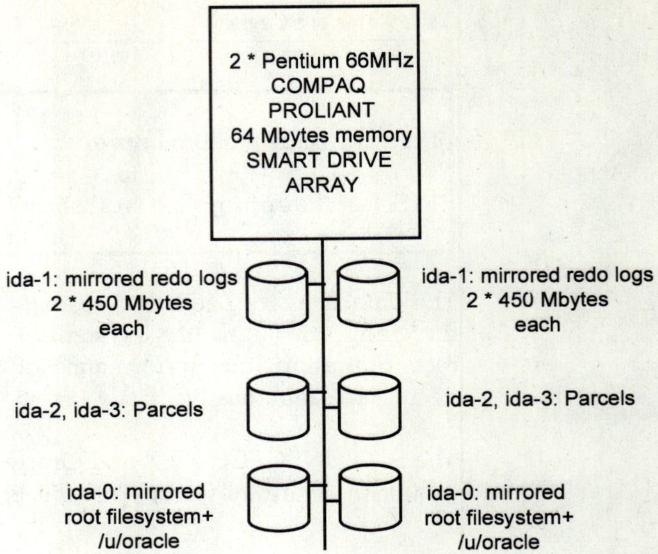

Figure 11-8: The redo logs are installed on two mirrored disks and are configured as 2*50 Mbyte divisions. The mirroring provides reliability. The parcel data is spread across two disks. The root filesystem and */u/oracle* filesystem are also installed on a pair of mirrored disks. The size of the database is increased from 150,000 to 300,000 records. The second CPU is enabled throughout this example.

⇩

Step 3. Determine how to measure the operation and test its current performance.

☑ Note the test result on the worksheet in the column marked **Now.**

The test program used in the previous example is still valid, so the same program and procedures will be used to determine the cause of the performance degradation.

After the database was reconfigured, the test results increased from 260 seconds to 1718 seconds.

Step 4. Set a realistic performance goal.

☑ Note this on the worksheet in the column marked **Your Goal.**

The goal is to restore the system to the level of performance achieved prior to reconfiguring the database.

Step 5. Identify the resources to monitor and decide which monitoring tools to use.

☑ The worksheets list the appropriate resources.

The operating system resources to monitor are identified on the SCO UNIX and SCO MPX Tuning worksheets. The key Oracle resources are identified on the Oracle Tuning worksheet.

As in the previous example, the sar, cpusar, and mpsar commands are used to monitor the operating system resources. The sar2wks, mpx2wks and oraclestat scripts are used to extract the appropriate worksheet data from the data files.

⇩

Step 6. Run the test with the monitoring tools and monitor the resource usage and record the test results.

☑ Enter the initial values of the tunables and note the resource usage in the column marked **Initial Values**. Note the test results under the column called **Monitoring.**

The test result with the monitoring enabled is equal to 1718 seconds.

Initial Observations

The key resources to examine are as follows:

- CPU
- memory
- direct disk access and the disk subsystem

The CPU statistics show that %wio on the first CPU has risen to 83% and on the second CPU to 75%. Figure 11-9 compares the CPU usage from the final test described in the previous example and the current monitoring run.

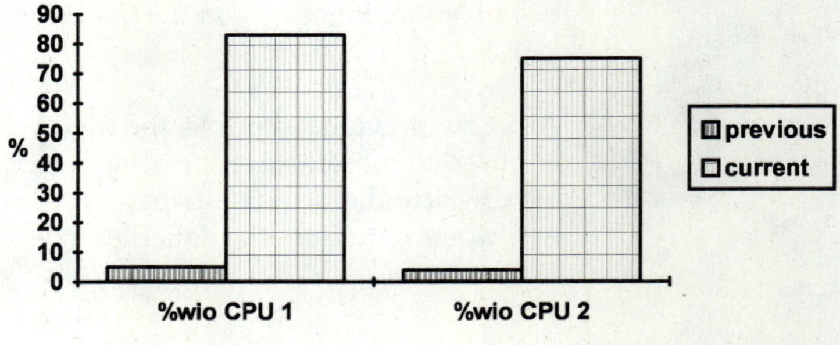

Figure 11-9: Changes in %wio Between Previous and Current Configuration

Neither CPU spends much time executing Oracle or the operating system in comparison to the amount of time they spend idle, waiting for I/O to complete.

The operating system is neither paging nor swapping, so a memory shortage is not causing the sudden drop in performance.

The frequency of direct disk access requests has increased from 64 in the previous configuration to 88 per second in the larger configuration.

The pattern has reverted to one that was seen when the value of db_block_buffers was less than it is now. However, the value of db_block_buffers has not changed, so some other problem must be causing the performance degradation.

Figures 11-10 and 11-11 show the avserv and number of blks/s handled by each logical volume in the new configuration.

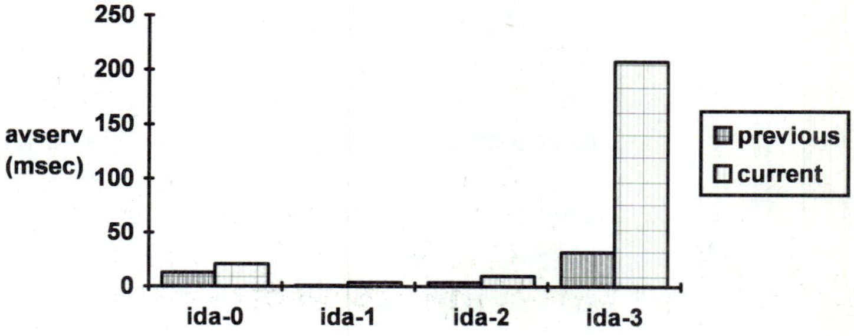

Figure 11-10: The avserv Time for Each Logical Volume for the Previous and Current Configuration

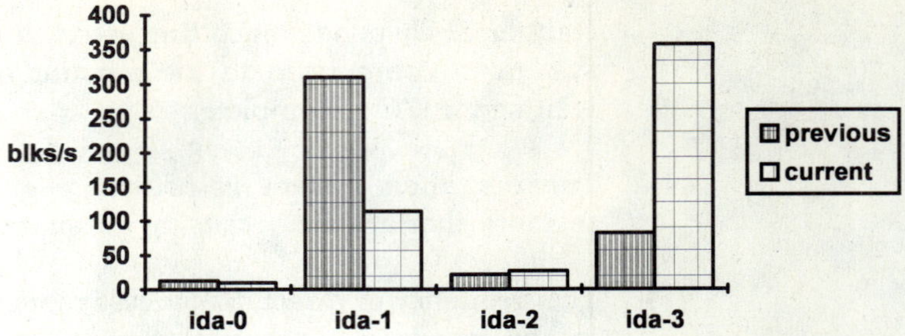

Figure 11-11: The number of blks/s for Each Logical Volume for the Previous and Current Configuration

The dramatic increase in disk activity coupled with the increase in direct disk access activity may mean that the Oracle cache is now working much less efficiently.

The operating system does not influence the efficiency of the Oracle cache, so some Oracle configuration must also need changing when the size of the database increases.

To determine if the cache efficiency is the cause of the performance degradation, we need to calculate the efficiency of the cache.

The ORACLE RDBMS Performance Tuning Guide in the section "Tuning the Buffer Cache" shows that the hit ratio is given by the following equation:

$$(1-(\frac{physical\_reads}{(db\_block\_gets+consistent\_gets)}))*100=hit\_ratio$$

The hit rate for the current configuration is equal to:

$$(1-(\frac{31477}{(69264+129056)}))*100=81.1\%$$

The efficiency ratio for the original run is close to 97%.

The reason for the change in efficiency is not clear, so we need to make a good guess. But first, more understanding of the configuration change is necessary.

The parcels database was originally configured to be 150,000 records and *hashing* was chosen as the index method. In some database configurations, hashing improves performance by shortening the amount of time necessary to locate a given database row that contains the requested database information.

hash key, hash value, hash function

Rather than searching the standard Oracle index segments for the disk location containing the database information, Oracle uses a special function to map an intermediate location pointer to the disk location where the database information is stored. The special mapping function is called a *hash function* and the intermediate location pointer is called a *hash value* or *hash key.* The smaller the number of hash keys, the greater the number of disk locations that map to the same hash key.

cluster key value

The *cluster key value* specifies the rows that are to be retrieved from the table covered by the hash function. When Oracle retrieves the requested data from the database, it executes the hash function using the cluster key value to determine the correct hash key. Each disk location mapped to the hash key is searched until the correct row(s) is found. This search is known as a *hash scan.* If a large number of disk locations map to the same hash key, then a long list must be searched to find the correct row(s), and performance is adversely affected. The smaller the number of disk locations that map to a hash key, the quicker the correct database row(s) can be retrieved.

CREATE CLUSTER, HASHKEYS

The CREATE CLUSTER command allocates an area on the disk where the tables that are covered by the hashing function are located. The tables covered by the CREATE CLUSTER command are known as *hash clusters.* The value of HASHKEYS is the number of hash keys. A complete description of hashing can be found in the Oracle RDBMS Database Administrator's Guide, Volume I.

The ORACLE RDBMS Performance Tuning Guide provides guidelines for hashing configuration. One of the guidelines is: "Store a table in a hash cluster if you can determine how much space is required to hold all rows with a given cluster key value, including rows to be inserted immediately as well as rows to be inserted in the future."

The ORACLE RDBMS Performance Tuning Guide also suggests: "For best performance of hash scans, choose a HASHKEYS value that is at least as large as the number of cluster key values."

The current number of cluster key values is equal to 300,000 and the value of HASHKEYS is equal to 150,000. A good guess, then, is to assume that the current value of HASHKEYS is not suitable for the larger database and the time required for the hash scans is causing the performance degradation.

Step 7. Decide how to change the resource allocation; rerun the tests and note progress toward the goal. Iterate until either the goal is reached, or until a limited resource is encountered.

☑ Determine whether to increase or decrease the resource/tunable. Note the new tunable values in the column marked **Test #1** and the test results under the column **Res #1.** Use the rest of the columns for the results of subsequent test iterations.

☑ When the goal is reached, implement the new resource allocation.

Test #1: HASHKEYS =300,000

To test this guess, the hash cluster for the parcels table was rebuilt with the value of HASHKEYS set to 300,000.

The duration of the test has fallen to 260 seconds, which is equal to the previous test result, so the guess proved correct.

The CPU efficiency has improved dramatically, as shown in Figure 11-12.

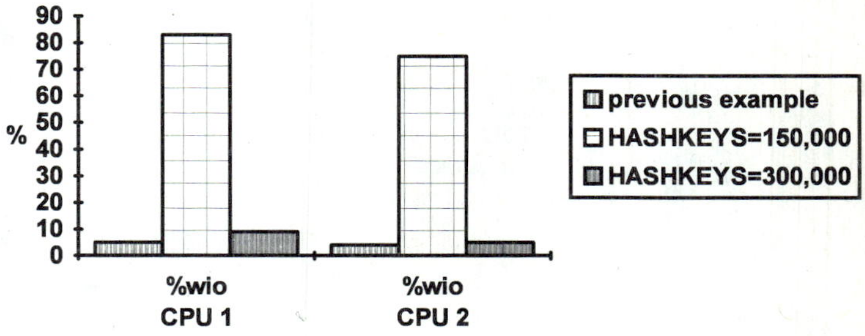

Figure 11-12: Comparison of %wio on CPU One and Two Between the Previous Example and the Different HASHKEYS values

The ratio of %usr to %sys time on both CPUs is close to optimal, with a ratio of 64% to 22% on CPU one and 66% and 23% on CPU two. The ratios could be more optimal if the more disks could be added.

The memory usage pattern shows that no memory shortage is occurring.

The number of direct disk access requests is once again close to the previous configuration, as pbufs/s is equal to 67. In the previous configuration, pbufs/s was equal to 64.

The total number of reads and writes from oraclestat is shown in Figure 11-13.

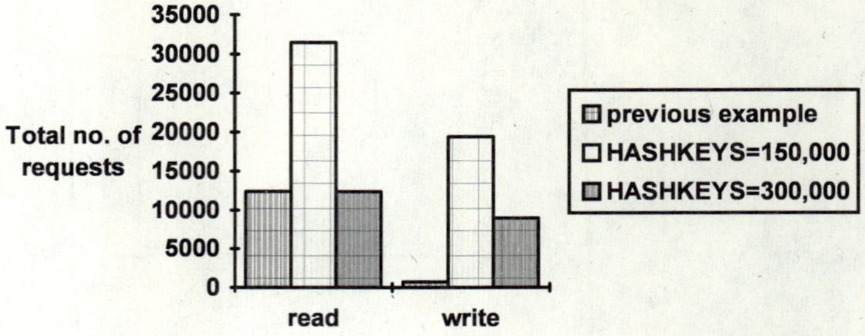

Figure 11-13: Comparison of Oracle Physical Reads and Writes

The Oracle cache efficiency statistic confirms the reasons for the change in behavior shown in Figure 11-13. The new cache statistic is equal to:

$$(1-(\frac{12401}{(514835+489597)}))*100=98.8\%$$

The cache is more efficient, so the amount of disk activity has decreased. When Oracle searches the list of locations mapped by the hash key, each disk location must be read into the Oracle cache. Since the lists are long when the value of HASHKEYS is equal to 150,000, many disk locations will be loaded into the cache before the requested row is found. Reading the disk locations forces other database data out of the cache, thereby reducing the Oracle cache efficiency. When the lists are short, only a small number of disk locations are read, so only a small amount of data will be forced out of the cache, and the cache can be more efficient.

This reduction is confirmed by the disk usage statistics reported by mpsar as shown in Figures 11-14 and 11-15.

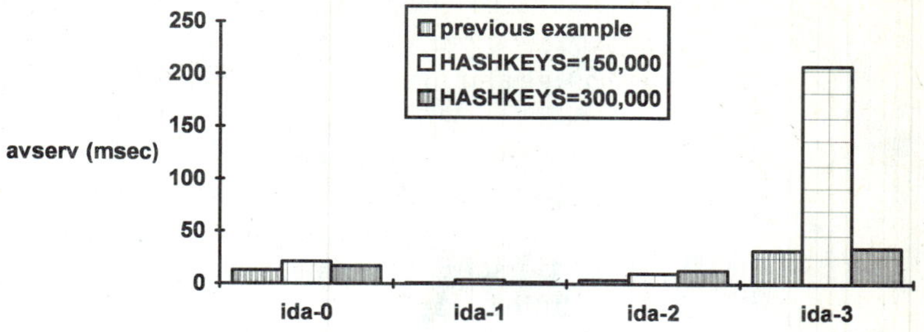

Figure 11-14: The avserv Time of Each Logical Volume for the Previous Example and the Different Values of HASHKEYS.

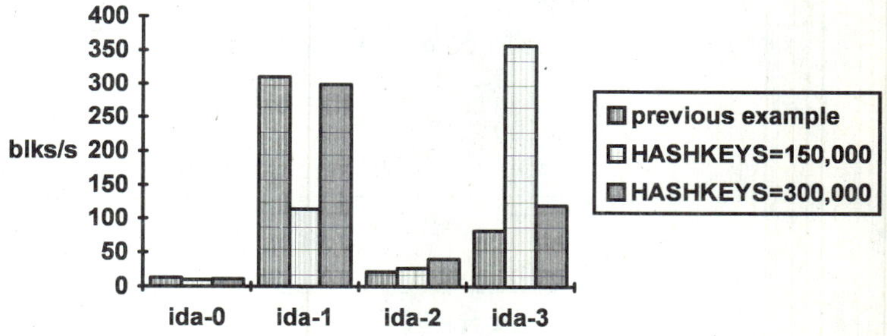

Figure 11-15: The number of blks/s for Each Logical Volume for the Previous Example and the Different Values of HASHKEYS.

The decrease in the frequency of blks/s confirms the reduction in disk activity that corresponds to the increase in Oracle cache efficiency.

Conclusions

This example shows the importance of correct Oracle configuration to Oracle database performance. In this case, the Oracle configuration was causing the performance degradation rather than the operating system configuration. In other situations, the operating system configuration may be preventing increased performance. Both the operating system and Oracle must be properly configured in order to achieve efficient resource usage and maximum performance.

This example also shows how systematic data analysis does not always lead to a conclusive decision to change resource allocation. In such cases, a good guess is necessary to decide which direction to pursue. Experimentation and guessing can often lead to a solution, especially if executed in a systematic fashion with a thorough analysis of the changes that occur as a result of the experiments.

Quick Diagnosis Summary

Table 11-1 summarizes the key operating system behaviors that should be monitored when the Oracle database is running.

Operating System Behavior	Command
CPU usage	mpsar -u/cpusar -u and sar -u
Direct disk access	mpsar -b/sar -b
Disk activity	mpsar -d/sar -d
Amount of swap space used	swap -l
Amount of paging	mpsar -p/sar -p

Table 11-1: Summary of Key Operating System Behavior When Oracle is Running

The oraclestat script extracts the statistics referred to in this example. Table 11-2 summarizes these statistics.

Oracle Behavior	Command
Physical reads and writes	oraclestat
Cache efficiency	oraclestat + equations
DBWR checkpoints	oraclestat

Table 11-2: Summary of Key Oracle Statistics

The essential tuning guidelines for Oracle are summarized as follows:

- Configure the database to use the direct disk access interface.
- Carefully plan the database layout so the level of disk activity is equal for all the disks containing database information. Spread the database records across as many disks as possible.
- If the database is configured with hashing, ensure that the number of HASHKEYS is greater than or equal to the number of cluster key values.
- Allocate a mirrored pair of disk drives for the sole use of the redo logs. The log disks are unique in that the database writes to these disks only in a sequential fashion. Since disks are at their quickest when writing data sequentially without disruption, separating the logs from the other random access activity is optimal for performance.
- Ensure that the post-wait driver is configured in the *init.ora* file. Configure Oracle to use AIO by setting the USE_AIO environment variable to TRUE.

- Set the checkpoint interval so data reliability is guaranteed without significantly increasing the amount of disk activity.

- Set the number of db_block_buffers to the highest value possible with the given memory configuration. Do not set db_block_buffers so high that paging and swapping occur.

The SCO MPX and SCO UNIX configuration recommendations are as follows:

- The optimal CPU usage values for non-networked systems are as follows: %usr between 70% and 80%, %sys between 20% and 30% and %wio and %idle less than 5%.

- Increase the amount of shared memory to accommodate the number of configured db_block_buffers.

- If Oracle is the primary application running on the system, reduce the amount of memory occupied by the operating system by reducing the size of minimally used operating system data structures. See Appendix B for suggestions.

- Configure the sleeper driver and asynchronous I/O.

- Configure the amount of AIO memory for use by Oracle, as defined by */usr/lib/aiomemlock*, to a value larger than the amount of memory configured for Oracle buffers.

- For SCO MPX, set loadbalance, preemptive, dopricalc and cache_affinity to zero.

- Minimize the amount of swapping/paging occurring on the client and server systems.

- In networked environments, ensure that both the client and server have sufficient CPU capacity to process the network traffic. In a networked environment, the CPU usage values are: %usr equal to 50-60%, %sys equal to 40-50% and %wio and %idle less than 5%.

Worksheet 11-1: SCO UNIX Tuning Worksheet (part 1) for the Oracle Installation Example

Tunables	Initial Values	Test #1	Test #2	Test #3	Test #4
*Installed Memory	64 Mbytes				
Application Storage	See Worksheet 11-4 and 11-5				
GPGSLO, GPGSHI	500 600				
MAXSC, AGEINTERVAL	8 31				
S5CACHEENTS, S5HASHQS	3072 8191				
NFILE	4700				
NINODE, NHINODE	5000 2048				
NBUF, NHBUF	2048 2048				
BDFLUSHR, NAUTOUP	30 10				
NCOPYBUF, PLOWBUFS	100 10				
NMPBUF, NMPHEADBUF	16 2048				
NPBUF, DMAABLEBUF	200 64				
SDSKOUT	4				
*Disk Configuration, Data Layout	See Worksheet 11-4 and 11-5				
NCLIST	2048				
NPROC, NREGION	3000 6000				
NSCRN, CTBUFSIZ	0 128				

Worksheet 11-2: SCO UNIX Tuning Worksheet (part 2) for the Oracle Installation Example

Resources to Monitor	Initial Values	Test #1	Test #2	Test #3	Test #4
Free Memory, Free swap	8975 196608	3746 196608	578 191941	1479 196608	1497 196608
Blocks Swapped in/out	0.0 0.0	0.0 0.0	0.0 0.9	0.0 0.0	0.0 0.0
Pages Reclaimed	0.00	0.00	0.21 (45)	0.00	0.00
CPU: %usr, %sys, %wio, %idle	28 16 54 1	74 26 0 0	74 26 0 0	74 26 0 0	70 23 4 1
Scheduling	1.7 0 643	13.1 0 930	10.4 0 782	11 0 791	10 0 917
Namei Cache	98%	100%	100%	100%	97%
File Table, Inode Table	326 0 161 0	326 0 161 0	327 0 161 0	326 0 160 0	333 0 167 0
Buffer Cache %rcache Reads: bread/s lread/s Writes: bwrit/s, lwrit/s	98 2 116 3 102	100 0 271 3 272	100 0 283 3 284	100 0 287 3 287	100 2 483 5 481
Scatter/Gather	0 0 1 0	0 0 2 0	0 0 2 0	0 0 2 0	0 0 3 0
Copy Buffers	0 0	0 0	0 0	0 0	0 0
Direct Disk Access	124 0	123 0	72 0	74 0	64 0
Disk Driver : %busy avque, r+w/s, blks/s, avwait, avserv (ida-0)	9 1 3 9 0 25	8 0 2 6 0 9	9 0 3 8 0 8	10 0 3 7 0 10	14 0 3 13 0 13
ida -1	7 1 46 184 0 1	12 1 85 344 0 1	7 1 58 256 0 1	7 1 59 256 0 1	8 1 61 310 0 1
ida-2	100 1 66 265 0 42	2 1 5 19 0 4	1 0 0 2 0 2	1 0 2 9 0 3	3 1 5 22 0 4
ida-3	100 1 89 358 0 178	99 1 64 257 0 35	29 1 19 77 0 19	30 1 20 81 0 22	25 1 20 82 0 32

Now	Your Goal	Monitoring	Res #1	Res #2	Res #3	Res #4
1031	460	1029	493	469	469	260

Worksheet 11-3: SCO MPX Tuning Worksheet for the Oracle Installation Example

Tunables	**Initial Values**	**Test #1**	**Test #2**	**Test #3**	**Test #4**
Number of CPUs	1	1	1	1	2
loadbalance					0
preemptive					0
dopricalc					0
primove					10
cache_affinity					0
Resources to Monitor	**Initial Values**	**Test #1**	**Test #2**	**Test #3**	**Test #4**
CPU 1: %usr, %sys, %wio, %idle					69 23 5 3
CPU 2: %usr, %sys, %wio, %idle					70 23 4 3
CPU 3: %usr, %sys, %wio, %idle					
CPU 4: %usr, %sys, %wio, %idle					
CPU 1 InterCPU interrupts					9 25 0
CPU 2 InterCPU interrupts					25 9 0
CPU 3 InterCPU interrupts					
CPU 4 InterCPU Interrupts					

Worksheet 11-4: Oracle Tuning Worksheet (part 1) for the Oracle Installation Example

Tunables	Initial Values	Test #1	Test #2	Test #3	Test #4
checkpoint_process	FALSE				
db_block_buffers	1000	10000	16500	14000	
db_block_checkpoint_ batch	2				
db_block_max_scan_cnt	30				
db_block_write_batch	8				
discrete_transactions_ enabled	TRUE				
dml_locks	400				
log_buffer	262144				
log_checkpoint_interval	9999999				
log_checkpoint_timeout	0				
use_post_wait_driver	TRUE				
USE_AIO	TRUE				
shared_pool_size					
Size of redo log	2*450 Mbytes				
Number of rollback segments	30				
Database Layout disk 1 disk 2 disk3, disk 4	 rootdisk logs: 2*450 Mbytes (mirrored) products				

Worksheet 11-5: Oracle Tuning Worksheet (part 2) for the Oracle Installation Example

Resources to Monitor	Initial Values	Test #1	Test #2	Test #3	Test #4
Total System Global Area	9016216	30104592	45328560	39474256	
Fixed Size	40088				
Variable Size	6665984	20480000	33792000	28672000	
Database buffers	2048000	2048000	33792000	28672000	
Redo buffers	262144				
Physical Writes	41450	22199	376	1130	721
Physical Reads	41602	14793	12111	12177	12415
redo log usage	57 Mbytes	56 Mbytes	55 Mbytes	54 Mbytes	53 Mbytes
DBWR checkpoints	0	0	0	0	0
Database file reads:					
Database file writes:					

Now	Your Goal	Monitoring	Res #1	Res #2	Res #3	Res #4

Worksheet 11-6: SCO UNIX Operating System Tuning Worksheet (part 1) for Oracle Reconfiguration Example

Tunables	Initial Values	Test #1	Test #2	Test #3	Test #4
*Installed Memory	64Mb				
Application Storage					
GPGSLO, GPGSHI	500 600				
MAXSC, AGEINTERVAL	8 31				
S5CACHEENTS, S5HASHQS	3072 8191				
NFILE	4700				
NINODE, NHINODE	5000 2048				
NBUF, NHBUF	2048 2048				
BDFLUSHR, NAUTOUP	30 10				
NCOPYBUF, PLOWBUFS	100 10				
NMPBUF, NMPHEADBUF	16 2048				
NPBUF, DMAABLEBUF	200 64				
SDSKOUT	4				
*Disk Configuration, Data Layout	See Oracle Worksheet 11-9, 11-10				
NCLIST	2048				
NPROC, NREGION	3000 6000				
NSCRN, CTBUFSIZ	0 128				

Worksheet 11-7: SCO UNIX Tuning Worksheet (part 1) for Oracle Reconfiguration Example

Resources to Monitor	Initial Values	Test #1
Free Memory, Free swap	1478 196608	1527 196608
Blocks Swapped in/out	0.0 0.0	0.0 0.0
Pages Reclaimed	0.00	0.00
CPU: %usr, %sys, %wio, %idle	11 7 79 3	65 23 8 5
Scheduling: runq-sz, swpq-sz, pswch/s	1.4 0 479	10.2 0 914
Namei Cache	98%	98%
File Table, Inode Table	329 0 163 0	329 0 164 0
Buffer Cache %rcache Reads: bread/s lread/s Writes: bwrit/s, lwrit/s	100 0 83 5 72	100 0 469 5 459
Scatter/Gather: mpbuf/s, ompb/s, mphbuf/s, omphbufs/s	0 0 3 0	0 0 3 0
Copy Buffers	0 0	0 0
Direct Disk Access	88 0	67 0
Copy Memory	0 0	0 0
Sdsk Request Blocks	0 0	0 0
Disk Driver : %busy avque, r+w/s, blks/s, avwait, avserv (ida-0)	16 0 3 10 0.02 21	15 0 3 11 0.02 17
ida-1	6 1 28 114 0.02 4	9 1 59 299 0.01 2
ida-2	7 1 7 27 0.01 10	9 0 10 40 0.05 13
ida-3	97 1 89 357 .01 208	32 1 30 120 0.05 34

Now	Your Goal	Monitoring	Res #1
1702	260	1718	260

Worksheet 11-8: SCO MPX Tuning Worksheet for Oracle Reconfiguration Example

Tunables	**Initial Values**	**Test #1**	**Test #2**	**Test #3**	**Test #4**
Number of CPUs	2				
loadbalance	0				
preemptive	0				
dopricalc	0				
primove	10				
cache_affinity	0				
Resources to Monitor	**Initial Values**	**Test #1**	**Test #2**	**Test #3**	**Test #4**
CPU 1: %usr, %sys, %wio, %idle	8 6 83 8	64 22 9 5			
CPU 2: %usr, %sys, %wio, %idle	14 9 75 2	66 23 6 4			
CPU 3: %usr, %sys, %wio, %idle					
CPU 4: %usr, %sys, %wio, %idle					
CPU 1 InterCPU interrupts	32 74 9	12 29 0			
CPU 2 InterCPU interrupts	74 32 0	29 12 0			
CPU 3 InterCPU interrupts					
CPU 4 InterCPU Interrupts					

Now	**Your Goal**	**Monitoring**	**Res #1**	**Res #2**	**Res #3**	**Res #4**

Worksheet 11-9: Oracle Tuning Worksheet (part 1) for Oracle Reconfiguration Example

Tunables	Initial Values	Test #1	Test #2	Test #3	Test #4
checkpoint_process	FALSE				
db_block_buffers	14000				
db_block_checkpoint_ batch	2				
db_block_max_scan_cnt	30				
db_block_write_batch	8				
discrete_transactions_ enabled	TRUE				
dml_locks	400				
log_buffer	262144				
log_checkpoint_interval	9999999				
log_checkpoint_timeout	0				
use_post_wait_driver	TRUE				
USE_AIO	TRUE				
shared_pool_size					
Size of redo log	2*50 Mbytes				
Number of rollback segments	30				
Database Layout disk 1 disk 2 disk 3, disk 4	 rootdisk logs:2*50 Mbytes (mirrored) parcels				

Worksheet 11-10: Oracle Tuning Worksheet (part 2) for Oracle Reconfiguration Example

Resources to Monitor	Initial Values	Test #1	Test #2	Test #3	Test #4
Total System Global Area	39474256				
Fixed Size	40088				
Variable Size	10500024				
Database buffers	286720000				
Redo buffers	66 Mbytes				
Physical Writes	31477	12401			
Physical Reads	19405	8935			
redo log usage	66 Mbytes	52 Mbytes			
DBWR checkpoints	1	1			
Database file reads:					
Database file writes:					
free_buffer_inspected	1451				
db_block_gets	69264	514835			
consistent_gets	129056	489597			
free_buffer_requested	48276	17194			

Now	Your Goal	Monitoring	Res #1	Res #2	Res #3	Res #4

Chapter 12

Informix-OnLine Case Study

This chapter describes how to tune Informix OnLine following the seven-step method. The objectives of this study are to show the importance of the following tuning principles:

- Database layout planning
- Having enough disks and a high capacity disk subsystem
- Database tuning
- Rechecking early conclusions after dramatic performance changes

The case starts out with a summary of the situation, then describes some guidelines for database layout. A description of the monitoring tools used in this study follows the discussion of database layout.

The section called The Seven Steps illustrates how the seven-step method and worksheets are used to understand the system resource usage patterns. The resource allocation step goes beyond how the steps might normally be used in order to illustrate the behavior of some key OnLine tunable variables in this environment.

After a description of tuning the basic Informix OnLine environment, a discussion of the tuning considerations for other configurations, such as installing OnLine on a filesystem or over the network, is presented. This discussion assumes an understanding of the concepts presented in The Seven Steps section.

The case concludes with a summary of the key Informix OnLine, SCO UNIX and SCO MPX tuning recommendations. Completed worksheets are included at the end of the chapter as a sort of appendix to show how resource allocation decisions can be made from the resource usage statistics.

The case assumes a familiarity with the common operation technical background and performance tuning concepts presented in this book and with OnLine terms, such as *extent*, *chunk*, and *tbstat*. In addition, this case study does not replace the tuning guidelines provided with Informix OnLine and instead provides complementary information that can be used alongside the suggestions provided with the application or the hardware. Please see the Informix-OnLine Administrator's Guide for more information on tuning and on the database terms used in the case study.

Situation Summary

The installation is a set of local computers that download inventory and order information to a central database. The central database is the system being tuned.

Each local database contains inventory information that is updated with the product purchase information as the cashier enters it. The local databases store the purchase transactions for the day, and then download them to the central database. During the download process, the local computers are connected to the central database via a high-speed wide-area network. The download operation must complete in time for new orders to be sent to the distribution center so the orders can be sent out to the local stores the next day.

Layout and Tools

The location of different parts of the database significantly affects database performance. Since the operating system provides no intermediate storage areas to enhance the performance of the direct disk access interface, how quickly the database can retrieve data from the disk is a key determinant of transaction performance. This section describes some OnLine database layout guidelines for use when deciding which sections of the database should go where. Time spent planning and optimizing the database layout is often rewarded with significantly increased performance.

Database Layout Suggestions

For optimal performance, carefully plan how to use the different disks in the disk subsystem. An understanding of the potential usage pattern of the different database *chunks* helps ensure that the disk activity is spread evenly over a number of disks or disk subsystems. If the usage information is not available, then try an initial allocation, but be prepared to rearrange the data after running some initial tests. The command tbstat -D provides information on the database server disk usage pattern. If some disks are experiencing more activity than others, consider rearranging the data so the disk usage is more equally spread over the disks. A more detailed description of the database layout guidelines can be found in the Informix OnLine Administrator's Guide.

In addition to the values shown by tbstat -D, use the values reported by sar -d to determine the level of disk activity for each disk. Some disks may have higher service times than other disks. Again be prepared to move the chunks used by the database from one disk to another to reduce the number of requests serviced by any one disk. Monitoring entire disks with sar -d is important because a disk may have multiple chunks and the usage pattern of those chunks may be such that the disk heads spend significant time moving between the chunks on that disk. Disk head travel causes additional delay to the servicing of disks and so should be minimized where possible.

Always configure Informix-OnLine to access the disks through the direct disk access interface. For example, if you create a division on the disk for use by OnLine with the name *database1*, then when specifying the disk area to OnLine use */dev/rdatabase1*. The assignment can be confirmed with the sar -h command and examining the pbuf/s columns. These columns monitor the amount of disk activity through the direct disk access interface, so should be greater than zero if the database is configured correctly.

Allocate the fastest disks and adapters on the system to the physical and logical logs. If the physical or logical log must be mirrored because of reliability, then consider using a disk adapter that supports mirroring directly in hardware. Hardware support means OnLine does not have to implement mirroring in the software. Hardware mirroring is generally faster than software mirroring.

Ensure that the number of checkpoints that occurs during a measurement is as low as possible, but high enough to meet any data recovery time requirement. The number of checkpoints can be found with the command tbstat -p. This command is described in more detail in the Informix OnLine Administrator's Guide. The less frequent checkpoints are, the longer the recovery time will be should the system unexpectedly fail. The time increases because more data is stored in the logs before being committed to the database. At each checkpoint, the data in the logs must be processed as part of the recovery mechanism. A checkpoint occurs for these reasons:

- The time interval specified by CKPTINTVL (in seconds) has elapsed since the last checkpoint, so all data in the log must be committed

- A system administrator forces a checkpoint using one of the utilities provide by OnLine

- The physical log is 75% full

- The logical files have wrapped so that the next file contains the most recent checkpoint mark

If the checkpoints occur more frequently than specified by CKPTINTVL, modify the resource allocation so the value in CKPTINTVL is the only mechanism that controls checkpoint frequency. Reallocation may include increasing the size of the physical log or using more files for the logical log.

Monitoring Tools

This case uses the standard SCO UNIX and SCO MPX monitoring tools, sar, mpsar, and cpusar. Informix OnLine provides a monitoring tool called tbstat that monitors both database resource usage and some hardware resource usage. The runinf script included on the floppy disk runs the necessary monitoring tools. See the Informix OnLine Administrator's Guide for more information on this command.

The Seven Steps

Step 1. Decide what to improve.

☑ Select the appropriate worksheet for the common operation.

The length of time for the download process is increasing because each store is generating more sales which generates more inventory update information. The time required for the database update is almost too long for the distribution center orders to be processed and sent out the next day for delivery.

The selected worksheets are shown in Worksheets 12-1 through 12-5.

⇩

> **Step 2.** Identify the limited and unlimited resources.
>
> ☑ Note any limited resources on the worksheet by marking them with an asterisk (*).

Figure 12-1 shows the current hardware configuration. The hardware resources are limited to what is currently available.

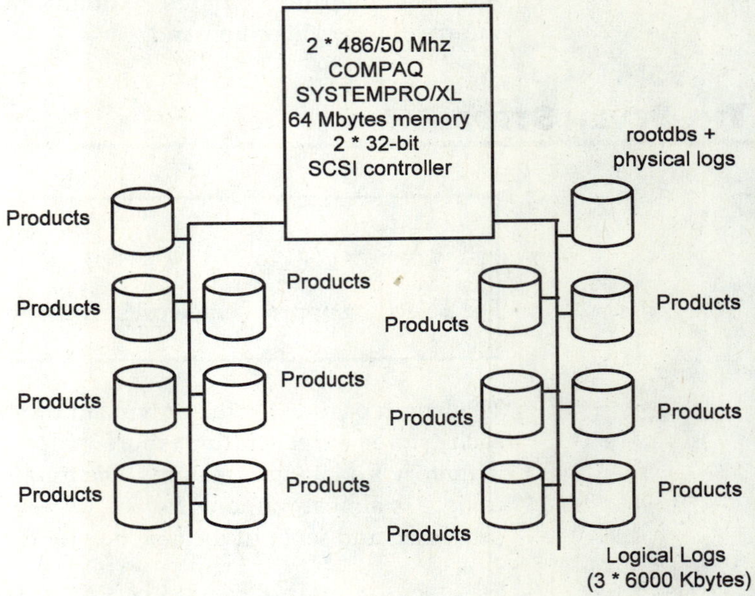

Figure 12-1: Hardware Configuration and Database Layout

⇩

Step 3. Determine how to measure the operation and test its current performance.

☑ Note the test result on the worksheet in the column marked **Now.**

A short program that does repeated query-modify transactions was written to simulate what occurs during peak periods. Since processing the normally large volume of transactions is impractical for a short test, the results for a smaller number of transactions will be used and the results extrapolated to a large number. 10,000 transactions should provide a reasonable basis for extrapolation. Currently, 10,000 transactions takes approximately 185 seconds to process.

⇩

Step 4. Set a realistic performance goal.

☑ Note this on the worksheet in the column marked **Your Goal.**

Because of the critical nature of the problem, the performance goal must be aggressive. The goal is to cut the amount of time required to process 10,000 transactions from 185 seconds to 90 seconds.

⇩

Step 5. Identify the resources to monitor and decide which monitoring tools to use.

☑ The worksheets list the appropriate resources.

The operating system resources that must be monitored are shown in the worksheet. The database resources are shown in the Informix worksheet.

The standard operating system monitoring tools, sar, mpsar, and cpusar are used to monitor operating system and hardware resource usage patterns. Informix-OnLine provides a monitoring command called tbstat for monitoring OnLine resource usage patterns. The runinf program automatically collects the appropriate resource usage statistics.

⇩

Step 6. Run the test with the monitoring tools and monitor the resource usage and record the test results.

☑ Enter the initial values of the tunables and note the resource usage in the column marked **Initial Values**. Note the test results under the column called **Monitoring.**

With monitoring, the test now takes 188 seconds.

Initial Observations

Because the performance of databases can be improved by setting the loadbalance, preemptive, and dopricalc variables to zero, these were set to zero before continuing. Changing these values can increase the amount of CPU time available to the database processes, which might then lead to increased disk activity, depending on the frequency of transactions.

Rerun the test. The new test results are 174 seconds.

⇩

Step 7. Decide how to change the resource allocation; rerun the tests and note progress toward the goal. Iterate until either the goal is reached, or until a limited resource is encountered.

☑ Determine whether to increase or decrease the resource/tunable. Note the new tunable values in the column marked **Test #1** and the test results under the column **Res #1.** Use the rest of the columns for the results of subsequent test iterations.

☑ When the goal is reached, implement the new resource allocation.

Test Series #2: Increase BUFFERS from 1000 to 12000

The key resource usage patterns to examine are CPU, memory and disk.

The CPU usage statistics show that CPU one spends 23% of its time %wio and 1% of its time %idle and CPU two spends 12% of its time %wio and 20% of its time %idle. The amount of time spent executing the operating system on CPU one is equal to 51% and on CPU two is equal to 40%. Increasing the amount of time spent executing in %usr space should result in an increase in performance.

The database is configured to use direct disk access. The resources used for the direct disk access operation are as follows:

- Application intermediate storage location as defined by the value of BUFFERS
- Copy memory (not used because the disk adapter can access all memory so it has been deleted from the Worksheet 12-2)
- Disk driver and disks

Informix OnLine maintains an intermediate storage area to reduce the amount of direct disk access activity. This area is also known as the direct disk access area. The OnLine intermediate storage area works in a fashion similar to the SCO UNIX filesystem buffer cache. More information about OnLine buffers can be found in the Informix-OnLine Administrator's Guide.

The size of this storage area is configured by either setting the value of BUFFERS in the configuration file defined by the environment variable TBCONFIG, or using the Shared Memory option on the Parameters menu with the tbmonitor command. The number of buffers should not be increased if paging and/or swapping are occurring, and instead should be reduced until paging and/or swapping stop. If additional memory is somehow made available, for example, by following the suggestions in Appendix B for reclaiming memory, then the number of BUFFERS can be increased.

When increasing the number of BUFFERS, always carefully monitor how performance is changing. More buffers do not always improve performance.

Changing the number of buffers may also requiring changing other parameters, such as LRU_MAX_DIRTY, LRU_MIN_DIRTY, and CLEANERS to ensure a larger number of buffers is managed most efficiently. The effect of these parameters is discussed later in this case study.

To determine the optimal number of OnLine buffers, a series of tests was run which tried a range of buffers.

Figure 12-2 shows the variation in test results as the value of BUFFERS is changed.

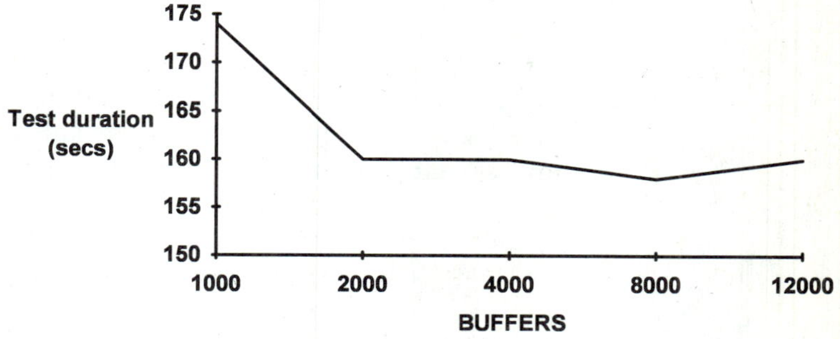

Figure 12-2: Test Duration as BUFFERS increased

Figure 12-2 shows how the test duration increased slightly with 12,000 buffers. Considering this trend, increasing the amount of memory and the number of buffers will not result in the performance target being achieved. This graph shows that increasing the number of buffers does not always result in increased performance. The CPU usage statistics for the different number of buffers is shown in Figure 12-3.

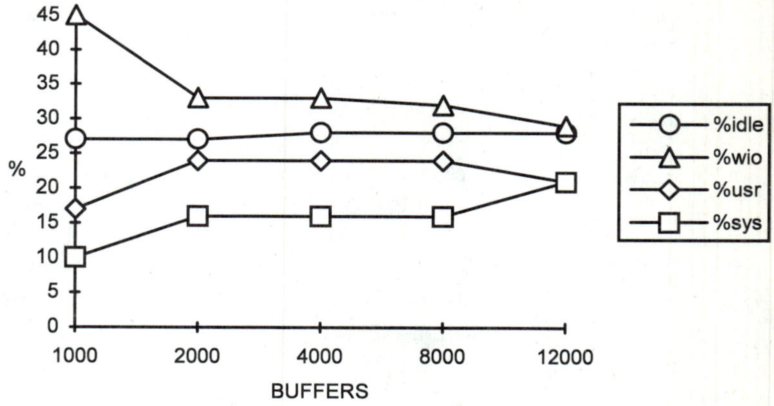

Figure 12-3: CPU Usage as BUFFERS increased

This graph shows the perplexing behavior of both %wio and %idle time increasing with the greater number of buffers. This result is the opposite of what would be expected when the application direct disk access area is increased to reduce the amount of disk activity. The trend of decreasing %sys is expected behavior.

To further investigate the reason for the high percentage of %wio and %idle, examine the disk usage statistics collected with mpsar and cpusar. Figure 12-4 shows the average number of blks/s to the disks containing the products information versus the average number of blks/s to only the rootdbs.

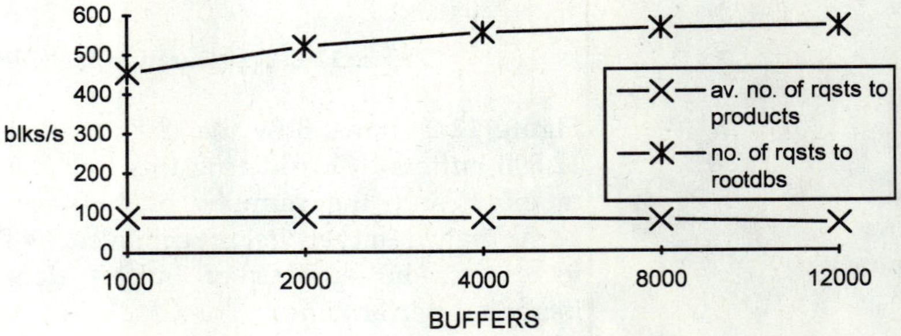

Figure 12-4: Average Number of Requests to the rootdbs and products Disks

As expected with an increasing number of buffers, the average number of blks/s requests to and from the products database decreased. However, the average number of requests to the rootdbs information increased except when BUFFERS is equal to 8000 and 12000 BUFFERS. Because the direct disk access interface allows the application complete control over the frequency of disk requests, the behavior of Informix OnLine must be examined to understand the underlying cause of the increase activity on rootdbs.

The tbstat -p command reports on the efficiency of the Informix OnLine buffer cache in a fashion similar to sar -b. Figure 12-5 shows the read and write cache hit ratios for the Informix cache.

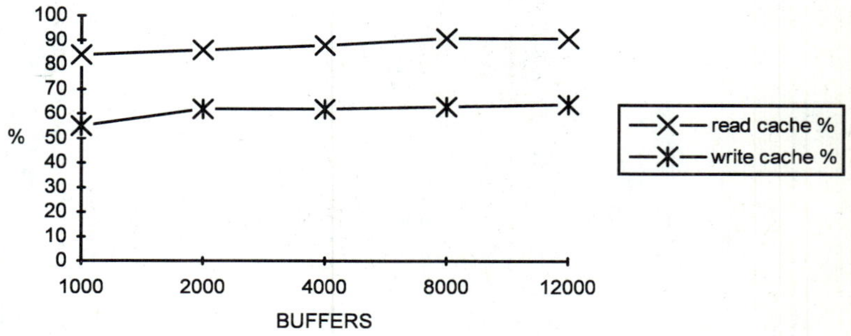

Figure 12-5: Informix OnLine Cache Efficiency Statistics

The read cache hit ratio is equal to the number of times the information requested by one of the OnLine servers is found in the OnLine buffer cache. The higher the percentage, the greater the efficiency of the cache. The write cache hit ratio is the percentage of times a buffer in the cache has been modified before being written to the disk. For more information see the OnLine Administrator's Guide.

As expected, the graph shows an increase in cache efficiency. However, the disk activity increased despite the greater cache efficiency, so further analysis is required.

The tbstat -D command provides information on the number of reads and writes to each disk area used by OnLine. The results are shown in Figure 12-6.

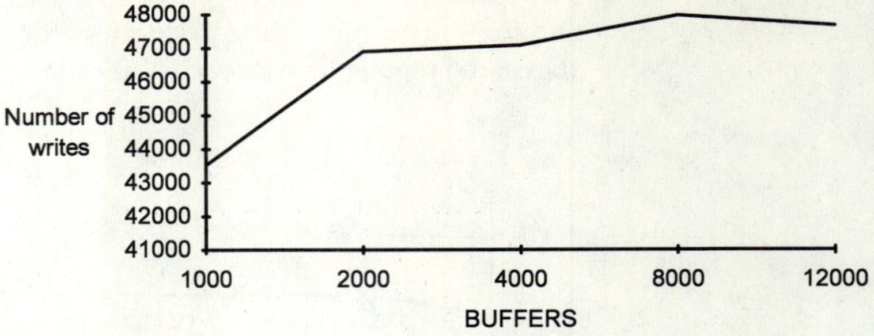

Figure 12-6: Changes in Number of Writes as BUFFERS Increases

This graph confirms the increase in the amount of disk activity to the rootdbs disk.

At this point, we do some routine checking of database parameters and behavior to see if increasing the buffer size has inadvertently caused some side effect that results in increased disk activity. The Informix OnLine Administrator's Guide provides a description of what to examine to improve performance. The first place to start is the number of checkpoints, because a greater number of checkpoints will cause a greater amount of disk activity.

The tbstat -p command shows the number of checkpoints that occurred during the test and the number of times an OnLine process had to wait while the checkpoint completed. When OnLine runs a checkpoint, all database update activity is suspended until the checkpoint completes. Figures 12-7 and 12-8 show the number of checkpoints and the number of waits.

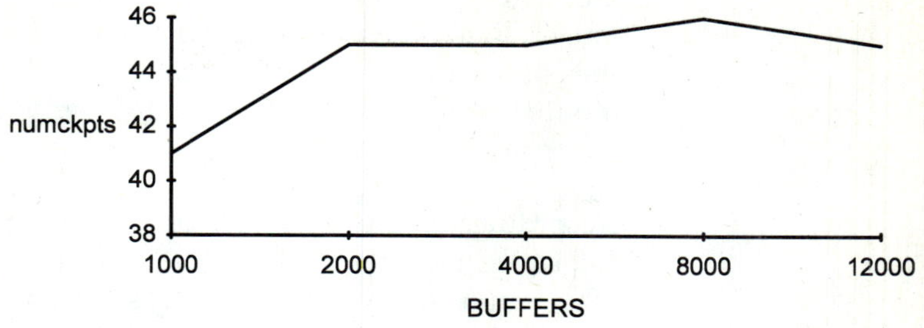

Figure 12-7: Number of checkpoints

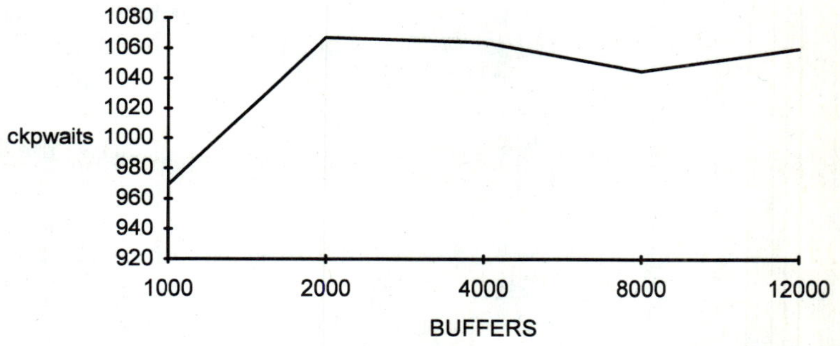

Figure 12-8: Number of ckpwaits

In this configuration, the value of CKPINTVL is equal to 300 seconds. The expected number of checkpoints during the test run is zero because the test duration is less than 300 seconds. One checkpoint might occur if the interval expires during the test run. Some checkpoints occur when the database is brought on line, so the actual number is often greater than one. The values reported by tbstat slightly greater than what is expected, so reducing the number of checkpoints is the next step in tuning the database.

When a checkpoint occurs, modified data is written to the disk. More frequent checkpoints reduce the efficiency of the cache because modified buffers may be written to the disk and then modified quite soon afterwards. If the checkpoint interval was longer, then only the modification that was last made is written to the disk, and the first modification is not. Since the first modification was transitory, a disk write is saved with a longer checkpoint interval.

According to the Informix-OnLine Administrator's Guide, the Informix processes must wait until a checkpoint completes before they can execute critical code sections. If checkpoints occur frequently, they can affect the duration of transactions. If checkpoints occur infrequently, however, then writing the modified data may take a long time, and that may also adversely affect performance.

Each checkpoint causes the buffers to be written to the appropriate disks. In addition, any data held in the internal physical and logical buffers is also written to the appropriate disks. More checkpoints means more disk activity. For more information on what a checkpoint does, see the INFORMIX OnLine Administrator's Guide.

The frequency of checkpoints must be balanced with the amount of data modified and the time-critical nature of the transactions and reliability issues, such as the time to bring up the database after an unexpected crash.

The number of times a process is suspended because a checkpoint is in progress also increases with a larger number of buffers. Suspended processes cannot use the increased amount of CPU time made available by reducing %sys, so the increase in %idle and %wio can now be explained.

As described previously, the following events can cause a checkpoint to occur:

- CKPINTVL seconds have elapsed since the last checkpoint
- A system administrator forces a checkpoint, using one of the utilities provided by OnLine
- The physical log is 75% full

- The logical log files have wrapped so that the next file contains the most recent checkpoint mark

Since the checkpoints occur more frequently than CKPINTVL and the system administrator has not forced a checkpoint, the first two causes can be eliminated. The second two can be investigated with the information provided by tbstat.

The command tbstat -l provides information on physical log usage. Examining the report displayed by tbstat showed the following physical log usage pattern:

```
......
phybegin physize  phypos   phyused  %used
400bc0   1450     225      110      7.59
......
phybegin physize  phypos   phyused  %used
400bc0   1450     929      748      51.59
.......
phybegin physize  phypos   phyused  %used
400bc0   1450     1312     1087     74.97
```

The heading for the last line shown above showed:

```
RSAM Version 5.00.UD1    -- On-Line (CKPT REQ) --
Up 00:01:19 -- 38480 Kbytes
```

This line indicates a checkpoint is necessary.

The pattern here shows that the filling up of the physical log is causing the checkpoints, so the physical log must be reconfigured.

Examining the report produced by tbstat for the logical log shows the following:

```
number flags    uniqid begin  size used    %used
4      F------ 0      200208 3000    0     0.00
5      F------ 0      200dc0 3000    0     0.00
6      U---C-L 598    201978 3000  516    17.20
7      F------ 0      202530 3000    0     0.00
8      F------ 0      2030e8 3000    0     0.00
9      F------ 0      203ca0 3000    0     0.00
10     F------ 0      204858 3000    0     0.00
11     F------ 0      205410 3000    0     0.00
.......
.......
.......
number flags     uniqid begin  size used   %used
4      U---C--   604    200208 3000  599   19.97
5      F------   0      200dc0 3000    0    0.00
6      F------   0      201978 3000    0    0.00
7      F------   0      202530 3000    0    0.00
8      F------   0      2030e8 3000    0    0.00
9      F------   0      203ca0 3000    0    0.00
10     F------   0      204858 3000    0    0.00
11     U-B---L   603    205410 3000 3000 100.00
```

In the interest of clarity, the address column is deleted from this display.

The logical log usage pattern shows that the logical logs are filled and freed faster than they are used. This usage pattern does not show any evidence of wrapping, so this is not the cause of the high number of check points.

Test #3: Increase Size of Physical Log and Move to High Performance Disk Adapter

The next step in tuning is to increase the size of the physical log and move it to a disk adapter with caching and striping. A disk adapter with caching and striping provides additional throughput and reduces the delay encountered by the OnLine processes while they wait for the checkpoint to complete.

Rerun the test with 1000 buffers. The test results are shown in the Informix worksheet. The duration of the test is longer than with the previous disk configuration, but the CPU usage pattern is very different.

The command sar -u reports a %wio value of 18% and %idle of 1%, so the CPU is idle due to waiting-for-device-I/O to complete rather than just plain idle. Waiting for I/O to complete is common behavior when the disk subsystem cannot keep up with the frequency of disk requests from the database.

Since performance increased in the previous test by increasing the number of buffers, we try it again now that the number of checkpoints and the amount of disk activity have decreased.

Figure 12-9 shows the test results for an increasing number of OnLine buffers in the new configuration.

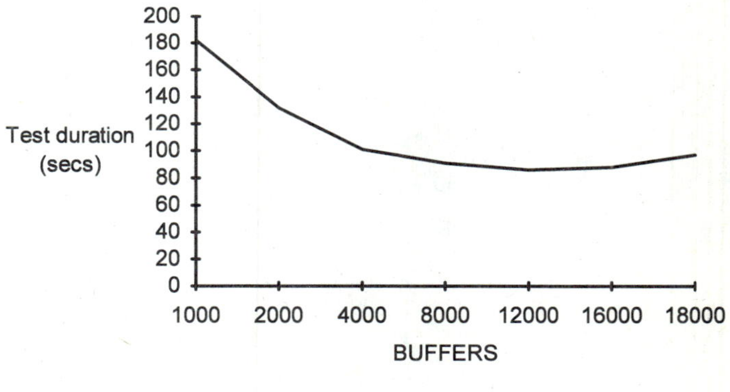

Figure 12-9: New Configuration Test Results

Rechecking the physical log usage statistics reported by tbstat -l shows that the log is filling slowly, approximately 1% every 20 seconds during the test run. In all cases, only three checkpoints occurred during the test.

Figure 12-10 shows the OnLine buffer cache efficiency statistics reported by OnLine for the new disk configuration.

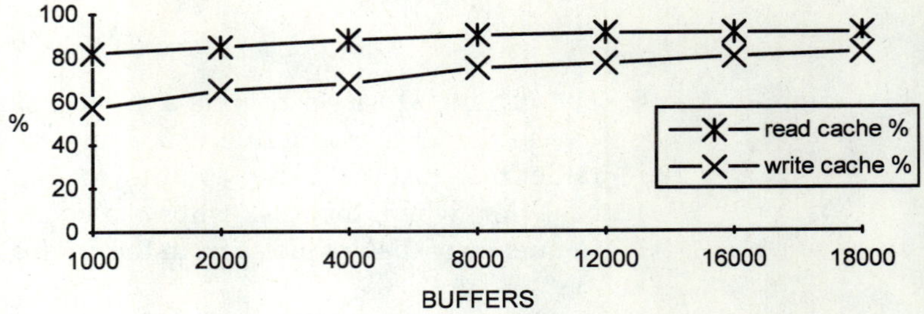

Figure 12-10: Informix OnLine Buffer Cache Efficiency Statistics in New Configuration

The efficiency statistics are significantly improved over the values reported for the previous disk configuration.

Figure 12-11 shows the CPU usage statistics for the new configuration.

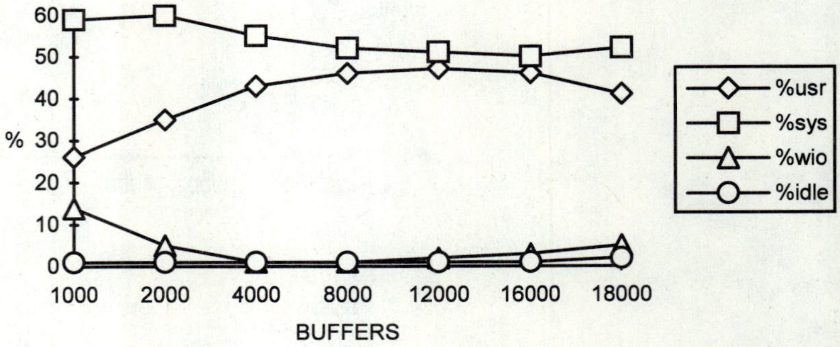

Figure 12-11: CPU Usage Statistics as BUFFERS increases

As the number of buffers increases, the system and waiting on I/O time decreases. The user time increases and idle time is minimal for all configurations. The application is therefore making much better use of the CPU as the number of buffers increases. However, the pattern changes when the buffers increase from 16,000 to 18,000. This decrease might arise because more information must be written to the disk at a checkpoint.

page cleaners

OnLine provides two tunable variables to determine how modified buffers in the cache are managed. Modified buffers are written to the disks by the *page cleaner* processes. The value of CLEANERS determines the number of cleaner processes that run simultaneously. The more cleaner processes that are defined, the more buffers that can be written to the disk at the same time.

The value of CLEANERS should be between 0 and 32. This variable specifies the number of page cleaners that should be created for writing modified buffers to the disk. These processes behave in a fashion similar to the bdflush system process in SCO UNIX. A larger number of processes allows more write disk requests to be in progress simultaneously. The number of processes that should be configured depends on the speed of the disk subsystem and the number of processors installed.

A disk subsystem becomes saturated when the time reported by sar -d in avserv rises over time. If the disk subsystem can keep up with the level of activity, the avserv time should not increase as the amount of disk activity increases. More page cleaners may cause a slight rise in the reported values, and too many page cleaners will cause this value to rise very quickly. More context switches can occur when there are more processes, because SCO UNIX switches from one page cleaner process to another to start disk writes. If a few page cleaners can keep up with the level of requests, then these context switches are unnecessary and simply cause %sys to be higher than it need be. With too few page cleaners, the number of dirty buffers may be higher than it needs to be, perhaps increasing the time taken by a checkpoint.

LRU_MIN_DIRTY,
LRU_MAX_DIRTY

The values of LRU_MIN_DIRTY and LRU_MAX_DIRTY are thresholds that determine when the cleaner processes start and stop writing buffers to the disk. The page cleaner processes start writing buffers to the disk when the percentage of modified buffers reaches LRU_MAX_DIRTY.

The page cleaner processes stop writing buffers when the percentage of modified buffers reaches LRU_MIN_DIRTY. Increasing the difference between these values increases the amount of disk activity that occurs when buffers are written, but the page cleaners execute less frequently.

In addition, increasing these values means that more modified data remains in the cache for a longer time period, which means that more data must be written during a checkpoint. More data written during a checkpoint may adversely affect performance, because server processes must wait until the checkpoint completes before completing additional transactions. Decreasing these values causes a larger number of disk writes, and more disk writes can increase disk service times. More frequent checkpoints may also decrease the efficiency of the OnLine cache because frequently modified data is repeatedly written to disk even though the value of that data changes rapidly.

In this environment, a record may be updated frequently if many customers buy it. If the product information is often updated in memory before being written to disk, then only the latest information is actually written to the disk instead of all of the intermediate, transient record values. When a checkpoint occurs, the OnLine servers cannot update records, so the length of the checkpoint affects the length of time required to update the database.

The original value specifying the number of page cleaner processes for this configuration was eight, following the recommendations in the INFORMIX OnLine Administrator's Guide. The values may need to change as the number of buffers increases, so run some tests to understand the performance effect of changing these values.

The results for various values of LRU_MIN_DIRTY and LRU_MAX_DIRTY are shown in Figure 12-12.

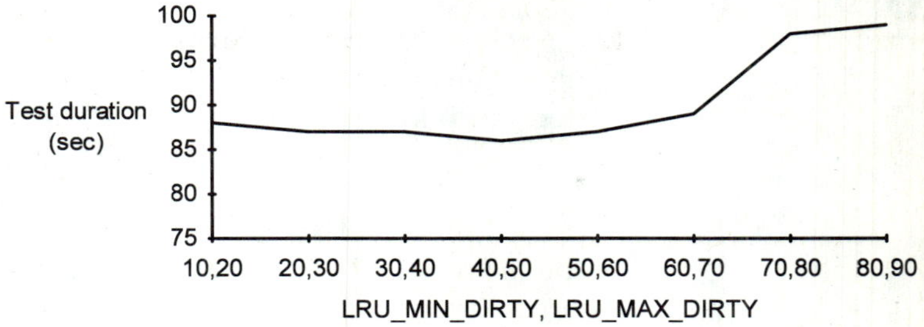

Figure 12-12: Test Results for Changing Values of LRU_MIN_DIRTY and LRU_MAX_DIRTY

The default difference between the two values is used for this test. This graph shows that the optimal values for LRU_MIN_DIRTY is 40 and LRU_MAX_DIRTY is 50 because the test duration is 86 seconds.

Since performance has improved significantly since the original test, rechecking the SCO MPX scheduling values to see that they are still set optimally is the final step in tuning.

Test #4: Recheck the SCO MPX Scheduling Variables

To check the operating system once again, the values for loadbalance, preemptive, and dopricalc are set back to one and the test is run again. The test duration increased to 124 seconds. The level of context switching increased from 1743 to 2626 per second, the amount of %usr time dropped from 46% to 35%, and the amount of %sys time increased from 50% to 62%. Setting these variables to zero is therefore still the optimal operating system configuration.

Other Configurations

This section provides some additional information on operating system and Informix tuning for other types of configurations: Informix OnLine on the filesystem and installed on a network.

With OnLine installed on the filesystem, tuning the performance of the file read and write operation is a much larger part of overall Informix and SCO tuning. All operating system intermediate storage locations, such as the namei and buffer caches, play a much larger part in the duration of database operations. To tune the system, follow the recommendations and tuning steps for the file read and write operation in addition to the Informix OnLine recommendations provided in this case study.

When Informix uses the filesystem, the guidelines for database layout must also be modified, since the filesystem configuration becomes part of what needs to be considered when designing the layout. The same basic layout guidelines apply, but the implementation of those guidelines will vary because of the filesystem configuration issues.

Informix OnLine and Informix-STAR can be used across a network in a client/server installation. The client OnLine processes communicate with the server OnLine processes via TCP/IP. Tuning in this environment follows the same principles as those described in the case and summarized in Quick Diagnosis, but the network should be tuned prior to tuning Informix and the operating system. The network efficiency and amount of streams resources should be checked at each step of the process, because an increase in Informix performance may increase the amount of network traffic, which in turn may cause a shortage of network resources. Please follow the procedures described in the Monitoring Client/Server Connections and Common Client/Server Operations chapters for tuning the client and server operating systems.

Because a database server machine typically serves many clients, the capacity of the memory, CPU, disk, and network subsystems must be large enough provide reasonable response time. In addition to the descriptions provided above, consider the following when tuning Informix in a networked environment:

- The increase in the amount of CPU resources consumed because of handling the network protocol may require either a faster CPU or the addition of more CPUs to the system so the clients encounter minimal delay.

- The networking software and streams use more memory so more memory may be required on the server when used in networked environment. The speed of the network card also affects the server's ability to keep up with requests.

- The Informix clients require sufficient memory and CPU time to handle the responses from the server. Since these clients may also be running memory-intensive applications such as those written for Open Desktop, memory usage must be balanced between these competing applications.

Quick Diagnosis Summary

The tuning tools and their options used for tuning the operating system and Informix OnLine are summarized in Tables 12-1 and 12-2.

Operating System Behavior	Command
CPU usage	mpsar -u/sar -u
Context switching	mpsar -w/sar -w
Disk activity	mpsar -d/sar -d
Amount of swapping	mpsar -w/sar -w
Amount of paging	mpsar -p/sar -p

Table 12-1: Operating System Monitoring Tools

Informix OnLine behavior	Command
Buffer cache efficiency	tbstat -p
Number of checkpoints	tbstat -p
Number of checkpoint waits	tbstat -p
Physical log usage	tbstat -l
Disk activity	tbstat -D

Table 12-2: Informix OnLine Monitoring Tools

The essential tuning guidelines for Informix OnLine are summarized as follows:

- Configure the database to use the direct disk access interface.
- Carefully plan the database layout so the level of disk activity is equal for all the disks.
- Allocate the fastest disk and adapters to the physical and logical logs.
- Monitor the number of checkpoints and ensure they occur at the expected frequency.
- Set the number of OnLine buffers to the highest value possible, but be careful of unexpected performance decreases as the number of buffers increases. Do not increase the number of buffers if the system starts to page or swap.
- Change the value of LRU_MAX_DIRTY and LRU_MIN_DIRTY if the value of BUFFERS changes.
- Balance the number of page cleaners, as specified by the variable CLEANERS, with the number of processors and the speed of the disk and disk adapters. A higher capacity disk subsystem that can support a large number of disk transfers may benefit from a larger number of page cleaners.

- In networked environments, ensure that the server has sufficient CPU capacity to process the network traffic and that the clients have sufficient memory to avoid paging and swapping.

The SCO MPX and SCO UNIX configuration recommendations are as follows:

- Increase the amount of shared memory to accommodate the number of BUFFERS configured.

- If OnLine is the only application using the machine, decrease the size of the SCO UNIX buffer cache by lowering the value of NBUF. Decrease NBUF in favor of Informix BUFFERS.

- For SCO MPX, set loadbalance, preemptive and dopricalc to 0. This setting works for many configurations, but test it to ensure it works for the particular test environment in use.

- Minimize the amount of swapping/paging occurring on the client and server systems.

Worksheet 12-1: SCO UNIX Tuning Worksheet (part 1)

Tunables	Initial Values	Test #1	Test #2	Test #3	Test #4
Installed Memory	64 Mbytes				
Application Storage	See Informix worksheet				
GPGSLO, GPGSHI	550 600				
MAXSC, AGEINTERVAL	8 31				
S5CACHEENTS, S5HASHQS	3072 8191				
NFILE	2700				
NINODE, NHINODE	2700 2048				
NBUF, NHBUF	4096 8192				
BDFLUSHR, NAUTOUP	30 10				
NCOPYBUF, PLOWBUFS	100 30				
NMPBUF, NMPHEADBUF	16 40				
NPBUF, DMAABLEBUF	200 64				
SDSKOUT	4				
Disk Configuration, Data Layout	See Informix worksheet				
NCLIST	2000				
NPROC, NREGION	600 2000				
NSCRN, CTBUFSIZ	0 128				

Worksheet 12-2: SCO UNIX Tuning Worksheet (part 2)

Resources to Monitor	**Initial Values**	**Test #1**	**Test #2**	**Test #3**	**Test #4**
Free Memory, Free swap	10218 65536	10154 65536	10476 65535	2267 65535	2302 65535
Blocks Swapped in/out	0 0	0 0	0 0	0 0	0 0
Pages Reclaimed	0	0	0	0	0
CPU: %usr, %sys, %wio, %idle	26 52 14 9	27 45 17 10	23 58 18 1	44 52 3 1	35 62 2 1
Scheduling:	11.3 0 2891	8.1 0 2247	6.6 0 3649	11 0 1628	19 0 3628
Namei Cache	98%	97%	98%	98%	98%
File Table, Inode Table	167 0 66 0	169 0 71 0	183 0 75 0	172 0 74 0	160 0 68 0
Buffer Cache %rcache Reads: bread/s lread/s Writes: bwrit/s, lwrit/s	100 0 338 6 335	100 1 378 10 375	100 0 322 8 323	100 0 720 8 720	100 0 498 1 497
Scatter/Gather:	6.43 0 0 0	7.9 0 0 0	1.6 0 0 0	1.7 0 0 0	1.2 0 0 0
Copy Buffers	0 0	0 0	0 0	0 0	0 0
Direct Disk Access	341 0	364 0	387 0	374 0	279 7
Disk Driver : %busy avque, r+w/s, blks/s, avwait, avserv (root)	12 1 4 404 0.3 32	14 1 4.4 478 0.0 32	0.3 1.3 0.3 1.5 2.9 9.4	0.3 1 0.2 1 0.3 13	0.2 1.2 0.2 1.4 1.7 11
products	22 1.3 16 66 4.2 12.4	26 1.5 21 83 6.5 13	25 1.4 20 79 5.0 13	37 1.7 29 18 9.4 13	26 1.5 21 83 5.7 12
logs	n/a	n/a	100 1 21 121 0.0 29	36 1 57 457 0.0 6	25 1 42 338 0.0 6

Now	**Your Goal**	**Monitoring**	**Res #1**	**Res #2**	**Res #3**	**Res #4**
185	90	188	174	182	86	124

Worksheet 12-3: SCO MPX Tuning Worksheet

Tunables	**Initial Values**	**Test #1**	**Test #2**	**Test #3**	**Test #4**
Number of CPUs	2	2	2	2	2
loadbalance	1	0	0	0	1
preemptive	1	0	0	0	1
dopricalc	1	0	0	0	1
primove	10	10	10	10	10
cache_affinity	1	1	1	1	1
Resources to Monitor	**Initial Values**	**Test #1**	**Test #2**	**Test #3**	**Test #4**
CPU 1: %usr, %sys, %wio, %idle	21 59 19 1	25 51 23 1	24 52 22 1	47 49 3 2	43 54 2 1
CPU 2: %usr, %sys, %wio, %idle	31 44 8 17	29 40 12 20	24 52 22 1	47 49 3 2	43 54 2 1
CPU 3: %usr, %sys, %wio, %idle					
CPU 4: %usr, %sys, %wio, %idle					
CPU 1 InterCPU interrupts	341 228 0	76 27 0	213 70 0	18 20 0	505 313 0
CPU 2 InterCPU interrupts	228 341 0	27 76 0	214 70 0	20 18 0	313 505 0
CPU 3 InterCPU interrupts					
CPU 4 InterCPU Interrupts					

Now	**Your Goal**	**Monitoring**	**Res #1**	**Res #2**	**Res #3**	**Res #4**

Worksheet 12-4: Informix Tuning Worksheet

Tunables	Initial Values	Test #1	Test #2	Test #3	Test #4
TBLSPACES	2000				
CHUNKS	20				
DBSPACES	20				
PHYSBUFF	128				
LOGBUFF	128				
LOGSMAX	20				
PHYSFILE	2900		29000		
LOGFILES	3				
LOGSIZE	6000				
CKPTINTVL	300				
BUFFERS	1000		12000		
CLEANERS	8				
LRUS	8				
LRU_MAX_DIRTY	60			50	50
LRU_MIN_DIRTY	50			40	40
LTXHWM	80				
LTXEHWM	90				
Database Layout	10 disks with products 1 disk with logs 1 disk rootdbs		move logs to their own faster disk with striping and caching		

Worksheet 12-5: Informix Tuning Worksheet (part 2)

Resources to Monitor	Initial Values	Test #1	Test #2	Test #3	Test #4
Checkpoints	43	37	3	3	3
Checkpoint waits	1024	869	24	25	24
Disk and page reads	793690 81642	77545 79863	83723 87508	80102 82024	60476 62371
Disk and page writes	48876 104924	43497 99205	70363 85816	45132 103127	75273 14869
Physical Log Usage					
Logical Log Usage					
Reads per division/pathname rootdbs product log Writes per division/pathname rootdbs product log	 135 5481 n/a 45129 1863 n/a	 137 5678 n/a 43520 1937 n/a	 151 5644 5 33 1650 20187	 114 7785 5 27 3308 31387	 146 5673 5 27 2176 42752

Now	Your Goal	Monitoring	Res #1	Res #2	Res #3	Res #4

Chapter 13

The Essential Elements of Tuning

This chapter brings together the essential concepts presented in this book by discussing the requirements of the computing environment, including applications and hardware.

The first section of this chapter poses a series of questions that help define the requirements of the environment in which you intend to run applications. The next section of the chapter discusses introduces the concept of matching complementary hardware technology for optimal performance.

The final section of the chapter collects the application requirements, optimal hardware configuration, and the tuning guidelines presented in this book and distills them into a set of key tuning principles.

Understanding Application Requirements

When selecting the application, remember to develop an understanding of the hardware and software requirements of the application in the intended environment. For example, if the application is graphical and client/server and you intend to use it in that fashion, then do the users require local processing capacity or will X terminals be sufficient? Understanding the requirements of the application goes beyond knowing how much memory is necessary per user, and instead should accurately reflect a thorough understanding of the intended use of the entire computing environment.

An inventory to help you understand the application requirements can be done for new and existing systems. For existing systems, completing the questions can help to identify any poorly configured areas in the current system and possibly generate some new ideas for improving these weak areas. Here are some questions that can help the inventory process:

Application features

What are the features of the application that will be used? Are they client/server? If so, where is the optimal place to store the data? From where will the applications be run? The server? The client? A combination? If a combination, then which applications will run where and how frequently?

Application data access

Will these applications need access to central data or only to local data? Will users need local copies of their data as well as centralized copies? If so, what mechanism, if any, will be used to guarantee data integrity? What are the networking protocols required by the application to access the data? What is the anticipated level of network activity?

User interface

Are there special graphical features that are particularly resource-intensive, such as Motif applications? Where (client or server) and how frequently will these applications be executed?

Will the users be accessing the system via character terminals? If so, how many and what is the nature of the application they will be running? Does the application update the screen frequently (a few times a second) under normal use? Does the user require rapid screen update (as when an experienced user enters data in a spreadsheet) for efficient user/application interaction?

Time-critical Tasks

Will users be executing time-critical tasks when using the centralized applications? Are customers kept waiting if the computer system slows down? Which features of the application will be used in a time-critical fashion?

Check the application documentation for CPU, memory, disk and network recommendations for the features that are time-critical; note these for all the applications that will be run, either on the client or the server. Time-critical tasks should be isolated so that a small program can be written to simulate them, using the guidelines presented in Chapter 1. This program can then be used to evaluate the hardware/software systems.

Databases

Is the application a database? Does the database support direct disk access as well as filesystem access? How much data is in the database? What is the nature of the typical transaction? What is the proportion of read to write queries?

Because databases vary considerably in their use, the proportion of reads versus writes is just one general indicator of the necessity of more advanced disk array technology to support the more write-intensive installations.

What kind of backup mechanisms, if any, are provided in the database to make backing up the direct disk or *raw* partitions easier? What are the hardware requirements of this backup mechanism?

How many users will be accessing the data in the database simultaneously? Are their tasks time-critical? How quickly does the transaction have to complete in order to avoid slowdowns in other parts of the business?

Future changes

How will numbers of users, size of database, types and numbers of applications change in the future?

Developing an understanding of the application requirements can be done prior to deciding on the actual hardware that is necessary. Technology must be kept in mind, however, as the choice of application may restrict the choice of technology. All such restrictions should be noted and taken into account when deciding on the hardware required.

PLANNING HARDWARE CONFIGURATIONS

The next phase is to match the needs of the applications with the appropriate complementary technology. Complementary technology refers to technology whose throughput and performance are equivalent. Configuring systems with these concepts in mind ensures that all the components of the system perform adequately without any imbalances. The following examples are not precise configurations, but rather provide an indication of where to begin designing a system with complementary technology.

Table 13-1 describes a sample complementary database server configuration for 150 active database clients connected to the Database Server With a TCP/IP Network.

Table 13-2 describes a sample non-complementary database server configuration for 32 database users with terminals connected directly to the server.

Table 13-3 describes a complementary Open Desktop client running Motif client/server applications accessing data over the network.

Component	Explanation
2 Pentium processors	The database server can use the CPU power provided by two processors as long as the database is optimally configured for the memory and disk subsystems.
256 Kbyte write-back L2 cache	The cache increases the performance by reducing the time to access memory.
96+ Mbytes memory	This amount of memory allows the database to be configured with a large direct disk access area so that the disk activity is minimized and the amount of data that can be reused is maximized.
8 - 12 disks (RAID 5, striped and/or mirrored)	The actual number of disks required depends on the size of the database. The larger the number of disks, the greater the flexibility in database layout, and the greater the potential for increased parallel servicing of disk requests.
8 Mbyte caching disk adapter	The cache increases the speed of disk transfers.
32-bit bus master DMA network interface card	No delays will occur at the network hardware level when transmitting or receiving packets. Maximum network efficiency is achieved and the CPU time spent processing packets is minimized.

Table 13-1: Complementary Network Database Server Supporting 150 Active Users

Non-Complementary Component	Explanation
1 Pentium processor	Will spend most of its time paging and swapping because of the memory shortage. Applications will not benefit from the increased speed of the Pentium because the CPU be busy paging and swapping.
16 Mbytes memory	This amount of memory is insufficient to allows the database to be configured with a large direct disk access area. Database performance will be adversely affected because of the increased disk activity.
2 disks	Two disks do not allow much flexibility in the design of the database layout. Two disks also do not allow much parallel servicing of disk requests to occur.
16-bit SCSI disk adapter	This disk adapter requires the CPU to complete its disk transfers, so more of the CPU time is spent executing the operating system rather than the database.
32-port intelligent multiport card	Necessary to connect 32 terminals to the database server without impacting the amount of CPU time available for the database. This hardware component is the only one that matches the capacity of the Pentium processor.

Table 13-2: Non-complementary Server Configuration for Running 32 Database Users With Terminals Connected Directly to the Server

Component	Explanation
1 486/66 Mhz processor	Ensures that user response time will be sufficient for productive interaction with the system.
24 - 32 Mbytes memory	This amount of memory is sufficient to avoid any memory shortages when running a reasonable number of Motif applications.
1 300 - 600 Mbyte disk	This disk provides a sufficient amount of disk space to store local data. The average seek time for the disk should be in the 10 - 12 msec range to complement the speed of the graphics adapter and CPU. If the machine is not swapping, then the disk will be most active when loading the applications or any local data required by them.
1 IDE disk adapter	Although this disk adapter requires the CPU to complete disk transfers, this type of could be a low cost alternative to SCSI in this type of configuration where disk throughput is not a critical factor in performance.
32-bit bus master DMA network interface card	Necessary to handle the frequency and intensity of network traffic, including those generated by the NFS environment.
Local bus graphics with enhanced graphics adapter	The enhanced graphics adapter will maximize the speed of display update and minimize the amount of additional work the CPU must do to complete those operations. This leaves more time for the CPU to execute applications.

Table 13-3: Open Desktop Client running Motif Client/Server Applications accessing data over the network.

When deciding how to configure the systems, be sure to take into account any application-specific recommendations. Application documentation often includes "minimum recommendations." These should not be confused with "optimal" recommendations, which are often much more generous, especially with respect to memory and disk requirements.

With an understanding of the needs of the application and how to build systems containing complementary technology, a modified version of the seven steps can be used as a framework for evaluating and configuring the systems.

Core Guidelines

This section highlights some of the key guidelines that have been presented in the previous chapters and case studies.

CPU Usage

Almost all operations benefit from minimizing %wio, %idle, and %sys time in favor of %usr time. If either %wio goes down and %idle goes up or %idle goes down and %wio goes up, then look in detail at resource usage pattern for all the processes running on the system to uncover the resource shortage preventing processes from becoming ready-to-run. An optimal configuration shows %wio and %idle less than 5% when ready-to-run processes exist. If no ready-to-run processes exist, then application contention may be preventing processes from becoming ready-to-run and the application configuration should be examined.

If the operation involves networking, sometimes the %sys time will go up when the system is running optimally because the system is handling more packets.

When considering the addition of another processor, examine the average number of ready-to-run processes. This number indicates the amount of potential work for the CPUs. The current CPU usage statistics indicate whether the system has sufficient resources to support the added CPU power, as well as sufficient work to require the added CPU power. If the current value of

%idle is greater than 10%, then a current resource shortage may prevent the additional CPU from bringing maximum benefit. Remember, when multiple processes run simultaneously, resource contention at any level - application, operating system or hardware - will introduce delay.

Memory

Memory shortages cause delay because the CPU and disk are busy compensating for the shortage rather than executing applications. All operations are adversely affected by memory shortages because paging and swapping use valuable CPU and disk throughput resources. Fixing a memory shortage does not always require installing additional hardware. Instead, unused applications can be removed from the system to increase the amount of memory. In some cases, this removal can free sufficient memory to stop paging and swapping. When more than 4 Mbytes are required to stop paging or swapping, then adding memory is often the quickest solution to improved performance.

Filesystem Operations

Filesystem operations can be improved by reducing the time taken to search for the data in the intermediate storage locations. The sooner the data is found, the more quickly the application runs. The following techniques reduce the time to locate the data:

- Tune the buffer cache to maximize %rcache value. When the cache hit rate is more than 98%, further increases to the size of the buffer cache minimally improve filesystem performance. Provided sufficient memory is available and the filesystem data is re-used, tune the cache to achieve a %rcache of least 90%.

- Plan the filesystem layout to maximize the ability of the disk subsystem to handle requests in parallel and to minimize the disk head travel. Striping the filesystem over multiple disks, installing swap on a separate disk, installing a ramdisk for pipes, are all techniques that can minimize head travel.

- Increase the capacity of the disk subsystem to match the level of activity required by the application processes. On-board caches, striping, mirroring, and 32-bit bus master DMA are features that improve performance. Match the throughput capacity of the CPU, memory and disk subsystem for optimal performance.

In all cases, do not increase filesystem resources if the system is paging or swapping. In such cases, performance may be improved by reducing the allocation of these resources.

Client/Server Operations

The primary tuning guidelines for maximizing network efficiency are as follows:

- Eliminate streams allocation errors by examining streams usage and increasing buffer allocations where shortages exist.

- Eliminate network errors, such as retransmission errors, by matching the speed of network interface cards on clients and servers and by ensuring that sufficient CPU time is available to process the incoming and outgoing messages.

- Minimize collisions by reorganizing network layout. Collisions require retransmissions and cause delay.

- Maximize CPU time for processing streams messages. The CPU is required to execute the protocol stack that sends and receives messages. If the CPU is not available, then a backlog occurs, resulting in longer network operations.

- Provide sufficient resources for the applications running on the client and the server, including eliminating, where possible, all paging and swapping activity. Client/server applications are structured as cooperating processes that communicate over the network. If either the client or the server does not have sufficient resources to run these applications, then delays will occur.

- Ensure the server has sufficient disk performance to cope with the synchronous write activity generated by the NFS environment.

Direct Disk Access

Performance of direct disk access can be improved by the following techniques:

- Ensure that a sufficient number of direct access control blocks are always available, because delays will occur if these control blocks are not available.

- Rearrange the database data on the disks so that the number of requests to each disk and disk adapter are spread evenly. If the requests are not evenly spread, then the disks that are receiving more requests may cause delays.

- Use disk mirroring and striping to improve the parallelization of disk read and write requests and to reduce service time. With no intermediate storage locations between the disk adapter and the application, any delay caused by the disk subsystem directly results in a delay to the completion of the operation. Disk mirroring allows multiple reads to be serviced simultaneously, thereby reducing request service times. Striping spreads the data over multiple disks, and so larger requests can be serviced by multiple disks simultaneously.

- Install a cache on the disk adapter, so that requests access the cache instead of waiting for the disk. With a cache, the time required to read or write to the disk is reduced. This feature improves performance of direct disk access more so than for filesystem operations because no intermediate storage locations are used.

Oracle

The essential tuning guidelines for Oracle are summarized as follows:

- Configure the database to use the direct disk access interface. The filesystem interface provides unnecessary data buffering that interferes with optimal database performance.

- Carefully plan the database layout so the level of disk activity is equal for all the disks containing database information. Spread the database records across as many disks as possible for maximum parallelization.

- Allocate a mirrored pair of disk drives for the sole use of the redo logs. The log disks are unique in that the database writes to these disks only in a sequential fashion. Since disks are at their quickest when writing data sequentially without disruption, separating the logs from the other random access activity is optimal for performance.

- Ensure that the sleeper/postwait driver and asynchronous I/O are configured in both the operating system and in the *init.ora* file. Configure Oracle to use AIO with the USE_AIO environment variable equal to TRUE..

- Configure the amount of AIO memory for use by Oracle, as defined by */usr/lib/aiomemlock,* to a value larger than the amount of memory configured for Oracle buffers.

- Set the checkpoint interval so data reliability is guaranteed without significantly increasing the amount of disk activity.

- Set the number of db_block_buffers to the highest value possible with the given memory configuration. Do not set db_block_buffers so high that paging and swapping occur.

- Increase the amount of shared memory to accommodate the number of configured db_block_buffers.

- For SCO MPX, set loadbalance, preemptive, dopricalc and cache_affinity to zero.

- In networked environments, ensure that the server has sufficient CPU capacity to process the network traffic and that the clients have sufficient memory to avoid paging and swapping.

- Minimize the amount of swapping and paging occurring on the client and server systems.

Informix

The essential tuning guidelines for Informix OnLine are summarized as follows:

- Configure the database to use the direct disk access interface.

- Carefully plan the database layout so the level of disk activity is equal for all the disks.

- Allocate the fastest disk and adapters to the physical and logical logs.

- Monitor the number of checkpoints and ensure they occur at the expected frequency.

- Set the number of OnLine buffers to the highest value possible, but be careful of unexpected performance decreases as the number of buffers increases. Do not increase the number of buffers if the system starts to page or swap.

- Increase the amount of shared memory to accommodate the number of BUFFERS configured.

- Change the value of LRU_MAX_DIRTY and LRU_MIN_DIRTY if the value of BUFFERS changes.

- Balance the value of CLEANERS with the number of processors and the speed of the disk and disk adapters. A higher capacity disk subsystem that can support a large number of disk transfers may benefit from a higher number of page cleaner processes.

- In networked environments, ensure that the server has sufficient CPU capacity to process the network traffic and that the clients have sufficient memory to avoid paging and swapping.

- If OnLine is the only application using the machine, decrease the size of the SCO UNIX buffer cache in favor of the OnLine buffer cache.

- For SCO MPX, set loadbalance, preemptive and dopricalc to zero. These settings increase performance in some configurations.

- Minimize the amount of swapping and paging occurring on the client and server systems.

Conclusion

This book is about understanding how the computer system uses resources to accomplish common operations. The operations are a framework for technical understanding and for optimal resource allocation. Before resources can be changed, data on the current behavior must be collected. The seven steps and the worksheets provide a systematic framework for collecting and analyzing that data.

Understanding is often developed through multiple attempts at solving the underlying problem. As shown by the case studies, a good guess is often an essential part of the method when no obvious way forward exists. Over time and repeated observations, and as your knowledge about the cause and effect of resource shortages develops, your guesses about system behavior become much more accurate.

Systematic experimentation is a great way to practice guessing, as such experiments will enhance your ability to analyze the data and to predict the results of any resource allocation changes. The technical information, framework and case studies described in this book provide a wide range of tools to start this journey toward an optimally performing system.

Appendix A

Worksheets

This appendix contains a set of annotated worksheets and a set of blank worksheets to use when collecting data on system resource usage patterns. The blank worksheets are at the end of this appendix.

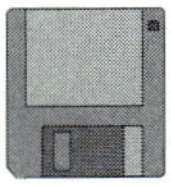

The tune2wks command provided on the floppy disk extracts the appropriate tunables information for entry into the SCO UNIX, SCO MPX and Network and Streams worksheets. The sar2oswks utility provided on the floppy disk automatically extracts the correct resource usage data for the SCO UNIX tuning worksheet. The sar2mpxwks utility extracts the correct resource usage for the SCO MPX tuning worksheet. Appendix C contains a full description of all the utilities provided on the floppy disk.

The net2wks utility automatically extracts the data from the netstat, nfsstat and llistat statistics for entry into the Network and Streams Tuning worksheet. The runinf utility extracts statistics from Informix-Online for entry into the Informix worksheet. The tunables specified in the worksheet can be found in the file pointed to by the environment variable called TBCONFIG. The oraclestat utility extracts the statistics from Oracle Version 7 for entry into the worksheet. The tunables can be found in the init.ora or equivalent file. Both runinf and oraclestat extract additional statistics that are not specified by the worksheet. These statistics can be useful in database tuning and analysis.

Worksheet A-1: SCO UNIX Tuning Worksheet (Part 1)

Tunables	Initial Values	Test #1	Test #2	Test #3	Test #4
Installed Memory	**1**				
Application Storage	**2**				
GPGSLO, GPGSHI					
MAXSC, AGEINTERVAL					
S5CACHEENTS, S5HASHQS					
NFILE					
NINODE, NHINODE					
NBUF, NHBUF					
BDFLUSHR, NAUTOUP					
NCOPYBUF, PLOWBUFS					
NMPBUF, NMPHEADBUF					
NPBUF, DMAABLEBUF					
SDSKOUT					
Disk Configuration, Data Layout	**3**				
NCLIST					
NPROC, NREGION					
NSCRN, CTBUFSIZE					
Display adapter, colors	**4**				
Mouse Settings	**5**				
Other Memory Used	**6**				

Cell #	Cell Description
1	Enter the amount of physical memory installed in the machine. If the CPU L2 cache only covers a certain portion of the memory, note that either in the cell or in the margin.
2	Enter the amount of application storage area allocated. In many cases, developing a special worksheet for complex applications may be necessary to adequately describe the tunables and resource usage patterns. In other cases, the application may only have one or two memory configuration options. If the application only has one or two tunables, then enter the names and values of these tunables in this cell.
3	Draw a small picture or describe the configuration of the filesystems on the disk subsystem. Use extra paper if necessary. Special extra space is allocated on the database worksheets for layout information because the database layout is often quite complex.
4	Enter the capabilities, such as amount and type of memory, and number of colors supported by the display adapter and X server. Fill in this cell only if you are tuning an Open Desktop display update operation.
5	Enter the setting for SENSITIVITY. If you are using a keyboard mouse, enter the values for kbm_poll, kbm_poll_max. Fill in this cell only if you are tuning an Open Desktop display update operation.
6	Enter any other major consumers of memory that may be configurable.

Figure A-1: Cell Descriptions for SCO UNIX Tuning Worksheet (part 1): For all the cells that have no number, enter the value of the corresponding tunables. Use tune2wks to extract all the information from the appropriate operating system files.

Worksheet A-2: SCO UNIX Tuning Worksheet (part 2)

Resources to Monitor	Initial Values	Test #1	Test #2	Test #3	Test #4
Free Memory, Free swap	**7**				
Blocks Swapped in/out	**8**				
Pages Reclaimed	**9**				
CPU: %usr, %sys, %wio, %idle	**10**				
Scheduling: runq-sz, swpq-sz, pswch/s	**11**				
Namei Cache	**12**				
File Table, Inode Table	**13**				
Buffer Cache %rcache Reads: bread/s lread/s Writes: bwrit/s, lwrit/s	**14**				
Scatter/Gather: mpbuf/s, ompb/s, mphbuf/s, omphbuf/s	**15**				
Copy Buffers	**16**				
Direct Disk Access	**17**				
Copy Memory	**18**				
Sdsk Request Blocks	**19**				
Disk Driver : %busy avque, r+w/s, blks/s, avwait, avserv	**20**				
Serial I/O, clists, Characters, Interrupts	**21**				

Now	Your Goal	Monitoring	Res #1	Res #2	Res #3	Res #4
22	**23**	**24**	**25**			

Cell #	Cell Description
7	Enter the amount of free memory (in pages) as reported by sar -r in the freemem column. Enter the amount of free swap space (in blocks) reported by sar -r in the freeswp column.
8	Enter the average number of blocks swapped in and out as reported by sar -w in the bswin/s and bswot/s columns.
9	Enter the average number of pages reclaimed per second as reported by sar -p in the rclm/s column.
10	Enter the CPU usage pattern as reported sar -u.
11	Enter the average size of the run queue as reported by sar -q in the runq-sz column. Enter the average size of the swap queue as reported by sar -q in the swpq-sz column. Enter the average number of context switches as reported by sar -w in the pswch/s column.
12	Enter the average namei cache efficiency statistic as reported by sar -n in the hit % column.
13	Enter the largest size that the open file table reached as reported by sar -v in the file-sz column. Enter the number of overflows that occurred as reported by the ov column. Enter the largest size that the inode table reached as reported by sar -v in the inod-sz column. Enter the number of overflows that occurred in each table as reported by the ov column.
14	Enter the buffer cache efficiency and utilization statistics as reported by the sar -b command. The columns are %rcache, bread/s, lread/s, bwrit/s and lwrit/s.
15	Enter the values reported by sar -h for scatter/gather temporary work area and buffer header usage. The columns are noted on the worksheet.
16	Enter the values reported by sar -B for copy buffer usage. The columns are cpybuf/s and slpcpybuf/s.

Figure A-2: Cell Descriptions for SCO UNIX Tuning Worksheet (part 2): Use the sar2oswks utility to extract the appropriate information for entry into this part of the worksheet. If you are monitoring SCO MPX, use the mpsar command instead of sar command. This figure is continued on the next page.

Cell #	Cell Description
17	Enter the number of direct disk access requests per second as reported by sar -h. The columns are pbuf/s and spbuf/s.
18	Enter the copy memory usage statistics as reported by sar -h. The columns are dmabuf/s and sdmabuf/s.
19	Enter the number of Sdsk control blocks allocated per second and the number of times processes were suspended per second because no control blocks were available. These values are reported by sar -S in the reqblk/s and oreqblk/s columns. These statistics are only available if the SCO MPX mpsar Maintenance Supplement is installed.
20	Enter the disk driver and disk usage statistics as reported by sar -d. The columns are specified in the worksheet.
21	Enter the serial connection statistics reported by sar -g and sar -y. The columns are ovsiohw/s, ovclist/s, rawch/s, canch/s, outch/s, rcvin/s and xmtin/s. Enter values in this column only if you are improving the performance of a display update or keyboard echo operation involving serial connections.
22	Enter the current duration of the test program.
23	Enter the desired test result.
24	Enter the duration of the test program with the monitoring tools running.
25	Enter the new test result with the monitoring tools running after the first change in configuration.

Figure A-2: Cell Descriptions for SCO UNIX Tuning Worksheet (part 2): Use the sar2oswks utility to extract the appropriate information for entry into this part of the worksheet. If you are monitoring SCO MPX, use the mpsar command instead of sar command. This figure is continued from the previous page.

Worksheet A-3: SCO MPX Tuning Worksheet

Tunables	Initial Values	Test #1	Test #2	Test #3	Test #4
Number of CPUs	1				
loadbalance					
preemptive					
dopricalc					
primove					
cache_affinity					
Resources to Monitor	**Initial Values**	**Test #1**	**Test #2**	**Test #3**	**Test #4**
CPU 1: %usr, %sys, %wio, %idle	2				
CPU 2: %usr, %sys, %wio, %idle	3				
CPU 3: %usr, %sys, %wio, %idle	4				
CPU 4: %usr, %sys, %wio, %idle	5				
CPU 1 InterCPU interrupts	6				
CPU 2 InterCPU interrupts	7				
CPU 3 InterCPU interrupts	8				
CPU 4 InterCPU Interrupts	9				

Now	Your Goal	Monitoring	Res #1	Res #2	Res #3	Res #4

Cell #	Cell Description
1	Enter the number of serialized CPUs.
2-5	Enter the CPU usage statistics reported by cpusar -u for this CPU. The columns are specified in the worksheet. If you have more than four CPUs installed, then use an additional worksheet to record the usage statistics.
6-9	Enter the number of interrupts sent and received by this CPU as reported by cpusar -i in the columns: cpuints_snd/s, cpuints_rcv/s. Enter the number of special I/O interrupts processed by this CPU as reported by cpusar -i in the IOcpuints/s column.

Figure A-3: Cell Description for SCO MPX Tuning Worksheet. Use sar2mpxwks to extract the data for this worksheet.

Worksheet A-4: Network and Streams Tuning Worksheet (Part 1)

Tunables	**Initial Values**	**Test #1**	**Test #2**	**Test #3**	**Test #4**
NBLK4, NBLK16					
NBLK64, NBLK128					
NBLK256, NBLK512					
NBLK1024, NBLK2048					
NBLK4096					
NQUEUE, NSTREAM					
STRLOFRAC, STRMEDFRAC					
nfsd, biod, nfsclnt, lckclnt	**1**				
TCPWINDOW, tcp_round_mss	**2**				
tcp_ttl, udp_ttl	**3**				

Worksheet A-5: Network and Streams Tuning Worksheet (part 2)

Resources to Monitor	Initial Values	Test #1	Test #2	Test #3	Test #4
Streams	**4**				
Input Packets/errors	**5**				
Output Packets/errors	**6**				
Collisions	**7**				
Octets Received	**8**				
Octets Transmitted	**9**				
NIC Interrupts	**10**				
RPC calls: total calls, badcalls, retrans, badxid, timeout, wait, newcred	**11**				
nclget, nclsleep	**12**				
RPC calls: null, getattr, setattr, root, lookup, readlink, read, wrcache, write, create, remove, rename, link, symlink, mkdir, rmdir, readdir, fsstat	**13**				
Network Topology	**14**				
Protocol Errors	**15**				
CPU time used by daemons	**16**				

Now	Your Goal	Monitoring	Res #1	Res #2	Res #3	Res #4

Cell #	Cell Description
1	The values for this column can be found by running the ps -el command. The column containing with the name of the process, such as nfsd, will also contain a number. The number is the number of these processes that have been started. Enter these values.
2	Enter the value found in the */etc/conf/pack.d/tcp/space.c* file corresponding to the name of the tunable.
3	Enter the values found in the */etc/conf/pack.d/tcp/space.c* and */etc/conf/pack.d/udp/space.c* file.
4	Enter any failures to obtain streams queues or streams buffers as reported by netstat -m in the fail column for each size streams buffer.
5	Enter the number of input packets and errors that were handled by the network interface card used in this test as reported by netstat -i in the Ipkts and Ierrs columns.
6	Enter the number of output packets and errors that were handled by the network interface card used in this test as reported by the netstat -i in the Opkts and Oerrs.
7	Enter the number of collisions that occurred as reported by netstat -i in the Collis row.
8	Enter the number of octets (bytes) received during the test as reported by llistat -i in the Received Octets row.
9	Enter the number of octets (bytes) transmitted during the test as reported by llistat -i in the Transmitted Octets row.
10	Enter the number of interrupts handled by the network interface card as reported by llitstat -i in the Device Interrupts row.

Figure A-4: Cell Descriptions for SCO Network and Streams Tuning Worksheet (parts 1 and 2). Use the tune2wks and net2wks commands to extract the data for this worksheet. Continued on the next page.

Cell #	Cell Description
11	Enter the number and status of the remote procedure calls made as reported in calls, badcalls, retrans, badxid, timeout, wait and newcred. These calls are reported by nfsstat -cr for the client and nfsstat -sr for the server. The appropriate values are shown in the first column of the display.
12	Enter the number of times a client handle was allocated as reported by nclget. Enter the number of times a process was suspended because no client handles were available as reported by nclsleep. These values are reported by nfsstat -cn.
13	Enter the number of times each of the possible types of remote procedure call occurred as reported by null, getattr, setattr, root, lookup, readlink, read, wrcache, write, create, remove, rename, link, symlink, mkdir, rmdir, readdir and fsstat. These values are reported by nfsstat -cn for the client and nfsstat -sn for the server. The appropriate values are shown in the first column of the display.
14	Briefly describe the network topology.
15	Enter any protocol specific errors that might be relevant as reported by netstat -s. Select the rows for the protocols used as follows: ip: bad header checksums, with size smaller than minimum, with data size < data length, with header length < data size with data length < header length tcp: discarded for bad checksums, discarded for bad header offset fields, discarded because packet too short udp: incomplete headers, bad data length fields, bad checksums
16	Enter any CPU time accumulated by the networking daemons as reported by ps -el in the TIME column corresponding to the daemon.

Figure A-4: Cell Descriptions for SCO Network and Streams Tuning Worksheet (parts 1 and 2). Use the tune2wks and net2wks commands to extract the data for this worksheet. This figure is continued from the previous page.

Worksheet A-6: Oracle Tuning Worksheet (part 1)

Tunables	**Initial Values**	**Test #1**	**Test #2**	**Test #3**	**Test #4**
checkpoint_process					
db_block_buffers					
db_block_checkpoint_ batch					
db_block_max_scan_cnt					
db_block_write_batch					
discrete_transactions_ enabled					
dml_locks					
log_buffer					
log_checkpoint_interval					
log_checkpoint_timeout					
use_post_wait_driver					
USE_AIO					
shared_pool_size					
Size of redo log					
Number of rollback segments					
Database Layout	**1**				

Worksheet A-7: Oracle Tuning Worksheet (part 2)

Resources to Monitor	Initial Values	Test #1	Test #2	Test #3	Test #4
Total System Global Area	2				
Fixed Size	3				
Variable Size	4				
Database buffers	5				
Redo buffers	6				
Physical Writes	7				
Physical Reads	8				
redo log usage	9				
DBWR checkpoints	10				
Database file reads:	11				
Database file writes:					

Now	Your Goal	Monitoring	Res #1	Res #2	Res #3	Res #4

Cell #	Cell Description
1	Briefly describe the database layout.
2	Enter the value Oracle reports as the Total System Global Area when the database instance is started.
3	Enter the size of the fixed portion of the System Global Area when the database instance is started.
4	Enter the size of the variable portion of the System Global Area when the database instance is started.
5	Enter the value of db_block_buffers.
6	Enter the number of redo buffers.
7	Enter the number of physical writes that occurred. This must be extracted by the oraclestat utility or similar program.
8	Enter the number of physical reads that occurred. This must be extracted by the oraclestat utility or similar program.
9	Enter the amount of the redo log that was used during the test. This usage is called redo size. This statistic must be extracted by the oraclestat utility or similar program.
10	Enter the number of checkpoints that occurred. This must be extracted by the oraclestat utility or similar program.
11	Enter the number of reads and writes per database. These numbers can be obtained with the oraclestat utility or similar program.

Figure A-5: Oracle Tuning Worksheet (parts 1 and 2). Use oraclestat to extract the information for parts of this worksheet. The oraclestat command reports additional statistics that might be useful for more specialized database tuning problems.

Worksheet A-8: Informix Tuning Worksheet (part 1)

Tunables	Initial Values	Test #1	Test #2	Test #3	Test #4
TBLSPACES					
CHUNKS					
DBSPACES					
PHYSBUFF					
LOGBUFF					
LOGSMAX					
PHYSFILE					
LOGFILES					
LOGSIZE					
CKPTINTVL					
BUFFERS					
CLEANERS					
LRUS					
LRU_MAX_DIRTY					
LRU_MIN_DIRTY					
LTXHWM					
LTXEHWM					
Database Layout	**1**				

Worksheet A-9: Informix Tuning Worksheet (part 2)

Resources to Monitor	Initial Values	Test #1	Test #2	Test #3	Test #4
Checkpoints	2				
Checkpoint waits	3				
Disk and page reads	4				
Disk and page writes	5				
Physical Log Usage	6				
Logical Log Usage	7				
Reads per division/pathname Writes per division/pathname	8				

Now	Your Goal	Monitoring	Res #1	Res #2	Res #3	Res #4

Cell #	Cell Description
1	Briefly describe the database layout.
2	Enter the number of checkpoints (numckpts) that occurred during the test as reported by tbstat -p.
3	Enter the number of checkpoint waits as indicated by ckpwaits as reported by tbstat -p.
4	Enter the number of disk and page reads (page reads, dskreads) as reported by tbstat -p.
5	Enter the number of disk and page writes (page writes, dskwrits) as reported by tbstat -p.
6	Enter the physical log usage as reported by tbstat -l.
7	Enter the logical log usage as reported by tbstat -l.
8	Enter the number of reads and writes per division or pathname as reported by tbstat -D.

Figure A-6: Cell Descriptions for Informix Tuning Worksheet (parts 1 and 2). Use runinf to collect and extract the appropriate statistics. The runinf command extracts additional statistics that can be useful for more specialized database tuning problems.

Worksheet A-10: SCO UNIX Tuning Worksheet (Part 1)

Tunables	**Initial Values**	**Test #1**	**Test #2**	**Test #3**	**Test #4**
Installed Memory					
Application Storage					
GPGSLO, GPGSHI					
MAXSC, AGEINTERVAL					
S5CACHEENTS, S5HASHQS					
NFILE					
NINODE, NHINODE					
NBUF, NHBUF					
BDFLUSHR, NAUTOUP					
NCOPYBUF, PLOWBUFS					
NMPBUF, NMPHEADBUF					
NPBUF, DMAABLEBUF					
SDSKOUT					
Disk Configuration, Data Layout					
NCLIST					
NPROC, NREGION					
NSCRN, CTBUFSIZ					
Display adapter, colors					
Mouse Settings					
Other Memory Used					

Worksheet A-11: SCO UNIX Tuning Worksheet (part 2)

Resources to Monitor	Initial Values	Test #1	Test #2	Test #3	Test #4
Free Memory, Free swap					
Blocks Swapped in/out					
Pages Reclaimed					
CPU: %usr, %sys, %wio, %idle					
Scheduling: runq-sz, swpq-sz, pswch/s					
Namei Cache					
File Table, Inode Table					
Buffer Cache %rcache Reads: bread/s lread/s Writes: bwrit/s, lwrit/s					
Scatter/Gather: mpbuf/s, ompb/s, mphbuf/s, omphbufs/s					
Copy Buffers					
Direct Disk Access					
Copy Memory					
Sdsk Request Blocks					
Disk Driver : %busy avque, r+w/s, blks/s, avwait, avserv					
Serial I/O, clists, Characters, Interrupts					

Now	Your Goal	Monitoring	Res #1	Res #2	Res #3	Res #4

Worksheet A-12: SCO MPX Tuning Worksheet

Tunables	Initial Values	Test #1	Test #2	Test #3	Test #4
Number of CPUs					
loadbalance					
preemptive					
dopricalc					
primove					
cache_affinity					
Resources to Monitor	**Initial Values**	**Test #1**	**Test #2**	**Test #3**	**Test #4**
CPU 1: %usr, %sys, %wio, %idle					
CPU 2: %usr, %sys, %wio, %idle					
CPU 3: %usr, %sys, %wio, %idle					
CPU 4: %usr, %sys, %wio, %idle					
CPU 1 InterCPU interrupts					
CPU 2 InterCPU interrupts					
CPU 3 InterCPU interrupts					
CPU 4 InterCPU Interrupts					

Now	Your Goal	Monitoring	Res #1	Res #2	Res #3	Res #4

Worksheet A-13: Network and Streams Tuning Worksheet (Part 1)

Tunables	Initial Values	Test #1	Test #2	Test #3	Test #4
NBLK4, NBLK16					
NBLK64, NBLK128					
NBLK256, NBLK512					
NBLK1024, NBLK2048					
NBLK4096					
NQUEUE, NSTREAM					
STRLOFRAC, STRMEDFRAC					
nfsd, biod, nfsclnt, lckclnt					
TCPWINDOW, tcp_round_mss					
tcp_ttl, udp_ttl					

Worksheet A-14: Network and Streams Tuning Worksheet (part 2)

Resources to Monitor	Initial Values	Test #1	Test #2	Test #3	Test #4
Streams					
Input Packets/errors					
Output Packets/errors					
Collisions					
Octets Received					
Octets Transmitted					
NIC Interrupts					
RPC calls: total calls, badcalls, retrans, badxid, timeout, wait, newcred					
nclget, nclsleep					
RPC calls: null, getattr, setattr, root, lookup, readlink, read, wrcache, write, create, remove, rename, link, symlink, mkdir, rmdir, readdir, fsstat					
Network Topology					
Protocol Errors					
CPU time used by daemons					

Now	Your Goal	Monitoring	Res #1	Res #2	Res #3	Res #4

Worksheet A-15: Oracle Tuning Worksheet (part 1)

Tunables	Initial Values	Test #1	Test #2	Test #3	Test #4
checkpoint_process					
db_block_buffers					
db_block_checkpoint_ batch					
db_block_max_scan_cnt					
db_block_write_batch					
discrete_transactions_ enabled					
dml_locks					
log_buffer					
log_checkpoint_interval					
log_checkpoint_timeout					
use_post_wait_driver					
USE_AIO					
shared_pool_size					
Size of redo log					
Number of rollback segments					
Database Layout					

Worksheet A-16: Oracle Tuning Worksheet (part 2)

Resources to Monitor	Initial Values	Test #1	Test #2	Test #3	Test #4
Total System Global Area					
Fixed Size					
Variable Size					
Database buffers					
Redo buffers					
Physical Writes					
Physical Reads					
redo log usage					
DBWR checkpoints					
Database file reads:					
Database file writes:					

Now	Your Goal	Monitoring	Res #1	Res #2	Res #3	Res #4

Worksheet A-17: Informix Tuning Worksheet (part 1)

Tunables	Initial Values	Test #1	Test #2	Test #3	Test #4
TBLSPACES					
CHUNKS					
DBSPACES					
PHYSBUFF					
LOGBUFF					
LOGSMAX					
PHYSFILE					
LOGFILES					
LOGSIZE					
CKPTINTVL					
BUFFERS					
CLEANERS					
LRUS					
LRU_MAX_DIRTY					
LRU_MIN_DIRTY					
LTXHWM					
LTXEHWM					
Database Layout					

Worksheet A-18: Informix Tuning Worksheet (part 2)

Resources to Monitor	Initial Values	Test #1	Test #2	Test #3	Test #4
Checkpoints					
Checkpoint waits					
Disk and page reads					
Disk and page writes					
Physical Log Usage					
Logical Log Usage					
Reads per division/pathname Writes per division/pathname					

Now	Your Goal	Monitoring	Res #1	Res #2	Res #3	Res #4

Appendix B

Making More Memory Available

This appendix offers suggestions for increasing the amount of memory available to application. Try the suggestions described in the following table that correspond to the amount of memory needed to stop paging and stopping. The amount of memory specified in the table applies to Open Desktop 3.0, SCO UNIX 3.2.4v2 and SCO MPX 3.0. Earlier releases may have slightly different values. For more information on how to implement the suggestion, see the relevant SCO manual.

The amount of additional required by the applications can be estimated with the swap -l command and the following equation:

$$\frac{(blocks\_column - free\_column)}{8} = swap\_space\_used(4\ Kbytes)$$

The value displayed in the blocks column is the total amount of swap space free. This value is displayed in units of 512-bytes. This value does not take into account those pages that are copied in from the filesystem, and so is an approximation. See the Common Open Desktop Operations chapter for more information on determining the required amount of memory.

Table B-1: How to Save Memory

Memory Saved	Action or Tunable	Comment
1.5 Mbytes	Disable the xdt desktop	See the Open Desktop System Administrator's Manual for instructions
1 Mbyte	Disable scologin	See the Open Desktop System Administrator's Manual for instructions
556-908 Kbytes	Stop tcp	If the TCP/IP networking capability is not actively in use, stop the TCP/IP support processes using this command. Open Desktop applications requiring access to the TCP/IP interfaces will still work as long as they do not require access to any remote machines. See the Open Desktop System Administrator's Guide for instructions.
Approx. 596 Kbytes	Remove TCP/IP	Use custom(ADM) to completely remove TCP/IP. Some applications require the interfaces supported by TCP/IP and so may not function correctly after TCP/IP is removed from the operating system. See the on-line manual page for custom for instructions.
Size of application	Close applications rather than minimize them	Minimizing still leaves the application's image in memory, while closing them removes the application's image from memory. The amount of memory saved can be considerable, since Open Desktop applications tend to be very large.
520 Kbytes	Use xterm(X) instead of scoterm(X)	In many cases, not all of the additional terminal emulator functionality provided by scoterm(X) is required. Try xterm(X) instead and see if the functionality is sufficient, and if so, replace scoterm(X) with xterm(X). See Open Desktop System Administrator's Manual for instructions.
500 Kbytes	Remove DOS Services	Use custom(ADM) to remove DOS services. The actual amount saved may vary as DOS services customizes itself extensively to the computing environment.
350 Kbytes	Stop nfs	If the remote file access capability of the NFS environment is not actively used, stop the NFS support processes. See the Open Desktop System Administrator's Guide for instructions.

Table B-1 (Continued): How to Save Memory

Memory Saved	Action or Tunable	Comment
286 Kbytes	Remove the NFS system from the operating system	If the remote file access capability of the NFS system is never used, then use custom(ADM) to completely remove NFS. See the on-line manual page for custom for instructions on how to remove software.
16 Kbytes + 76 bytes each	NMPBUF	Use sar -h to determine the usage pattern of this data structure. See the Common SCO UNIX Operations chapter for more information on these tunables.
1104 bytes	NBUF	Use sysadmsh(ADM) to change this variable. See the Common SCO UNIX Operations chapter for more information on this tunable.
Various sizes	Streams configuration	Careful monitoring of streams usage patterns with netstat -m can reveal unused sizes of streams buffers. If only a maximum of three 4 Kbyte buffers are used and eight are allocated, reduce the number of 4 Kbyte buffers and save 20 Kbytes of memory. Be sure the new allocation does not cause a buffer shortage, as that will degrade network and X server performance.
Various sizes	mail and print services	If mail or print services are not actively in use, then remove them with custom(ADM). The amount of memory saved depends on which mail and print services are installed.
1 Kbyte each	CTBUFSIZE	This tunable controls the size of buffer used by the tape. Can be reduced in fairly large increments, such as from 128 to 64.
76 bytes each	NMPHEADBUF	Use sar -h to determine the usage pattern of these buffer headers. See the Common SCO UNIX Operations chapter for more information on these tunables.
16 bytes each	NHBUF	NHBUF should always be a power of two. See the Common SCO UNIX Operations chapter for more information on this tunable.
76 bytes each	NPBUF	Use sar -b to check control block usage. If the number configured is more than sufficient, then decrease NPBUF.

Table B-1(Continued): How to Save Memory

Memory Saved	Action or Tunable	Comment
12 bytes each	NFILE	Use sar -v to check open file table usage. Set NFILE to 10% more than the maximum value reported by sar -v.
172 bytes each	NINODE	Use sar -v to check the inode table usage. Set NINODE to 10% more than the maximum value reported by sar -v.
8 bytes each	NHINODE	When NINODE is reduced, NHINODE may also be reduced. See the Common SCO UNIX chapter for more information on reducing NHINODE.
372 bytes each	NPROC	Use sar -v to check process table usage. Set NPROC to be 10% more than the maximum used. If the operating system runs out of process data structures, the following message is displayed: `CONFIG: newproc - Process table overflow (NPROC = x exceeded)` where x is the current value of NPROC.
76 bytes each	NREGION (must be at least 3*NPROC + 20)	If the operating system runs out of regions, the following error message is displayed: `CONFIG: allocreg - Region table overflow (NREGION = x exceeded)` where x is the current value of NREGION.
34 bytes each	FLCKREC	Use sar -v to check file locking table usage. Set FLCKREC to be 5% more than the maximum used.
40 bytes each	S5CACHEENTS	For Open Desktop systems that are paging and swapping, reducing the size of these tunables will not affect performance of the filesystem operations. See the SCO UNIX chapter for more information on these tunables.
8 bytes	S5HASHQS	See the Common SCO UNIX Operations chapter for recommendations on how to tune this variable.

Table B-1(Continued): How to Save Memory

Memory Saved	Action or Tunable	Comment
6 Kbytes each	NSCRN	If not all of the multiscreens™ are used, then reduce the amount of memory allocated for them by setting NSCRN to the number of multiscreens that are in use. If the value of NSCRN is zero, then the operating system automatically allocates the number appropriate for the amount of physical memory in the system.

Appendix C

Manual Pages for Floppy Disk Utilities

This appendix contains the manual pages describing all the utilities provided on the floppy disk. The copyright and warranty information is included on the floppy disk. Table C-1 summarizes the programs that are included on the floppy disk.

Name	Description
calcop	Provides a framework for measuring the performance of CPU-intensive operations
ctree	Creates a directory hierarchy
fileop	Provides a framework for measuring the performance of file read and write operations
float.awk	Executes many different floating point computations
makeram	Creates ramdisks
net2wks	Produces a summary of the key network usage statistics for entry into the SCO Networking and Streams Tuning Worksheet

Table C-1: Summary of Utilities Provided on Floppy Disk

Name	Description
netdata	Writes network statistics to standard output
nfsop	Provides a framework for measuring the performance of remote file read and write operations using the NFS environment
odtop	Provides a framework for measuring the performance of display update operations on Open Desktop
oraclestat	Extracts Oracle resource usage statistics
rcpop	Provides a framework for measuring the performance of remote file read and write operations when rcp is used
runinf	Provides a framework for measuring performance on Informix-OnLine
sar2mpxwks	Produces a summary of the key operating system resource usage statistics for entry into the SCO MPX Tuning Worksheet
sar2oswks	Produces a summary of the key operating system resource usage statistics for entry into the SCO UNIX Tuning Worksheet
saravg	Calculates resource usage at specified intervals
tune2wks	Generates the appropriate configuration information for entry into the tunables section of the SCO UNIX and Networking Tuning Worksheets.

Table C-1 (Continued): Summary of Utilities Provided on Floppy Disk

Name

calcop

Syntax

calcop [-sar] [-procs number] [-help]

Description

The calcop script provides a framework for measuring the performance of calculation operations. The calcop script forks 10 processes, each of which execute calculation operations. The time taken for all the processes to complete their tests is measured. The operations performed by these processes are defined in the calc_ulm script, which uses the float.awk script by default. The calc_ulm script can be modified to use scripts other than float.awk.

The -sar option enables sar data collection during the test.

The -procs option specifies the number of processes that should be created for the test. The default value is 10 processes.

The -help option will display a usage message.

Returns

At the end of the test the amount of real, system and user time is displayed. This information is also recorded in the file *results/log_x*, where x is the run identifier displayed by calcop. The *results* directory is automatically created if it does not exist. If the -sar option is specified, then a sar file will be created in the *results* directory called *sar_x*. The current run identifier is stored in the file called *.runid* in the directory where calcop is executed.

Example

calcop -procs 20

This command measures the time required for 20 processes to complete the calculation operations.

The results of the tests will be displayed and recorded in the file *results/log_x*, where x is the run identifier displayed by calcop.

calcop -sar -procs 20

This command repeats the previous test but this time also executes sar to monitor the resource usage. The statistics are stored in the file called *results/sar_x,* where x is the run identifier displayed by calcop.

Warning

The calc_ulm script must be located in a directory specified by the PATH environment variable.

Ensure that the number of processes that will be created by the script will not exceed the kernel tunables NPROC and MAXUP.

See Also

float.awk

Name

ctree

Syntax

ctree [-s size] [-d depth] [-f number_of_files] [-n name]

Description

The ctree utility builds a directory hierarchy. The lowest level directories are the only directories that contain files. The directory hierarchy is built in the current directory. If no options are specified, the hierarchy that is built consists of a single directory with 100 files, each 1024 bytes in size.

The -s option specifies the size of the files that are created at the lowest level. The size value is specified in bytes. The default value is 1024.

The -d option specifies the depth of the directory hierarchy that will be created. For example, if the depth is set to two, then the ctree utility builds one directory in the current directory and then two further directories in that directory. The default value is one.

The -f option specifies the number of files that are created in each of the lowest level directories. The default value is 100.

The -n option specifies the name of the directory that is created in the user's current working directory. If this option is omitted, then the utility automatically generates a name. ctree automatically generates the names for the other directories and files created.

Warning

Ensure that sufficient disk space is available to store the directory hierarchy created by ctree. Check the amount of available space with the df(C) command. Specifying a very deep hierarchy can use a large amount of disk space.

Output

When ctree has completed building the directory hierarchy a summary is displayed:

```
Created directory hierarchy in name of directory.
Depth of directory hierarchy is depth.
All the lowest level directories contain number
files.
Each file is size bytes.
Total amount of data in directory hierarchy = number
bytes.
```

Example

ctree -s 1024 -d 1 -f 100 -n testdir

This command creates a directory called testdir in the current directory. Within the testdir directory there will be 100 files with a size of 1024 bytes.

See Also

df(C) du(C)

Name

fileop

Syntax

fileop [-sar] [-procs number] [-files number] [-iterations number] [-testdir directory name] [-filesize number] [-help]

Description

The fileop script provides a framework for measuring the performance of file read and file write operations. fileop forks a set of processes that execute file read and write operations. The time taken for all the processes to complete their tests is measured.

The fileop script does the following:

1. Reads the names of files held in a test directory, as specified by -testdir
2. Creates one file list for each process that describes what files should be accessed during the test
3. Creates the processes

Each process works through the file lists by executing three reads and then a file copy (read+write) operation. When executing the copy operation, the process seeks to a position in the file, reads from the seek position to the end of file, and then writes the data from the source file to a target file located in a temporary directory. This temporary directory, *tmp*, is located in the same directory from which fileop is started.

The file_ulm script defines the operations performed by these processes. This script can be modified to simulate different behavior.

If fileop is used a second time and the previous file lists still exist, then the following question is asked:

```
File lists exist from previous run, reuse? (y/n)
```

If the files in the test directory have not been modified then enter 'y' otherwise 'n' should be entered.

The -sar option specifies that sar monitoring should take place during the test.

The -files option specifies the number of files that are used by each created process. The default is 100.

The -iterations option specifies the number of times the processes repeat their operations. The default is one.

The -testdir option specifies the pathname(s) of the directory(ies) storing the test files. If multiple directories are specified, then they should be enclosed in quotes, for example, "directory1 directory2". If no test directory is specified, then the default name is data1.

The -filesize option specifies the size of the smallest file in the test directory. This value is used for file seeks. All files in the test directory should be the same or similar size. The default value for filesize is 32768.

The -help option displays a usage message.

Returns

At the end of the test the amount of real, system and user time is displayed. This information is also recorded in the file *results/log_x*, where x is the run identifier displayed by fileop. If the -sar option is used then there will be a file *results/sar_x* containing the sar output. The *results* directory will automatically be created if it does not exist. The current run identifier is stored in the file *.runid* in the directory where fileop is executed.

Examples

ctree -n data1 -f 200 -d 1 -s 32768
fileop

This command creates a directory *data1* in the current directory containing 200 files.

A test is run with these files. 10 processes are forked and each process acts on 100 files. The processes only execute the tests once.

The results of the tests are displayed and recorded in *results/log_x*, where x is the run identifier displayed by fileop.

fileop -sar

This command repeats the test while running sar. The sar data is stored in the file *results/sar_y*, where y is the run identifier displayed by fileop.

Warning

The file_ulm script must be located in a directory specified by the PATH environment variable.

Ensure that NPROC and MAXUP are sufficiently large to accommodate the processes that are started by fileop.

See Also

ctree

Name

float.awk

Syntax

awk -f float.awk [STEPS=number] [TESTS=number]

Description

The float.awk script calculates a series of trigonometric functions to a specified accuracy. The accuracy is determined by the value of STEPS, as this value controls the number of iterations executed If no value is specified, then a default of 25,000 will be used.

The TESTS option can be used to limit the number of iterations when the value set by STEPS is so large that overflow or underflow will occur on some calculations.

This script can be used to measure the performance of calculations on a given system.

Example

awk -f float.awk STEPS=1000

This command executes 1000 iterations for each trigonometric operation.

See Also

awk(C)

Name

makeram

Syntax

makeram [-help] [-pipe] [-device name] [-mount name]
64K | 128K | 256K | 512K | 1Mb | 2Mb | 4Mb | 8Mb | 16Mb | 32Mb

Description

The makeram utility provides a convenient way of creating ramdisks that can also be used for pipes.

The -pipe option specifies that after the ramdisk is initialized, any new pipes should use the ramdisk disk. If this option is omitted, then pipes will not use the ramdisk.

The -device option specifies the name of the device node, for the ramdisk. The name following -device is used for the device node's name. If this option is not used the default name is */dev/ramx,* where x is the size of the ramdisk.

The -mount option specifies the mount point for the ramdisk. The ramdisk is mounted on the directory specified by the name following -mount. If -mount is not specified, the default mount point is */mnt.*

The -help option displays a usage message.

Warnings

The memory used by a ramdisk is not available for use by applications, so always check the amount of available memory before creating a ramdisk.

A small ramdisk may not be large enough to handle the amount of data being transferred with pipes. Use df to monitor how much space is available in the ramdisk.

Examples

makeram -pipe 2Mb

This command creates a ramdisk mounted on */mnt* that is 2 Mbytes in size. Pipes will use the ramdisk to store data.

makeram -pipe -mount /ram_mnt 512K

This command creates a ramdisk mounted on */ram_mnt* that is 512 Kbytes in size. Pipes will use the ramdisk to store data.

See Also

pipe (C) ramdisk (HW) df(C)

Name

net2wks

Syntax

net2wks [-titles] [-interface name] [-client] [-server] [-help] [-tabs] [-help] file1 file2

Description

net2wks takes the output from the network utilities netstat, nfsstat and llistat and produces a summary that is suitable for insertion into the **Resources to be monitored** section of the Network Tuning Worksheet.

The file specified by *file1* should contain all the network statistics prior to the start of the test, and the file specified by *file2* should contain the statistics after the test was run.

net2wks computes the changes in the statistics and displays the differences. The *file1* and *file2* files should contain the information obtained from netstat with the -i, -m, -s, and -a options, from llistat -l and from nfsstat -cs. The netdata utility can provide all of this information.

The -titles option provides additional information describing each statistic.

The -interface option specifies the name of the network interface card. Statistics are only produced for a single interface card. If -interface is omitted then the first interface card reported by netstat -a will be used.

The -client and -server options specify whether the system is acting as a client or as a server. One or the other should be specified when analyzing the NFS statistics. When -client is specified ".cl" will be post-fixed to the names specified by *file1* and *file2*. For servers the post-fix is ".se".

The -tabs option specifies that tabs delimit each number that is displayed rather than spaces. Spaces are the default delimiter.

The -help option provides a usage message.

Examples

net2wks -client before after

This command produces statistics for a client based on the data contained in the files *before.cl* and *after.cl*.

net2wks -server -interface cet0 before after

This command produces statistics for the network interface card called cet0 for a server based on the data contained in the files *before.se* and *after.se*.

See Also

netstat (TC) llistat(ADM) , nfsstat(NADM), netdata

Name

netdata

Syntax

netdata [-nfs] [-stats] [-start] [-end] [-help]

Description

The netdata utility writes network statistics to standard output. The utility can also be used by a client to start and stop sar on a server using rcmd.

The -nfs option generates nfs statistics.

The -stats option generates netstat and llistat statistics.

The -start option starts sar data gathering.

The -stop option stops sar data gathering.

The -help option provides a usage message.

Examples

netdata -nfs -stats > start.cl

This command records the current values for the network statistics in the file *start.cl.*

For additional examples, please refer to the rcpop and nfsop scripts.

See Also

netstat (TC) llistat(ADM) nfsstat(NADM)

Name

nfsop

Syntax

nfsop [-sar] [-procs number] [-files number] [-iterations number] [-cpus number] [-tmp directory name] [-testdir directory name] [-serverwka directory name] [-help] name_of_server

Description

The nfsop script provides a framework for measuring the performance of remote file read and file write operations using an NFS-mounted filesystem to access data held on the specified server.

nfsop starts a number of processes that execute file read and write operations. The time taken for all the processes to complete their tests is measured.

nfsop executes the following:

1. Reads the names of files located in the test directory specified by the - testdir option
2. Creates file lists for each the processes that will run as part of the test
3. Creates the processes

Each process works through its file list executing three read operations followed by a file read and write, or copy, operation. The copy operation uses cp to copy a file on the server to the client and cp to copy the file back to the server.

The operations performed by these processes are defined in the nfs_ulm script and can be modified to simulate different behavior.

If nfsop is used a second time and the previous file lists still exist then the question will be asked:

```
File lists exist from previous run, reuse? (y/n)
```

If the files in the test directory have not been modified then enter 'y' otherwise 'n' should be entered.

The -sar option specifies that sar monitoring should take place during the test.

The -files option specifies the number of files that are used by each process. The default is 100.

The -iterations option specifies the number of times processes repeat their operations. The default is 1.

The -cpus option specifies the number of processors on the server. If the server is not a multiprocessor system then 0 (the default) should be used. -cpus only needs to be specified when -sar is used.

The -tmp option specifies a temporary directory on the server. The default directory is */tmp*.

The -testdir option specifies the pathname(s) of the directory(ies) storing the test files. If multiple directories are used, then their names should be included in quotes, for example, "directory1 directory2". The directory pathname(s) should always include the mount point. For example, if the server's filesystem is mounted on */servermnt* the directory pathname should include this. If no test directory is specified then the default name is */mnt/data1*.

The -serverwka option specifies the directory where data will be copied for the copy operation. The default is the value specified using the -testdir option.

The -help option provides a usage message.

Returns

At the end of the test the amount of real, system and user time will be displayed. This information is also recorded in the file *results/log_x*, where x is the run identifier displayed by nfsop.

If the -sar option is used then there will be two sar files in the results directory, *ssar_x* contains server sar data and *csar_x* contains client sar data. If the server is running SCO MPX, then a sar file called *ssar_x.y* will be created for each of the active CPUs; y identifies the CPU for which the data was collected.

The *results* directory will also contain four log files containing network statistics. The files *log_sx.cl* and *log_ex.cl* store the before and after network statistics for the client and *log_sx.se* and *log_ex.se* store the before and after network statistics for the server. The current run identifier is stored in the file *.runid* in the directory where nfsop is executed.

Example

nfsop -testdir /mnt/w/test mainhost

This command executes the nfs test using mainhost as the server system. The directory */mnt/w/testdir* is remotely mounted using NFS and should contain the files that are to be accessed for the test. The test will consist of 10 processes accessing these files. The processes will only perform the tests once.

The results of the tests will be displayed and recorded in *results/log_x*, where x is the run identifier displayed by nfsop.

Warning

The nfs_ulm script must be located in a directory specified by the PATH environment variable.

Ensure that NPROC and MAXUP are sufficiently large to accommodate the number of processes created by nfsop.

Also check the client and server *.rhosts* files to ensure that both the client and server can access each other.

See Also

ctree

Name

odtop

Syntax

odtop [-sar] [-help]

Description

The odtop script provides a framework for measuring the performance of operations running on SCO Open Desktop. The operations are defined in the file odt_ulm. The default operation is to refresh the display 20 times with xrefresh(X).

The -sar option specifies that sar monitoring should take place during the test.

The -help option will provide a usage message.

Returns

At the end of the test the amount of real, system and user time will be displayed. This information is also recorded in the file *results/log_x*, where x is the run identifier displayed by odtop. If the -sar option is used then there will be a sar file, *sar_x*, in the *results* directory. The *results* directory is automatically created if it does not exist. The current run identifier is stored in the file *.runid* in the directory where odtop is executed.

Example

odtop -sar

This command refreshes the X display 20 times. The result of this test is displayed and recorded in *results/log_x*, where x is the run identifier displayed by odtop. The file *results/sar_x* stores the sar data collected during the run.

Warning

The odt_ulm script must be located in a directory specified by the PATH environment variable.

Name

oraclestat

Syntax

oraclestat [-sysstat] [-filestat] [-help]

Description

The oraclestat script provides a mechanism for obtaining statistics when running Oracle. Before this script can be used, the database that is to be monitored must be mounted. The data generated by this script should be recorded before and after a test. Changes in values due to the test can then be easily determined.

This script can be extended to provide other information. For a description of all the statistics kept by the Oracle RDBMS please refer to "The Dynamic Performance Tables" section in ORACLE RDBMS Database Administrator's Guide Volume III.

The -help option provides a usage message.

The output displayed with the -filestat option is based on the information held in the V$FILESTAT table. For more information please refer to "The Dynamic Performance Tables" section in the ORACLE RDBMS Database Administrator's Guide Volume III. This option is based on the SQL query provided in the ORACLE RDBMS Performance Tuning Guide, please see the chapter on Tuning I/O.

The output displayed with the -sysstat option is the information held in the V$SYSSTAT table.

Example

oraclestat -filestat

This command displays the number of reads and writes that have occurred to the different database files in the currently mounted databases.

See Also

"The Dynamic Performance Tables" and "Statistics Monitor" sections in the ORACLE RDBMS Database Administrator's Guide Volume III.

Name

rcpop

Syntax

rcpop [-sar] [-procs number] [-files number] [-iterations number] [-cpus number] [-tmp directory name] [-testdir directory name] [-help] name of server

Description

The rcpop script provides a framework for measuring the performance of remote file read and file write operations when rcp is used to access data held on the specified server.

rcpop creates processes that execute file read and write operations. The time taken for all the processes to complete their tests is measured.

rcpop executes the following actions:

1. Reads the names of files held in a test directory, as specified by -testdir
2. Creates file lists for each the processes that will run as part of the test
3. Creates the processes

Each process works through its file list executing three reads using rcp and then a file copy (read+write) operation. The copy operation uses rcp to copy a file on the server to the client and then uses rcp to copy the file back to the server.

The operations executed by these processes are defined in the rcp_ulm script and can be modified to simulate different behavior.

If rcpop is used a second time and the previous file lists still exist then the following question will be asked:

```
File lists exist from previous run, reuse? (y/n)
```

If the files in the test directory have not been modified then enter 'y' otherwise 'n' should be entered.

The -sar option specifies that sar monitoring should take place during the test.

The -files option specifies the number of files that are used by each process. The default is 100.

The -iterations option specifies the number of times the processes repeat the file operations. The default is one.

The -cpus option specifies the number of processors on the server. If the server is not a multiprocessor system then zero (the default) should be used. -cpus only needs to be specified when -sar is also used.

The -tmp option specifies a temporary directory on the server. The default directory is */tmp*.

The -testdir option specifies the pathname(s) of the directory(ies) storing the test files. If multiple directories are used, then their names should be included in quotes, for example, "directory1 directory2". The directories should either be specified relative to the home directory (on the server) of the user running the test or from root. If no test directory is specified then the default name is data1.

The -help option provides a usage message.

Returns

At the end of the test the amount of real, system and user time is displayed. This information is also recorded in the file *results/log_x*, where x is the run identifier displayed by rcpop.

If the -sar option is used then there will be two sar files in the results directory, *ssar_x* contains server sar data and *csar_x* contains client sar data. The *results* directory also contains four log files containing network statistics. The files *log_sx.cl* and *log_ex.cl* store the before and after network statistics for the client and *log_sx.se* and *log_ex.se* store the before and after network statistics for the server.

If the server is running SCO MPX, then a sar file called *ssar_x.y* will be created for each of the active CPUs; y identifies the CPU for which the data was collected. The current run identifier is stored in the file *.runid* in the directory where rcpop is executed.

Example

rcpop -testdir /w/test mainhost

This command executes the rcp test using mainhost as the server system. The directory */w/testdir* should contain the files that are to be accessed for the test. The test consists of 10 processes accessing these files. The processes will only perform the tests once.

The results of the tests will be displayed and recorded in *results/log_x,* where x is the run identifier displayed by rcpop.

rcpop -sar -testdir /w/test mainhost

This command repeats the previous test, but this time runs the monitoring tools. The monitoring data can be read using the sar2oswks and net2wks scripts. For example, for the client the following commands should be used:

```
sar2oswks results/csar_x
net2wks -client results/log_sx results/log_ex
```

For the server, the following commands should be used:

```
sar2oswks results/ssar_x
net2wks -server results/log_sx results/log_ex
```

Warning

The rcp_ulm script must be located in a directory specified by the PATH environment variable.

Ensure that NPROC and MAXUP are sufficiently large to accommodate the number of processes that will be created.

Also check the client and server *.rhosts* files to ensure that both the client and server can access each other.

See Also

ctree

Name

runinf

Syntax

runinf

Description

The runinf script provides a framework for running tests with Informix and maintaining test output and monitoring data.

The script creates a directory *results* and stores the test results and sar output in this directory. Results are written in files named *log_x* and sar output is written in files named *sar_x,* where x is the run identifier displayed by runinf. The log files also include information obtained from tbstat.

Before runinf can be used the script runinf_ulm should be modified to include the test operations that will be measured.

See Also

Please refer to the Informix OnLine Administrator's Guide.

Name

sar2mpxwks

Syntax

sar2mpxwks [-titles] [-sartitles] [-tabs] [-help] [-cpus number of cpus] [-saropt saroptions] filename

Description

sar2mpxwks takes sar output files that have been created using the -o option of mpsar and produces a summary of the data suitable for inclusion in the SCO MPX Tuning Worksheet.

The filename specified on the command line must be a valid sar output file. The sar output files for each processor must exist.

The options allow the output of this utility to be varied to suit different needs.

The -titles option displays a title for each of the statistics shown. The title shows which resources match which statistics, as given in the "Resources to be monitored" column of the SCO MPX Tuning Worksheet.

The -sartitles option displays the sar column title for each of the statistics shown.

The -tabs option specifies that tabs should be used to delimit each number that is displayed rather than the default delimiter. The default delimiter is spaces.

-help provides a usage message.

The -cpus option specifies the number of processors for which output is required. If no -cpus option is given, then the default value is two. The sar output files must exist for each of the processors. For example, if the filename specified to sar was *sardata*, then for two processors the files *sardata.1* and *sardata.2* must exist.

The -saropt option allows additional options, specified after the -saropt switch, to be passed to sar. When multiple options are specified, they should be enclosed within quotes.

Examples

sar2mpxwks sar.10

This command produces output for two CPUs suitable for entry into the SCO MPX Tuning Worksheet from the sar information stored in the files *sar.10.1* and *sar.10.2*.

sar2mpxwks -cpus 3 sar.10

This command produces output for three CPUs suitable for entry into the SCO MPX Tuning Worksheet from the sar information stored in the files *sar.10.1, sar.10.2* and *sar.10.3*.

See Also

mpsar(MP) cpusar(MP) sar2oswks

Name

sar2oswks

Syntax

sar2oswks [-titles] [-sartitles] [-mpxsarsls] [-noconcise] [-tabs] [-help] [-saropt saroptions] filename

Description

sar2oswks takes sar output files that have been created using the -o option of sar (or mpsar) and produces a summary of the data held in the file suitable for inclusion in the SCO UNIX Tuning Worksheet.

The filename specified on the command line to sar2oswks must be a valid sar output file. With the exception of the file table and inode table statistics, the values obtained are based on the averages produced by sar. Where appropriate, the values are rounded to the nearest integer value. For the file table and inode table usage statistics, the maximum recorded value is shown.

The options allow the output of this utility to be varied to suit different needs.

The -titles option displays a title for each of the statistics shown. The title identifies which resource the statistics relates to, as given in the "Resources to be monitored" column of the SCO UNIX Tuning Worksheet.

The -sartitles option displays the sar column title for each of the statistics shown.

The -mpxsarsls option should be used when the SCO MPX mpsar Maintenance Supplement has been installed on a system. Additional information about the SCSI subsystem will be displayed.

The -noconcise option stops sar2oswks from rounding and truncating any of the output produced by sar, so that the values obtained will be exactly those produced by sar.

The -tabs option specifies that tabs should be used to delimit each number that is displayed rather than the default delimiter of spaces.

The -help option displays a usage message.

The -saropt option allows additional options, specified after the -saropt switch, to be passed to sar. When multiple options need to be specified, they should be enclosed within quotes.

Examples

sar2oswks sar.10

This command produces output suitable for the SCO UNIX Tuning Worksheet from the sar information stored in the file *sar.10*.

sar2oswks -saropt "-s 12:20:00 -e 12:30:00" sar.12

This command generates output for the SCO UNIX Tuning Worksheet from the file *sar.12* but only for the times from 12:20 to 12:30.

See Also

sar(ADM)

Name

saravg

Syntax

saravg [-help] [-tabs] [-period number] -file filename [-cpu] [-runqueue] [-memory] [-paging] [-nameicache] [-buffercache] [-directio] [-alldisk] [-disk diskname]

Description

saravg takes the information normally displayed by sar (or mpsar) and produces averages for the specified resources. The average values are obtained by grouping the values produced by sar into groups of 10. For example, if sar has been used to take measurements every second, then saravg can be used to produce averages for the specified resources over 10 second periods. This information can be useful for determining how resource usage varies over extended periods of time.

The -help option displays a usage message.

The -tabs option specifies that tabs should be used to delimit each number that is displayed rather than the default delimiter. The default delimiter is a space.

The -period option allows the period over which the average is computed to be varied. The number following the -period switch specifies how many sar readings should be grouped together for each average produced. The period of time the average is based on depends on how sar was used. For example, if sar was used to take measurements every 10 seconds then -period 6 will produce averages based on 1 minute intervals.

The -saropt option allows additional options, specified after the -saropt switch, to be passed to sar. When multiple options need to be specified, they should be enclosed within quotes.

The -filename switch must be specified and the filename given must be a file that was written with the -o option of sar (or mpsar).

The -cpu option produces averages for CPU usage.

The -runqueue option produces averages for run queue size.

The -memory option produces averages for free memory and free swap.

The -paging option produces averages for paging activity.

The -nameicache option produces averages for namei cache usage.

The -buffercache option produces averages for the buffer cache sar statistics.

The -directio option produces averages for the direct i/o sar statistics.

The -alldisk option produces averages for all the disks installed in the system. The -disk option produces averages for the disk specified by the name following -disk. The name specified should match the name that sar -d uses to identify a given disk. Both -disk and -alldisk can be useful for obtaining a matrix of disk results because, unlike sar -d, disks with no activity will have output produced for them. If averaging is not required, use -period 1.

Examples

saravg -file sarfile -cpu

If *sarfile* was produced with sar -o *sarfile* 1 200 then this example will produce CPU usage statistics averaged over 10 second intervals. If *sarfile* had been produced with sar -o *sarfile* 10 200 then the averages would be based on 100 second intervals.

saravg -period 1 -file sarfile -disk ida-0

If *sarfile* was produced with sar -o *sarfile* 1 200 then this example will produce a complete set of statistics for the ida-0 disk. Where the disk has no activity the values shown will be 0.

Warning

When unsure about the sampling period used by sar, use sar -f to see how frequently the sar statistics were produced.

See Also

sar(ADM)

Name

tune2wks

Syntax

tune2wks -file filename [-help] [-network]

Description

tune2wks generates appropriate information for the tunables section of the SCO UNIX and Networking Tuning Worksheets. The data generated is stored in the file specified by the -file switch. The default output is suitable for use with the SCO UNIX Tuning Worksheet. In order to provide complete output the utility will prompt for additional information. The prompts are:

```
Please enter total amount of memory installed:
```

Enter either the amount of memory reported at boot time or that reported by memsize (users must be root to use memsize).

```
Please enter any application specific memory
tunables:
```

Enter any additional information relating to tunables for the application being used.

```
Please enter a summary of the disk arrangement:
```

Enter information describing how the disks are configured on the system for the test.

```
Please enter a summary of the display configuration:
```

Enter how the display adapter has been configured. For example, the number of horizontal and vertical pixels used and the number of colors. This information is also used when configuring the display adapter with mkdev graphics.

```
Please enter a summary for the configuration of the
mouse:
```

Enter how the mouse has been configured. For example, enter the current value of SENSITIVITY and for keyboard mice, the current values of kbm_poll and kbm_poll_max.

```
Please enter a summary for other memory usage:
```

Enter any additional information that relates to how memory is being used during the test.

To produce output for the Network Tuning Worksheet, use the -network option. The prompts that will appear are as follows:

```
Please enter number of nfsd daemons:
Please enter number of biod daemons:
Please enter number of nfsclnt daemons:
Please enter number of lckclnt daemons:
```

This information can be derived either from using ps or by checking the startup scripts. For more information, please refer to the nfs (NADM) manual pages.

-help displays a usage message.

Warnings

The information obtained by tune2wks is based on the current state of the system link kit and not on the currently running operating system. If the link kit has been modified since the operating system for the test was linked, then the information produced by this utility may be incorrect.

See Also

memsize (ADM) nfs(NADM)

Appendix D

SCO NFS Patch

This appendix provides a patch for the SCO NFS environment on SCO Open Server 3.0 and SCO Open Desktop 3.0 systems. This patch allows NFS clients to increase the usage of the buffer cache for client write operations without compromising the NFS system requirement that writes between client and server must be executed synchronously. This patch can significantly reduce the number of write remote procedure calls executed by the client.

Performance is improved only if the number of write remote procedure calls executed by the client is consuming a significant proportion of the resources required to access remote files. If the client is primarily reading files from the server, then the patch is unlikely to benefit performance, and should not be installed. Prior to installing the patch, monitoring the amount of write activity should allow you to assess whether installing the patch would benefit your system.

This patch is unlikely to improve performance if the remote filesystem is mounted with the wsize=xx options. In some cases, SCO systems that contain this patch may be more responsive when changing the buffer cache tunables.

This patch is supplied on an AS IS basis and installation of the patch is at your own risk. This patch is not sponsored nor supported by SCO. This patch can only be applied by the superuser. Please ensure that the system is in single user mode before installing this patch.

How to Install the Patch

The commands in **bold** should be entered at either the shell or debugger command-line prompt.

The steps to install the patch are as follows:

Step 1: Enter:

cp /unix unix.orig

This command provides a backup of the operating system prior to installing the NFS patch. If problems are experienced while installing the patch, then the backup operating system can be easily restored.

Step 2: Enter:

cd /etc/conf/pack.d/nfs

This command sets the current working directory to the directory that contains the SCO NFS driver.

Step 3: Enter:

cp Driver.o Driver.o.orig

This command provides a backup of the original NFS driver in the file Driver.o.orig. Making backup copies of any essential files prior to changing them is a critical part of any system maintenance task such as installing a patch. On some systems, a file called *Driver.a,* rather than *Driver.o*, may be found in this directory. If you have such a system, carefully match the correctness of the SCO NFS object module you are modifying with the information described here. If the information matches, then continue to apply the patch, but substitute *Driver.a* for *Driver.o*.

Step 4: Enter:

/etc/_fst -w Driver.o

This command provides you with a mechanism for applying the patch. If a mistake is made, enter $q and copy the original driver from *Driver.o.orig* to *Driver.o* before starting another attempt to re-apply the patch.

Step 5: Enter:

nfswritei+0x574,7?ai

The following lines should appear on the screen:

```
nfswritei+0x574:  .....
nfswritei+0x574:  lea eax,[edi+ebx]
nfswritei+0x577:  cmp eax,[ebp-0x20]
nfswritei+0x57a:  jne nfswritei+0x590
nfswritei+0x57c:  mov eax, [ebp-0x8]
nfswritei+0x57f:  or Byte Ptr[eax+0x30],0x1
nfswritei+0x583:  push  [ebp-0xc]
nfswritei+0x586:  call near 0x17:0x0
```

The first two lines should appear as one line on your screen. If the output displayed on your system does not precisely match that shown above (with the exception of the first two lines), then the patch should NOT be applied. Use $q to quit at this step.

Step 6: Enter:

nfswritei+0x57a?x

The following output should appear on your screen:

```
nfswritei+0x57a:  1475
```

If the output displayed on your screen does not precisely match that shown above, then the patch should not be applied. Use $q to quit at this step.

Step 7: Enter:

nfswritei+0x57a?w 14eb

The following output should appear on your screen:

```
nfswritei+0x57a:  0x1475=0x14eb
```

If the output on your screen does not precisely match that shown above, exit the operation by typing $q.

The display may not match because a mistake may have been made in a previous step. To try again, copy the original *Driver.o.orig* file to *Driver.o* and start the process from Step 4.

Step 8. Enter:

nfswritei+0x574,7?ai

You can check the correctness of what you have done by matching the following output with what is displayed on your screen.

The following lines should appear on your screen:

```
nfswritei+0x574:  .......
nfswritei+0x574:  lea eax,[edi+ebx]
nfswritei+0x577:  cmp eax,[ebp-0x20]
nfswritei+0x57a:  jmp near nfswritei+0x590
nfswritei+0x57c:  mov eax, [ebp-0x8]
nfswritei+0x57f:  or Byte Ptr[eax+0x30],0x1
nfswritei+0x583:  push  [ebp-0xc]
nfswritei+0x586:  call near 0x17:0x0
```

The first two lines of this display should appear as one line on your screen. If your display does not precisely match (with the exception of the first two lines), then exit the operation by typing $q. Copy the *Driver.o.orig* file to *Driver.o* and either try again by starting at Step 4 or abandon the entire operation.

Step 9: Enter:

$q

This command exits the debugger. The patch to the NFS driver has been successfully made.

Step 10: Enter:

cd /etc/conf/cf.d

This command sets the current directory to the directory where a new kernel can be created.

Step 11: Enter:

./link_unix

Follow the normal procedure described in the SCO Open Desktop System Administrator's Guide when creating a new operating system. After the operating system is successfully created, reboot the system to activate the changes.

Sample Performance Test

This example uses adapted versions of the nfsop_ulm and nfsop scripts provided on the floppy disk. The changes consisted of having the client machine execute only copy operations to the server. In this case, the client machine executed 10 processes that each copied 100 32K files to the server.

The files used by each process were stored in separate directories so that they could be copied to the server with the following command:

cp * srvr_mount_point/ directory.

The test was adapted to execute only file write operations because the patch affects the performance of the NFS system file write rather than file read operations.

The client and server machines are the same as those used in the Remote File Access Case Studies described in chapter 10. In the interest of brevity, completed worksheets are not included at the end of this appendix.

Figure D-1 compares the duration of the test before and after installing the NFS patch.

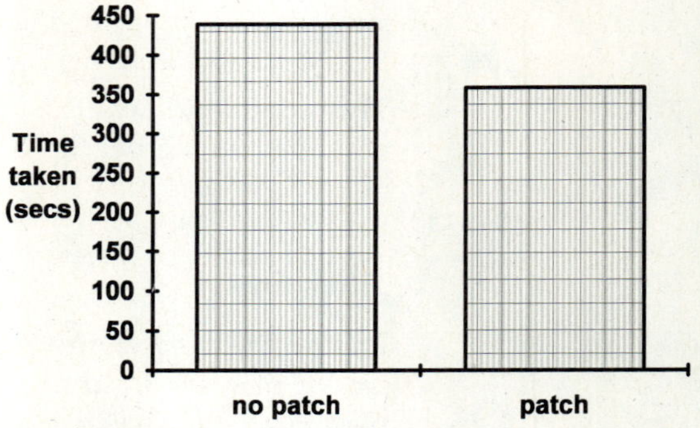

Figure D-1: Comparison Between Test Duration Before and After the Installation of the Patch

Figure D-1 shows how the time taken to write the files from the client to the server decreased after the patch was applied to the operating system. Figure D-2 shows the number of input and output packets handled by the client without and with the patch.

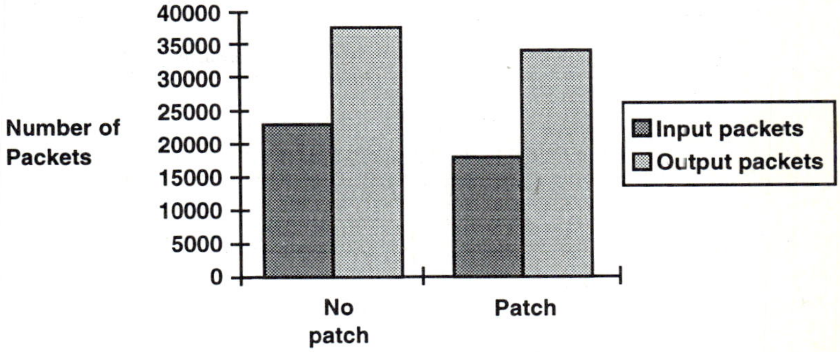

Figure D-2: Number of Input and Output Packets Handled Before and After the Installation of the Patch

Both the number of input and output packets fell after the patch was installed. The reason both fall is that the patch allows more grouping of write requests to be made, and so fewer remote procedure calls should be necessary for the same test.

Figure D-3 shows the change in number of remote procedure calls made by the client.

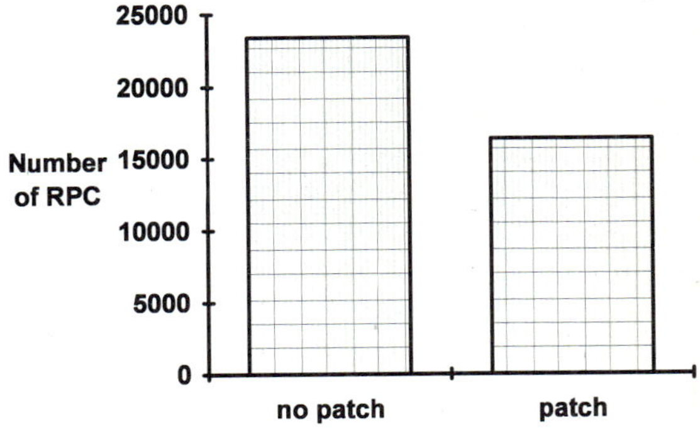

Figure D-3: Number of remote procedure calls executed by Client Before and After the Installation of the Patch

Examining the remaining remote procedure call data shows a similar reduction in nclget. This reduction is expected because each remote procedure call requires a client handle. With the exception of the write remote procedure, there was little change in the number of remote procedure calls executed. Figure D-4 shows the change in the number of write remote procedure calls executed by the client.

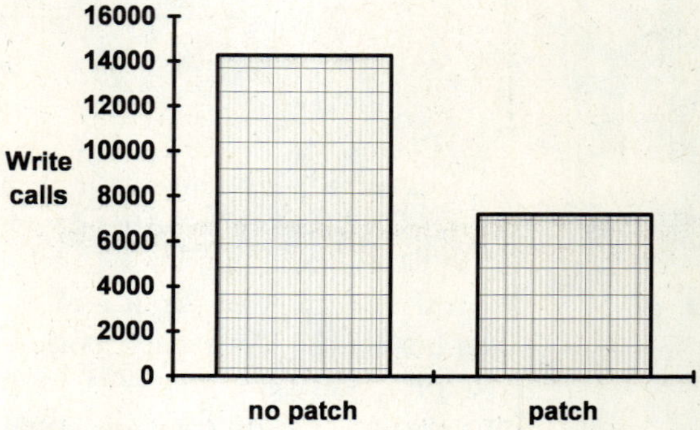

Figure D-4: Comparison Between Number of Write Remote Procedure Calls Before and After the Installation of the Patch

Figure D-4 shows that the number of write remote procedure calls reduced by nearly 50%.

The statistics for the server show similar trends as those described for the client.

Both client and server disk usage statistics show the disks handling an increased frequency of blks/s. This is consistent with transferring the same amount of data in less time. The test duration is shorter, but the amount of data remains the same, so the frequency of blks/s should increase.

Conclusions

This test shows one scenario where the NFS patch can improve performance. If the client frequently executes write operations, then the installation of the patch should benefit performance.

Prior to installing the patch, we recommend monitoring the frequency of remote file write operations and remote write procedure calls. These statistics should allow you to judge whether a significant amount of write activity is occurring, and if so, to estimate what the potential benefit of patch installation versus the cost of reconfiguring the operating system to install the modification.

Index

D

M

N

Q

R

S